YOUR DAILY LIGHT

SIMON T. MUNGWA

YOUR DAILY LIGHT

365 devotionals for daily illumination   Vol.1

Impressum

Unless otherwise indicated, all scripture quotations are taken from the **New King James Version** of the bible.

YOUR DAILY LIGHT Vol. 1 (paperback)
ISBN: 978-3-98733-000-1
Copyright © 2022 LIGHTHOUSE GLOBAL MISSIONS
Wuerzburg, Germany
Email: yourdailylight@gmail.com
www.lgmissions.org
www.lighthouseglobalmissions.org
Facebook, Instagram, YouTube @YOUR DAILY LIGHT

Published by PHOTIZO PUBLISHERS
Wuerzburg, Germany
www.photizopublishers.com
Phone: +4917657761915

Cover and layout design by Christina Brandl

All rights reserved. Contents and/or cover may not be reproduced in anyway in whole or in part without the express written consent of the publisher.

Illumination for every day

YOUR DAILY LIGHT is a non-denominational devotional with a growing global audience that seeks to bring the word of God daily to people across the globe for a victorious and fulfilling life in Christ. Since March 2019, it has been authored and distributed principally through private messaging and social media platforms. Its principal platform and channel to the world has been Facebook where it has been able to reach a growing audience of over 75,000 followers.

For the first time, we have YOUR DAILY LIGHT in print. This is the first volume of a sequel of this devotional that will continue as an annual publication for the illumination and edification of saints around the world. It covers every relevant subject for practical Christian living, touching on faith, prayer, the Holy Spirit, purpose, spiritual gifts, relationships and more.

With sound scriptural backing, you will find trust-worthy nourishment for your spirit daily. It is guaranteed to inspire your faith and bring about results in your life as you walk into a richer fellowship with God and an experience of his supernatural power. As a lighthouse to a sailor at sea, so is YOUR DAILY LIGHT to a soul in the world, bringing them God's word for their journey in life. Like the Psalmist would say, "Your word is a lamp to my feet and a light to my path" (Psalm 119:105). And it is my prayer that you will find light for every day through these pages of YOUR DAILY LIGHT and God will cause His glory to be revealed in you.

How to make the most of this devotional

1. Follow the structure

As evident, each day has a structured lesson for you. The caption highlights the theme of the day and helps you set your gaze on what specific light or knowledge the Lord is bringing to you. Don't make assumptions on the writing that follows, even when the caption seems to echo the clear thought. Through the expounding writing, you will gain spiritual insight as many other verses are connected. Remember, "Wisdom is the principal thing; Therefore, get wisdom. **And in all your getting, get understanding**" (Proverbs 4:7).

Make out time to go through the lesson itself. You will be missing out on a lot by assuming what follows. The thought of the day brings you the summary of all things, it is the one thought you should carry along with you even if you were to forget everything else that was written. The verse of the day is your verse to memorize for the day. In this way, you will be building a reservoir of God's word in your spirit that will serve you in the day of need. End with the prayer and say it in faith. You can always go ahead to pray more according to your need and as the Lord gives you inspiration.

2. Meditate on the word

YOUR DAILY LIGHT gives you material for meditation. This is what God's word is intended to provide us – something to ponder upon. Don't just speed-read like a novel. Read meditatively with goal to understand and assimilate the spiritual truths for practical living. This is how you get results through God's word (Joshua 1:8).

3. Share your thoughts

There is no better way to extend the impact of the word of God in your life than to share with others. In the process of sharing, you also consolidate the knowledge you have gained. Social media platforms offer us such avenues. The lesson might also awaken questions. Don't leave them unanswered. We are also always willing to respond to your questions when they come. Do not hesitate to reach us with feedbacks, testimonies, and questions via our social media pages or website.

JANUARY

Your word is a lamp to my feet and a light to my path. // **Psalm 119:105**

JAN 1

A light for every day

The Psalmist declared, "Your word is a lamp to my feet and a light to my path" (Psalm 119:105). How true that is. The word of God is light. It illuminates in many ways and pro-vides us with a daily dose of divine light for our paths. Without God's word, we will grope in darkness, without the word of God, we will be uninformed, we will be in the dark regarding many things. God's word is illuminating, it enlightens us about life, its origin, its purpose, and ultimate end. God's word shines the light on Himself, bringing us into the true knowledge of who God really is and how we can come into relationship with Him. The word of God also shines the light on us, so we can see who we are and what God has made us to be, enabling us to live the good life His has planned for us. And without exhausting the list, the word of God shines the light on our paths, so we can see our way and ponder out paths to a glorious destiny.

God neither wants you to walk in the dark regarding life, nor does he want you to live in assumptions and guesses of His purpose for your existence. He has a plan for your life, a plan He wants you to discover and fulfill. This is the reason He has given us His word, to give us light for every day. And through Your Daily Light, we are serving you with God's word in season, a timely word to light your world daily with the word of God for a fulfilling and a victorious life in Christ. And if you happen to be one who questions if the bible can be trusted as the true word of God, then this is the material for you on the path to discovery.

Your Daily Light is a daily devotional born by a divine vision to shine the light of God's word to every soul, bringing them into the knowledge of God's plan and purpose for their lives, and leading them on their paths to destiny. With sound scriptural backing, it captures spiritual truths, breaking them down into bits and pieces, easy to comprehend and implement for practical results in life. Through a progressive journey, covering diverse relevant topics for practical Christian living, you will find inspiration for each day. This devotional builds your faith through the word, brings you into a deeper fellowship with God and ushers you into a glorious experience of ever-increasing measure in Christ.

> **Through the word of God, you find light for every day, a light that illuminates your path and brings you into a rich experience with God.**

Prayer

Heavenly Father, thank you for bringing to me your light through the word, that I might see things the way they really are. Thank you for your word as a light for my path and a lamp to my feet. For by it I have direction and will not walk in darkness. I have the light of life. In Jesus' name.

Bible in one year // **Genesis 1-3, Matthew 1**

If anyone loves Me, he will keep My word; and My Father will love him, and We will come to him and make Our home with him. // **John 14:23**

A fellowship with the Father

God's greatest desire is to have fellowship with you. That is the principal reason for creation, God was seeking a people to relate with, and that purpose still stands. It is God's longing that you know Him as a father and come into fulfilling fellowship or intimacy with Him. And this is one main reason Your Daily Light found its way to you, for the Father desires to reveal Himself to you and bring you into an experiential fellowship with Him. John wrote to his readers, "That which we have seen and heard we declare to you, that you also may have fellowship with us; and truly our fellowship is with the Father and with His Son Jesus Christ" (1 John 1:3).

The apostle John had come to know and experience a fellowship with the Father. And in His writing to the readers, he was doing so with goal to bring them into an experience of that fellowship. John was trying to bring his readers into a fellowship with himself and the other apostles, but much more, a fellowship that was truly with the Father and with His son Jesus Christ. And this is what the word of God will do for you. As you spend a moment daily in the word of God, He will speak to you and bring you into an experience with Himself. He will reveal Himself to you and make His word real in your life. God will bring you into a rich fellowship where you can know and experience Him.

> The word of God has as purpose to bring you into a living fellowship and experience with the Father as you meditate on the word and pattern your life after its teachings.

Jesus spoke of it in this way, "He who has My commandments and keeps them, it is he who loves Me. And he who loves Me will be loved by My Father, and I will love him and manifest Myself to him". And then He added, "If anyone loves Me, he will keep My word; and My Father will love him, and We will come to him and make Our home with him" (John 14:21 & 23). The end purpose of God's word to you is not to bring you into vain philosophical ideas. A thousand times no! It is God's material to invitation to draw you into a living fellowship and experience with Him as your Father, where He reveals Himself to you and bring you into a glorious experience in life.

Prayer

Heavenly Father thank you for your word that I receive today. As I receive your word, my heart is open and my life is made ready for your abiding presence. Lord have free course in my life this year and let your manifest presence be evident as I walk in your word. In Jesus' name.

Bible in one year // **Genesis 4-6, Matthew 2**

You are all children of the light and children of the day. We do not belong to the night or to the darkness. // **1 Thessalonians 5:5**

Children of the light

Paul wrote to the Thessalonians, "You are all sons of light and sons of the day. We are not of the night nor of darkness. Therefore, let us not sleep, as others do, but let us watch and be sober. For those who sleep, sleep at night, and those who get drunk are drunk at night. But let us who are of the day be sober, putting on the breastplate of faith and love, and as a helmet the hope of salvation" (1 Thessalonians 5:5 -8). He reminded them of their identity and called them to live accordingly, they were children of Light.

John wrote about Jesus, "In Him was life, and the life was the light of men" (John 1:3). He spelled out a fundamental truth: Those who receive Jesus are lit and are made children of Light. So, if you have received Jesus, that is your identity, you are a child of light. Across that line is the identity no one should desire. It is the identity of being a child of darkness. That is the identity of the person without Jesus, they are in the dark and under the dominion of Satan. Knowingly or unknowingly, the devil is their Lord and has power and authority over their lives. There is no middle ground. You are either a child of light or a child of darkness. If you never made that decision before, then this is the occasion to invite Jesus into your life.

> As many as have received Jesus into their lives are children of light. They have the light of life and have been translated from the dominion of darkness and authority of Satan into the kingdom of light.

Don't let another day go by without this decision. It makes all the difference to be a child of light. Jesus Himself declared, "I am the light of the world. He who follows Me shall not walk in darkness but have the light of life" (John 8:12). You have light for your life, light for your path and spiritual darkness with all its demonic entities are excluded from your life. In Colossians 1:13, the bible tells us, "He has delivered us from the power of darkness and conveyed us into the kingdom of the Son of His love". As a child of light, you are no longer under the dominion and control of the devil. He has no legal right over your life. By accepting Jesus, one is made a child of light. They are also delivered out of darkness and brought into the Kingdom of light.

Prayer

Heavenly Father, thank you for the gift of Jesus Christ to me as the sacrifice for my sins. Because I accept Him as Lord and savior of my life, I have the light of life. This year I will not walk in darkness nor stumble on my journey because my paths are illuminated. The devil also has no authority over me. In Jesus' name.

Bible in one year // **Genesis 7-9, Matthew 3**

Most assuredly, I say to you, unless one is born again, he cannot see the kingdom of God. // **John 3:3**

The necessity of a new birth

A teacher of the law came to Jesus one night and Jesus said to him, "Most assuredly, I say to you, unless one is born again, he cannot see the kingdom of God" (John 3:3). Jesus made it unequivocally clear that the new birth is a necessity. He said unless a person is born again, they CANNOT see the Kingdom of God. And the reason is simple. Romans 5:12 tells us, "When Adam sinned, sin entered the world. Adam's sin brought death, so death spread to everyone, for everyone sinned" (NLT). By our natural birth, descending from our biological parents, we all inherit the sinful nature of Adam and by that sinful nature, we were separated from God – that is spiritual death.

> The new birth is a necessity if anyone will see the Kingdom of God and have fellowship with Him. And that new birth takes place when a person receives Jesus as Lord and savior.

Spiritual death is the state we would be in if we are not born again, it is the state of being separated from God. In this state, an individual is blind to the realities of the spirit and their spiritual senses cannot perceive the Kingdom of God. Just as a corpse is to this physical world, non-responsive to its environment, so also is the natural man to God. This is the reason why anyone must be born again if they will see or enter the Kingdom of God. And this new birth happens when a person believes in Jesus, receiving him based on the testimony He gave of himself as the savior of the world. He declares, "For God so loved the world that He gave His only begotten Son, that whoever believes in Him should not perish but have everlasting life" (John 3:16).

Without the new birth, a soul is bound for destruction. But God offers us salvation through Jesus, giving us also a new life through the new birth so we can live for Him and fulfill His purpose for us. John writes, "As many as received Him, to them He gave the right to become children of God, to those who believe in His name: who were born, not of blood, nor of the will of the flesh, nor of the will of man, but of God" (John 1:12-13). This is what it means to be born again. For the first birth was a natural birth by your natural parents, but the second birth is the new birth by God himself, giving you a new life. You become alive to God and alive in the Kingdom of God. An all new and exciting spiritual journey begins. God is now your father, and you are His Child. Are you born again? If not, today is the day for you to invite Him in.

Prayer

Heavenly Father, thank you for the gift of your son Jesus Christ through whom we have forgiveness of sins. I accept Him as my Lord and savior. I am born again and born into your Kingdom. I am alive to you, called into a living fellowship. Thank you, Father, for giving me new life. In Jesus' name.

Bible in one year // **Genesis 10-12, Matthew 4**

Make the most of every opportunity in these evil days. // **Ephesians 5:16 NLT**

JAN 5

A blank cheque

A blank cheque is one of the most generous gifts anyone could ever receive in human terms. It gives you the opportunity to decide on what and how you spend from a bank account. This is what we are getting with a new year, it is a blank cheque to us from the Lord. And it is in our hands to decide how we use the time, what we invest it in and with whom we share that time. A year ahead of us is a blank cheque and even so is every day. Ephesians 5:15-17 tells us, "See then that you walk circumspectly, not as fools but as wise, redeeming the time, because the days are evil. Therefore, do not be unwise, but understand what the will of the Lord is".

Time is of the essence. And you cannot afford to be unintentional with your use of time. The year is given to us and as much time as we have ahead of us to be part of God's plan. He has measured to us a window of opportunity to use as we choose. And He is trusting us to make the right decision with our use of that time. You can choose to invest that time in serving the Lord or burn it away in self-gratifying ventures that have no eternal value or purpose. We must not let the things of lesser significance become the major things on which our time is invested.

> The year ahead of us is a blank cheque from the Lord, to use the time as we choose. Do well to use it in such a way that counts to your advantage for eternity.

Like you would be accountable with money entrusted to your care, even so you should be accountable for your time this year and always. Face every day with a sense of duty and make concrete goals. Give your time to those goals and maintain the necessary balance with family, friends, work, career, and kingdom service. Define boundaries and work at maintaining them. Educate yourself on time management if you need to. Buy and read a book on time management. Do all in your ability to make the most of this blank cheque of time given to us by the Lord as He counts us among the living on this day. Above all, remember there is no better way to invest time than investing it in a way that counts for us in eternity.

Prayer

Thank you Lord for a new day and the opportunity to glorify you in the flesh. Today I receive grace to do the things I ought to do. Thank you for the Holy Spirit that lives in me, that by Him I can know your will and use my time wisely for your glory. In Jesus name.

Bible in one year // **Genesis 13-15, Matthew 5:1-26**

> I press toward the goal for the prize of the upward call of God in Christ Jesus.
> // Philippians 3:14

Set concrete goals

Living life without goals is like playing a football match without goal posts. There are no targets and therefore no scales to measure progress and achievements. That is not the life God calls us to live. He has made us achievers. That is the very reason for your creation, He had a vision for your life and created you for that purpose. However, you can only measure your progress and evaluate how much of that purpose you are living out when you can set concrete goals. Setting goals also gives you an opportunity to evaluate your speed and adjust it for destiny. Whatever vision you have for life can be broken down into concrete goals for the season. Whatever dream God has placed in your heart can be accomplished one tiny piece at a time. So, set concrete goals this year and go after them.

> **Set concrete goals for your life for this season and beyond based on God's purpose and plan for you.**

Paul lived a goal-oriented life after he found His purpose in God. He wrote, "Not that I have already attained, or am already perfected; but I press on, that I may lay hold of that for which Christ Jesus has also laid hold of me. Brethren, I do not count myself to have apprehended; but one thing I do, forgetting those things which are behind and reaching forward to those things which are ahead, I press toward the goal for the prize of the upward call of God in Christ Jesus" (Philippians 3:12-14). He was set with his gaze on the goal, to lay hold on the very thing for which Christ had called him. This is the kind of goal-setting that guarantees accomplishment – when your goals are set and defined by God's plan for your life.

God's plan for your life should inspire the goals you define. And that divine plan for you is not mysterious. Hopefully you have discovered it already. If not, stay with me on this journey of illumination through the word of God and you will find out what His plan for you is. This is the purpose for which the Lord has called me. He has called me as a lighthouse to my generation to shine the light of the gospel and to bring men and women into their inheritance in God. This is what I am all set for. This is the reason for Your Daily Light, to bring to you that light in daily bits so you can see your paths for life and destiny.

Prayer

Almighty God, thank you for the plans you have for me, plans of good and not of evil, to give me a hope and a future. As you unveil to me these plans by the Holy Spirit, I receive grace to set concrete goals and the discipline to accomplish them for your glory. In Jesus name.

Bible in one year // **Genesis 16-17, Matthew 27-48**

For we are His workmanship, created in Christ Jesus for good works, which God prepared beforehand that we should walk in them. // **Ephesians 2:10**

Along traced paths

Imagine how difficult life would be if every time you had to travel to a place, you had the responsibility to create a path to that destination. Imagine needing to travel from where you are to the next city close to you and having to make your own road for the journey because there was none. That would make most journeys practically impossible and sometimes, reaching the destination will be a myth. But how easy it is when there are already traced paths connecting you to your destination. Much so, with today's technology of navigation apps and gadgets, you could almost navigate yourself to any known address or destination. This is possible just by finding and walking in the right paths traced already.

This is the same thing spiritually. God's plan for your life was predestined and the paths for its fulfillment traced out for you ahead of time. Paul wrote to the Ephesians, "For we are His workmanship, created in Christ Jesus for good works, which God prepared beforehand that we should walk in them". When we read same verse from the Amplified version, it gives it an even much better rendition. It says, "For we are God's [own] handiwork (His workmanship), recreated in Christ Jesus, [born anew] that we may do those good works which God predestined (planned beforehand) for us [taking paths which He prepared ahead of time], that we should walk in them [living the good life which He prearranged and made ready for us to live] (Amp).

> As much as God has a plan for your life, He also has a path for it. And as you learn to walk with Him, the Lord will lead you along His traced paths for you, bringing you into a glorious and a fulfilling destiny.

There is a traced-out path for your life in Christ Jesus, a good path that is. If you will discover God's plan for your life and be willing to be led by the Spirit of God, He will guide you along a traced path for your life. Like a trusted navigation, He will tell you where to turn left and where to go right, where to drive on and where to turn away from. He will guide you along paths that bring you into the supply of all that you need for the fulfillment of your destiny. It is just as the prophet Isaiah foretold, "Whether you turn to the right or to the left, your ears will hear a voice behind you, saying, 'This is the way; walk in it'" (Isaiah 30:21 NIV).

Prayer

Heavenly Father, thank you for predestination in Christ Jesus, that before you formed me, you knew me and prearranged for me good works, that I might walk in them. Now I am here and yield myself to walk in your paths and to fulfill your plans for my life. Lead me by your Spirit, now and always. In Jesus name.

Bible in one year // **Genesis 18-19, Matthew 6:1-18**

You guide me with your counsel, leading me to a glorious destiny.
// **Psalm 73:24 NLT**

Give heed to His counsel

The Psalmist made a confident declaration, "You guide me with your counsel, leading me to a glorious destiny" (Psalm 73:24 NLT). This has always proven true. No one who was led by the Lord and gave heed to His counsel ever failed to walk into the fullness of the glory of their lives. Therefore, this should be our resolution, to give heed to divine counsel. It will guarantee your safety and spare you losses. His counsel will keep you out of harm's way and bring you into a place of bountiful harvest. His counsel will indeed lead you to a glorious destiny.

When Joshua took over the mission to lead the children of Israel into the promised land, the Lord spoke to him saying, "Only be strong and very courageous, that you may observe to do according to all the law which Moses My servant commanded you; do not turn from it to the right hand or to the left, that you may prosper wherever you go. This Book of the Law shall not depart from your mouth, but you shall meditate in it day and night, that you may observe to do according to all that is written in it. For then you will make your way prosperous, and then you will have good success" (Joshua 1:6-8). The guarantee of their safety and possession of the land they were going to inherit was tied to how well they could hold on to the counsel of Lord.

> We have God's written word and the Holy Spirit. And by these two avenues we can find trusted counsel for life that will lead us to a glorious destiny.

God gives us counsel on many things through His written word, guiding us on how to go about life. Don't be one of such persons who ignore what the word says and do what they think. Some even consciously act in opposition to God's word. You can also have counsel from the Holy Spirit if you find yourself at crossroads, He is always willing to give you direction and guide you into the right paths. That is one reason He came. Jesus spoke of Him saying, "When He, the Spirit of truth, has come, He will guide you into all truth; for He will not speak on His own authority, but whatever He hears He will speak; and He will tell you things to come" (John 16:13). It is God's desire to give you counsel through His word and by His Spirit, but you must take responsibility and give heed to His counsel. For then indeed you will make your way prosperous and have good success.

Prayer

God, thank you for ears that hear your voice, eyes that can see what you show and a heart that is willing to follow in your paths. And as I take steps with you, the crooked paths are made straight, mountains are brought low, the valleys are raised, and a way is made where there was no way. In Jesus' name.

Bible in one year // **Genesis 20-22, Matthew 6:19-34**

Do not be like the horse or like the mule, which have no understanding, which must be harnessed with bit and bridle, else they will not come near you.
// Psalm 32:9

Spare yourself the trouble

The bible teaches us clearly that we can spare ourselves much trouble by our choices. And we can also get ourselves into much trouble by our choices. The interesting part is that when things go contrary to our expectation, even when we are the orchestrators of a mishap, we blame the Lord for it. It is like the writer of Proverbs puts it, "A person's own folly leads to their ruin, yet their heart rages against the Lord" (Proverbs 19:3). You don't have to be that person. You can spare yourself the trouble by walking in the word of God and being yielded to the Holy Spirit.

David was quick to recognize his mistakes and take responsibility for his own troubles. He wrote, "Before I was afflicted, I went astray, but now I keep Your word" (Psalm 119:67). David could look at the trouble he got into, the afflictions he suffered because he strayed. This is not to say every difficulty or mishap is a product of our own errors. No. Job is one bible example of one who suffered much ill that was no consequence of him going astray. The emphasis here is on the blessedness of walking in the word of God and being led by His spirit and the opposite thereof. You don't have to learn the hard way.

A practical example of what we are sharing takes place when Paul is brought along to Rome as a prisoner (Acts 27). Paul, inspired by the Holy Spirit, advised the people to shelter for a while until the storm was over. He told them, "Men, I perceive that this voyage will end with disaster and much loss, not only of the cargo and ship, but also our lives" (Acts 27:10). But they would not listen. In the end, it was by God's mercy that they all survived a shipwreck. They lost the sheep and all the cargo. The prophet Jonah and his troubles at sea is another example (Jonah 1). The psalmist cautions us, "Do not be like the horse or like the mule, which have no understanding, which must be harnessed with bit and bridle, else they will not come near you" (Psalm 32:9). You don't have to suffer the consequences of rebellion before you learn to take heed to divine counsel. You can spare yourself the trouble and do His will.

You can spare yourself much trouble by living by the word of God and being yielded to the Holy Spirit as He guides you. You don't have to learn through disobedience.

Prayer

Heavenly Father, thank you for you are working in me to will and to do according to your good pleasure. My ears are inclined to your sayings, and I look out for your paths and walk in them. Therefore, my feet are kept from stumbling as you uphold me by the power of your mighty hand. In Jesus' name.

Bible in one year: Genesis 23-24, Matthew 7

We all, with unveiled face, beholding the glory of the Lord, are being transformed into the same image from one degree of glory to another. For this comes from the Lord who is the Spirit. // **2 Corinthians 3:18 ESV**

Transfiguration by the word

Matthew shares an account in the life of Jesus during His earthly work. "After six days Jesus took with him Peter, James, and John the brother of James, and led them up a high mountain by themselves. There he was transfigured before them. His face shone like the sun, and his clothes became as white as the light" (Matthew 17:1-2). Jesus was literally transfigured in full view of the disciples with Him. He was transformed to a more glorious state, reflecting a light that could not be hidden.

> When you give attention to the word of God, beholding His glory as in a mirror, you will be transfigured to reflect same glory to your world.

This event of the transfiguration was not new when it happened with Jesus. Long before Jesus, Moses lived such a moment. "When Moses came down from Mount Sinai with the two tablets of the covenant law in his hands, he was not aware that his face was radiant because he had spoken with the Lord. When Aaron and all the Israelites saw Moses, his face was radiant, and they were afraid to come near him" (Exodus 34:29-30). Moses was himself transfigured because he had spoken with the Lord. This is a transfiguration as the glory of God is infused into an individual through a time of holy communion so they can reflect that glory too.

This is what Paul wrote to the Corinthians. "We all, with unveiled face, beholding the glory of the Lord, are being transformed into the same image from one degree of glory to another. For this comes from the Lord who is the Spirit" (2 Corinthians 3:18 ESV). As we meditate in the word, having fellowship with the Father, we are also transfigured from one degree of glory to another. Even if physically our faces do not give off such light, we can be sure that such a thing is happening with our spirits. We are transfigured by the word. The Greek word used to mean transfigure in Matthew 17:2, is the same word used in 2 Corinthians 3:18 to mean transform. It is the word "Metamorphoo". The word means a metamorphosis, changing from one state to another like a caterpillar turns to a butterfly. This is the power the word of God has on our lives; it continually causes in us a transfiguration to reflect increasing degrees of glory.

Prayer

Father of all glory, thank you for Christ in me is my hope of glory. As I meditate in your word and give it attention, your glory is infused and multiplied in my life and I am continually transfigured, from one degree of glory to another. Let this glory shine out that men may see and glorify you in Jesus' name.

Bible in one year // **Genesis 25-26, Matthew 8:1-17**

The light shines in the darkness, and the darkness can never extinguish it. // **John 1:5 NLT**

JAN 11

An approaching light

Once I was invited to minister at a women's Church retreat. After sharing the word of God with the precious saints in attendance, I went on to pray for them. As I walked through the isle and approached one of the sisters who had her hands lifted to the Lord in prayer, I could notice the Lord was reaching her. So, I stretched forth my hands in prayer towards her. And before I could hardly touch her head, she was on the ground, overwhelmed by the power of God. The Lord was at work.

But what was more striking later was her testimony. At the end of the meeting, she came forward to share her experience with everyone. She told us how she had been healed of a migraine. She said as I walked towards her, all she saw was an approaching light of great intensity that was difficult to look into. And as the light approached and got stronger, she felt something leave her like a bird would fly away. And the migraine was gone. It was a miracle, a supernatural manifestation of God. It reminds us of the verse that says, "The light shines in the darkness, and the darkness did not comprehend it" (John 1:5). A demonic affliction had been expelled by the approaching Light of God's glory reflected through me.

> Commit yourself to meditation in the word of God and it will work in you a transfiguration, making you a reflector of the Father's glory.

Two things unfold in this experience. I had been transfigured by the glory of God in me and that glory was being reflected to others as God's light that shines into darkness and expels all demonic works. The Lord opened her eyes to see spiritually what was happening in reality. This was part of the thoughts shared in yesterday's writing – transfiguration by the word. Not only is Jesus the Light of the world. He lit us up and made us also the light to our world. And that light gets brighter and reflects itself to others as we continue to behold His glory as in a mirror through the word. So, make it your priority this year to give a committed attention to the word of God and experience a transfiguration by the word. And you will become a walking embodiment of divine glory, expelling the darkness wherever you go.

Prayer

Heavenly Father, thank you for you word of illumination that enlightens me and brings understanding. Therefore, I act as one who is enlightened, giving your word the attention necessary as you work in me a transformation that will be evident to all. In Jesus' name.

Bible in one year // **Genesis 27-28, Matthew 8:18-34**

He sent His word and healed them, and delivered them from their destructions. // **Psalm 107:20**

Healing in the word

There is healing in the word of God for your body. It does not matter what medical condition it is. It does not count if there is a medical treatment or not. Whatever malady there is, the word provides the cure. The Psalmist declared, "He sent His word and healed them, and delivered them from their destructions" (Psalm 107:20). The word of God you receive into your spirit has capacity to bring healing to your body. Not only that, it has power to keep you in health. The purpose of God's word is beyond providing us with a moral code of conduct. It also has supernatural power to heal us from every kind of sickness. The word of God carries with it the power of God to cause the changes even in our bodies.

> **The word of God you receive is medicine to all your flesh, it brings healing to every kind of medical condition as you receive it in your spirit.**

The Lord speaks to us in this manner, "My son, give attention to my words; incline your ear to my sayings. Do not let them depart from your eyes; keep them in the midst of your heart; for they are life to those who find them, and HEALTH TO ALL THEIR FLESH" (Proverbs 4:20-22). He declares His word to be health to all our flesh.

In Proverbs 4:22, the Hebrew word translated "Health" is the word "Marpe" (pronounced "Mar-pay"). The word means "Medicine". This goes to say that the word of God is medicine to all your flesh. Jesus went throughout Galilee, teaching in their synagogues, proclaiming the good news of the kingdom, and healing every disease and sickness among the people" (Matthew 4:23). Jesus was the word that became flesh and dwelled amongst men. And in His earthly work, He brought healing to every kind of sickness. The word provides a medium by which we can continue to live this reality of God's supernatural healing power in our bodies. The word of God is medicine to all your flesh and will bring you healing as you continually meditate in it.

Prayer

Heavenly Father, thank you for your word that is sent to me daily, for it is healing to my body and health to all my flesh. As I continually meditate in your word, my body is healed and vitalized. I walk in health. I am fit and strong to live out my purpose. In Jesus' name.

Bible in one year // **Genesis 29-30, Matthew 9:1-17**

Do not be conformed to this world, but be transformed by the renewing of your mind, that you may prove what is that good and acceptable and perfect will of God. // **Romans 12:2**

JAN 13

Be renewed in your mind

Being renewed in your mind is a must as a child of God if you will experience the fullness of His glory. Your mind is like a databank with capacity to store information that can be retrieved, processed, and used. And you will process, evaluate, and see things based on the kind of information your mind contains. So the kind of information you have will define your mindset and shape your perspective which ultimately guides your actions. And when we come to know the Lord, we come from a world with its own systems and ideologies, its way of seeing and evaluating things, its own definition of what is right or wrong.

Mind renewal is therefore necessary. This has to do with the receiving of new information to replace the old information in our databank, the mind. This happens through the word of God as we receive God's teachings and accept His perspectives on things. We learn to see things from His perspective, call right what He defines as right and define wrong by what He declares as wrong. As it is written, "Do not be conformed to this world, but be transformed by the renewing of your mind, that you may prove what is that good and acceptable and perfect will of God" (Romans 12:2).

> Being renewed in your mind is a must as a child of God if you will walk in His perfect will and experience the fullness of His glory in your life.

As you meditate in the word of God and learn His word, accept His thoughts, and exchange your old opinions for His new perspectives. That is mind renewal. If you don't do this, you will find yourself in argument with the word of God always, with baseless opinions and philosophies from the world that will not necessarily help you in making progress as a Christian. Neither will it help you to experience the fullness of Gods glory. Failing to renew your mind will blind your heart from discerning the good, perfect, and acceptable will of the Lord, making it difficult for you to walk in His perfect will for your life. Therefore, be renewed in your mind through the word.

Prayer

Almighty God, thank you for your word that has power to renew my thinking as I receive new information and perspective through your word. I receive grace to grow in my knowledge of you and to discern what is your good, perfect, and acceptable will for me. In Jesus' name.

Bible in one year // **Genesis 31-32, Matthew 9:18-38**

JAN 14

Be anxious for nothing, but in everything by prayer and supplication, with thanksgiving, let your requests be made known to God. // **Philippians 4:6**

Be anxious for nothing

Every season comes with reasons for anxiety. There could always be concerns about us, situations with uncertain outcomes, misunderstanding in relationships, such as necessitate anxiety. But you don't have to respond by being anxious. God wants your life free of anxiety and He has made provisions for you to live such a life. Philippians 4:6 & 7 tell us, "Be anxious for nothing, but in everything by prayer and supplication, with thanksgiving, let your requests be made known to God; and the peace of God, which surpasses all understanding, will guard your hearts and minds through Christ Jesus".

> Refuse to be anxious for anything and trust God with your life for He will never leave you nor forsake you.

Anxiety, if anything, can only work against you. This fact alone should encourage you to avoid being anxious. Say it to yourself, "I refuse to be anxious". Refuse to be anxious about your job, your future, your ministry, your life, a pandemic, or anything else. Unless you are doing something about a thing, don't let it cheat you of peace and make you restless. This is not the will of God for you. Anxiety can also impact your health negatively; it is an established path to hypertension.

Jesus said, "I tell you, do not worry about your life, what you will eat or drink, or about your body, what you will wear. Isn't there more to life than food and more to the body than clothing? Look at the birds in the sky: They do not sow, or reap, or gather into barns, yet your heavenly Father feeds them. Aren't you more valuable than they are? And which of you by worrying can add even one hour to his life?" (Matthew 6:25-27 NET). Do not worry about your life, and do not let anything move you to anxiety. Rather pray about every concern and trust God in everything for He has promised never to leave nor forsake you (Hebrews 13:5).

Prayer

Heavenly Father, thank you for the assurance we have in you, the rest we can enjoy in Christ, knowing that you will never leave nor forsake me. You have called me by name and predestined me for glory. I will be still and know that you are God over all things. In Jesus' name.

Bible in one year // **Genesis 33-35, Matthew 10:1-20**

However, when He, the Spirit of truth, has come, He will guide you into all truth; for He will not speak on His own authority, but whatever He hears He will speak; and He will tell you things to come. // **John 16:13**

Listen for His voice

God wants to talk to you. And you can know His voice. Jesus said, "My sheep hear My voice, and I know them, and they follow Me" (John 10:27). It is in the ability of the sheep to know and recognize the shepherd's voice. This is true for you too if you are a child of God. He wants to talk to you, lead you and guide you into His plans for your life. You can know His voice and walk with Him. But you will have to start by listening for His voice. The prophet Habakkuk shows us how. After spending time to pray, he said to Himself, "I will stand at my guard post and station myself on the watchtower; and I will keep watch to see what He will say to me, and how I may reply when I am reprimanded" (Habakkuk 2:1 NASB).

Habakkuk was going to take active steps in listening for the voice of God. He was going look out for the Master's voice. This, we also are to do. Give time and attention to God and look out for His voice. When you are at crossroads, ask the Lord for guidance. If you seek clarity on certain issues, you can also ask the Lord for insight. It is His delight to lead us and to make known His secrets to us. He promised, "Call to Me, and I will answer you, and show you great and mighty things, which you do not know" (Jeremiah 33:3).

Before Jesus would return to heaven, He promised the Holy Spirit to as many as believed in Him. He also talked a lot about what the Holy Spirit will do in our lives. Jesus said, "However, when He, the Spirit of truth, has come, He will guide you into all truth; for He will not speak on His own authority, but whatever He hears He will speak; and He will tell you things to come. He will glorify Me, for He will take of what is Mine and declare it to you" (John 16:13-14). The Holy Spirit is here and ready to reveal to us things beyond human scrutiny. He is willing to give you trust-worthy counsel, encourage you in times of despair and bring you into the fullness of God's plan for your life. But you will have to give Him attention in prayer, meditate on His word and listen for His voice.

> **The Holy Spirit was sent to be our guide and helper. He is willing to talk to you, but you will have to listen for His voice.**

Prayer

Heavenly Father, thank you for the gift of the Holy Spirit to me. My ears are open to hear from Him, my eyes are open to see visions of the spirit and my heart is willing to walk in His paths. Help me Lord to be in tune with your voice, in Jesus' name.

Bible in one year // **Genesis 36-38, Matthew 10:21-42**

> Test everything that is said. Hold on to what is good.
> // 1 Thessalonians 5:21 NLT

Recognize the voice of God

As we grow in the Lord, one question every believer gets to struggle with at some point in time is this: How can I know the voice of God? It is a very valid question. The bible lets us know that God is spirit and therefore His voice is also spiritual. John 4:4 says, "God is Spirit". That is a statement of fact. It also goes to say that He communicates as the Spirit He is. And there are a few things you must get straight if you will recognize His voice.

One key thing to note if you seek to recognize the voice of God is that it takes faith. It takes faith to hear Him and it takes faith to associate what is heard with God as the source. It takes faith to accept the voice of God. Just as the writer of Hebrews puts it, "Without faith it is impossible to please Him, for he who comes to God must believe that He is, and that He is a rewarder of those who diligently seek Him" (Hebrews 11:6). You must of necessity believe that He is Spirit and His voice also is spiritual. Don't look out for a physical sound from outside like you would expect when someone talks to you. Although that sometimes happens, it is not the norm. Lookout for the voice of the Spirit from your inside where He dwells.

God's voice can come to us in many ways, but it will never be in opposition to the revelations of His written word. This is how to recognize His voice.

This is a subject to be addressed in a book, on how to hear and recognize the voice of God. For God speaks in many ways. Hebrews 1:1 tells us, "Long ago God spoke to the fathers by the prophets at different times and in different ways. In these last days, He has spoken to us by His Son... (Hebrews 1:1-2). In whichever way God speaks to us, it is more important that we can evaluate the voice to be His own. You will need to verify what you are supposing to be His voice with the revealed truth of God's word in scripture. The two must NOT be in opposition of each other. For God will NOT contradict himself. His voice is always in line with scripture and seeks to bring glory to His name. We are admonished, "Test everything that is said. Hold on to what is good" (1 Thessalonians 5:21 NLT).

Prayer

Heavenly Father, thank you for a discerning heart to recognize your voice. A stranger's voice I will not follow. I walk in your paths that lead me into your will and purpose for my life. Thank you for giving me the capacity to hear you in the spirit and to recognize your voice to me. In Jesus' name.

Bible in one year // Genesis 39-40, Matthew 11

Like newborn babies, crave pure spiritual milk, so that by it you may grow up in your salvation. // **1 Peter 2:2 NIV**

Like newborn babes

The bible commands, "Like newborn babies, crave pure spiritual milk, so that by it you may grow up in your salvation" (1 Peter 2:2 NIV). It defines an attitude in our craving for the word of God and tells us the purpose for this craving. It is an instinct for a newborn babe to move their mouth about even while their eyes are closed, and they are yet to know or recognize the mother. They are craving milk, the one food that best serves them for growth and development. Though they do it instinctively, the reward is evident to all as they gain mass and height. And if given only to milk for the first months as most parents do, the growth and change becomes evident to all.

This is the picture Peter paints for us. This is the craving God desires we have of the word. Such craving that makes us reach for the word of God as if our lives depend on it – and sure it does. All that you will ever experience in God is hidden in His word. Even if you had amazing experiences with God without His word, you would be shaky in your faith. You will lack the substance and foundation that holds all things. The writer of Hebrews wrote of Jesus, "The Son is the radiance of God's glory and the exact representation of his being, sustaining all things by his powerful word" (Hebrews 1:3 NIV). He sustains and keeps all things by His word.

> Have a hunger for the word of God and go after it. For through your nourishment by the word of God, you will grow in your experience of salvation.

You must have such an attitude towards the word of God as a newborn craves milk and takes active steps to satisfy the craving. In this, Peter says you will grow in your salvation. That highlights the second emphasis of our opening verse. Our experience in the salvation God brought to us through Christ Jesus is a progressive experience. After you are saved from sin, there is a lot more to experience in Christ. But this experience that follows salvation is anchored on your knowledge of God's word. For through the word, you learn to appropriate all that God has made available for you in Christ Jesus.

Prayer

Heavenly Father, thank you for the salvation I have received through Jesus my Lord. I pray that you give me hunger for your word and the grace to go for it. And as I grow in this knowledge, I will also grow in my experience of the salvation brought to me on the cross. In Jesus' name.

Bible in one year // *Genesis 41-42, Matthew 12:1-13*

> Now, brethren, I commend you to God and to the word of His grace, which is able to build you up and give you an inheritance among all those who are sanctified. // **Acts 20:32**

Take a hold of your inheritance

Paul said to the elders in Ephesus as he took his leave, "So now, brethren, I commend you to God and to the word of His grace, which is able to build you up and give you an inheritance among all those who are sanctified" (Acts 20:32). This word is true for you today. The word of God can build you up and give you an inheritance among the sanctified. You have an inheritance in Christ. You are one of many saints who share in the inheritance in theKingdom of God. Just as Paul wrote to the Colossians, "Giving thanks to the Father, who has qualified us to share in the inheritance of the saints in light" (Colossians 1:12 NASB).

> Commit yourself to God and the word of His grace which can build you up and give you an inheritance among the saved.

Your inheritance in Christ is all that is rightfully yours by virtue of being a child of God. There are things that have been willed to you. It is a full package you have to discover and appropriate for yourself. However, that discovery that leads to total possession of what is yours only comes as you are enlightened through the knowledge of God's word. Just as Paul prayed for the Ephesians, I pray that the eyes of your heart may be enlightened in order that you may know the hope to which he has called you, the riches of his glorious inheritance in his holy people" (Ephesians 1:18 NIV).

As you go through the word of God, you will discover that health is yours in Christ Jesus and you will understand how to make that a living-reality in your life (1 Peter 2:24). You will understand that it is the Father's will that you prosper in all things and you will learn how to make that your story (3 John 1:2). You will understand that God has delivered you from the power of darkness and brought you into the Kingdom of the Son He loves, giving you authority over the devil and His cohorts (Colossians 1:13). You will also learn how to exercise that authority and live free of demonic oppression. These and more are aspects of your inheritance in Christ. But you will only lay hold on them through the word of God.

Prayer

Heavenly Father, thank you for the inheritance I have in Christ Jesus, pure and incorruptible. As I commit myself to the word of your grace, I am continually built up. Therefore, I am enlightened and take hold of all that is mine in Christ, to the praise of your glory. In Jesus' name.

Bible in one year // **Genesis 43-45, Matthew 12:24-50**

Blessed be the God and Father of our Lord Jesus Christ, who according to His abundant mercy has begotten us again to a living hope through the resurrection of Jesus Christ from the dead. // **1 Peter 1:3**

JAN 19

A living hope

Blessed be the God and Father of our Lord Jesus Christ, who according to His abundant mercy has begotten us again to a living hope through the resurrection of Jesus Christ from the dead, to an inheritance incorruptible and undefiled and that does not fade away, reserved in heaven for you, who are kept by the power of God through faith for salvation ready to be revealed in the last time (1 Peter 1:3-5). A lot to be said from this writing. But today, we want to highlight the fact that when one becomes born again, they are born into a living hope. There is no hopeless child of God. There are only those who because of their circumstances are blinded from seeing the hope they have.

You were born again into a living hope, a hope that cannot fail. Paul writes of this hope, he declared as a fact that it does not disappoint. "Now hope does not disappoint, because the love of God has been poured out in our hearts by the Holy Spirit who was given to us (Romans 5:5). It does not matter what you are facing. You have hope in Christ Jesus, a hope that is sure. You are never without hope.

Even if what you are holding unto in hope proved otherwise, you can be sure of the word that says "We know that all things work together for good to those who loveGod, to those who are the called according to His purpose" (Romans 8:28). Don't talk hopelessness. Lift your eyes beyond circumstances and take hold of the hope offered us in the gospel (Colossians 1:23). Like Paul's word of instruction to the Colossians, "Don't drift away from the assurance (hope) you received when you heard the Good News" (Colossians 1:23 NLT). The one thing you can do if you really feel hopeless is to get back to reading and meditation on the word of God as youare doing now. As it is written, "For whatever things were written before were written for our learning, that we through the patience and comfort of the Scriptures might have hope" (Romans 15:4).

> **You were born again into a living hope that cannot disappoint. There is no child of God without hope. If ever you feel hopeless, it is because you are drifting from the hope offered you in the gospel.**

Prayer

Heavenly Father thank you for all that was written for my learning and comfort so that through the enlightenment of scriptures I can have hope, a hope that does not disappoint. My hope is renewed, and my faith strengthened to produce results accordingly. In Jesus' name.

Bible in one year // **Genesis 46-48, Matthew 13:1-30**

JAN 20

> You have come to Mount Zion, to the city of the living God, the heavenly Jerusalem, and to countless thousands of angels in a joyful gathering.
> // **Hebrews 12:22**

The land of our inheritance

God called Abraham out of the land of Ur to bring him into a Land he and his descendants would inherit. Many centuries later after the descendants of Abraham had become enslaved in Egypt, God appeared to Moses with an assignment for Him: "I have surely seen the oppression of My people who are in Egypt, and have heard their cry because of their taskmasters, for I know their sorrows. So I have come down to deliver them out of the hand of the Egyptians, and to bring them up from that land to a good and large land, to a land flowing with milk and honey" (Exodus 3:7-8). The Lord was bringing them into the Land of their inheritance.

Then the people were brought into the promised land and the territory shared among the tribes and families (Numbers 34:29). Everyone got an inheritance as the Lord had purposed. But they all soon disctovered that the promised land was only a shadow of what God had planned for His people. The writer of Hebrews puts it this way, "All these died in faith [guided and sustained by it], without receiving the promises... The truth is that they were longing for a better country, that is, a heavenly one. For that reason God is not ashamed [of them or] to be called their God; for He has prepared a city for them" (Hebrews 11:13 & 16 Amp). The land of Canaan was only a shadow of the greater things to come, the reality of which things are in Christ (Hebrews 10:1).

> **If you are born again, you are in Zion, the city of our inheritance, and you can now possess that which God has for you in Christ Jesus.**

God had prepared a heavenly city – Zion. He prepared it with us in mind and the patriarchs were not getting it without us. For, "God had us in mind and had something better for us, so that they [these men and women of authentic faith] would not be made perfect apart from us" (Hebrews 11:40 Amp). When we received Christ, we were born into that city, we were born into Zion. So, we have come into the land of our inheritance. As the writer of Hebrews puts it, "You have come to Mount Zion, to the city of the living God, the heavenly Jerusalem, and to countless thousands of angels in a joyful gathering" (Hebrews 12:22-23). We are presently in Zion, the land of our inheritance.

Prayer

Heavenly Father, thank you for bringing me into the land of my inheritance, to Zion, the heavenly city. Thank you for qualifying me to share in the inheritance of the saints who are in the light. I receive gladly all that you have for me. In Jesus' name.

Bible in one year // **Genesis 49-50, Matthew 13:31-58**

The Lord will record, when He registers the peoples: "This one was born there". // **Psalm 87:6**

Your true birthplace

The Psalmist often wrote in prophetic terms, declaring of things to come as he was inspired by the Holy Spirit. One of such prophetic inspirations is this, "I will make mention of Rahab and Babylon to those who know Me; Behold, O Philistia and Tyre, with Ethiopia: 'This one was born there'" And of Zion it will be said, "This one and that one were born in her; and the Most High Himself shall establish her". The Lord will record, when He registers the peoples: "This one was born there" (Psalm 87:4-6).

The Psalmist looking forward with the eyes of the Spirit, saw a time when the Lord was going to do a census of His people, making a record of their places of birth. He saw the Lord declare, "I will make mention of those who know me". And he went on to list the names of these foreign nations which by nature were not a part of Israel nor shared in the covenants of God. He was talking of a time when the non-Jew and all who believe would be counted as God's people. Just as Paul would later explain about the gospel reaching the gentiles, "I was found by those who did not seek Me; I was made manifest to those who did not ask for Me" (Romans 10:20).

> When you believed in Jesus, you became born of God and born into Zion, the heavenly city. Zion is therefore your true birthplace and with this are great implications.

The Psalmist added, "And of Zion it will be said, "This one and that one were born in her; and the Most High Himself shall establish her". The Lord will record, when He registers the peoples: "This one was born there". The Psalmist saw a time coming for a spiritual census when the Lord will make a registry of His people and their birthplace would be declared as Zion. This prophecy is fulfilled in Christ. Just as we all were born into this physical world at birth, even so we, at new birth, were born into Zion. We were born into the heavenly city of God. As it is written, "You have come to Mount Zion, to the city of the living God, the heavenly Jerusalem. You have come to thousands upon thousands of angels in joyful assembly, to the church of the firstborn, whose names are written in heaven (Hebrews 12:22-23). Indeed, when the Lord makes a census of His people, He says of you, "This one was born in Zion". That is your true birthplace, and with this are implications.

Prayer

Heavenly Father, thank you for giving me new birth into Zion, your heavenly City. Thank you for delivering me from the dominion of darkness and translating me into the Kingdom of the son you love where I can live free of demonic oppressions and the consequences of sin. In Jesus' name.

Bible in one year // **Exodus 1-3, Matthew 14:1-21**

JAN 22

> Not that I have already attained, or am already perfected; but I press on, that I may lay hold of that for which Christ Jesus has also laid hold of me.
> // **Phil 3:12**

Make it your own

Paul did well on many occasions to record his prayers for the saints in his letters. In one such writings to the Church in Ephesus, Paul wrote, "I pray that you, being rooted and established in love, may have power, together with all the Lord's holy people, to grasp how wide and long and high and deep is the love of Christ, and to know this love that surpasses knowledge–that you may be filled to the measure of all the fullness of God" (Ephesians 3:18-19 NIV). Paul prayed that the saints would be able to grasp somethings. However, there is more to that word than just grasping. The King James Version of the bible renders same verse as follows: "May be able to comprehend with all the saints". It uses another word, "comprehend".

> God's will for you is that you will grasp the truths of His word and make it your own. Bring the word home to yourself and make them your personal truths. This is the word that has power in your life.

In translation, some meaning of Paul's prayer is lost because both words (grasp and comprehend) as used above do not fully communicate his thoughts. The word translated to mean grasp or comprehend is the Greek work "Katalambano". It literally means to "seize something and make it yours". Another word in English closer to meaning is the word apprehend. Like when thieves or armed rebels are apprehended by the forces of law and order. It has to do with a forceful taking of something. But more than just grasping, you take it and make it yours.

It is the same word that Paul uses in Philippians 3:12, Not that I have already attained, or am already perfected; but I press on, that I may lay hold of that for which Christ Jesus has also laid hold of me". Paul was pressing on to "Katalambano" that for which Christ had taken hold of him. He was making efforts to seize and make it his own. This is what you have to do with the word of God. Just as Paul prayed that the Ephesians would comprehend together with the saints, he really was saying they would grasp with full understanding the truth of God's word and make it theirs. That is the knowledge that benefits you, the knowledge that has been personalized, the knowledge you take hold of and make your own.

Prayer

Heavenly Father, thank you, for we have received, not the spirit that is of the world, but the Spirit that is of you; that we might know the things that are freely given to us. As we meditate in the word and discover these things, we lay hold on the truths and make them ours. In Jesus' name.

Bible in one year // **Exodus 4-6, Matthew 12:22-36**

> This charge I commit to you... according to the prophecies previously made concerning you, that by them you may wage the good warfare.
> // 1 Timothy 1:18

JAN 23

A prophetic people

While there can be so much controversy about prophecy, it is important that such controversies and abuse of a heavenly gift does not blind us from what it really is. We are a prophetic people and we will be making a big mistake to not walk with that consciousness. Even your life is a prophecy, it was conceived long ago by God and its paths traced long before you ever were born. And this is true for every life. However, we only become positioned to flow with the prophetic move of God when we become born again by receiving Jesus Christ. This is where a destiny and life in God begins.

Ephesians 2:10 tells us, "For we are His workmanship [His own master work, a work of art], created in Christ Jesus [reborn from above–spiritually transformed, renewed, ready to be used] for good works, which God prepared [for us] beforehand [taking paths which He set], so that we would walk in them [living the good life which He prearranged and made ready for us] (Amplified). In this light, your life is the unfolding of a prophecy. Together in Christ, we are a prophetic people. Paul wrote to Timothy, "This charge I commit to you, son Timothy, according to the prophecies previously made concerning you, that by them you may wage the good warfare" (1 Timothy 1:18).

We are a people of prophecy. Our very lives are prophecies in God. So, we must walk with this consciousness and give heed to prophetic guidance in our lives.

This implies we must give attention to prophecies, looking out for what the Lord is saying to you as an individual or the church as His people. Then give heed to the prophetic word and act accordingly. The King Jehoshaphat told his people, "Believe in the LORD your God, and you shall be established; believe His prophets, and you shall prosper" (2 Chronicles 20:20). He understood the purpose of prophecy and the benefits it offers to those who heed them. Prophecy is the unfolding of divine secrets; it is God making known His plans to His people. Sometimes, He reveals the schemes of the devil so that we might outwit him. We are a people of prophecy, and by watching for the word of the Lord, we can take advantage of His prophetic guidance and navigate our way in destiny.

Prayer

Father thank you for the Spirit of revelation given to me in Christ Jesus. For through the Holy Spirit, your plan is made know to me. And as I give heed to your prophetic leading in my life, I outwit the devil and take advantage of great opportunities for my progress and wellbeing. In Jesus' name.

Bible in one year // **Exodus 7-8, Matthew 15:1-20**

Humbly accept the word God has planted in your hearts, for it has the power to save your souls. // **James 1:21 NLT**

Receive the word with meekness

James wrote, "Receive with meekness the implanted word, which is able to save your souls" (James 1:21). This is a commendable attitude with which to receive the word of God. Meekness has to do with the quality of being submissive, not being puffed-up with how much you know such that receiving new knowledge becomes difficult (Colossians 2:18). Meekness is that attitude that receives the word with a heart willing to embrace and submit to the truth it communicates, as you say to yourself, "I don't know better". It is an attitude of humility that receives God's word from the standpoint of "He knows better". In this case, if you find something that is opposed to your thinking, you don't argue with the word of God but seek understanding and receive God's perspective.

You will hear some people say things like, "I know the bible says, but personally I think that...". Then they go ahead to express a contrary opinion. They negate the word of God and argue it away with vain human philosophies. That is the converse of meekness. That is being puffed-up with vain knowledge. Such people know too much to be informed by the word of God. They seek to explain spiritual principles away with fruitless human ideas. Never find yourself in such a situation where you stand opposed to God's word. It can only harm you.

> **Never find yourself disputing God's word with empty human opinions. That will only work to your disadvantage. Receive with meekness the word of God which has power to save you.**

Paul describes such a person when he wrote to the Colossians, "Do not let anyone who delights in false humility and the worship of angels disqualify you. Such a person also goes into great detail about what they have seen; they are puffed-up with idle notions by their unspiritual mind" (Colossians 2:18 NIV). Paul says such a person is puffed-up with idle notions, crazy ideas resulting from an unspiritual mind (1 Corinthians 2:14). The word has power to save your soul and bring salvation to every area of your life. But that will not happen until you receive the word with meekness and put it to use in your life.

Prayer

Almighty God, thank you for your wisdom made available to me through the scriptures. For though it be foolishness to many, it has the potency to save me in all things. I rejoice in your word and accept it for my life so it can produce its results as promised. In Jesus' name.

Bible in one year // **Exodus 9-11, Matthew 15:21-39**

For indeed the gospel was preached to us as well as to them; but the word which they heard did not profit them, lnot being mixed with faith in those who heard it. // **Hebrews 4:2**

JAN 25

Make profit in the Word

"For indeed the gospel was preached to us as well as to them; but the word which they heard did not profit them, not being mixed with faith in those who heard it" (Hebrews 4:2). The writer of Hebrews explains to us in this verse above a reason why the word of God did not profit a group of people – they did not mix the word of God with faith. The missing component for these people was faith. The word of God produces results in those who receive it with faith. It can make you prosper; it can bring healing to your body; it can make you effective in Kingdom service. All these results are possible by the word of God when it is received with faith.

Make profit in the word by receiving it with a heart of faith that dares to act on its truths, and you will see the results it talks about. The message does not profit some people because they received it without faith. Jesus gave a parable, "Behold, a sower went out to sow. And as he sowed, some seed fell by the wayside; and the birds came and devoured them. Some fell on stony places, where they did not have much earth; and they immediately sprang up because they had no depth of earth. But when the sun was up they were scorched, and because they had no root they withered away. And some fell among thorns, and the thorns sprang up and choked them. But others fell on good ground and yielded a crop: some a hundredfold, some sixty, some thirty" (Matthew 13:4-8).

Make profit in the word by receiving it with a heart of faith that dares to act on its truths, and you will see the results it talks about.

The problem is never with the word. The problem is always with the heart that receives it. It is up to you to make profit with the word of God, making a harvest of the results it guarantees. Jesus later explained the parable to show why the word was not fruitful in three groups of people. For the first, they lacked understanding, so the enemy came and snatched the word. The second had no root in themselves and could not stand challenges, so the word failed for them. The third class refers to those who because of cares and the deceptions of this world, fail to bear fruit because these things choke the word. But there is a final class, these receive the word and yield a harvest in different proportions (Matthew 13:21-23). This is the class you want to belong to, such as make profit by the word of God.

Prayer

Heavenly Father, My heart is plowed by your Spirit and made a receptive and fruitful ground for your word. The word works in me, bringing forth fruit to its maximum capacity in all things. I receive grace for quick understanding of the word so the evil one will not outsmart me. In Jesus' name.

Bible in one year // **Exodus 12-13, Matthew 16**

JAN 26

He Himself has said, "I will never leave you nor forsake you." So we may boldly say: "The Lord is my helper; I will not fear. What can man do to me?" // **Hebrews 13:5-6**

Our response to the word

There is a response to the word of God that we need to practice if we have not yet cultivated such an approach. For our response to the word of God is what positions us for results by the word of God. The writer of Hebrews shows us how to respond to the word of God. He wrote, "He Himself has said, "I will never leave you nor forsake you." So we may boldly say: "The Lord is my helper; I will not fear. What can man do to me?" (Hebrews 13:5-6). In his writing, he shows us a simple principle: What God says to us is so that we can say something in response. He said He will never leave nor forsake us. We process that, understand the implications, then declare the implications as our response to God's word.

> Our response to the word of God is to proclaim in unison with Him the things that are said concerning us. For in doing so, His works will be manifested in our lives.

This is the word that produces result. We receive the word and prophesy that word in response, speaking the word of God to ourselves or to circumstances. This is how come scriptures declare, "They overcame him by the blood of the Lamb and by the word of their testimony" (Revelation 12:11). As we receive the word of God, our response is to testify to that word, speaking in unison with the Lord, what things have been said concerning us.

So when you read Ephesians 2:10 that says, "For we are God's masterpiece. He has created us anew in Christ Jesus, so we can do the good things he planned for us long ago" (NLT), you don't just go away and say you are blessed by the verse. You do more than that. Your response is to testify in line with that word. You declare in response, "I am a masterpiece of God's creation. I am a new creation in Christ Jesus. My life was predestined for good works. I walk in ordained paths and my life brings glory to the Lord". And as you respond in this manner to the word of God always, circumstances will adjust to your response. For the word of God on your lips is creative, producing the results it talks about. Just as Proverbs 18:21 tells us, "Death and life are in the power of the tongue".

Prayer

Almighty God, thank you for your word that has power on my lips to cause changes as I testify in unison with it. Therefore, I flourish in all things, producing results byw your word. By my testimony, the enemy is paralyzed, and my victory is made evident to all. In Jesus' name.

Bible in one year // **Exodus 14-15, Matthew 17**

By faith we understand that the worlds were framed by the word of God, so that the things which are seen were not made of things which are visible.
// **Hebrews 11:3**

JAN 27

Frame your world

By faith we understand that the worlds were framed by the word of God, so that the things which are seen were not made of things which are visible (Hebrews 11:3). What a profound saying! That the worlds were framed by the word of God and the things we all see in creation came into existence through words. This is a fundamental fact of life and all origins. Man can conjure every theory to explain our origins and justify them with every logical explanation of the big bang theory and evolution. Even then they all conclude that all that is seen came from nowhere. But we are not ignorant. We have light, we have spiritual information, and we know how it all came about.

The writer of Hebrew summarizes it in this one verse, "By faith we understand that the worlds were framed by the word of God, so that the things which are seen were not made of things which are visible". John gives us more insight to this creative power of God's word. "In the beginning was the Word, and the Word was with God, and the Word was God. He was in the beginning with God. All things were made through Him, and without Him nothing was made that was made (John 1:1-3). So, all things were made by the word, and without it, was nothing made. That is a repetition with emphasis – of all that is seen, there is nothing that came forth without having its origin from the word.

The word "Framed" as used in Hebrews 11:3 is the Greek word "Katartizo". In this context it is used as a word in architecture when you set the frame of a structure around which the rest of its components are fitted. It means to define the course of events. This goes to say the word of God framed the worlds, defining the course of events. This same law is still at work today and you can use it to your advantage as you consistently speak the word of God in your life, declaring the things you want to see. Don't speak failure, sickness, and poverty. Speak health, wealth, freedom, progress and all the good things made available to you in Christ Jesus. You will be framing your world with the word, defining the course of your life (Proverbs 18:21).

> The word of God on your lips is potent and able to define the course of your life, shaping events and defining outcomes as you speak words of faith and order your life in the way things should go.

Prayer

Heavenly Father, thank you for the potency of the word that it can do and undo. As we use the word in proclamations, we denounce whatever is not in accordance with your will in our lives and call into being the things that should be for your glory. In Jesus' name.

Bible in one year // **Exodus 16-18, Matthew 18:1-20**

JAN 28

*For assuredly, I say to you, whoever says to this mountain, 'Be removed and be cast into the sea,' and does not doubt in his heart, but believes that those things he says will be done, he will have whatever he says. // **Mark 11:23***

Speak to that situation

Mark records of us the words of Jesus, "For assuredly, I say to you, whoever says to this mountain, 'Be removed and be cast into the sea,' and does not doubt in his heart, but believes that those things he says will be done, he will have whatever he says" (Mark 11:23). In His words, Jesus showed us the power we have to command results through words. He said we would have whatever we say. However, to this guaranteed outcome was attached some duty. He shows us how to obtain results by words. In this verse are hidden many principles to apply.

The very first principle is to direct your words to the specific situation and declare what you want to see. If you feel sick, then speak healing to your body. Direct your words to whatever challenge it is and declare the outcome you want to see. The second thing is to believe in your hearts the words you have spoken. Don't just utter words. Speak out by faith, being confident that what you are saying produces the results. Remember the words of Jesus, "If you can believe, all things are possible to him who believes" (Mark 9:23).

> Whatever the challenge might be, you can fix the situation by speaking the word of God to it. And when you do, apply the basic principles that govern obtaining results by words.

Jesus also emphasized the need to not doubt. He said, "...and does not doubt in his heart". You have to overcome all doubts and give no room for any, if you want to see results by your words. Just like the Apostle James wrote, "Let him ask in faith, with no doubting, for he who doubts is like a wave of the sea driven and tossed by the wind. For let not that man suppose that he will receive anything from the Lord... (James 1:6-8). And finally, "...believe that those things which you said will be done". Don't make declarations and turn around to question if it will happen. You should know that it will be as you have declared. That is what it means to believe that those things which you have said shall be done. When someone puts all these simple principles to work and speak to that situation, Jesus guarantees, "He will have whatever he says".

Prayer

Heavenly Father, thank you for my words are powerful, able to bring into being the results they proclaim. So, as I speak words of faith in accordance with your will, the results declared come to manifestation to the praise of your glory. In Jesus' name.

Bible in one year // **Exodus 19-20, Matthew 18:21-35**

Where the word of the King is, there is power... // **Ecclesiastes 8:4**

JAN 29

The words of a king

"Where the word of the King is, there is power" (Ecclesiastes 8:4). This is a spiritual law. There is always power available to propel the words of a king into the accomplishment of the purpose for which it was sent. Now the bible records of such an incident with Jesus, "Now it happened on a certain day, as He was teaching, that there were Pharisees and teachers of the law sitting by, who had come out of every town of Galilee, Judea, and Jerusalem. And the power of the Lord was present to heal them" (Luke 5:17). Jesus the King of Kings was teaching, and "The power of the Lord was present to heal".

This also explains something true about you. Revelation 1:5-6 says, "From Jesus Christ, the faithful witness, the firstborn from the dead, and the ruler over the kings of the earth. To Him who loved us and washed us from our sins in His own blood, and has made us KINGS and PRIESTS to His God and Father, to Him be glory and dominion forever and ever". We are Kings and priests unto God in Christ Jesus. It is a sovereign decree. God has made you a king, and with that, His power is made available to you to fulfill the proclamations of your mouth. Just as the Ecclesiastes 8:4 puts it, "Where the word of the King is, there is power".

As the king God has made you in Christ, He also makes available His power to make manifest the words you proclaim. Have this understanding when proclaiming the word of God. There is power to make it happen.

This plays out on several instances throughout scriptures. You must understand these spiritual principles and take full advantage of them for a victorious and fulfilling life in Christ. One such instance when God honors the words of His servants is in Acts 3:1-8. You can read the whole story for yourself. Peter said to the cripple, "Silver and gold I do not have, but what I do have I give you: In the name of Jesus Christ of Nazareth, rise up and walk." And he took him by the right hand and lifted him up, and immediately his feet and ankle bones received strength. So he, leaping up, stood and walked and entered the temple with them –walking, leaping, and praising God" (Acts 3:6-8). Peter spoke to the situation directly defining the outcome he desired. Notice that following Peter's declarations, the man's legs received strength. For the power of God was present to honor the word of the kings.

Prayer

Heavenly Father, thank you for making me a King in Christ Jesus and calling me to reign with Him in life. Thank you for your power that is made available to me for the fulfillment of the words I speak. We this awareness I speak words of life, prosperity, progress, and increase. In Jesus' name.

Bible in one year // **Exodus 21-22, Matthew 19**

JAN 30

A good man out of the good treasure of his heart brings forth good; and an evil man out of the evil treasure of his heart brings forth evil. For out of the abundance of the heart his mouth speaks. // Luke 6:45

Take with you words

Take words with you, and return to the LORD. Say to Him, "Take away all iniquity; Receive us graciously, for we will offer the sacrifices of our lips (Hosea 14:2). The prophet Hosea was instructing the people to take with them words and turn to the Lord. Then He went on to tell them what to say with regards to that specific situation. He even likened their words to be sacrifices of the lips. And indeed, words are a form of sacrifice which when rightly offered, moves heaven to action with results that will be evident to all. Be it God's word uttered in prayer or proclaimed towards situations needing a change.

> Take with you words by building in your spirit, a reservoir of verses through meditation. These will serve you in times of need. Be it in prayer, in addressing situations or in resisting the devil when he attacks.

You have to take words with you, that is to say, have with you words stored up in your spirit and ready for use when the situation comes. Jesus taught us how this can be done. He said to the disciples, "A good man out of the good treasure of his heart brings forth good; and an evil man out of the evil treasure of his heart brings forth evil. For out of the abundance of the heart his mouth speaks" (Luke 6:45). Your heart is a reservoir that will spill out its content in the face of a situation. Like a loaded gun, you can store up the word of God in you, the right scriptures for diverse situations. And these words, you take along with you in life for the day of need.

When Jesus encountered the devil in the wilderness, He had words with Him. Jesus answered the Devil with words of scripture. He had words with Him in the wilderness, a reservoir of words He had stocked as He mastered the scriptures. Remember in Luke 2:46, even as a little boy, it is written of Jesus, "They found him in the temple courts, sitting among the teachers, listening to them and asking them questions" (Luke 12:46). As you meditate in God's word, memorize verses, and let these be on your lips always. Often, as I go about my affairs, I speak the word of God to myself, declaring "The Lord is my shepherd, I shall not be in want". I declare, "I will not see shame"; as it is written, "Those who look to him for help will be radiant with joy; no shadow of shame will darken their faces" (Psalm 34:5 NLT).

Prayer

Heavenly Father, thank you for a heart that can store up your word for the time of need. I receive grace to memorize and retain potent scriptures that will serve me at the right time. From the abundance of my heart, I speak words of life, faith, prosperity, and progress and see them come to pass in Jesus' name.

Bible in one year // **Exodus 23-24, Matthew 20:1-16**

Be doers of the word, and not hearers only, deceiving yourselves.
// James 1:22

JAN 31

Build on the rock

This first month of devotionals was a journey aimed at inspiring your love for the word of God, motivating you into a consistent life of meditation in scriptures and showing you how to put that word to work for practical results. It is worth ending on this note with an emphasis on the need to be a doer of the word and not a hearer only. Jesus shared a parable of two builders, a foolish and a wise builder. He said, ""Therefore whoever hears these sayings of Mine, and does them, I will liken him to a wise man who built his house on the rock: and the rain descended, the floods came, and the winds blew and beat on that house; and it did not fall, for it was founded on the rock" (Matthew 7:24-25).

Jesus went ahead to exemplify in pictures what the reverse will do. "Everyone who hears these sayings of Mine, and does not do them, will be like a foolish man who built his house on the sand: and the rain descended, the floods came, and the winds blew and beat on that house; and it fell. And great was its fall" (Matthew 7:26-27). Be a doer of the word of God. don't just read and feel blessed and enlightened. Use the knowledge you are gaining. If of faith, then walk in faith; if a call to a change of habit or character, respond accordingly; if a call to duty or responsibility, take action. Be a doer of the word, one who puts to use in their own life, the knowledge they have gained.

James echoes this in another way in His writing, "Be doers of the word, and not hearers only, deceiving yourselves. For if anyone is a hearer of the word and not a doer, he is like a man observing his natural face in a mirror; for he observes himself, goes away, and immediately forgets what kind of man he was. But he who looks into the perfect law of liberty and continues in it, and is not a forgetful hearer but a doer of the work, this one will be blessed in what he does" (James 1:22-25). James shows by writing: As a doer of the word, not only will you be building on the rock, you will also be blessed in all you do.

Build upon the rock by living your life according to the knowledge you are gaining from the word of God. And you will stand the challenges of life. To do otherwise is to be foolish, deceiving your own self.

Prayer

Heavenly Father, thank you for you are working in me to will and to do according to your good pleasure. I am yielded to your word and to your spirit. Today I receive grace to live by the word, so my life is established on the rock, firmly planted and able to withstand the storms of life. And by your word, I make progress from glory to glory. In Jesus' name.

Bible in one year // **Exodus 25-26, Matthew 20:17-34**

FEBRUARY

> If My people who are called by My name will humble themselves, and pray and seek My face, and turn from their wicked ways, then I will hear from heaven, and will forgive their sin and heal their land. // **2 Chronicles 7:14**

FEB 1

A call to prayer

Jesus spoke a parable to His disciples to show that men always ought to pray and not lose heart, saying: "There was in a certain city a judge who did not fear God nor regard man. Now there was a widow in that city; and she came to him, saying, 'Get justice for me from my adversary.' And he would not for a while; but afterward he said within himself, 'Though I do not fear God nor regard man, yet because this widow troubles me I will avenge her, lest by her continual coming she weary me.'" Then the Lord said, "Hear what the unjust judge said. And shall God not avenge His own elect who cry out day and night to Him, though He bears long with them? I tell you that He will avenge them speedily" (Luke 18:1-8).

Someone has rightly said, "If there is someone to pray, then there is God to answer". And that is the call we have from the Lord – a call to prayer. James wrote, "Is anyone among you in trouble? Let them pray" (James 5:13). As we look around us and find things that are not where they should be, or situations contrary to God's plans and purposes for us, it is a call to prayer – the sufferings in the world and the challenges of life all call us to pray.

Jesus in this parable emphasized not just the call to pray, but also the need for persistent prayer – prayer that doesn't stop at anything until the change is established. God is willing and ready to grant our requests. That is the reason He calls us to pray. Like the prophet of old wrote, „If My people who are called by My name will humble themselves, and pray and seek My face, and turn from their wicked ways, then I will hear from heaven, and will forgive their sin and heal their land" (2 Chronicles 7:14).

> **There is a call to pray for everything that is contrary to God's plan and purpose for our lives, a call to pray for the establishment of God's plans in our lives and our world.**

Prayer

Gracious God, thank you for the blessing of a new month and the opportunities therein. We receive grace this season to respond to the call to prayer, knowing that you will hear and answer us. In Jesus' name.

Bible in one year // **Exodus 27-28, Matthew 21:1-22**

FEB 2

> God is faithful, through whom you were called into fellowship with His Son, Jesus Christ our Lord. // **1 Corinthians 1:9**

A call to fellowship

Paul wrote, "God is faithful, through whom you were called into fellowship with His Son, Jesus Christ our Lord" (1 Corinthians 1:9). The call to prayer is more than a call to present an endless list of requests; it is first and foremost, a call to fellowship with the divine. It is a time of communion with the Lord, when you get to have a moment of conversation with your heavenly Father. It is more than a shopping stop where you come over with your list of things to be handed over to you (Although there is time and avenue for that). It is a time to recognize the divine and to walk into that communion with the trinity. That is the greater purpose of prayer – the time spent with God.

> The call to prayer is more than a call to make requests, it is a call to a time of fellowship with the divine.

Communion or fellowship is the very reason Jesus came in the first place, there was a separation with God which He came to restore. He emphasized communion as the reason why He comes into our lives. He says, "Behold, I stand at the door and knock. If anyone hears My voice and opens the door, I will come in to him and dine with him, and he with Me" (Revelation 3:20). Then he talked about them making their home with us who live by His word (John 14:21-23).

God longs to spend time with you. He has called you into a fellowship with His son Jesus, and prayer gives you an opportunity for that fellowship, a time with God in conversation. Think of meeting the leader of your country, even if on a specific mission with specific requests, there is going to be a conversation and a moment of exchange. That is fellowship – when we take out time, not necessarily to make requests, but to spend time with the Lord, meditating in His word and waiting on His response and His touch on our lives. Prayer only becomes richer, when it goes beyond a time of just making requests to a time of fellowship.

Prayer

Thank You Heavenly Father for calling us into fellowship with yourself and with your Son Jesus. Help us to recognize this privilege of being alone with the monarch of the universe in a time of communion and grant us the grace to seek your face and presence through prayer. Even as you promised, make known yourself to us through personal revelations as we pray. In Jesus name.

Bible in one year // **Exodus 29-30, Matthew 21:23-46**

The heaven, even the heavens, are the Lord's; but the earth He has given to the children of men. // **Psalm 115:16**

FEB 3

Why prayer

Often, some people ask the question: If God is all-knowing, why then do we have to make requests through prayers? The reason for this question is simple. They are yet to understand God's relationship and manner of dealing with humanity. As for being all knowing, God truly is. Jesus said this about prayer: "When you pray, do not keep on babbling like pagans, for they think they will be heard because of their many words. Do not be like them, for your Father knows what you need before you ask him" (Matthew 6:7-8 NIV). So, in prayer, you are not telling someone who is uninformed about your plight. The Psalmist declared this about the Lord, "You know when I sit and when I rise; you perceive my thoughts from afar" (Psalm 139:2). He understood even before thoughts crossed his mind, the Lord already knew them.

So why then do we have to pray? We have to make requests because God's relationship with humanity is like that of a landlord and his tenants. Like the Psalmist wrote, "The heaven, even the heavens, are the Lord's; but the earth He has given to the children of men" (Psalm 115:16). Starting from Eden, what God did was create an environment for us in which we could live and have fellowship with him. Like tenants, He has entrusted the earth to us.

Now the landlord has no legal right to walk in and out of the building as he wills just because it is his property, so long as that building is on lease. The landlord needs our invitation and formal permission to come into the building even for works of maintenance and repairs. That is what prayers do. In prayer, we give the Landlord of the earth the official invitation and right of way to get involved with the affairs of men. So, though He loves us and is informed of our concerns, He waits on our invitation because he would not overwrite our will. Therefore, make no assumptions about God being all-knowing. If there is a concern, then there is a call to prayer.

> **The Lord is all knowing but needs our invitation and permission to get involved with the affairs of men in the earth as we call on him through prayer.**

Prayer

Almighty God, thank you for the illumination in your word. Thank you for the privilege of prayer, that we can come boldly to the throne of grace to obtain mercy and find help in times of need. Today we receive grace to pray about things even as you have called us to do for a supernatural change. In Jesus' name.

Bible in one year // **Exodus 31-33, Matthew 22:1-22**

FEB 4

If you abide in Me, and My words abide in you, you will ask what you desire, and it shall be done for you. // **John 15:7**

A key to answered prayers

"If you abide in Me, and My words abide in you, you will ask what you desire, and it shall be done for you" (John 15:7). That was Jesus himself talking. He literally gave us the key to answered prayers. He said that for good reason and meant what He said. For it is the case that if His word abides in us as we continually meditate in it, we will know His will and be able to pray accordingly. For His word will define our expectations and tailor our desires to conform to His purpose. And by that, whatever we ask will already be in line with the things He is willing to do for us. Such prayers always get answered.

James explained why sometimes prayers go unanswered. "You desire but do not have, so you kill. You covet but you cannot get what you want, so you quarrel and fight. You do not have because you do not ask God. When you ask, you do not receive, because you ask with wrong motives, that you may spend what you get on your pleasures" (James 4:2-3 NIV). Remember Jesus said, "Ask and it will be given to you; seek and you will find; knock and the door will be opened to you. For everyone who asks receives; the one who seeks finds; and to the one who knocks, the door will be opened" (Matthew 7:7-8 NIV). Now James tells us why this promise might not be true for everyone – they ask with wrong motives.

> Through meditation in the word, our desires and inclinations are tailored to align with the will of the Father, guaranteeing for us answered prayers.

We have the key to answered prayers – praying from a place of understanding of the word of God with knowledge of His will and purpose for our lives and the rest of the world. You can always find through scriptures what God wants for your life and for the world and let these guide and shape your requests. Such requests made in accordance with the will of the Father never go unanswered. This makes for an exciting prayer life – when you continually watch the things you pray for come to pass.

Prayer

Thank you, Heavenly Father, for the blessing of a new day. We receive grace today to abide in you and have your word abiding in our hearts. That as we know and pray in line with your will and purposes, no request will go unanswered. In Jesus name.

Bible in one year // Exodus 34-35, Matthew 22:23-46

Now this is the confidence that we have in Him, that if we ask anything according to His will, He hears us. // **1 John 5:14**

FEB 5

Here is our confidence

One reason for faithlessness in prayer is the lack of knowledge on God's will on an issue while we pray. On the contrary, knowledge of His will breaths confidence in us, a confidence that translates to potent faith. John wrote, "Now this is the confidence that we have in Him, that if we ask anything according to His will, He hears us. And if we know that He hears us, whatever we ask, we know that we have the petitions that we have asked of Him" (1 John 5:14-15). John goes ahead in his letter to emphasize this confidence that He hears us, is as good as the result expected

> Our Confidence in answered prayers which eventually breathes out the faith for results, is anchored on praying according to the will of the Father.

But how do we know God's will about a situation? The very first is to go back to scriptures and find out what the Lord says regarding that subject. For an example, considering healing, you can tell from scriptures that it is the Father's will for you to be in health as you read through many verses that emphasize this truth. It is His will that you prosper and be in health, even as your soul prospers (3 John 1:2). Healing was also made available for us through the cross. Just as it is written, "By His wounds we are healed" (Isaiah 53:5).

Sometimes there are situations that are not spelled out in the word of God, things for which you might not directly discern the will of the Father. That is where we get help from the Holy Spirit. Sometimes the Holy Spirit reveals to us the Father's will. Or as Paul wrote, "In the same way, the Spirit helps us in our weakness. We do not know what we ought to pray for, but the Spirit himself intercedes for us through wordless groans. And he who searches our hearts knows the mind of the Spirit, because the Spirit intercedes for God's people in accordance with the will of God" (Romans 8:26-27). That is one advantage and reason we pray in tongues, giving the Spirit an opportunity to pray according to the will of God.

Prayer

> Almighty God, as we pray and give you invitation to work in the things that concerns us, your will is established, and your glory revealed in our lives and communities. Thank you for the Holy Spirit who helps us to pray in accordance with your will in all things. In Jesus name.

Bible in one year // **Exodus 36-38, Matthew 23:1-22**

FEB 6

> He is also able to save to the uttermost those who come to God through Him, since He always lives to make intercession for them. // **Hebrews 7:25**

A fitting intercessor

He (Jesus) holds his priesthood permanently since he lives forever. So, he is able to save completely those who come to God through him, because he always lives to intercede for them. For it is indeed fitting for us to have such a high priest: holy, innocent, undefiled, separate from sinners, and exalted above the heavens (Hebrews 7:24-26 NET). As much as we are called to pray with guaranteed divine intervention, it is helpful to know that you have a fitting intercessor – the Lord Jesus himself. And He is able to save to the uttermost those who come to God through Him because He continually pleads our cause.

When you think you are failing in prayer and seem not to get all the support in prayer from the saints, remember that you have Jesus as your fitting intercessor. He lives and forever intercedes for you.

For all the things you fail to pray about, for all the times loved ones forget to mention you in prayer, He continually bears your name in the throne room, speaking on your behalf and in your favor. He is your intercessor in the presence of the Father. Now, to intercede means to plead a cause on behalf of another, soliciting assistance or cooperation from an authority or one who stands in a position to influence things for the one we are interceding for. You can think of your local representative in Government, who bears and brings your concerns to the right quarters.

Hebrews 4:15 tells us, "For we do not have a high priest who is unable to empathize with our weaknesses, but we have one who has been tempted in every way, just as we are - yet he did not sin". Moreover, He is fit for the office. Like our opening passage puts it, "Such a High Priest was fitting for us, who is holy, harmless, undefiled, separate from sinners, and has become higher than the heavens". Therefore Jesus, like one of us, effectively represents us in the Father's presence. While this is not a call to prayerlessness, it really means you can rest assured that Jesus makes up for all your inadequacies in prayer. He forever lives and intercedes for you. He is your fitting intercessor.

Prayer

Heavenly Father, as much as we labor in prayer, we rest assured in your love and in the ministry of Jesus our High Priest who lives to make intercessions on our behalf. Being confident that you would perfect all that concerns us, even where we fall short in prayers. In Jesus' name.

Bible in one year // **Exodus 39-40, Matthew 23:23-39**

> I will stand my watch and set myself on the rampart, and watch to see what He will say to me, and what I will answer when I am corrected. // **Habakkuk 2:1**

FEB 7

Do well to listen

Habakkuk had been praying to the Lord, inquiring why the Lord seemed silent despite the sufferings of His people. The second chapter of his book opens up with him making a declaration to himself – to position himself to listen: "I will stand my watch and set myself on the rampart, and watch to see what He will say to me, and what I will answer when I am corrected" (Habakkuk 2:1). He understood prayer was more than a one-way conversation. That we should recognize too. It is not sufficient that you pour out your heart to the Lord in prayer. It is equally important that you give Him attention to Listen – looking out for what He would answer and say.

In fact, it is not so much as important how much you can tell the Lord in prayer. It matters more what you hear from Him after you have prayed. For in His response, there is a lot more to be blessed with. Sometimes that information is all you need, just to be reminded even that He has it checked. Other times, it could be the specific instruction that will flip things around for your good. It is not sufficient that you prayed. It is much more necessary that you give attention to listen to the Lord. That is what Habakkuk set in his heart to do. And the Lord responded saying, "Write the vision and make it plain on tablets, that he may run who reads it" (Habakkuk 2:2).

> Do well to listen to what the Lord would say when you pray, He might have a word of response or instruction for you.

Learn to be quiet in His presence and listen when you pray. Sometimes just close your eyes and be calm, don't utter a word, just wait in an atmosphere of worship with ears open to hear what the Lord will say. Have your mind fixed on Him and be keen as you look out for any visions or pictures that might flash through your mind. You will be surprised what the Lord might bring to your attention as you begin or maintain this Holy practice. Don't just pray. Also do well to Listen when you pray, for the Lord will speak to you in response to your prayers.

Prayer

Thank You Heavenly Father, for the fellowship we have with you in Christ Jesus. That like your sheep, we can know your voice and follow as you lead us. Today we receive the grace to wait on you and to hear you when you answer us with words. In Jesus' name..

Bible in one year // **Leviticus 1-3, Matthew 24:1-28**

FEB 8

> When he brings out his own sheep, he goes before them; and the sheep follow him, for they know his voice. // **John 10:4**

You can know His voice

John wrote, "The gatekeeper opens the gate for him, and the sheep listen to his voice. He calls his own sheep by name and leads them out. When he has brought out all his own, he goes on ahead of them, and his sheep follow him because they know his voice. But they will never follow a stranger; in fact, they will run away from him because they do not recognize a stranger's voice" (John 10:3-5 NIV). From when you believe in Jesus and start your walk with Him, there is a lot of learning unto spiritual maturity. One such area of growth is to come to know the voice of the Lord and to distinguish it from other voices.

Maybe you are reading this today as one who knows the voice of our shepherd. Then glory to God. Or maybe as one who still has lots of questions about how God speaks and if we can know His voice today. In any category, I pray you find helpful illumination on the subject in the ensuing pages of this devotional. That was Jesus talking in our opening passage. He said He is the good shepherd and calls His sheep by name. They follow Him because THEY KNOW HIS VOICE. A stranger's voice they would not follow. This is true for every child of God; we have the capacity to know His voice.

> It is in your capacity to know and recognize the voice of God if you would give it time and remain in an atmosphere of spiritual growth through knowledge in the word of God.

Nonetheless, like a child born to a couple, you would have to grow to know that voice. A child doesn't necessarily come out knowing the voice of the parents. Rather, with time and exposure, they become acquainted with their voices. Generally, when the shepherd leads the sheep, the sheep follow the shepherd because they know his voice. But lambs follow the sheep because they know their mother. In the process, because they abide with the shepherd, the lamb becomes exposed to the shepherd's voice. Even so, if you fellowship with other mature believers who can guide you, you will be in the right atmosphere to know His voice. With Your Daily Light in your hands, you are also on that path.

Prayer

Thank You LORD for the privilege that we can know your voice and follow you in the paths you have traced out for us in destiny, fulfilling your purpose and bringing glory to you. We receive grace to always discern and recognize your voice. In Jesus' name.

Bible in one year // **Leviticus 4-5, Matthew 24:29-51**

The one who has My commands and keeps them is the one who loves Me. And the one who loves Me will be loved by My Father. I also will love him and will reveal Myself to him. // **John 14:21 HCSB**

FEB 9

Start with the written Word

"For gaining wisdom and instruction, for understanding words of insight.... let the wise listen and add to their learning, and let the discerning get guidance – for understanding proverbs and parables, the sayings and riddles of the wise" (Proverbs 1:1-6 NIV). This introductory writing of the author of proverbs spells out some fundamental truths about knowing and discerning the voice of God. Like the rest of the Bible, the author highlights the purpose of the book. Among other things, it serves for gaining wisdom and for understanding words of insight. The sixth verse of the opening passage crowns it all with these words, "For understanding proverbs and parables, the sayings and riddles of the wise".

You might remember the words of the Lord to Moses when He said, "If there were prophets among you, I, the LORD, would reveal myself in visions. I would speak to them in dreams. But not with my servant Moses. Of all my house, he is the one I trust. I speak to him face to face, clearly, and not in riddles! (Numbers 12:6-8 NLT). Paraphrased, the Lord said to Moses, "If there were prophets among you, I, the LORD, would reveal myself in visions. I would speak to them in dreams, and I will do so in riddles.

> *If you will come to know and recognize the voice of the Lord, you will have to start by meditating in the written word.*

Together, this tells us giving attention to these written words will program an individual's mind to be able to understand and make sense of the riddles and parables of the wise when they speak. So, if you will get to know and recognize the voice of the Lord and be able to comprehend Him when He speaks, you will have to begin with the right attitude towards the written word. That is where it all begins. Jesus said, "The one who has My commands and keeps them is the one who loves Me. And the one who loves Me will be loved by My Father. I also will love him and will reveal Myself to him" (John 14:21 HCSB).

Prayer

Thank You Heavenly Father for the words long preserved for us, that we might meditate therein and walk by. Thank you for through your Word you will reveal yourself to us continually as we live by it. We receive grace to delight in your written word that by it we might experience you. In Jesus' name.

Bible in one year // **Leviticus 6-7, Matthew 25:1-30**

FEB 10

One thing I have desired of the Lord, that will I seek: That I may dwell in the house of the Lord all the days of my life, to behold the beauty of the Lord, and to inquire in His temple. // **Psalm 27:4**

Be inquisitive in His presence

One thing I have often said is this, "If the disciples of Jesus did not ask him questions, there is much we never would have known". As you go through scriptures, particularly the gospels, that is one thing that stands out. The Lord often spoke in response to the curiosity of men. And that is something David understood. He made the declaration: "One thing I have desired of the Lord, that will I seek: That I may dwell in the house of the Lord all the days of my life, to behold the beauty of the Lord, and to inquire in His temple (Psalm 27:4). He desired to dwell in the house of the Lord and to inquire in His presence. He had an inquisitive spirit in the presence of the Lord. Even as a King, it was His attitude to inquire of the Lord even when the one thing that ought to be done seemed evident.

> Have an inquisitive spirit in the presence of God if you would like to hear him on issues. Learn to ask God questions.

In 1 Samuel 30, after the Amalekites raided Ziklag, taking away the wives of David and His men, and bringing away everything with them as plunder, there seemed just one thing to do – chase down the raiders. But not David, he would first inquire of the Lord. He asked specific questions. The bible tells us, "David inquired of the Lord, "Shall I pursue this raiding party? Will I overtake them?" "Pursue them," he answered. "You will certainly overtake them and succeed in the rescue" (1 Samuel 30:8 NIV).

On the other hand, we have Joshua. One of the biggest errors of His life and ministry was a result of not asking questions. You might have read the story from Joshua 9, when the Gibeonites resorted to deception to save their lives from the Israelites who had proven invincible to every army that had come up against them. Joshua 9:14 records, "The Israelites sampled their provisions BUT DID NOT INQUIRE of the Lord". And the Lord too did not interrupt Joshua to say, "It's a lie". For often, the Lord talks to an inquisitive spirit in His presence, and in response to our inquiries. Be inquisitive in His presence.

Prayer

Thank you, Gracious Lord, that we can come boldly to the throne of grace to find mercy and obtain help in times of need. Help me to recognize you in my day and to seek your will in all things, being attentive to hear when you speak to me. In Jesus' name.

Bible in one year // Leviticus 8-10, Matthew 25:31-46

Do you not know that you are the temple of God and that the Spirit of God dwells in you? // **1 Corinthians 3:16**

FEB 11

Listen from the inside

Could it be we sometimes miss the word of the Lord for us or His voice because we are listening wrongly? One such can even result from an expectation suggested in this verse: Your ears shall hear a word behind you, saying, "This is the way, walk in it," Whenever you turn to the right hand or whenever you turn to the left (Isaiah 30:21). It says your ears will hear a word behind you, it seems to literally suggest the direction from where the voice will come. It might leave you waiting to hear the voice of God with your physical ears. While that might happen and does happen, that is the spectacular. For we do not necessarily hear the voice of God with our ears like we hear our friends and those around talk to us.

Remember, your body is the temple of God and God dwells in you by His Spirit (1 Cor 3:16, 6:19). So if He is going to talk to you, He is normally going to do so from the inside. Generally, not from behind. And you do not necessarily hear Him with your physical ears, for God is spirit and speaks therefore to our spirits. Even as we have physical senses, even so we have spiritual senses that relate and receive from the Spirit of God. Paul wrote in 1 Corinthians 2:14, "The natural man does not receive the things of the Spirit of God, for they are foolishness to him; nor can he know them, because they are spiritually discerned". So it goes, that the voice of the Lord is not meant for your natural ears.

> **Do not look out for a physical voice from outside when listening to the Lord, listen on the inside with your spirit, for there He resides by His Spirit and speaks to you from the inside.**

A few verses earlier, Paul emphasized some truths. Among many things, Paul said: "Now we have received, not the spirit of the world, but the Spirit who is from God, that we might know the things that have been freely given to us by God. These things we also speak, not in words which man's wisdom teaches but which the Holy Spirit teaches, comparing spiritual things with spiritual" (1 Corinthians 2:12-13). God speaks to us by His spirit, usually from the inside, from within us where He lives.

Prayer

Thank you, Lord, for the illumination in your word that comes to me daily, helping me to grow in my knowledge of you on to perfection in Christ. As I exercise my spiritual senses in living by your word, they are enhanced and refined to discern your voice even better in the name of Jesus.

Bible in one year // **Leviticus 11-12, Matthew 26:1-25**

FEB 12

> And after the earthquake there was a fire, but the LORD was not in the fire. And after the fire there was the sound of a gentle whisper.
> // 1 Kings 19:12 NLT

Don't expect the spectacular

Elijah was told, "Go out, and stand on the mountain before the Lord." And behold, the Lord passed by, and a great and strong wind tore into the mountains and broke the rocks in pieces before the Lord, but the Lord was not in the wind; and after the wind an earthquake, but the Lord was not in the earthquake; and after the earthquake a fire, but the Lord was not in the fire; and after the fire a still small voice. So it was, when Elijah heard it, that he wrapped his face in his mantle and went out and stood in the entrance of the cave. Suddenly a voice came to him, and said, "What are you doing here, Elijah?" (1 Kings 19:11-13 NIV)

The prophet Elijah had this encounter with the Lord at a time of desperation. He most certainly had been longing to hear Him say a word. Elijah had just prevailed over the false prophets of Baal, calling down fire from heaven and displaying such miraculous works of God. Though such a heavenly move, his zeal and work for God had now gotten him into some real trouble with the queen Jezebel who vowed to kill the prophet. For Jezebel sent him words saying, "So let the gods do to me, and more also, if I do not make your life as the life of one of them by tomorrow about this time." (1 Kings 19:2 NIV).

> When waiting upon the Lord, it is important to not look out for the spectacular. While that could indeed happen, it is not generally the norm. It is often a still small voice.

Elijah in response to threat, took off for the wilderness, running for his life. There was an earthquake that shook the mountains, but the Lord was not in it. Then came the fire but the Lord also did not speak from there. It was a still small voice that came. It is easy to imagine a spectacular loud voice from heaven, calling your name with blinding and blazing lights, sounding like thunder. While all that is described at certain instances in scriptures, it is not the norm. If you look out for the spectacular, you will miss the voice of God. It is often the still small voice. Don't expect the spectacular.

Prayer

Gracious Lord, thank You for being a very present help in trouble, reaching us always at the point of our needs. We receive grace to recognize you amid the chaos and to hear your still small voice calling out to us. That we might not miss you because we were looking out for the spectacular. In Jesus' name.

Bible in one year // Leviticus 13, Matthew 26:26-50

Now we have received, not the spirit of the world, but the Spirit who is from God, that we might know the things that have been freely given to us by God. // **1 Corinthians 2:12**

A knowing by the spirit

FEB 13

Have you ever had a situation when you had a certain outcome and you said to yourself or to others, "I knew it?" In this case, I am not referring to things for which you could make a logical prediction. It was intuitive. If someone asked, how did you know, the only answer you would give is, "I just knew in my spirit or in my heart". Generally, such knowledge is not from you, it is a knowing by the Spirit. When you just know that you know. It is an illumination on the inner man as the Lord turns on His light in us to see.

You can liken such knowledge to that moment when you are standing in a dark room and the lights come on. You just suddenly take notice of the elements in that room. No one needs to list out to you the things, you just recognize and know them. This is what you would term the inner witness. Just as Paul wrote, "The Spirit Himself bears witness with our spirit that we are children of God" (Romans 8:16 NKJV). That is to say, the spirit of God who lives in you deposits that know-ledge in your spirit, and suddenly there is an awareness in your heart about things you do not necessarily have an explanation or a justification for. And we will do well to learn to trust that; particularly if you have been in an atmosphere of prayer, worship, and meditation in the word of God, with specific questions on the issue.

> **The Holy Spirit in us gives us knowledge of the things of God, not necessarily by an audible voice of communication but by bearing witness to our spirits on things that concern us.**

Others may call it intuition, but if you are a child of God filled with the Holy Spirit, it is more than an intuition. It is a knowing by the Spirit. Just as it is written, "Now we have received, not the spirit of the world, but the Spirit who is from God, that we might know the things that have been freely given to us by God" (1 Corinthians 2:12). Many testimonies abound of people who because of such intuitive knowledge, have either walked into great blessings or spared themselves from great losses. All by a knowing of the Spirit.

Prayer

Heavenly Father, thank you for the Holy Spirit given to us that we might know the things that you have freely given to us. We pray to be more alert and responsive to such ministrations from you. In Jesus' name.

Bible in one year // **Leviticus 14, Matthew 26:51-75**

FEB 14

He speaks in dreams, in visions of the night, when deep sleep falls on people as they lie in their beds. // **Job 33:15 NLT**

Dreams and visions

While dreams might truly result from the activities of our days and other sources outside God, they remain a major gateway of divine communication for the child of God. Particularly during our early years in the faith and walk with God while we are yet to know how to recognize and ascertain His voice. And that for a good reason. When we are awake and alert, due to the noise around us, the many distractions, and our own inner contemplations, it could be difficult to filter the source of thoughts and ideas racing through our minds. Is this from me, from the Lord, or because of what people are saying, we would ask.

> Dreams and visions remain a gateway of divine communication. As a child of God, do not take your dreams lightly.

The book of Job tells us: "For God may speak in one way, or in another, yet man does not perceive it. In a dream, in a vision of the night, when deep sleep falls upon men, while slumbering on their beds, then He opens the ears of men, and seals their instruction. In order to turn man from his deed, and conceal pride from man, He keeps back his soul from the pit, and his life from perishing by the sword" (Job 33:14-18).

This is the reason you should never take dreams lightly as a child of God. Now we do not ignore the manipulative schemes of the devil who will try to hijack this channel of communication with false dreams. That is why you should pray and declare your life shielded from demonic activity and live in a heavenly atmosphere created through a life that walks in the light of God's word. For in such an atmosphere, you can always trust your dreams to be of God. And if ever it were not of him, you will be able to discern the presence in the dream to be demonic and not divine. Like the opening passage puts it, "God speaks in one way, or in another, yet man does not perceive it. In a dream, in a vision of the night, when deep sleep falls upon men, while slumbering on their beds".

Prayer

Heavenly Father, thank you that even in sleep, you are with us. We receive grace to see the things you show and hear the things you say through dreams and visions, being able to remember them when we awake. We forbid every form of demonic communications in our dreams. In Jesus' name.

Bible in one year // **Leviticus 15-16, Matthew 27:1-26**

I will praise the LORD, who counsels me; even at night my heart instructs me. // **Psalm 16:7 NIV**

FEB 15

Listen to your heart

"I will praise the LORD, who counsels me; even at night my heart instructs me" (Psalm 16:7 NIV). This was David declaring the work of the Lord in his life, how He gives him counsel. By extension, he recognized how his heart instructed him. It reminds me of a lesson I once learned from Andrew Wommack in a teaching on how to be led by the Spirit. He shared with an example, how by a loss of desire to honor an invitation to preach, he cancelled a flight that never made it to its destination. He was led by the spirit. He had been expounding on the verse, "Take delight in the LORD, and he will give you the desires of your heart" (Psalm 37:4). In his explanation, he presented a twist to this verse that made a lot more sense than the common interpretation many will quickly make.

Generally, that verse seems to say whatever we desire, if we delight ourselves in the Lord, He will grant it to us. Well, I guess your experiences might have taught you by now that God does not necessarily give us what we desire but what we need and that which is fitting for his purpose for our lives. Andrew in his discuss on being led by the Spirit, rather emphasized this verse means to say, "If you delight yourself in the Lord, He will place his desires in your heart".

Suddenly, you want what God wants. And what God does not want, you resent. Your desires now come from him; the desires you have in your heart become a reflection of the things God is instructing you towards. And to delight yourself, Andrew emphasized to mean taking time to seek the Lord, in prayer, meditation and fasting – glorying in His presence. Such that when you come from such an atmosphere, you can trust the inclinations of your heart to be God's will. Then you can listen to your heart. And like David, you will be able to say, "I will praise the LORD, who counsels me; even at night my heart instructs me".

> If you sincerely seek the Lord, He will bring you in sync with His desires, making your heart a place of instructions from where he compels you towards his paths for your life and away from snares.

Prayer

Gracious Father, thank you for the blessing of a new day and all that is in it for us. As we delight ourselves in you, our hearts get in sync with your spirit and desires and our hearts instruct us. And like a river course, you will direct it in the line of your plans and purposes. In Jesus' name.

Bible in one year // **Leviticus 17-18, Matthew 27:27-50**

FEB 16

> For who knows a person's thoughts except their own spirit within them? In the same way no one knows the thoughts of God except the Spirit of God. // **1 Corinthians 2:11 NIV**

Concise divine thoughts

The greater truth is this: as children of God, we all have had the Lord talk to us in many ways and on many occasions. The only difference is that some have come to know and recognize divine communication when it comes, while others are yet to know how to filter and distinguish if it was of God or another source. It is like the story of little Samuel who ran to Eli many times as the Lord called out to him, mistaken Eli had spoken.

As it is written, "Again the Lord called, "Samuel!" And Samuel got up and went to Eli and said, "Here I am; you called me." "My son," Eli said, "I did not call; go back and lie down." Now Samuel did not yet know the Lord: The word of the Lord had not yet been revealed to him. A third time the Lord called, "Samuel!" And Samuel got up and went to Eli and said, "Here I am; you called me." Then Eli realized that the Lord was calling the boy. So Eli told Samuel, "Go and lie down, and if he calls you, say, 'Speak, Lord, for your servant is listening.'" So Samuel went and lay down in his place. (1 Samuel 3:6-9).

Because we have the mind of Christ and God lives in us by His spirit, He impresses concise thoughts on our minds that make known to us His plans and counsel.

Paul wrote, "For who knows a person's thoughts except their own spirit within them? In the same way no one knows the thoughts of God except the Spirit of God. What we have received is not the spirit of the world, but the Spirit who is from God, so that we may understand what God has freely given us (1 Corinthians 2:11-12 NIV). Just like this verse puts it, no one knows the thoughts of God except the spirit of God. However, God lives in us by His Spirit. This therefore means His thoughts can be impressed on our minds. And God does communicate like that to us on many occasions, by concise divine thoughts. By concise divine thoughts, I mean very clear comprehensive sentences that are full of information or ideas, such that you yourself can recognize you did not think that through or formulate it.

Prayer

Thank You, Heavenly Father that you have made your residence in me. Thank you that I have the mind of Christ and therefore can know and receive your thoughts impressed on my mind. I receive grace to recognize such inspirations that I might walk by them and see the blessings thereof. In Jesus name.

Bible in one year // **Leviticus 19-20, Matthew 27:51-66**

We have also a more sure word of prophecy; whereunto ye do well that ye take heed, as unto a light that shineth in a dark place, until the day dawn, and the day star arise in your hearts. // **2 Peter 1:19 KJV**

FEB 17

A more sure word

If we would be effective in our walk with God and fulfil His purpose for us, we would have to know His word and His voice. While there are those who care little about divine direction and walking in God's plans for their lives, there are also the extremists who in their pursuit of "What god is saying" without a grasp on the written word, also stumble. In this case, they fail to evaluate accurately the things they believe to be hearing from God and in the process, sometimes believe a lie. But God has been gracious to preserve the scope of His knowledge (the written word) by which we should judge everything else we believe to be hearing.

The Bible is God's surest word to us, a collection of books by inspired men who in every sense wrote the thoughts of God for us through different generations. Most of these things having been fulfilled, indeed place the written word as a surer word for us to cling to. It also provides for us the measuring rod by which every other claimed revelation or divine leading should be judged. Just like Paul admonished, "Examine everything carefully; hold fast to that which is good" (1 Thessalonians 5:21 NASB).

> The written word of God is a more sure word preserved through the ages for us, and by it every other revelation is to be evaluated. Never trust revelations outside the context of God's revealed truths.

Peter wrote, "We have also a more sure word of prophecy; whereunto ye do well that ye take heed, as unto a light that shineth in a dark place, until the day dawn, and the day star arise in your hearts" (2 Peter 1:19 KJV). As Hebrews 1:1 makes it clear, God speaks to us in diverse ways. Be it directly to us as individuals or through those He has placed on our paths who are also His children, we would in every instance need to prove and examine all things in line with the written word. This is the sure word we are called to heed like a lamp shining in the darkness until the day dawns and the morning star, Christ Himself is revealed to us.

Prayer

Forever Lord, your word is indeed settled. And you have exalted your word above all your names. We receive grace for right comprehension as we build our lives by its truths. That we would not be tossed back and forth by any false revelation but will be grounded and rooted in your word. In Jesus' name.

Bible in one year // **Leviticus 21-22, Matthew 28**

FEB 18

> From the first day that you set your heart to understand, and to humble yourself before your God, your words were heard; and I have come because of your words. // Daniel 10:12

A call to fast

One reason we are called upon to fast is to enhance our spiritual alertness and to be spiritually positioned to hear from the Lord. As a baby in the faith, my initial understanding of fasting was wrong. In recent years, I have come across persons too who think like I used to. They ask, why do we have to fast to get something from the Lord. In their minds, they think fasting is hunger-strike – a time you boycott food to get the attention of someone on something. You are not going to eat until they recognize how desperate or angry you are about things. That is not the purpose of fasting. It is far from that. We do not fast to get God's attention.

Fasting helps position your spirit to receive from the Lord as you withdraw your attention from other things to be more inclined to Him.

We always have God's attention. Remember, "He that watches over you neither sleeps nor slumber" (Psalm 121:4). God even says these words which are true for you too, "I have engraved you on the palms of my hands; your walls are ever before me" (Isaiah 49:16). So, we always indeed have God's attention. Rather, we fast to give God our attention, to be rightly positioned spiritually to perceive and receive from the Lord. We become better positioned for Him to reach us with the things He might even have been trying to tell us, but we could not get because our attention was everywhere else.

In that record of Daniel, when you read the whole story (Daniel 10:1-14), you will find out that Daniel set his face to fast and to seek the Lord. And God, knowing that Daniel was positioned to receive, sent forth the angel with revelations for Daniel. The angel spoke to Daniel saying: "Do not fear, Daniel, for from the first day that you set your heart to understand, and to humble yourself before your God, your words were heard; and I have come because of your words (Daniel 10:12). That call to prayer and seeking the Lord only gets better when we really take out time to fast and pray, depriving our flesh of its routine and pleasures that our spirits might be better positioned to receive from the Lord.

Prayer

Almighty God, thank you for the blessing of a new day and your grace that continually abounds towards us in all things. Even this season, we receive grace to be disciplined in seeking you in prayers and fasting, that we might be rightly positioned to hear from you. In Jesus' name.

Bible in one year // Leviticus 23-24, Mark 1:1-22

As the Holy Spirit says: "Today, if you hear his voice, do not harden your hearts" // **Hebrews 3:7-8 NIV**

FEB 19

Yield to the Lord

The human nature is a rebellious one, with a tendency to have its own inclinations, desires and plans that are away from the divine. Paul wrote His struggle with himself as he wrestled to do the will of God. However, that was before Christ took resident in him. For in his writing, he shared an experience under the law as he struggled in his own ability to live up to God's expectations (Romans 7). Sadly, many people end there with their reading and use this passage of Paul's struggle to say how difficult it is to be a Christian. On the contrary, it is an exciting life in Christ. And that is why Jesus came, that we might have life; and that to the fullest (John 10:10).

The call today is to be yielded to the Lord. It might not always be the most convenient, but it is always in our best interest. The word of God that comes to us will not serve us until we become yielded to that word. To yield means to bring yourself under the submission and directives of the word of instruction or counsel you have received. That is where the blessing is. We are admonished, As the Holy Spirit says: "Today, if you hear his voice, do not harden your hearts..." (Hebrews 3:7-8 NIV)

> **Be yielded to the Lord, embracing His perspective and plans particularly when it is contrary to your expectations or entails some inconvenience you'd rather not have.**

The bible records of Jesus, "For the joy set before him he endured the cross, scorning its shame, and sat down at the right hand of the throne of God" (Hebrews 12:2). He was yielded to the will of the Father even when it was inconvenient. This is God's call to us today, to be yielded to His will. When we embrace His perspective, look pass our plans and follow on His purpose. That is the very reason His voice comes to us. And sometimes, your willingness to do according to His will may be the reason He makes known his purpose to you or not. So, as you hear the voice of the Lord, harden not your heart. Be yielded to Him and do His will even when it seems inconvenient. It is always in your best interest.

Prayer

Heavenly Father, thank you for the blessing of a new day. Thank you for working in me to will and to do according to your good pleasure. Today, I receive grace to be yielded to you, that I might gladly say, "Not my will but your will be done in all things". In Jesus' name.

Bible in one year // **Leviticus 25, Mark 1:23-45**

FEB 20

Enter his gates with thanksgiving and his courts with praise; give thanks to him and praise his name. // **Psalm 100:4**

A response of praise

Psalm 100 is a parallel of Psalm 23. In both psalms, David who had been a shepherd himself, reflects his relationship with the Lord as one between the sheep and the shepherd. In Psalm 23, probably the most popular Psalm, David declares, "The Lord is my shepherd; I shall not want. He makes me lie down in green pastures; He leads me beside the still waters. He restores my soul; He leads me in the paths of righteousness For His name's sake".

In Psalm 100, worthy of note is the verse that reads, "Know that the Lord is God. It is he who made us, and we are his; we are his people, the sheep of his pasture" Psalm 100:3 NIV. How good to know that the Lord has pasture, all reserved for His flock. That one can boldly declare, "I am the sheep of His pasture". In a more contemporary manner, you might declare, "My name is written on the Lord's bank card, it is mine to use". Mindful of such a privilege, David calls for a response in praise. "Enter his gates with thanksgiving and his courts with praise; give thanks to him and praise his name" – Psalm 100:4.

> Recognize the blessedness of having the Lord as your shepherd and all the benefits to it and let your response be praise to Him.

In its entirety, Psalm 100 reads, "Shout for joy to the Lord, all the earth. Worship the Lord with gladness; come before him with joyful songs. Know that the Lord is God. It is he who made us, and we are his; we are his people, the sheep of his pasture. Enter his gates with thanksgiving and his courts with praise; give thanks to him and praise his name. For the Lord is good and his love endures forever; his faithfulness continues through all generations". Psalm 100 is indeed a parallel of Psalm 23 that calls for a response of praise. Recognize these truths today for your life and respond in accordance.

Prayer

Heavenly Father, thank you for the love you have lavished upon us that we might be called your sons, brought into your family, and made joint heirs with Christ to your throne. Thank you for the Holy Spirit given to us. You have raised us up and made us to sit in heavenly places far above principalities and powers, giving us authority over Satan and his cohorts. Thank you for these blessings. In Jesus' name.

Bible in one year // **Leviticus 26-27, Mark 2**

I trust in the LORD for protection. So why do you say to me, "Fly like a bird to the mountains for safety!" // **Psalm 11:1 NLT**

FEB 21

Do not fret

The Psalmist had much confidence in the Lord as his refuge, he was not moved into panic and anxiety. And even if you read his writings where he expressed concerns and fears, they always had a spin-off to a declaration of hissecurity in the Lord. David wrote, "I trust in the LORD for protection. So why do you say to me, "Fly like a bird to the mountains for safety!" (Psalm 11:1 NLT). Have you ever had a situation in your life when things seemed to be falling apart and everyone around you expected you to be under such panic? In fact, they think something is wrong with you because you do not panic.

> Do not panic over whatever circumstances or uncertainties surround you but rest assured in the Lord. He is your sure refuge!

While it could be worthwhile taking a second look at things when those around you panic for your sake, it is great to know like David that because you take refuge in the Lord, you need not run helter-skelter in panic. You need not fret. In my favorite Psalm, David wrote, "The Lord is my light and my salvation – whom shall I fear? The Lord is the stronghold of my life – of whom shall I be afraid? When the wicked advance against me to devour me, it is my enemies and my foes who will stumble and fall. Though an army besiege me, my heart will not fear; though war break out against me, even then I will be confident" (Psalm 27:1-3 NIV).

David had a resolve not to fret, not even if an army came up against him. He was indeed confident in the refuge he had come to find in the Lord. This was the reason David would not fret. And how we all need this at a time of global pandemic when life seems more uncertain than ever, and systems and governments are buckling under pressure. You might have lost a job and other things seem they would fail along with it. Or you might be trusting the Lord on something, and time seems passing. Do not fret but find refuge in the Lord. He has promised, "I will never leave you nor forsake you" (Hebrews 13:5).

Prayer

Heavenly Father, we rejoice in the fact that as the mountains surrounds Jerusalem, so you surround your people now and forever. Our lives are hidden in you in Christ, and we are secured. We remain confident to see your goodness in the land of the living. In Jesus' name.

Bible in one year // **Numbers 1-3, Mark 3**

FEB 22

I have loved you, my people, with an everlasting love. With unfailing love, I have drawn you to myself. // **Jeremiah 31:3 NLT**

Rest assured in His Love

Who shall separate us from the love of Christ? Shall trouble or hardship or persecution or famine or nakedness or danger or sword? As it is written: "For your sake we face death all day long; we are considered as sheep to be slaughtered." No, in all these things we are more than conquerors through him who loved us. For I am convinced that neither death nor life, neither angels nor demons, neither the present nor the future, nor any powers, neither height nor depth, nor anything else in all creation, will be able to separate us from the love of God that is in Christ Jesus our Lord – Romans 8:35-9 NIV.

> Rest assured in the love of God for you in Christ Jesus this season, knowing that God will always cause all things to work together for your good.

Paul desired for the Ephesians that they would know the love of God that surpasses knowledge (Ephesians 3:19). And that for many good reasons. One of these reasons is the very assurance the knowledge of that love brings. Such an assurance that is highlighted in this passage. To know that you are loved, and God has you covered. To know that you are loved, and that love is unconditional. To know that you are loved, and that love seeks your good in all things, particularly when it seems to hurt.

Many times, I have pondered on the example of a little baby who watches their parent hand them over to a nurse for an injection. Often, the look on their face would suggest the question, "Mom, how can you let them do this to me?". But the parents, even with a moment of temporal distress, have the child's interest at heart. It is all out of love. I encourage you to rest assured in the love of God for you. He won't love you less because you missed the mark. He won't love you more because you did better. For He says, "I have loved you, my people, with an everlasting love. With unfailing love, I have drawn you to myself" (Jeremiah 31:3 NLT).

Prayer

Gracious Father, thank you for your love that you richly lavish on us, calling us to be your children. Thank you for we know that you cause all things to work together for the good of those who love you and are called according to your purpose. This is true in my life this season. In Jesus' name.

Bible in one year // **Numbers 4-6, Mark 4:1-20**

Let us therefore come boldly to the throne of grace, that we may obtain mercy and find grace to help in time of need. // **Hebrews 4:16**

FEB 23

Come boldly to the throne

Approaching any authority or a monarch can be such an intimidating thing particularly when you approach as one guilty of a crime. This can easily be the case spiritually. That with guilt lingering on our hearts, we would rather do anything but pray or read the bible. In fact, there are people who would feel too sinful to join in for a Christian fellowship. "How can I join the holy assembly?", they ask. When that happens, we are only falling for a deception of darkness, the devil trying to keep us away from the place of spiritual fortitude, he tries to take us out of our vantage position.

The writer calls us to have an attitude in approaching God's throne. He shows us, "We do not have a High Priest who cannot sympathize with our weaknesses, but was in all points tempted as we are, yet without sin. Let us therefore come boldly to the throne of grace, that we may obtain mercy and find grace to help in time of need" (Hebrews 4:15-16). He charges us to "come boldly". He wrote this because He had such an understanding of what Christ had accomplished for us on the cross. He paid it all on our behalf and gave us a clean slate to walk boldly into the throne room.

Ask yourself the alternative question like Peter. If you do not run to the throne room because you feel unworthy where else would you go? Peter had come to the realization that only with Christ he could find life. So, he asked, "Lord, to whom shall we go? You have the words of eternal life" (John 6:68 NKJV). That should be your attitude. Come boldly to the throne of grace.

> **It does not matter how far you have wandered away from the Lord, you can always come boldly to the throne of grace, for there you will find mercy and grace in time of need.**

Prayer

Heavenly Father, thank you for reconciling the world to yourself, not counting our sins against us. Thank you for the invitation to come boldly to the throne of grace that we might find mercy and obtain grace in times of need. In Jesus' name.

Bible in one year // **Numbers 7-8, Mark 4:21-41**

FEB 24

I lift up my eyes to the mountains– where does my help come from? My help comes from the Lord, the Maker of heaven and earth.
// **Psalm 121:1-2**

Look to the Lord

David wrote, "I lift up my eyes to the mountains– where does my help come from? My help comes from the Lord, the Maker of heaven and earth. He will not let your foot slip– he who watches over you will not slumber; indeed, he who watches over Israel will neither slumber nor sleep. The Lord watches over you– the Lord is your shade at your right hand; the sun will not harm you by day, nor the moon by night. The Lord will keep you from all harm– he will watch over your life; the Lord will watch over your coming and going both now and forevermore" (Psalm 121).

The Psalmist sure knew what it meant to look to the Lord. He echoes this throughout his writings in many ways. He looked to the Lord as His shepherd. He was confident He would have all his needs supplied. He looked to the Lord for direction and boasted on how the Lord instructed him even in the nighttime. He even could declare, "You guide me with your counsel, leading me to a glorious destiny" (Psalm 73:24 NLT). He needed not boast in chariots, for he wrote, "Some boast in chariots and some in horses, but we will boast in the name of the LORD, our God" (Psalm 20:7 NASB).

> Look to the Lord for your everything, and you will not be disappointed. Your face will be radiant with joy.

He looked to the Lord for protection and was confident in Him as a shield. David wrote, The LORD is my fortress, protecting me from danger, so why should I tremble? When evil people come to devour me, when my enemies and foes attack me, they will stumble and fall. Though a mighty army surrounds me, my heart will not be afraid. Even if I am attacked, I will remain confident (Psalm 27:1-3 NLT). David knew, "Those who look to him are radiant; their faces are never covered with shame" (Psalm 34:5 NIV). Therefore, I charge you today the author and finisher of your faith your face will not be covered with shame.

Prayer

Thank you, Lord, for being everything to us, that in every way we can look to you and not be disappointed. We receive grace today to fix our eyes on Jesus, the author and finisher of our faith, knowing that you would lead us to refreshing places as we fulfill your purpose in life. In Jesus name.

Bible in one year // **Numbers 9-11, Mark 5:1-20**

Call upon Me in the day of trouble; I will deliver you, and you shall glorify Me. // **Psalm 50:15**

FEB 25

Call upon the Lord

David wrote, "I WILL bless the LORD at all times; His praise shall continually be in my mouth. My soul shall make its boast in the LORD; The humble shall hear of it and be glad. Oh, magnify the LORD with me, and let us exalt His name together. I sought the LORD, and He heard me, and delivered me from all my fears. They looked to Him and were radiant, and their faces were not ashamed. This poor man cried out, and the LORD heard him, and saved him out of all his troubles (Psalm 34:1-6)

> When we call upon the Lord in our time of need, He hears and answers us. Call on Him.

To call upon the name of the Lord means to seek his attention, with purpose to give him the praise due His name or to solicit his intervention. To call upon the Lord is to pray. The Psalmist recounts how he sought the Lord and was heard. He wrote, "This poor man cried out, and the LORD heard him, And saved him out of all his troubles" (Psalm 34:1 - 6). When it says this poor man, it is an expression of the state of helplessness he was in, yet his prayer was heard. You are no different.

The New Living Translation puts it this way, "In my desperation I prayed, and the Lord listened; he saved me from all my troubles" (Psalm 34:6 NLT). If there is a situation, let's call upon the Lord. How a minister of the Gospel once said, "If there is a person to pray, then there is a God to answer". The Lord Himself having declared, "Call upon Me in the day of trouble; I will deliver you, and you shall glorify Me" (Psalm 50:51).

Prayer

>Thank You Father for your love and ever-present help in trouble. Indeed we will not fear, though the mountains tremble, the land quakes and the oceans roar. You dwell in the midst of us and we shall not be destroyed. You shall come to our rescue just in time. In Jesus name!

Bible in one year // **Numbers 12-14, Mark 5:21-43**

FEB 26

And let the peace of God rule in your hearts, to which also you were called in one body; and be thankful. // **Colossians 3:15**

Be thankful

This profound instruction comes up as a short phrase among others as Paul writes to the Colossians regarding Christian living. "And let the peace of God rule in your hearts, to which also you were called in one body; AND BE THANKFUL. Let the word of Christ dwell in you richly in all wisdom, teaching and admonishing one another in psalms and hymns and spiritual songs, singing with grace in your hearts to the Lord. (Colossians 3:15-16).

Be thankful! It also features in one of my favorite verses of scriptures, Colossians 1:12. In fact, it is an anchor verse of my assignment to the body of Christ. That verse says, "Giving thanks to the Father who has qualified us to be partakers of the inheritance of the saints in the light". He has qualified us, we are not trying to qualify for it – to be partakers, sharers of the inheritance of the saints in the light. What a cause to be thankful. That is the reason for Your Daily Light, shining to you the Light of God's world so you can see and fully appropriate your inheritance in the Light. Even for this, we are to be thankful.

> Be thankful. Whatever you do, whatever the situation might be, you can be thankful, for even then, He has guaranteed, "Weeping may endure for the night, but Joy comes in the morning"

What amazing thoughts of the Spirit Paul was privileged to pen down for our benefit. Another such is in Colossians where He wrote, "As you therefore have received Christ Jesus the Lord, so walk in Him, rooted and built up in Him and established in the faith, as you have been taught, abounding in it with thanksgiving" (Colossians 2:6-7). This is the life we are called to live, a life overflowing with thankfulness of all that the Lord has done. Even if you have a lot you are believing the Lord for, a true sign of your faith in answered prayers is a heart of thanksgiving.

Prayer

Heavenly Father, I am forever grateful that you sacrificed your son. You saved my life and changed my destiny, thank you for your purpose in me. Thank you for answered prayers and all the blessings we are yet to see. In Jesus name.

Bible in one year // **Numbers 15-16, Mark 6:1-29**

Therefore, I say to you, whatever things you ask when you pray, believe that you receive them, and you will have them. // **Mark 11:24**

FEB 27

Believe you have received

A story has been told of a town that had been experiencing a season of drought. So, the inhabitants decided to meet at the town square and together, pray for rain. The day came and everyone showed up for the prayer meeting. However, only a young boy came along with an umbrella. The boy's faith was alive, he expected the rain after the prayers. He knew He would be needing his umbrella to get home. He was one who believed in prayers and practiced what Jesus commanded. The rest just went to pray.

Jesus taught on prayer saying, "Therefore I say to you, whatever things you ask when you pray, believe that you receive them, and you will have them" (Mark 11:24). What many do is that they pray and wait to see if they have what was prayed for. That is wrong. Jesus said when you pray, believe that you have received. You don't wait to see to know that you have received.
After you pray, believe you have received it. And then the manifestation will be hastened. Before long, you will realize you have it indeed. You believe you have received after your prayers. You accept in your heart that it is as good and done.

You cannot finish praying and still be downcast. It just means you have not believed that you received. You cannot leave the place of prayer still confused and frustrated. You cannot finish praying and be asking God, "When will you answer me?". Then you have not believed you received. Hannah had been desperately praying for a son. The priest Eli came to her and said, "Go in peace, and the God of Israel grant your petition which you have asked of Him." And Hannah said, "Let your maidservant find favor in your sight." So, the woman went her way and ate, and her face was no longer sad (1 Samuel 1:17-18). You see, Hannah believed she had received, and it was evident on her countenance. Even so the word proved true. She had a son, Samuel.

> You believe you have received after you pray. You don't wait to see the manifestation of the things you prayed for to know you have received. When you believe, you will see it come to pass.

Prayer

Heavenly Father, thank you for the privilege to make requests and to see the results come to pass. Thank you for the capacity to believe your word and to act on it. This season, as I make requests, I believe I receive the very things prayed for and watch them come to pass. In Jesus' name.

Bible in one year // **Numbers 17-19, Mark 6:30-56**

FEB 28

If we know that He hears us, whatever we ask, we know that we have the petitions that we have asked of Him. // 1 John 5:15

A note of victory

Many people have asked, "When do I stop praying for something I am expecting? Do I have to continue praying for that thing until it is fully manifested?". The answer is no. At some point in time, your prayer requests should turn to songs of praise or proclamations of faith. By this we mean you should be able to recognize that your prayer has been answered even if the manifestation is not yet evident to the eyes. This is when you have a note of victory in your spirit, you have a testimony from the Lord in response to the requests you have been making.

A practical example is with Hannah's story from yesterday. A note of victory was when she had a word from the priest Eli telling her it was done. Once we have such a response, your prayer should change to a testimony and a proclamation of faith. If you have been praying for healing and you received a word of healing or had a dream and saw yourself whole, that's your note of victory. If you have been praying for something and the Lord led you to a verse that is an answer to your prayer, that is your note of victory.

> A note of victory is the feedback you receive in your spirit from the Lord after you have prayed. Even before the manifestation is evident, your prayer changes to testimonies and proclamations of faith.

You don't have to continue with the same prayer point over and over. That will be unbelief; it means you do not know you have received. You will be making requests for things that have been given. Start proclaiming the word rather. If sickness, start declaring I am the healed of the Lord, even when you still feel sick. If not pregnant, proclaim in thanksgiving, I am bringing forth my child. Because of a note of victory, your prayer moves from requests to testimonies and faith proclamations. It is as John puts it, "Now this is the confidence that we have in Him, that if we ask anything according to His will, He hears us. And if we know that He hears us, whatever we ask, we know that we have the petitions that we have asked of Him" (1 John 5:14-15).

Prayer

Heavenly Father, thank you for my heart is open to discern when I have prevailed in prayer. You hear my prayer and I have the things prayed for according to your will. The feedback to my requests in the throne room are received and my joy abounds as I testify to the note of victory. In Jesus' name.

Bible in one year // **Numbers 20-22, Mark 7:1-13**

MARCH

Whatever is born of God overcomes the world. And this is the victory that has overcome the world – our faith. // 1 John 5:4

MAR 1

Prevailing faith

Prevailing faith is faith that does not buckle under pressure but stands its ground until it has the victory to show forth. And that is the faith God has called us to have. This is the kind of faith the author of Hebrews testifies to: "And what more shall I say? For the time would fail me to tell of Gideon and Barak and Samson and Jephthah, also of David and Samuel and the prophets: who through faith subdued kingdoms, worked righteousness, obtained promises, stopped the mouths of lions, quenched the violence of fire, escaped the edge of the sword, out of weakness were made strong, became valiant in battle, turned to flight the armies of the aliens" (Hebrews 11:32-34).

Just as scripture says, "Therefore put on the full armor of God, so that when the day of evil comes, you may be able to stand your ground, and after you have done everything, to stand" (Ephesians 6:13). Your faith can prevail. When you think you can't hold up anymore, it is just the devil bringing you to a place of surrender from a battle you already won.

> **Prevailing faith is faith that does not buckle under pressure but endures until it has the victory to show forth, and that is the kind of faith given to us in Christ Jesus.**

You have prevailing faith. It is the nature of faith that was given to you in Christ Jesus, a faith that has the capacity to come through all things victoriously. That is why the apostle John wrote, "Whatever is born of God overcomes the world. And this is the victory that has overcome the world– our faith" (1 John 5:4 NKJV). A simpler version has this rendering, "For every child of God defeats this evil world, and we achieve this victory through our faith" (NLT). So as a child of God, you indeed have prevailing faith. Your faith has the capacity to survive under pressure and overcome in all things, if only you will stand your ground till the end. Like the examples in our opening passage, they all had prevailing faith, accomplishing great and impossible feats by their faith.

Prayer

Almighty God, thank you for such a privilege and heritage in Christ Jesus, that whatever is born of you overcomes the world through faith. This season, as I stand my ground in the word and hold fast to your promises for me, my faith prevails in all things. In Jesus name.

Bible in one year // **Numbers 23-25, Mark 7:14-37**

MAR 2

Be honest in your evaluation of yourselves, measuring yourselves by the faith God has given us. // **Romans 12:3 NIV**

You have faith

Paul wrote, "Because of the privilege and authority God has given me, I give each of you this warning: Don't think you are better than you really are. Be honest in your evaluation of yourselves, measuring yourselves by the faith God has given us" (Romans 12:3 NIV). If you are born again, then you have faith. It doesn't matter how faithless you feel. The very knowledge you have that there is a God whom you might have never seen, and the fact that you believe in His son Jesus whom you never saw dying on the cross is a testimonial to your faith.

> If you are born again, you have faith. It might not be sufficient for everything and for every season, but you have the minimum faith with which you can thrive and prevail.

Even if you are at a place right now where you feel pressed and almost crushed, the very fact that you are still looking out to God and hoping for a divine intervention is an indication of your faith. You might be on certain issues, but it does not cancel that fact that you have faith as a child of God. As our opening verse puts it, you received a measure of faith from the Lord when you became born again. That seed of faith was deposited into your spirit by God himself. That is the initial faith we all receive, the faith that comes with the capacity to believe in things we cannot see and to accept as real the things we cannot prove by ourselves to be there (Hebrews 11:1).

Nonetheless, that initial faith you received at the new birth is not sufficient for everything on your journey as a Christian. That initial faith was only a deposit which you would have to develop to great and strong faith. It is your responsibility to grow your faith to the capacity where nothing is insurmountable, nothing is impossible, and nothing is a limitation on your journey with God - a faith that will engrave your name in "Faith's Hall of fame" (Hebrews 11). You too can be listed among those whose faith prevailed despite the diverse difficulties life brought them. It is your heritage for your faith to prevail (1 John 5:4).

Prayer

Heavenly Father thank you for giving me the capacity to see the invisible, believe the incomprehensible and expect the impossible. Thank you for the seed of faith in my spirit. I receive grace to grow my faith through meditation in the word and to prevail in all things. In Jesus' name.

Bible in one year // **Numbers 26-27, Mark 8:1-21**

Let us hold tightly without wavering to the hope we affirm, for God can be trusted to keep his promise. // **Hebrews 10:23**

MAR 3

Wavering faith

If any of you lacks wisdom, you should ask God, who gives generously to all without finding fault, and it will be given to you. But when you ask, you must believe and not doubt, because the one who doubts is like a wave of the sea, blown and tossed by the wind. That person should not expect to receive anything from the Lord (James 1:5-7 NIV). This echoes a scriptural truth written by James in our opening passage: Wavering faith is costly! Wavering faith is faith spiced with unbelief, the one moment you believe and the next you are doubting.

James wrote to inform the saints that wavering faith could cost us blessings that are rightfully ours to receive. Wavering faith can make you quit on projects that have the potential to transform lives and give many people a future. If you talk to some of the founders of the world's biggest companies, you might be surprised to find out how many times they probably considered quitting. What would have been told of their stories if they did not believe through in the possibility of success and the glorious end?

Our faith will be challenged in diverse ways at different times in life. But I pray we will reflect the faith of Abraham. The bible records, "Against all hope, Abraham in hope believed and so became the father of many nations, just as it had been said to him, "So shall your offspring be." Without weakening in his faith, he faced the fact that his body was as good as dead—since he was about a hundred years old—and that Sarah's womb was also dead. Yet he did not waver through unbelief regarding the promise of God but was strengthened in his faith and gave glory to God, being fully persuaded that God had power to do what he had promised. Romans 4:18-21. We are charged in Hebrews 10:23, Let us hold tightly without wavering to the hope we affirm, for God can be trusted to keep his promise NLT.

> **Wavering faith is costly, it can abort a divine miracle and prevent you for receiving all that God has for you. Keep your gaze on the lord and be strong in faith.**

Prayer

Almighty God, we acknowledge your greatness and magnify you above all else, knowing indeed that you who has started a good work in our lives will bring it to completion. We fix our gaze on you and hold fast to your word, knowing that you who promised is faithful to keep to His word. In Jesus name.

Bible in one year // **Numbers 28-30, Mark 8:22-38**

MAR 4

> It was by faith that Moses left the land of Egypt, not fearing the king's anger. He kept right on going because he kept his eyes on the one who is invisible. // **Heb 11:27 NLT**

Developing unwavering faith

You too can have unwavering faith; the kind of faith Abraham was commended for. The bible says, "He did not waver through unbelief regarding the promise of God, but was strengthened in his faith and gave glory to God (Romans 4:20). If you look carefully to how come Abraham had such faith, you would realize the very first was his focus on God and the knowledge of Him. Abraham looked away from the fact that he was advanced in age. He also looked away from the fact that Sarah had gone pass the age of childbearing; in fact, her womb was as good as dead. Abraham turned his eyes away from the facts and focused on God.

The secret to unwavering faith in the face of a challenge is to ignore the facts and the circumstances and fix your eyes on the Lord and His power to make manifest His word.

Abraham had a knowledge of God to which he clung, "Abraham believed in the God who brings the dead back to life and creates new things out of nothing. Without weakening in his faith, he faced the fact that his body was as good as dead—since he was about a hundred years old— and that Sarah's womb was also dead. In fact, his faith grew stronger, and in this he brought glory to God. He was fully convinced that God is able to do whatever he promises" (Romans 4:20-21 NLT).

Moses also had unwavering faith for the same reason as Abraham, "It was by faith that Moses left the land of Egypt, not fearing the king's anger. He kept right on going because he kept his eyes on the one who is invisible" Hebrews 11:27 (NLT). And that is the secret to unwavering faith. Is it regarding your health, the fruit of the womb or your finance? Stop considering the facts and circumstances and fix your eyes on God and His word. Let that knowledge of His ability to do exceedingly abundantly above all we ask or think overwhelm you. Then your faith will be firm and unwavering in the face of great challenges.

Prayer

Thank you Ancient of days for your infinite love towards us. Thank you for revealing yourself to us in the word so that we are not ignorant of the God who raises the dead and creates things from nothing. Even this season we fix our gaze on you and hold fast to your word knowing that those who look to you will be radiant with joy. No shadow of sham shall cover our faces. Receive all the praise in Jesus name.

Bible in one year // **Numbers 31-33, Mark 9:1-29**

In every situation take the shield of faith, and with it you will be able to extinguish all the flaming arrows of the evil one.
// **Ephesians 6:16 HCSB**

MAR 5

Your most prized possession

Jesus said to Simon, "Satan has asked to sift each of you like wheat. But I have pleaded in prayer for you, Simon, that your faith should not fail. So when you have repented and turned to me again, strengthen your brothers" (Luke 22:31-32 NLT). It is my prayer for you that your faith will prevail through all circumstances and your challenges would become testimonies in the unfolding time. I pray that where you thought the battle was fiercest, you would realize even the victory is closest. And with renewed faith you would face life like on unstoppable warrior.

> **Faith is your most prized possession, the one thing the devil is truly after, but God desires your faith to prevail always in all things.**

God's desire for us is that our faith would not fail but prevail over every situation. While a global pandemic might seem the main reason most people are under pressure, some individuals are dealing with issues far overwhelming and challenging, issues that overshadow all concerns over a world pandemic, its threat to life and the financial uncertainties that it announces to many. And just as Jesus said, men's heart fail for fear. Whereas we have not even reached the climax of the difficulties coming into the world as we await His second coming.

That is all part of the Devil's plan, to cripple faith and sift us as wheat through diverse oppressions. The devil is after your most prized possession - your faith. Jesus prayed that no matter what happens, our faith would not fail. For until your faith fails, the devil cannot get a hold of you. No doubt Paul wrote, "In every situation take the shield of faith, and with it you will be able to extinguish all the flaming arrows of the evil one" (Ephesians 6:16 HCSB). That faith is also your only ticket to God, „For without faith it is impossible to please Him" (Hebrews 10:6). And so long your faith is alive, it does not matter what else seems to be failing around you, your faith will always turn the tides around if it does not fail. Remember, "All things are possible to him who believes" (Mark 9:23).

Prayer

Heavenly Father, thank you for preserving us for your purpose and for your glory. We rejoice in the opportunities and blessings this season. With prevailing faith, we will see your goodness in the land of the living as we push back the devil and his cohorts from our lives and families. In Jesus name.

Bible in one year // **Numbers 34-36, Mark 9:30-50**

MAR 6

> Let us hold fast the confession of our hope without wavering, for He who promised is faithful. // **Hebrews 10:23**

Do not cast away hope

We have this call: "Let us hold fast the confession of our hope without wavering, for He who promised is faithful" (Hebrews 10:23). And how that is important, to not cast hope away particularly when situations challenge your faith. Remember, "Faith is the substance of things hoped for" (Hebrews 11:1). In other words, without hope, there is no talking of faith. I have defined faith by the inspiration of the Holy Spirit as, "Unshakable confidence in the manifestation of unseen divine realities that gets you acting and talking like it". Whichever way you look at it, Faith all begins with Hope. Before your faith ever fails, it will be because you cast hope away.

> You cannot have faith without hope, for that is where faith begins. Therefore, do not cast away your hope but go to the word of God to find the inspiration you need in trying times.

I have been in that place where I said to myself, "I will stop hoping and just have faith". Because it seemed every time my hope was being deferred. Like most of us have said at some point regarding something, "I don't want to get my hopes up". This tendency sometimes echoes too in our spiritual walk with God as we look to him for the things He has promised. Particularly when time counts down and lots of other things seem to be at stake. We must remember who we have believed in. Hold tightly without wavering to the hope you have affirmed, for God can be trusted to keep his promise.

This is what Abraham did. The bible records, "Even when there was no reason for hope, Abraham kept hoping-believing that he would become the father of many nations. For God had said to him, "That's how many descendants you will have!" And Abraham's faith did not weaken, even though, at about 100 years of age, he figured his body was as good as dead-and so was Sarah's womb. Abraham never wavered in believing God's promise. In fact, his faith grew stronger, and in this he brought glory to God" (Romans 4:18-20 NLT). Like Abraham, never cast away your hope in God. His word always proves true.

Prayer

Thank you, Faithful God for being reliable and dependable, unchanging through time. Thank you for your word preserved through the ages for our learning, that through its encouragement we will find hope that does not disappoint. We receive grace to be unwavering. In Jesus' name.

Bible in one year // Deuteronomy 1-2, Mark 10:1-31

> We have this hope as an anchor for the soul, sure and steadfast, which reaches inside behind the curtain, where Jesus our forerunner entered on our behalf. // **Hebrews 6:19-20 NET**

MAR 7

A sure anchor

When a ship reaches its destination or a stop, to keep it from drifting with the waves, the anchor is immediately lowered. This keeps the ship at the shore on which it is anchored. And that is what hope is to your soul, the hope in God given to us in Christ Jesus. It is a sure anchor for your soul, firm through the fiercest storms. It keeps you planted in God no matter what circumstances come your way, like a chord holding you in place, it is anchored on Christ himself. As it is written, "We have this hope as an anchor for the soul, sure and steadfast, which reaches inside behind the curtain, where Jesus our forerunner entered on our behalf" (Hebrews 6:19-20 NET).

The writer of Hebrews shows us why we could have unwavering hope. He argued, "Now when people take an oath, they call on someone greater than themselves to hold them to it. And without any question that oath is binding. God also bound himself with an oath, so that those who received the promise could be perfectly sure that he would never change his mind. So, God has given both his promise and his oath. These two things are unchangeable because it is impossible for God to lie (Hebrews 6:16-28 NLT)

He was referring to the oath God made when He gave a promise to Abraham, promises that were all fulfilled in Christ Jesus. As a double assurance, God who cannot lie gave a promise and bound himself to that promise with an oath. So indeed, we who have fled to God to take hold of this hope might have great encouragement, first because God won't lie and second, an oath obliges him to His promises. Now this hope is an anchor to your soul, keeping you steadfast in God and immovable from His presence. When you have this hope, even in the face of greatest difficulty and pressure, you will remain planted and immovable in God.

> **Unwavering hope in God inspired by His sure promises is a firm anchor for your soul, keeping you planted and firm in God irrespective of life's circumstances.**

Prayer
Heavenly Father thank you for the hope I have in you through Jesus Christ. Open my eyes to see your purpose even through the darkest night and seasons of turbulence, that I will remain steadfast, grounded, and rooted in you. In Jesus' name.

Bible in one year // Deuteronomy 3-4, Mark 10:32-52

MAR 8

> Those who look to him are radiant with joy; their faces will never be ashamed. // **Psalm 34:5**

Hope won't dissappoint

The Psalmist made a bold declaration, "Those who look to him are radiant with joy; their faces will never be ashamed (Psalm 34:5). And that is our story, when our hope is truly in God. It is a hope that will not disappoint. As it is written, "Now hope does not disappoint" (Romans 5:5). Now, you might have hoped in God for a specific thing that did not come forth as expected, or something that played out differently. That does not nullify the word of God about hope not making ashamed. For in these specific situations, it is often the case that our hope was not inspired by a specific word of promise that was given to us on that issue. That was not the kind of hope Paul referred to in His writing.

> **The hope we have in Christ Jesus is one that will not disappoint, it is the hope that no matter what happens, God's glory will be revealed in us in the end.**

Paul wrote, "Therefore, since we have been justified through faith, we have peace with God through our Lord Jesus Christ, through whom we have gained access by faith into this grace in which we now stand. And we boast in the hope of the glory of God" (Romans 5:1-2). It is the hope of the glory of God being revealed in your life through all situations. This is the hope that no matter what happens, the overall outcome will echo itself in the revelation of God's glory.

Indeed, this hope does not disappoint, the Hope we have in Christ Jesus. How the song writer puts it. "My hope is built on nothing less, than Jesus' blood and righteousness, I dare not trust the sweetest frame but wholly lean on Jesus' name. On Christ the solid rock I stand, all other ground is sinking sand". He added, "When all around my soul gives way, He then is all my hope and stay". He had come to understand, that this hope we have in Christ Jesus does not disappoint.

Prayer

Thank you, Heavenly Father, for the hope we have in Christ Jesus. We know that all things work together for good for us who love you and are called according to your purpose. You know the plans you have for us, to give us a hope and a future, to bring us to an expected end. In Jesus' name.

Bible in one year // **Deuteronomy 5-7, Mark 11:1-18**

> For whatever things were written before were written for our learning, that we through the patience and comfort of the Scriptures might have hope.
> // Romans 15:4

MAR 9

A fuel for divine service

Most times, people go to work not because of passion for what they do, but because of the very hope they have for the salary. The thought of the salary is their driving force, getting them out of bed when it is dark and cold, rainy or sunny, sometimes weak, sick and tired. They find the drive and the energy for service because of the reward they look to. Their hope is the fuel for their committed service. This is even more true when it comes to your service in the Kingdom of God. As Paul testified, "It is because of my hope in what God has promised our ancestors that I am on trial today. This is the promise our twelve tribes are hoping to see fulfilled as they earnestly serve God day and night. King Agrippa, it is because of this hope that these Jews are accusing me" (Acts 26:6-7 NIV).

Your hope in God is the fuel for your service. In the absence of that hope, we will faint, grow weary and quit. In Philippians 3:12-14 he wrote, "Not that I have already obtained all this, or have already arrived at my goal, but I press on to take hold of that for which Christ Jesus took hold of me. Brothers and sisters, I do not consider myself yet to have taken hold of it. But one thing I do: Forgetting what is behind and straining toward what is ahead, I press on toward the goal to win the prize for which God has called me heavenward in Christ Jesus".

Unwavering hope in the fulfillment of divine promises is the fuel for committed kingdom service even when you can't directly see an immediate reward for your sacrifices.

Jesus had the same attitude, He kept hope alive and it became the fuel for His mission. As it is written, "Who for the joy that was set before him endured the cross, despising the shame, and is set down at the right hand of the throne of God (Hebrews 12:2). His gaze was on the rewards thereof, the salvation for our sins and the glorious reign ahead. This is same hope you will need to keep alive through meditation in scriptures if you will be steadfast in Kingdom service (Romans 15:4).

Prayer

> Almighty God, thank You for the great and precious promises laid ahead of us in Christ. As we serve in hope, we will not grow weary as you renew our strength by your Spirit. We receive grace to keep your promises in foreview that they might inspire commitment and zeal in every day. In Jesus name.

Bible in one year // **Deuteronomy 8-10, Mark 11:19-33**

MAR 10

> Now these three remain: faith, hope, and love – but the greatest of these is love. // **1 Corinthians 13:13**

Three principal pillars

When you read beginning from Chapter 12 of the first letter to the Corinthians, you will realize Paul had been writing about spiritual gifts. In the next chapter, he builds on that foundation with the call to walk in love. And on a conclusive note, he writes, "Now these three remain: faith, hope, and love—but the greatest of these is love" (1 Corinthians 13:13). He emphasized faith, hope and love above spiritual gifts, highlighting that even prophecy as great as it is, would come to an end. These three, I call them principal pillars of the effective Christian life.

Faith hope and love together make three principal pillars of the Christian life. Irrespective of your gifts and calling, these three great factors are essential for effectiveness.

This is because if they are in place, you will always have spiritual buoyancy, like an architectural edifice, your life would have the principal elements about which everything else anchors. And just as pillars give form, structure and strength to a building, your life would be suited to survive the fiercest of storms, being fully fruitful to the glory of God. And when I talk about principal pillars of the effective Christian life, it is not just a play with words. It does not matter the spiritual giftings of God invested in you, without these three factors in place, you will be barren in God's vineyard.

Peter wrote in his second letter, "For this very reason, make every effort to add to your faith excellence, to excellence, knowledge; to knowledge, self-control; to self-control, perseverance; to perseverance, godliness; to godliness, brotherly affection; to brotherly affection, unselfish love. For if these things are really yours and are continually increasing, they will keep you from becoming ineffective and unproductive in your knowledge of our Lord Jesus Christ" (2 Peter 1:5-8). And it was guaranteed they would be effective and fruitful in their knowledge of Christ. The same is true for you today. Faith, love and hope are three elements that must abide in your life to the fullest for greater effectiveness in Christ.

Prayer

Heavenly Father, thank you for today and the illumination in your word. That we also, being built up for you would always have these elements of faith, hope, and love in overflow. That we would be effective in service for you as we bring your message and love to the world. In Jesus' name.

Bible in one year // Deuteronomy 11-13, Mark 12:1-27

God demonstrates His own love toward us, in that while we were still sinners, Christ died for us. // **Romans 5:8**

MAR 11

God's kind of love

While love might be a very common word, its true meaning and definition is often twisted by the human nature and understanding because of man's own limitations to know and express love. Such that the definition of love can only be in context and reference to what kind of love is in focus. In scriptures, there are many different words translated from the Greek to mean love. And that for good reason. There is the human kind of love and the God kind of love. While we will try to have an understanding today of the God kind of love, it is important to note that this love cannot be understood without spiritual revelation.

Just as Paul prayed for the Ephesian Church that they would "Know this love that SURPASSES KNOWLEDGE –that you may be filled to the measure of all the fullness of God" (Ephesians 3:18-19 NIV). And how important it is to know and be able to express this kind of love, for that is the secret to manifesting divinity to your world. This is the reason many people cannot experience supernatural manifestations of the power of God, particularly those in front-line ministry. Paul explained that knowing this love and being able to express it will bring you into the fullness of God, God being resident and expressed through you in all His totality.

> Knowing and being able to express the God kind of love is the secret to experiencing and manifesting the fullness of divinity in your life.

You see, And the easiest way to know this love and distinguish it from others is to recognize its characteristics. The very first is that it is unconditional love, a love we never have to qualify for, a love we don't get to earn. He of His own nature and will, loves us. Like scripture puts it, "God demonstrates his own love for us in this: While we were still sinners, Christ died for us" (Romans 5:6-8 NIV). the God kind of love seeks your good and well-being even when He has nothing to profit in it, it is selfless. Yes, this love is unconditional, it is unchanging, it is unending, and it is selfless in nature –the God kind of love.

Prayer

Thank you, Heavenly Father, for your loved us and chosen us to be called your sons. We pray that you would grant us revelational knowledge that we might know this love and express it one for another, that together, rooted and grounded in this love, we will experience your fullness in every day. In Jesus name.

Bible in one year // **Deuteronomy 14-16, Mark 12:28-44**

MAR 12

God's love has been poured out into our hearts through the Holy Spirit, who has been given to us. // **Romans 5:5 NIV**

You have the capacity

A passage from the bible where two types of love are in play is this verse in John 21:15: Jesus said to Simon Peter, „Simon son of John, do you love me more than these?" „Yes, Lord," he said, „you know that I love you." Jesus used another word for love. Jesus used the word "Agapao", a word corresponding to agape, the kind of love with which God loves. Peter in his response chose to use another word "Phileo", which is the tender affection humanly possible, not measuring up to the unchanging, unconditional, unending, and selfless love of Christ. He could love him and stand with him so long as it was fitting and convenient. When his life was at stake, Peter withdrew into the shadows and denied Jesus.

It does not pass our notice also that even as Peter loved and followed Jesus, it was initially interest-driven. On one occasion, Peter openly inquired what his gain would be for all he was sacrificing. Peter asked Jesus, "We've given up everything to follow you. What will we get?" (Matthew 19:27 NLT). And we all might have come through that phase in our walk with God where you felt you were laying it all down for Him and wondering what your benefit would be. Nonetheless, as we grow spiritually, we realize our love for Him ought not to be motivated by that but because of who He is. In fact, our love for Him is a response to His love for us. Just as John wrote, "We love Him because He first loved us" (1 John 4:19).

It is in your capacity to love like God if you are born again, to love unconditionally and selflessly.

However, that kind of love peter demonstrated was before he received the Holy Spirit. Until then, he lacked the capacity to love with the God kind of love - the unconditional love that was going to stand up boldly for the Lord in all places and in all things as He later demonstrated in his life and ministry. Just as the opening verse today puts it, "The love of God had been poured into his heart". The same is true for you today if you are born again. The Holy Spirit gives you the capacity to love like God does. Yes, it is in your capacity to love like God, to love even those who are so undeserving.

Prayer

Heavenly Father thank you for pouring your love into our hearts by your Spirit, giving us the capacity to love just as you love. Help us to overcome the cage and tendencies of our flesh that we might express your pure love to our world as you draw men to yourself through us. In Jesus name.

Bible in one year // **Deuteronomy 17-19, Mark 13:1-20**

A new commandment I give unto you, that you love one another;
AS I HAVE LOVED YOU, that you also love one another.
// John 13:34 KJV

MAR 13

A greater commandment

"You have heard that it was said, 'Love your neighbor and hate your enemy.' But I tell you, love your enemies and pray for those who persecute you, that you may be children of your Father in heaven. He causes his sun to rise on the evil and the good; and sends rain on the righteous and the unrighteous. If you love those who love you, what reward will you get? Are not even the tax collectors doing that? And if you greet only your own people, what are you doing more than others? Do not even pagans do that? Be perfect, therefore, as your heavenly Father is perfect" (Matthew 5:43-48 NIV).

When you understand the covenants of God and the life that has been given to us in Christ Jesus, you will truly appreciate the saying of Jesus, "From everyone who has been given much, much will be required" (Luke 12:48). For indeed, in Christ Jesus, we have received surpassingly much more than those who were under the old covenant received. And with that comes greater expectations. One such greater call is on love. To the people guided by the laws of Moses, they were told, "You shall love your neighbor as yourself". This was the most expected of them and that for two reasons.

> To love your neighbor as yourself is a lesser commandment. To love everyone with God's love indiscriminately as God does is the actual commandment given to us in Christ Jesus.

First, they lacked the spiritual capacity comprehend the love of God. They were a natural people, unregenerate and trapped in the flesh. But we are a new creation, born of the Spirit and given the Holy Spirit who makes Spiritual truths clear to us (1 Cor 2:12-14). Secondly, it was the best way love could be exemplified to the people under the law. In simple terms, the Lord was telling the people, "Put yourself in the shoes of the other person when you act towards them". But to us he said, "A new commandment I give unto you, that you love one another; AS I HAVE LOVED YOU, that you also love one another" (John 13:34 KJV). He calls us to such love that causes one to lay down his life for the other, a love that knows no bounds in its expression (John 15:13).

Prayer

Gracious an Everlasting Father, thank you for giving us so much in Christ Jesus and with it the grace to live up to the higher standards you have called us to. We pray that even in this aspect of love we will grow unto perfection, loving others unconditionally and indiscriminately just as you love. In Jesus name.

Bible in one year // **Deuteronomy 20-22, Mark 13:21-37**

MAR 14

> Now then, we are ambassadors for Christ, as though God were pleading through us: we implore you on Christ's behalf, be reconciled to God. // **2 1 Corinthians 5:18-20**

A ministry of reconciliation

One reason there is so much confusion among believers when it comes to understanding scriptures and living it out is because many have not understood the covenants. They have neither understood the old and the new covenants and their separation. As a result, what some have is an amalgamation of both covenants, sometimes bringing them to a place where they fail to understand who they really are in Christ and what life we have been given in him. The people of old were told, "Thou shalt not suffer a witch to live" (Exodus 22:18). And surprising enough, you hear this among many believers as they pray against their enemies with that as a reference – praying for the death of their enemies. Now it doesn't matter who's doing that, it is unscriptural and substandard for those in Christ Jesus.

> *Love your enemies and pray for their salvation. To you was given the ministry of reconciliation to bring all men to the Lord – even those hating and working against you.*

To the people of old was given a mission of annihilation - they were commissioned to destroy those who were not of God and had the potential to lead them away to idol worshiping. In fact, what they were doing was a reflection of a divine principle, "Whatever will cause you to sin, take it out of the way" (Matthew 5:29-30). Also, the people lacked the authority to cast out the demons at work in such persons (Ephesians 2:1-3). Therefore, they killed the witch to stop their activities. But that was then.

To us was given the power and authority over unclean spirits. More than that, we were told, nothing shall by any means harm us. And unlike the people of old, we have a mission towards these people, to set them free from the bondage of Satan and bring them into the light of God. As it is written, "Now all things are of God, who has reconciled us to Himself through Jesus Christ, and has given us the ministry of reconciliation... Now then, we are ambassadors for Christ, as though God were pleading through us: we implore you on Christ's behalf, be reconciled to God" (2 Corinthians 5:18-20).

Prayer

Heavenly Father thank you for the illumination in your word. We receive grace to walk in love today towards all men, to pray for our enemies, that the scales from their eyes will fall, that they might see the light and glory of the gospel in the face of Jesus and find salvation for their souls. In Jesus' name.

Bible in one year // **Deuteronomy 23-25, Mark 14:1-26**

He who does not love does not know God, for God is love .
// 1 John 4:8

MAR 15

No room for hatred

A lot to be shared on love, the God kind of love. It leaves no room for hatred. And that is the life we are called to live, a life that expresses indiscriminate love. Jesus called that perfection. So long as you find reasons to justify why you resent a person, you are yet to be perfected in love. God appeared unto Abraham and said unto Him, walk before me and be perfect. And a lot many times, people have questioned if perfection is indeed attainable. My answer is this, If the Lord called us to it, then it is indeed a standard we can attain. And it is made even simple and reachable when we realize this call to perfection is a call to walk in indiscriminate love. That is what Jesus illustrated in Matthew 5.

Jesus told the disciples, "You have heard that it was said, 'Love your neighbor and hate your enemy. But I tell you, love your enemies and pray for those who persecute you, that you may be children of your Father in heaven. He causes his sun to rise on the evil and the good, and sends rain on the righteous and the unrighteous. If you love those who love you, what reward will you get? Are not even the tax collectors doing that?... Be perfect, therefore, as your heavenly Father is perfect" (Matt 5:43-48). He connected such capacity to walk in love indiscriminately with being perfect like the father. And it is all possible.

Personally, when I search my heart, there is no one in the world I hate. In fact, I no longer have that capacity for hatred. Yes, because I have learned to see the image of God on everyone, for in His image, he indeed made us all. No matter who they are, no matter what they do. Scripture enjoins us, "Beloved, let us love one another, for love is of God; and everyone who loves is born of God and knows God. He who does not love does not know God, for God is love... If someone says, "I love God," and hates his brother, he is a liar; for he who does not love his brother whom he has seen, how can he love God whom he has not seen?" (1 John 4:7-20).

> **Make no room for hatred, it is not in the nature given to us in Christ Jesus. Ours is a nature with the capacity to love indiscriminately like the Father.**

Prayer

Heavenly Father thank you for your love that is poured into our hearts, giving us the capacity to love as you do. We receive grace to be perfected in love, irrespective of who we are dealing with. We receive healing for hurting souls that feel abused because they loved. In Jesus' name.

Bible in one year // **Deuteronomy 26-27, Mark 14:27-53**

MAR 16

> For [if we are] in Christ Jesus, neither circumcision nor uncircumcision counts for anything, but only faith activated and energized and expressed and working through love. // **Galatians 5:6 AMPC**

An atmosphere for miracles

There are laws of the Spirit, spiritual principles that govern life in the spiritual realm. And unless understood, we would struggle. The reason we have such technological developments is because we have been able to harness natural laws and principles for our good. Be it flying planes or the use of wireless technologies, all these are a direct result of understanding basic principles of the natural world and harnessing them for our good. It is no different with the spiritual environment in which we live. That is one reason we must be illuminated through the word of God – the main reason for Your Daily Light.

In this light, there is something we can do about creating an atmosphere for miracles. God, throughout scriptures, shows us how. One of them is to walk in love. I remember a lesson from the Lord taught me when I began public ministry, and that was in a dream. In this dream, I had been praying for a lady as I laid a hand on her forehead. But nothing was happening as I had my attention elsewhere. Then a voice came to me saying, "Show some love". As I looked at her with compassion in response to that voice, she fell under the power of God. Then I realized I had been dreaming. At that moment, the lesson came home straight. In ministering to people, it does not matter how great a faith you have, it is your love expressed towards them that will bring the power of God on the scene.

> **Walking in love creates about us an atmosphere for the manifestation of God's presence, an atmosphere for miracles.**

This is what is written, "For [if we are] in Christ Jesus, neither circumcision nor uncircumcision counts for anything, but only faith activated and energized and expressed and working through love" (Galatians 5:6 AMPC). Remember, "If I have faith that can move mountains, but do not have love, I am nothing" (1 Cor 13:2). Love on its own is the igniting force for miracles. We create an atmosphere for miracles when we walk in love, for where there is love, the power of God will flow. That is why faith works by love, for it is love that gives faith expression.

Prayer

Thank You Father for your word of illumination, making known your ways to us that we might walk in them. Today as we walk in love, we receive your presence and the atmosphere for miracles it brings. That our faith would be potent, working wonders and bringing glory to you. In Jesus' name.

Bible in one year // **Deuteronomy 28-29, Mark 14:54-72**

> We do not want you to become lazy, but to imitate those who through faith and patience inherit what has been promised.
> // **Hebrews 6:12 NIV**

MAR 17

Imitate them

We have many testimonies of heroes of faith and the record of their journeys, testimonies that provide us with examples to emulate. And the writer of Hebrews highlights two things which were particular about them and how their faith proved true. It was their FAITH and PATIENCE. And how patience is important. For no matter how great a faith you have, if it is not accompanied by corresponding patience, that faith might prove abortive and impotent. Not because the promise was not sure, but because you gave up before the time of manifestation. In fact, someone has defined patience as faith exercised over a prolonged period. Just as is written, "You have need of patient endurance [to bear up under difficult circumstances without compromising], so that when you have carried out the will of God, you may receive and enjoy to the full what is promised" (Hebrews 10:36 AMP).

Testimonies of many men and women of faith abound, in scriptures and in Church history whose faith and patience we can emulate and inherit divine promises just as they did.

The author of Hebrews went on to share amazing stories of prevailing faith, people he calls us to imitate. Starting with Abel, he climaxed his writing with these lines, "And what more shall I say? For the time would fail me to tell of Gideon and Barak and Samson and Jephthah, also of David and Samuel and the prophets: who through faith subdued kingdoms, worked righteousness, obtained promises, stopped the mouths of lions, quenched the violence of fire, escaped the edge of the sword, out of weakness were made strong, became valiant in battle, turned to flight the armies of the aliens (Hebrews 11:32 NKJV).

These heroes of faith who now are in glory, he called them a cloud of witnesses as he encourages us to emulate their example of faith and patience. Imitate them, therefore. Be inspired by their stories and act in their steps that in our own generation, we can also be remembered for our faith and be to others tomorrow more witnesses to this prevailing life of faith.

Prayer

Thank You God almighty for witnesses that abound to inspire and help my faith, people gone before me who show this life of conquering faith is possible. I receive grace for corresponding patience to wait until the full manifestation of your blessings and promises in my life. In Jesus name.

Bible in one year // **Deuteronomy 30-31, Mark 15:1-25**

MAR 18

So then faith comes by hearing, and hearing by the word of God.
// **Romans 10:17 NKJV**

Grow your faith

As Romans 12:3 puts it, God has given to everyone a measure of faith. However, that faith was only a seed given to you, a seed that has the potential to grow into great and strong faith – a faith that sees nothing to be impossible for God, a faith that doesn't buckle under pressure. It is your responsibility to grow that faith as you continuously meditate in the word of God. For in receiving the word of God, faith naturally grows as you get to know his power. Even the nonbeliever will only believe if they hear the word. As it is written, „How then shall they call on Him in whom they have not believed? And how shall they believe in Him of whom they have not heard?" (Romans 10:14)

> **It is your responsibility to grow in faith through meditation in the word of God and a conscious choice of association with men and women of faith.**

It was hearing about Jesus that Blind Bartimaeus had faith to receive his sight. We read, "A blind man, Bartimaeus, was sitting by the roadside begging. When he heard that it was Jesus of Nazareth, he began to shout, "Jesus, Son of David, have mercy on me!" (Mark 10 46-47). Just like the woman with the issue of blood, He had heard a lot about Jesus and what He could do. The woman because of all the miracles she heard were happening, had such great faith to tap off virtue from the Lord without His permission. For she said to herself, "If only I may touch His garment, I shall be made well." (Matthew 9:21).

There is no other way about growing your faith. It will be by the word and by the testimony of others who are prevailing by faith. This is also one reason you need to mind your associations. Belong to a local church and find a community of believers with whom you can grow and be encouraged together. Remember, the church is called the household of faith (Galatians 6:10). Like the writer of Hebrews admonishes, „Let us not neglect meeting together, as some have made a habit, BUT LET US ENCOURAGE ONE ANOTHER, and all the more as you see the Day approaching" (Hebrews 10:25). Don't forget, "Walk with the wise and become wise; associate with fools and get in trouble" (Proverbs 13:20 NLT). In the same light, if you walk with people of faith, your faith will grow and the reverse is also true.

Prayer

Thank you, Lord, for your word and the admonition to grow in faith. I receive a fresh desire for your word that by it I might grow. Help me in this season to make the right associations with persons who inspire my faith and not hinder it. So my faith will be more effective, prevailing in all things. In Jesus' name.

Bible in one year // **Deuteronomy 32-34, Mark 15:26-47**

Though he slay me, yet will I trust in him: but I will maintain mine own ways before him. // **Job 13:15**

A little snare

It is worth calling your attention to watch against the snare of anchoring your faith in God on the things He will do for you. If that is your focus, you are on the wrong footing. For in such a disposition, what happens is that your faith will easily be shaken when things do not go according to your expectation. Your faith in God should be based on your Knowledge of His character and person. When you know for a fact that God is your healer even if your health is not restored, you know that God is your provider even when your bills are not paid, and you know that God is your deliverer though you are in chains and even locked up in prison falsely.

The right faith in God is such that is anchored on God for His person and Character. And such a faith will always prevail in the end. For after all, it is not just about a faith to get things and make our lives on earth comfortable. It is about the faith that keeps you going in God, enduring till the end no matter what comes your way. Just as Jesus said, "He who endures to the end shall be saved" (Matt 24:13 NKJ). But if your faith is anchored on what God will do for you and what you can get in this life, that faith is sure to be unstable as this life itself. Your faith will soar high when prayers are answered and plunge low when expectations are contradicted. Job had the right faith in God. No doubt he could say, "Though he slay me, yet will I trust in him: but I will maintain mine own ways before him" (Job 13:15 KJV)

> **A stable faith is anchored on the person and character of God, not on what He does for you.**

The three Hebrew boys, Shadrach, Meshach, and Abednego in a time of Babylonian captivity demonstrated such a faith in God, a faith that was not anchored on what God would do for them, a faith anchored on who God is. They said, "King Nebuchadnezzar, we do not need to defend ourselves before you in this matter. If we are thrown into the blazing furnace, the God we serve is able to deliver us from it, and he will deliver us from Your Majesty's hand. But even if he does not, we want you to know, Your Majesty, that we will not serve your gods or worship the image of gold you have set up" (Daniel 3:16-18 NIV). They had a faith that was not anchored on what God would do for them, but on His person.

Prayer

God almighty, thank you for the blessing of a new day and the continuous illumination in your word. I pray that as you reveal and make known yourself to me, my faith will be based on your Character and person, not on the results I get. In Jesus' name.

Bible in one year // **Joshua 1-3, Mark 16**

MAR 20

And as you go, preach, saying, 'The kingdom of heaven is at hand.' Heal the sick, cleanse the lepers, raise the dead, cast out demons. Freely you have received, freely give. // **Matthew 10:7-8**

Dare out in faith

I remember a summer holiday almost a decade back. With such a hunger for the Lord, I spent the early hours until midday indoors in prayer and meditation. The thing that kept me in there was a sincere desire and longing for a fresh impartation of spiritual gifts. As much as every day had a delightful experience, I was feeling unsatisfied and prayed the more for a fresh touch from the Lord, a touch that would fill me with new spiritual abilities. But one morning as I spent time in prayer, I slept off for a moment and had a vision. It was a vision of the Lord saying to me these words, „For all the time you have been in my presence, I have been depositing on you spiritual blessings. But you will not see them until you step out". When I looked around in the vision, I could see it drizzling on me, then I awoke. And I have indeed experienced miracles of instant healings and diverse manifestations of the gifts of the Spirit by daring out in faith.

> If you are going to see the manifestations of the gifts of God in you, you will have to there out in faith into God's call for you.

This story is true for you too. You just might never know all the spiritual blessings and gifts of the Spirit bestowed on you until you dare out in faith to fulfill God's call for your life. This was true of Gideon. He had been hiding from the Midianites when the Angel of the Lord appeared to him and said, "Go in the strength you have and save Israel out of Midian's hand" (Judges 6:14 NIV). The gift was already in him, deposited by the Lord.

Jesus said to the disciples, „ As you go..." (Matthew 10:7-8). Same is true for you. You will not see the sick healed seating in your room and praying for the gift of healing. You will at most see visions of you praying for the sick. That is the Lord confirming to you that He has given you the gift of healing. You will have to dare out in faith and pray for the sick. Point is, whatever God has called you into, quit waiting and praying for spiritual gifts, dare out in faith for that's when the miracles begin.

Prayer

Heavenly Father thank you for the call to serve you and men. Today I receive grace to recognize the gifts in me and the opportunities to employ them for your glory. As I go, reveal yourself to men by the Holy Spirit and grace my labor with supernatural impact. In Jesus' name.

Bible in one year // **Joshua 4-6, Luke 1:1-20**

Finally, my brethren, be strong in the Lord and in the power of His might. // **Ephesians 6:10**

MAR 21

Be strong in the Lord

Be strong in the Lord and in the power of His might (Ephesians 6:10). Such a profound instruction. For if you are strong in the Lord, you are guaranteed to be victorious in all things. For you will stand fully equipped always, ready for every good work, alert to the leading of the Holy Spirit who will lead you to green pastures and away from losses. And all the while you will be strong, resisting the devil and his cohorts, putting them under your feet where they belong. So, I indeed write to you my dear brothers and sisters, be strong in the Lord and in the power of His might.

> Be strong in the Lord and in the power of His might. For therein is the guarantee of blessings and victory throughout the year.

Paul did not leave us in the dark as to how to make that happen. He added, "Put on the whole armor of God, that you may be able to stand against the wiles of the devil. For we do not wrestle against flesh and blood, but against principalities, against powers, against the rulers of the darkness of this age, against spiritual hosts of wickedness in the heavenly places. Therefore, take up the whole armor of God, that you may be able to withstand in the evil day, and having done all, to stand. Stand therefore, having girded your waist with truth, having put on the breastplate of righteousness, and having shod your feet with the preparation of the gospel of peace (Ephesians 6:11 - 15)

Above all, "Taking the shield of faith with which you will be able to quench all the fiery darts of the wicked one. And take the helmet of salvation, and the sword of the Spirit, which is the word of God; praying always with all prayer and supplication in the Spirit" (Ephesians 6:16 - 18). Same things I charge you to do. Be consistent in the word of God even as Your Daily Light has a responsibility to bring to you a daily dose of light from God's word. Continue in prayer and don't forsake your gathering with other believers. And the Lord will bless you and bring you through every situation in singing.

Prayer

> Thank You Father for your steadfast love. In Your strength we can crush an army; with you our God, we can scale any wall. We receive grace to be strong in you and in the power of your might in every passing day. So, we will be unstoppable and victorious in all things this year for your glory. In Jesus' name.

Bible in one year // **Joshua 7-9, Luke 1:21-38**

MAR 22

> Blessed is the one who perseveres under trial because, having stood the test, that person will receive the crown of life that the Lord has promised to those who love him . // **James 1:12 NIV**

You can stand

The above verse came to me many years ago at a season I needed it most. As a young believer, I had been contemplating going into the world as a mark of rebellion because of the challenges I was facing. This verse gave me such renewed zeal and strength to stand that season of test. And the knowledge from that book has followed me through the years. I am still standing in the faith by the grace of God. You too can stand. Just like Ephesians 6:13 puts it, "Put on the full armor of God, so that when the day of evil comes, you may be able to stand your ground, and after you have done everything, to stand".

> God will not allow you to be tempted beyond what you can bear. If he let it come your way, it is because He trusts you to be able to face it and remain standing in the end.

1 Corinthians 13 tells us, "The temptations in your life are no different from what others experience. And God is faithful. He will not allow the temptation to be more than you can stand. When you are tempted, he will show you a way out so that you can endure (NLT). That's a word of assurance, that God will not allow you to be tempted beyond your ability. So never say I cannot take it anymore. You can stand. Don't say "I give up". If God let it come your way, it is because He knows you can stand. Don't entertain any lies from the devil. Often the battle is fiercest when the victory is closest, and just when you almost get a hold of everything, that's where he tries to get you to quit. Stand your ground.

Consider this exhortation to us from Hebrews, "So do not throw away this confident trust in the Lord. Remember the great reward it brings you! Patient endurance is what you need now, so that you will continue to do God's will. Then you will receive all that he has promised. "For in just a little while, the Coming One will come and not delay. And my righteous ones will live by faith. But I will take no pleasure in anyone who turns away." But we are not like those who turn away from God to their own destruction. We are the faithful ones, whose souls will be saved" (NLT). This is our testimony, we are not of those who turn back, but of those who stand until the end. You can indeed stand through your trials!

Prayer

Thank You Heavenly Father for your love and mercies that are new every morning. Thank you for the assurance that you will never let us to be tempted beyond that which we can bear. We pray for renewed strength this season for they that feel exhausted and worn out. In Jesus' name.

Bible in one year // **Joshua 10-12, Luke 1:39-56**

> Let no one say when he is tempted, "I am tempted by God"; for God cannot be tempted by evil, nor does He Himself tempt anyone.
> // **James 1:13**

MAR 23

Know the difference

Know the difference between temptations and tests. One thing is sure: every child of God will be tested; your faith will be tried. It probably already was tested and is being tested even now. There is no way around it if your faith will grow. James was exhorting his readers here with these words, "My brethren, count it all joy when you fall into various trials, knowing that the testing of your faith produces patience. But let patience have its perfect work, that you may be perfect and complete, lacking nothing" (James 1:2-4). He informed them that the testing of their faith was necessary. The same is true for you today.

Nonetheless, in a twist in his writing, he moves from testing to temptations and emphasizes the source of temptations – they are never from God. "Let no one say when he is tempted, 'I am tempted by God'; for God cannot be tempted by evil, nor does He Himself tempt anyone. But each one is tempted when he is drawn away by his own desires and enticed. Then, when desire has conceived, it gives birth to sin; and sin, when it is full-grown, brings forth death" (James 1:13-15)

He tests us, but he does not tempt us. In testing, God brings you to a place where you would have to exercise your faith in Him, He puts you in a trying situation where you will have to act on His word no matter the alternatives you have, particularly when things suggest otherwise. That is testing. We will be brought into diverse situations where we would have to choose to do his will. In fact, Jesus himself learned obedience by the things he suffered even though He was a son (Hebrews 5:8). Recognize therefore that tests come from God and are intended for our spiritual development. But God is not the author of temptations.

> **Tests come from God. They are those situations God brings us into where our confidence and obedience in His word is tested.**

Prayer

Almighty God thank you for the blessing of today. Thank you for the trials and tests which provide us with opportunity for growth. We pray that the eyes of our spirits will be opened to see your loving arms holding us through it all that we might not loose heart but develop to the perfect man. In Jesus' name.

Bible in one year // **Joshua 13-15, Luke 1:57-80**

MAR 24

> Be sober, be vigilant; because your adversary the devil walks about like a roaring lion, seeking whom he may devour. // **1 Peter 5:8**

Satan the opportunist

Luke gives account of the temptations of Jesus. He highlights a truth in passing: Satan is an opportunist and the author of temptations. He seeks occasions and settings when God's people are most vulnerable to get them off course. And that is his sole business in the earth, to bring along to hell as many as he can. Or at minimum, he seeks to cheat us out of enjoying God's best for our lives. That's why Peter admonished us, "Be sober, be vigilant; because your adversary the devil walks about like a roaring lion, seeking whom he may devour. Resist him, steadfast in the faith, knowing that the same sufferings are experienced by your brotherhood in the world" (1 Peter 5:8-9).

Luke records, "Then Jesus, being filled with the Holy Spirit, returned from the Jordan and was led by the Spirit into the wilderness, being tempted for forty days by the devil" (Luke 4:1-3). See the full story from Luke 4:1-13. Now, Jesus was not led into the wilderness just to be tempted by Satan like Matthew's account suggests (4:1-11). You get this fuller picture when you read the accounts of Luke (Luke 4:1-13) and Mark (Mark 1:9-13). Jesus was led into the wilderness for a time of communion with God in fasting and prayers. Then Satan the uninvited guest showed up with same old agenda, to lure him away from the divine path. And when Satan failed, "He departed from Him until an opportune time" (Luke 4:13).

> **Satan is the author of temptations and takes opportunities when we are most vulnerable in times of testing to throw his best shots. But if you resist him, he will flee from you.**

The Devil takes advantage or immediate needs to lure us away from God's best. Because Jesus was hungry, he tempted with turning stones to bread. This attempt to derail God's people was not new. It started off with Eve in the garden. The good news is this: he will not prevail so long as you hold up your shield of faith with which to quench every fiery dart he throws at you (Ephesians 6:13). Remember, "Resist the devil, and he will flee from you" (James 4:7 NIV). Satan the opportunist has no alternatives but to flee if you will stand your ground. You have the victory over him.

Prayer

Thank You Heavenly Father for giving us authority and power over the devil and his cohorts who roam the earth seeking whom to devour. We forbid their activities in our lives and communities. All that concerns us is set apart and protected from their reach and manipulations in the name of Jesus.

Bible in one year // Joshua 16-18, Luke 2:1-24

For our light affliction, which is but for a moment, is working for us a far more exceeding and eternal weight of glory. // **2 Corinthians 4:17**

MAR 25

A crown for you

One thing that is true about seasons of trials and testing is that they are never pleasant. If we could, we would gladly do without them. These are those seasons when we pray like Jesus, „My Father, if it is possible, may this cup be taken from me. Yet not as I will, but as you will"(Matthew 26:39). Just like the writer of Hebrews would say, "No discipline seems pleasant at the time, but painful. Later, however, it produces a harvest of righteousness and peace for those who have been trained by it" (Hebrews 12:11). It is never pleasant, but the reward thereof is worth it. Like our lead passage today puts it, there is a crown for you if you will persevere under testing and not give up your faith but endure to the end.

> **Our light affliction, which is but for a moment, is working for us a far more greater weight of glory.**

Paul wrote about the overall outcome after a season of testing, "Yet what we suffer now is nothing compared to the glory he will reveal to us later" (Romans 8:18 NLT). In another place he added, "For our light affliction, which is but for a moment, is working for us a far more exceeding and eternal weight of glory" (2 Corinthians 4:17). These both echo the same truth, "If you consider the crown beyond the test, you will realize it is a very little price to pay. That is what enabled Jesus to face the cross. So, "Let us fix our eyes on Jesus, the author and perfecter of our faith, who for the joy set before Him endured the cross, scorning its shame, and sat down at the right hand of the throne of God" (Hebrews 12:2 BSB).

I therefore charge you to be encouraged today and have a renewed attitude towards those things that seem to put you at a tight spot on your journey with God, the challenges that you are dealing with this season. Even as I pray for you that God will meet you at the point of your need, strengthen you where you need it most, and raise you up on wings like eagles. I pray for you that you will run and not faint, walk and not grow weary, that indeed no matter what comes your way, you will stand the test and receive your crown.

Prayer

> Heavenly Father thank you for calling me and placing me on the path of the just that only gets brighter unto a perfect day as you bring us from glory to glory. Today I receive grace to stand the tests of life and receive the glories that follow. That my faith and results will inspire others for your glory. In Jesus name.

Bible in one year // **Joshua 19-21, Luke 2:25-52**

MAR 26

> My brethren, count it all joy when you fall into various trials, knowing that the testing of your faith produces patience.
> // James 1:2-3

Count it all joy

Another translation says, "When troubles of any kind come your way, consider it an opportunity for great joy" (NLT). What a word of admonition! It is not time to cry and feel sorry for yourself because of all the things that seem to pose themselves as obstacles on your course, rather count it an opportunity for great joy. And James tells us why: "Knowing that the testing of your faith produces patience. But let patience have its perfect work, that you may be perfect and complete, lacking nothing" (James 1:4).

> **Count it all joy if you are facing some challenges this season, knowing that it is an opportunity for growth and development.**

A time of testing is inevitable on your journey of spiritual growth. In our walk with God, this is guaranteed, a time of testing of your faith. Generally, this does not happen at the start of your walk with God. It comes when He knows you have learned enough to endure His testing. Of Abraham it is written, "Sometime later, God tested Abraham's faith" (Genesis 22:1 NLT). In fact, the writer of Hebrews makes it clear that going through trials authenticates your sonship, it validates your legitimacy as a child of God. He wrote, "Endure your suffering as discipline; God is treating you as sons. For what son is there that a father does not discipline? But if you do not experience discipline, something all sons have shared in, then you are illegitimate and are not sons" (Hebrews 12:6-7 NET).

In another place, reference is made of Jesus in the same light. In Hebrews 5:8-9, "Even though Jesus was God's Son, he learned obedience from the things he suffered. In this way, God qualified him as a perfect High Priest, and he became the source of eternal salvation for all those who obey him" (NLT). Jesus himself was perfected through the things He suffered and qualified to be the captain of our salvation. So, count it indeed all joy if you are facing some trials this season because of all the associated reasons. It is an opportunity for growth, it authenticates your sonship and qualifies you for more in God. And remember this, He will never leave nor forsake you; He is with you in and through every trial.

Prayer

Heavenly Lord, thank you for your grace is sufficient for me in every day, and I am enabled and strengthened by the Holy spirit to stand even in times of trials and difficulty. Thank you for you cause all things to work for good for us who love you and are called according to your purpose. In Jesus' name.

Bible in one year // **Joshua 22-24, Luke 3**

The god of this age has blinded the minds of unbelievers, so that they cannot see the light of the gospel that displays the glory of Christ, who is the image of God. // **2 Corinthians 4:4**

MAR 27

The atheist fails to know

"The heavens declare the glory of God; the skies proclaim the work of his hands. Day after day they pour forth speech; night after night they reveal knowledge. They have no speech, they use no words; no sound is heard from them. Yet their voice goes out into all the earth" (Psalm 19:1-4 NIV). This is the Psalmist looking at creation and writing by inspiration of God this simple fact: When we look at nature in all its diversity and beauty, all things testify to the ingenuity of a skillful artist – God. Sadly, it is such a subject of controversy to many that there is the possibility that a God exists, one that was all powerful and wise enough to create all things. And in the wake of this argument, is the very extreme group of those who don't believe in the existence of a god.

These are the atheists who are falling for a lie of the opportunist, the devil. Satan the opportunist is taking a hold on men's curiosity and leading them off into a very dangerous conclusion – that there is no God. They argue we are a product of chance events through billions of years, from a big bang to a process of spontaneous evolution. But like the Psalmists puts it, if we would just observe creation and be intentional about listening to the voice of nature, it indeed screams out, "We were skillfully made".

No doubt in another place David could boldly declare, "Only fools say in their hearts, 'There is no God.'" (Psalms 14:1). Because you must look away from all the evidence of intelligent design in nature to come to such a conclusion, and that is unwise. However, the bible tells us, it takes faith to understand human origins (Hebrews 11:3). Nonetheless, Satan the opportunist uses the curiosity of humanity to lure them away to a path for destruction with alternative theories. Atheists fail to know this, "The god of this age has blinded the minds of unbelievers" (2 Corinthians 4:4). But it is our prayer that they will find truth for the salvation of their souls and the glorious life in Christ that awaits them.

> Atheists and non-believers fail to know that there is Satan the opportunist blinding them with alternative philosophies and luring them away from God and His purposes for them.
> Let's not give up on their souls.

Prayer

Almighty God thank you for the privilege to be among the enlightened ones, for bringing me into fellowship with you through the sacrifice of Jesus. I receive grace to share the light I have received with those in darkness. That they too might believe unto salvation. In Jesus' name.

Bible in one year // **Judges 1-3, Luke 4:1-30**

MAR 28

The heavens belong to the LORD, but he has given the earth to all humanity. // **Psalm 115:16 NLT**

One common question

Often, when you meet an atheist, one main reason for not believing in the existence of God is summed in one question, "If there is such a being so powerful that created the world, why are all these bad things happening?" But God is real, and God is good. What the atheist fails to understand is this: it is all part of the scheme to lure them away from God. In their minds, they think if there is a God who created all things, He is all powerful to stop all these bad things from happening, and rightly so. However, God does not operate like that. What God did was to create a complete self-sustaining system as a habitation for humanity and entrust into our care that we might be responsible over it. And where we are limited, we ought to recognize our need for him and bring Him in by invitation -that is through prayer.

> **Never let the bad things happening in the world make you question God's sovereignty, power and love for humanity. It is all part of a satanic scheme to lure you away from God.**

Among those who believe in God, there is a comparable and parallel question that is common. Why do bad things happen to good people? Underlying this question sometimes is another question, "Why did God do that or let that happen?". And the whole time, God is himself, figuratively speaking, with hands raised saying, "It is not from me, I am myself asking how we got here". That's not to say he didn't know or did not see. He is saying, "That wasn't part of my plan. I envisaged something else".

Remember this parable by Jesus. "The kingdom of heaven is like a man who sowed good seed in his field. But while everyone was sleeping, his enemy came and sowed weeds among the wheat, and went away. When the wheat sprouted and formed heads, then the weeds also appeared. "The owner's servants came to him and said, 'Sir, didn't you sow good seed in your field? Where then did the weeds come from?' "'An enemy did this,' he replied" (Matthew 13:24-28). God is not so much as responsible for the world as many people think. The bible says after He finished His works, He rested. And He is still doing that, God is resting. The heavens belong to the LORD, but he has given the earth to all humanity (Psalm 115:16 NLT).

Prayer

> Heavenly Father thank you for enlightening us daily through your word that we might not be ignorant of the schemes of the devil. For just as he out-smarted Eve in the garden of Eden, he is still at it today, trying to deceive as many as he can. But we are spared from his deceptions. In Jesus' name.

Bible in one year // Judges 4-6, Luke 4:31-44

Ask, and it will be given to you; seek, and you will find; knock, and it will be opened to you. // **Matthew 7:7**

MAR 29

An open invitation

The misconception some people have is that the life of faith is the escape route for people who do not want to find "real answers" to life's origin and therefore choose to anchor every unexplained phenomenon to some invisible and magical being. Then there are those who assume those of us who are this given to a life of faith are also a group of people who in their difficulties and limitations, embrace "Religion" as a soothing for our lives. Well, that might be true for some religions. However, Christianity is not another religion though by English terminology it might be defined as one. Christianity is more than a religion.

Nonetheless, until a person lives a personal experience of the spiritual realities thereof, they would think it is the same thing. And even sadly sometimes, you hear people say I was a Christian before I became an atheist. That is an impossibility! You can't encounter God and turn around to deny His existence. Such an individual was never a Christian. They walked the corridors of Christianity, interacted with other Christians, and even religiously practiced Christian principles and traditions but they never had a personal encounter with the Lord Jesus.

> Jesus gave us an open invitation which still stands today, if only you will seek Him, you will find Him, experience Him, and know the truth for yourself.

Then there are those who because of their ancestral heritage and allegiance to inherited traditions, think of Christianity as an opposing and foreign religion that should never be embraced over their inherited practices. They also miss out on a reality – the opportunity to know and experience the one true God. Jesus gave such an open invitation as the verse of the day indicates. Then He went on to give the guaranteed outcome, "Everyone who asks receives; the one who seeks finds; and to the one who knocks, the door will be opened" (Matthew 7:8). Even now He says, "Look! I stand at the door and knock. If you hear my voice and open the door, I will come in, and we will share a meal together as friends" (Revelation 3:20 NLT).

Prayer

Gracious God thank you for today and an open invitation for me. That I can know you for myself if only I would seek. I receive the knowledge of the truth in Christ Jesus and welcome the Holy Spirit to guide me into truths beyond human scrutiny. That I might know you and the truths of life. In Jesus' name.

Bible in one year // **Judges 7-8, Luke 5:1-16**

For we walk by faith, not by sight. // **2 Corinthians 5:7**

We walk by faith

It is amazing when I look back and see how much growth and transformation in the Lord I have had through the years. I remember about 2005, being in Church and hearing a minister preach on the verse, "For we walk by faith, not by sight" (2 Cor 5:7). And the whole time I am seating there and thinking it's a misuse of English. He was probably trying to say, "We walk by sight". It is worth noting that I had been born again a long time and had been in church all my life. At 19 years of age at this point, it was already 6 years gone since I made the conscious decision to have Jesus as my Lord and savior. However, I was missing out on the basics of faith.

> We walk by faith and not by sight, conducting our lives according to the word of God and the leading by His Spirit.

And this is the condition of too many believers in the Lord. They have been in Church so long, that they don't realize they are missing out on the basics of our faith or walk with God. We have heard so little of every subject, that people don't stop in their steps to ponder on what is it they don't understand and need education in. As far as I was concerned sitting down there that blessed Sunday and listening to the minister, how could he be making such a blunder to keep emphasizing we walk by faith and not by sight. I thought we walk by sight. He needed correction!

That is the condition of the carnal believer, the one who is in Christ but doesn't yet has a grasp on spiritual realities. They find themselves thinking the word of God is wrong, as far as they are concerned, some chapters of the bible should be re-written. But it only fulfills what the scripture says, "The natural man does not receive the things of the Spirit of God, for they are foolishness to him; nor can he know them, because they are spiritually discerned (1 Cor 2:14 NKJV). It was simple all the while what the verse meant, "We walk by faith and not by sight". We do not conduct our lives, guided and led by our sensuality but rather by the word of God and by His Spirit. And that is God's reminder to you today.

Prayer

Heavenly Father thank you for opening our eyes to spiritual realities, that we might not be limited by our natural perception or understanding. We receive grace to comprehend the deep things of God and to know the mysteries of Christ. Then we can walk by faith and not by sight. In Jesus' name.

Bible in one year // **Judges 9-10, Luke 5:17-39**

Thanks be to God who always leads us in triumphal procession in Christ and who makes known through us the fragrance that consists of the knowledge of him in every place. // **2 Corinthians 2:14 NET**

MAR 31

A perpetual victory parade

When Israel left Egypt, when the family of Jacob left a foreign nation behind, Judah became his sanctuary, Israel his kingdom. The sea looked and fled; the Jordan River turned back. The mountains skipped like rams, the hills like lambs. Why do you flee, O sea? Why do you turn back, O Jordan River? Why do you skip like rams, O mountains, like lambs, O hills? Tremble, O earth, before the Lord – before the God of Jacob, who turned a rock into a pool of water, a hard rock into springs of water! (Psalms 114:1

When Israel journeyed for the Promised Land, the people traveled as a procession, organized according to tribes as God instructed Moses. God led the way and was ahead of His people, and they became one unstoppable triumphant procession, overcoming every obstacle, subduing every opposition, making it through all barriers until they reached their destination. That is also true for us in Christ. We are a people in a triumphant procession.

In 2 Cor 2:14, it is written, „But thanks be to God who always leads us in triumphal procession in Christ and who makes known through us the fragrance that consists of the knowledge of him in every place (NET). The message Bible puts same verse this way, „In the Messiah, in Christ, God leads us from place to place in one perpetual victory parade. Through us, he brings knowledge of Christ. Even as we begin a new month today, it is my prayer for you that the victory we have in Christ Jesus will be evident in your every move, that in all things, you will indeed show yourself to be more than a conqueror.

> In Christ we are Part of a victorious parade, one great triumphal procession, overcoming all the way.

Prayer

Thank you, Heavenly Father for making us more than conquerors and numbering us in Christ's triumphal procession. As part of a perpetual victory parade, we continue to overcome every opposition, surmounting all obstacles as you lead us to a glorious destiny. In Jesus' name.

Bible in one year // **Judges 11-12, Luke 6:1-26**

APRIL

He was wounded for our transgressions, He was bruised for our iniquities; the chastisement for our peace was upon Him, and by His stripes we are healed.
// **Isaiah 53:5**

APR 1

Where justice and mercy meet

To many, it has never made sense why one should die for another, why Jesus should die for the salvation of all. It was a matter of Justice and mercy, God wanting to meet the full demand of Justice, and in the process being merciful. This caption of today's lesson is inspired by lines in a song, "Jesus You are worth", by Brenton Brown – a song you should listen to. The song contains these lines: "Perfect sacrifice crushed by God for us, bearing in Your hurt all that I deserve… With Your blood, You purchased us for God. Jesus, You are worthy, that is what You are!… Justice and mercy meet on the cross".

> The cross was the wisdom of God displayed in meeting the demands of justice for sin; yet displaying his mercy to let us walk away without condemnation.

How true that is! Justice and mercy meet at the cross. Hopefully an illustration with the human court system can paint a better picture. Imagine being convicted for a crime in the court of law. The judge who precides over the case and declares you guilty would be unjust to let you go without the penalty for the crime, though he might be celebrated for being merciful. He will be unjust to let you walk away. So as the judge, he rules your sentence. But then does something surprising. He leaves his seat as the judge, then comes to take your place. He pays the penalty on your behalf so you can walk away guiltless and free. He serves justice, but also serves mercy. And this is what happened on the cross.

This is one reason it is difficult to grasp the mystery of the trinity. That Jesus himself is God. And as God he held man to account for their sin. But then he took on flesh and was made like one of us and fulfilled the demands. The prophet Isaiah saw this coming when he declared of Jesus, "Surely he took up our pain and bore our suffering, yet we considered him punished by God, stricken by him, and afflicted. But he was pierced for our transgressions, he was crushed for our iniquities; the punishment that brought us peace was on him, and by his wounds we are healed" (Isaiah 53:4-5 NIV). Jesus being fully God, took our place and met the demands of divine justice on our behalf, so we might be acquitted.

Prayer

> Heavenly Father, thank you for the sacrifice of Jesus, who took upon himself our sin that He might pay the price for our salvation, giving us a clean slate in your sight. Now we might come boldly to the throne of grace and find help in times of need. In Jesus' name.

Bible in one year // **Judges 13-15, Luke 6:27-49**

APR 2

Jesus said to her, "I am the resurrection and the life. He who believes in Me, though he may die, he shall live. // **John 11:25**

A rebirth of hope

Now that same day two of them were going to a village called Emmaus... As they talked and discussed, Jesus himself came up and walked along with them; but they were kept from recognizing him. He asked them, "What are you discussing together as you walk along?" They stood still, their faces downcast. One of them, named Cleopas, asked him, "Are you the only one visiting Jerusalem who does not know the things that have happened there in these days?" "What things?" he asked. "About Jesus of Nazareth," they replied... We had hoped that he was the one who was going to redeem Israel. And what is more, it is the third day since all this took place" (Luke 24:13-21 NIV).

Easter celebrations provide us an occasion for the rebirth of hope as we a reminder through the events of Christ death and resurrection that it is never too late with the Lord.

What strikes me always is their sense of hopelessness and failed dreams, the feeling that their hope which seemed so sure for a season was all dashed away in His death. They said to him, "We had hoped that he was the one who was going to redeem Israel. And what is more, it is the third day since all this took place". How they failed to realize the surety of divine promises and to know that nothing was ever going to get in the way of its fulfilment. And how hope was restored as Jesus opened their eyes to see from scriptures that the Messiah was to suffer and die, then would be raised from the death for the salvation of all.

And this is what the commemoration of the resurrection at Easter really announces, a rebirth of hope on several fronts. Sometimes, God lets things deteriorate before the miracle. Just as we have a record of Lazarus' experience. Jesus was told he was sick, however, he tarried a while. Then the man died finally. Then Jesus went to raise Lazarus from the dead (John 11). And what a hope that inspired again in the hearts of men, for God had given them a deliverer who is the resurrection and the life. Even so Easter is one occasion that should inspire hope in us, that even when all seems lost, God always has a way out.among those whose faith prevailed despite the diverse difficulties life brought them. It is your heritage for your faith to prevail (1 John 5:4).

Prayer

Heavenly Father, thank you for the hope we have in you, a sure and steadfast anchor for our souls. Even as we celebrate easter, may hope arise in every heart and faith rekindled throughout the world as you bring more people to the light. In Jesus' name.

Bible in one year // **Judges 16-18, Luke 7:1-30**

"He himself bore our sins" in his body on the cross, so that we might die to sins and live for righteousness; "by his wounds you have been healed.
// 1 Peter 2:24 NIV

APR 3

By his stripes

This is Peter, looking behind to the cross and testifying to what had been accomplished. The Prophet Isaiah had seen this coming, he prophesied it, but less as an accomplished event. For at the time, Jesus was yet to be revealed. Isaiah declared, "He was pierced for our transgressions, he was crushed for our iniquities; the punishment that brought us peace was on him, and by his wounds we are healed" (Isaiah 53:5 NIV). And that which he proclaimed was fulfilled at the cross – By His stripes, you were healed. And this is a reality. If you are in Christ, you are not sick. In fact, you are never sick. You were healed already.

About Jesus, Matthew wrote, "When evening came, many who were demon-possessed were brought to Jesus, and He drove out the spirits with a word and healed all the sick. This was to fulfill what was spoken through the prophet Isaiah: "He took on our infirmities and carried our diseases." (Matthew 8:16-17). He indeed took all our infirmities and bore all our diseases. If that is true that He took it, then you don't have it. But someone might say, why then am I not experiencing total health? That is where faith comes in, when we reach out and take hold of that which is ours from the Lord; when we refuse to endorse the medical facts and statistics but continually testify to the fact that by His stripes we were healed.

In essence, when we feel sick or receive a negative medical report, this is the alternative voice of circumstances or the devil trying to question what the Lord has accomplished for us in Christ Jesus. Just as he asked Eve regarding the tree, the devil is also trying to ask us a similar trying question that puts doubts in our minds regarding the works of the Lord. "Did God really make healing available for you in Christ Jesus?" Therefore, you must remember and hold firm to your confession of divine health. Say it like you know it even when your body seems battered by the worst of diseases. Proclaim it, "I am the healed of the Lord, for by His stripes I was healed". And God will cause a manifestation of His word.

> **By the stripes of Jesus, you were healed from all manner of diseases. Walk in the consciousness of this reality and proclaim it until it becomes your personal experience.**

Prayer

Heavenly Father, thank You for all that is made available for us in Christ Jesus, especially healing at such a time when the world is plagued with all kinds of diseases. We receive renewal in our flesh. Even natural genetic patterns shall have no rule over our health, for we share your divine nature. In Jesus' name.

Bible in one year // **Judges 19-21, Luke 7:31-50**

Having been justified by faith, we have peace with God through our Lord Jesus Christ. // Romans 5:1

APR 4

Acquitted

While we have so much joy in knowing that God has forgiven us all our sins in Christ Jesus, there is even a greater truth and call for celebration. It is the fact that we are justified in Christ Jesus. That is a greater blessing. To be forgiven means justice recognizes you as the culprit, as one guilty. Nonetheless, they are merciful enough to pardon you and not deal with you as your crime deserves. This is what the Psalmist wrote about in Psalm 103:10-12, "He does not treat us as our sins deserve or repay us according to our iniquities. For as high as the heavens are above the earth, so great is his love for those who fear him; as far as the east is from the west, so far has he removed our transgressions from us".

In Christ Jesus, God shows even more grace to us. He goes beyond forgiving us. He acquitted us of our transgressions. We were declared "Not guilty". That is what it means to be justified, to be declared innocent. How could that be? For at the new birth, we were reckoned in the death of Christ, that we, being raised to life, came forth as totally new creations, born again. We were brought forth like newborn babies without a past and therefore no record of wrong for which they needed forgiveness. Paul pictures this when he writes, "Therefore we have been buried with him through baptism into death, in order that just as Christ was raised from the dead through the glory of the Father, so we too may live a new life. For if we have become united with him in the likeness of his death, we will certainly also be united in the likeness of his resurrection" (Romans 6:4-5 NET).

> **More than being forgiven, in Christ Jesus, you were acquitted – declared not guilty.**

So then is the saying true, "If anyone is in Christ, he is a new creation; old things have passed away; behold, all things have become new" (2 Corinthians 5:17 NKJV). When you receive Jesus as Lord, you are counted in His death, so that you can share in His resurrection. On this account, the "old you" does not exist and therefore needed not be forgiven. Rather, a "new you", was born, one without a past, one without a record of sin, one innocent and justified in the sight of God. So, Paul writes, "He was delivered over to death for our trespasses and was raised to life for our justification" (Romans 4:25 BSB).

Prayer

Gracious Heavenly Father, what manner of love indeed you have bestowed upon us that we should be called your sons. Thank you for a clean slate in Christ Jesus, declaring us not guilty and making us accepted in the beloved. To you be all the praise. In Jesus' name.

Bible in one year // **Ruth 1-4, Luke 8:1-25**

Who shall bring a charge against God's elect? It is God who justifies.
// **Romans 8:33**

APR 5

Guilt – a weapon of darkness

In yesterday's meditation, we looked at the fact that you were acquitted in Christ Jesus – declared "Not guilty". While this is true, it does not necessarily translate to a guiltless life. Sometimes, we might have really had a hunting past in which our former way of life might have hurt so many people, our errors might have cost lives and inflicted irreparable damage on others or things. If you are such a one, a haunting past of guilt might stick with you a long time unless the right knowledge is received and accepted – the right knowledge of who you are in Christ Jesus and the newness of life you have received.

> Guilt can be such a weapon of darkness to make you lay down your weapons of prayer and the word, or make you feel unfit for divine tasks. Don't give the devil that opportunity.

While guilt is good, in the sense that it can bring us to repentance and cause us to seek restitution where need be, it can be such a weapon in the hands of the devil. He can use guilt to make you feel unworthy of many heavenly blessings and therefore cripple your faith for receiving things that are rightfully yours from the Lord. He can also very much use guilt to make you feel unfit to serve the Lord in certain capacities, and in that way, weaken the army of the Lord by making a few soldiers unwilling for service. As a young believer myself, there were days I felt too guilty to pray, too guilty to read my bible or too guilty to get involved with responsibilities in the house of the Lord.

If you are doing something wrong, there is sure a call to repentance, to walk in the way of the Lord. Do not stay in it. But much more, do not let the guilt of your errors become the impediment on your Christian journey and duties. Even if you feel guilty over things, it does not mean God is holding it against you, it just means you are holding it against yourself. Like our opening verse says, "Who shall bring a charge against God's elect? It is God who justifies". He declared you "Not guilty", He acquitted you so that no one else will have anything to against you in His court of law.

Prayer

> Thank you Heavenly Father, that there is no condemnation for us who are in Christ Jesus, who walk after the spirit. For the Law of the spirit of life in Him has set us free from the law of sin and death. Thank you for cleansing us from all unrighteousness and making us fit to share in your glory. In Jesus' name.

Bible in one year // **1 Samuel 1-3, Luke 8:26-56**

APR 6

> If our hearts condemn us, we know that God is greater than our hearts, and he knows everything. // **1 John 3:20 NIV**

Neither do I condemn you

John wrote, "When Jesus had raised Himself up and saw no one but the woman, He said to her, 'Woman, where are those accusers of yours? Has no one condemned you?' She said, 'No one, Lord.' And Jesus said to her, 'Neither do I condemn you; go and sin no more.'" (John 8:10-11). "Neither do I condemn you" were the words of Jesus to one who had been caught in adultery. The people had brought to him the woman expecting him to enforce the law of Moses, for such a sin was worthy of death. The actual rationale behind these instructions was to put fear in the hearts of the people towards certain acts, in hope that the fear of death will keep them from sin.

> God's testimony is greater than your feelings, so irrespective of how guilty you might feel, know that you are acquitted in Christ Jesus and not under condemnation.

Now the people were looking for an occasion to call Jesus a false prophet, for anyone who opposed the laws of Moses would have been false. But Jesus in wisdom, looked at them and said, "He who is without sin among you, let him throw a stone at her first" (John 8:7). And at His words, the people left, one after the other. Then Jesus cognizant of her sin, said to her, "Neither do I condemn you". These are the same words He would say to you today if you are overwhelmed with guilt, feeling unworthy of God's love and unqualified for His blessings. He is more interested that you recognize your errors and can make the right decision to run to Him.

If there is any voice of condemnation, it is not of God. It might be the voice of the Devil. For that is one of his earthly duties. In fact, He is called the accuser of the brethren (Revelation 12:10). It could also really be you, condemning yourself. But it is more important to remember scriptures. John wrote it this way, "If our hearts condemn us, we know that God is greater than our hearts, and he knows everything" (1 John 3:20 NIV). God who knows everything has acquitted you. So irrespective of how guilty you feel, shake off the feeling, for God's testimony is greater than that of your heart.

Prayer

Gracious God thank you for a new day and the blessings therein. Thank you for not dealing with us according as our sins deserve. Rather, as far as the east is from the west, so you have taken away our sins and guilt that we might serve you freely. We receive grace to walk in this light. In Jesus' name.

Bible in one year // **1 Samuel 4-6, Luke 9:1-17**

From everyone who has been given much, much will be demanded; and from the one who has been entrusted with much, much more will be asked.
// **Luke 12:48 NIV**

APR 7

To whom much is given

Some ministers of the gospel and Christians who are unskilled in the word of righteousness, find fault with teachings that emphasize that we are righteous in Christ because Jesus paid it all. They worry that those who emphasize such truths are leading the people to a reckless life of sin, where they become careless because of the knowledge that they are righteous, not because of their works but because God has imputed it to them as a gift. To such people, they think the more we emphasize how people are sinners, the more we will call them to holy living. But that is a misconception.

The ignorance of this knowledge of being righteous in Christ because of the finished work on the cross is the reason many people struggle with sin. Because they are trying to attain a righteousness by the law, they end up missing the mark each time. And often, in their frustration, the resort to quit trying to the standards of the word. In fact, they have concluded that no one can live without sin. On the contrary, when people know that they are righteous in Christ Jesus because of His finished work, it is so liberating that they don't have to labor for righteousness. Suddenly they will realize sin no longer has dominion over them and they have the capacity to express the righteousness of God as He works in them to will and to do of His good pleasure (Philippians 2:13).

Jesus said, "To whom much is given, much is expected" (Luke 12:48). This is even more true for us in Christ Jesus. We were sanctified by the blood of Jesus, so precious and costly. That we might recognize the worth and value of what we received freely. Not so that we would continue in sin that grace might abound, but rather overflow in thankfulness that reflects itself in holy living, a life guided by divine principles (Romans 6:1-4). God calls us to higher moral standards in Christ than he did the people of old. He expects more from us because we have received a lot more from Him.

> **Do not continue in sin that grace might abound. Rather, let the knowledge of your righteousness in Christ Jesus inspire a holy lifestyle that echoes your gratitude to God.**

Prayer

Heavenly Father, thank you for your Spirit who lives in us, working in us to will and to do of your good pleasure. That we walk by your principles, and they are not burdensome to us. We receive grace to overcome sinful habits and to walk in the newness of life purchased for us by the blood. In Jesus' name.

Bible in one year // **1 Samuel 7-9, Luke 9:18-36**

APR 8

Put on the new man which was created according to God, in true righteousness and holiness. // **Ephesians 4:24**

Your true worship

We are exhorted, "Brothers and sisters, in view of God's mercy, to offer your bodies as a living sacrifice, holy and pleasing to God–this is your true and proper worship. Do not conform to the pattern of this world; but be transformed by the renewing of your mind. Then you will be able to test and approve what God's will is–his good, pleasing, and perfect will (Romans 12:1-2 NIV). To whom much is given, much is expected. That was the emphasis of yesterday's meditation. As we highlighted the need to walk in the light of God's word and not continue in sin that grace might abound. For the knowledge of righteousness in Christ Jesus because of the finished work on the cross is not a license to a life of sin. Rather, it calls us to an even greater commitment to live to please the Lord, far more than those under the old covenant.

Paul wrote this to the Ephesians, "So I tell you this, and insist on it in the Lord, that you must no longer live as the Gentiles do, in the futility of their thinking. They are darkened in their understanding and separated from the life of God because of the ignorance that is in them due to the hardening of their hearts. Having lost all sensitivity, they have given themselves over to sensuality so as to indulge in every kind of impurity, and they are full of greed" (Ephesians 4:17-23 NIV).

> Your true act of worship is beyond songs. It is a life consecrated to God and submitted to the authority of His word, a life conducted in true righteousness and holiness.

Do not become complacent with any sin or thing clearly stated as inappropriate for God's people and justify it with the saying "We are under grace". It is a deception from the devil. There is still a moral code for God's people, a way of life that is commended. And that is your truest and most acceptable worship, a life consecrated unto the Lord and submitted to His principles. There is a way of life that has been given to us, a manner of living that we are expected to express. We received righteousness as a gift, not so we could have our freedom in sin, but so we would have the nature of God and express his righteous character. So, Paul urges, "Put off your old self, which is being corrupted by its deceitful desires; to be made new in the attitude of your minds; and to put on the new self, created to be like God in true righteousness and holiness" (Ephesians 4:22-24).

Prayer

Heavenly Father, thank you for calling us out of the world, that we might be separated unto you. That you might be our Father, and we, your sons and daughters. We receive grace to reflect your true righteousness and holiness in all things as we are transformed by the word daily. In Jesus' name.

Bible in one year // **1 Samuel 10-12, Luke 9:37-62**

Nevertheless, the solid foundation of God stands, having this seal: "The Lord knows those who are His," and, "Let everyone who names the name of Christ depart from iniquity". // **2 Timothy 2:19**

APR 9

Walk as children of light

Therefore, be imitators of God as dear children. And walk in love, as Christ also has loved us and given Himself for us, an offering and a sacrifice to God for a sweet-smelling aroma. But fornication and all uncleanness or covetousness, let it not even be named among you, as is fitting for saints; neither filthiness, nor foolish talking, nor coarse jesting, which are not fitting, but rather giving of thanks. For this you know, that no fornicator, unclean person, nor covetous man, who is an idolater, has any inheritance in the kingdom of Christ and God. Let no one deceive you with empty words, for because of these things the wrath of God comes upon the sons of disobedience. Therefore, do not be partakers with them. For you were once darkness, but now you are light in the Lord. Walk as children of light (Ephesians 5:1-8)

Paul's call to his readers is the same call I have for you today, the call to be imitators of God. The call to walk as children of light in a dark world. In this dispensation where evil is labeled as good and what people ought to be ashamed of is publicly displayed, we have the call to be the light of the world and not conform to their patterns and trends, particularly the decaying moral standards.

> **Do not let the world which has no moralcompass tell you what moral standards should be accepted in Christ. Do not deceive yourself with alternative views contrary to God's word. Walk as a child of Light!**

Paul cautioned his readers to not be deceived, listing the very things that are not fitting for God's people, the very reason for which his judgement will come upon the children of disobedience. That's the other thing to note. Any teaching about grace that does not call you to a transformed life is partial truth and should be checked The worst deception is when you are the very person deceiving yourself with alternative opinions, consciously living in sin misguided by the world that lacks a moral compass. God has a moral standard for His people. "Walk as children of light", He says. The bible is clear, "Nevertheless the solid foundation of God stands, having this seal: "The Lord knows those who are His," and, "Let everyone who names the name of Christ depart from iniquity" (2 Timothy 2:19).

Prayer

> Heavenly Father, thank you for calling us out of darkness into your marvelous light that we might show forth your praises. Even so, may our light shine so brightly that men might see our good works and glorify you. That our lives will be a sweet-smelling aroma to you in all places. In Jesus name.

Bible in one year // **1 Samuel 13-14, Luke 10:1-24**

APR 10

For God is working in you, giving you the desire and the power to do what pleases him. // **Philippians 2:13 NLT**

You are enabled

When you read the book of Romans and the account of Paul's struggle with sin, many end there to conclude that living a life guided by the word of God is impossible, and the life of sin is normal so long as we are in this world. But that was not the purpose of Paul's explanation in Romans 7. The focus was to show how on his own, he was a slave to sin, programmed to be dominated and ruled by the sinful nature. But he ends his account of such a struggle with a word of thanksgiving for the freedom from sin through Christ Jesus. "What a wretched man I am! Who will rescue me from this body that is subject to death?

In Christ Jesus, the power and dominion of sin over us was broken and we are enabled to lead righteous and holy lifestyles.

Thanks be to God, who delivers me through Jesus Christ our Lord!" (Romans 7:25 NIV). In Christ Jesus we were freed from the dominion of sin. So Paul writes, For sin shall not have dominion over you, for you are not under law but under grace (Romans 6:14). Rather, you have received the Holy Spirit who enables you to live above sin. Just like the prophet Jeremiah saw it coming, a time when God was going to put his laws in our hearts and make us willing and able to do his will. He prophesied saying, "This is the covenant I will make with the people of Israel after that time," declares the Lord. "I will put my law in their minds and write it on their hearts. I will be their God, and they will be my people. No longer will they teach their neighbor, or say to one another, 'Know the Lord,' because they will all know me, from the least of them to the greatest" (Jeremiah 31:33-34 NIV).

Therefore, it is written, "For God is working in you, giving you the desire and the power to do what pleases him" (Philippians 2:13 NLT). You are enabled to live a life above sin and the dictates of our human nature in Christ Jesus. If only you will take simple responsibilities. Like the Psalmist declared, "Your word I have hidden in my heart that I might not sin against you" (Psalm 119:11). Paul added, "Walk by the Spirit and you will not fulfil the lusts of the flesh" (Galatians 5:16).

Prayer

Heavenly Father, thank you for you work in us to will and to do of your good pleasure. And this is love for you that we do your commandments, and they are not burdensome. As we walk in love towards one another and serve you, we receive grace to say no to things are not for us your children. In Jesus' name.

Bible in one year // **1 Samuel 15-16, Luke 10: 25-42**

For he who sows to his flesh will of the flesh reap corruption, but he who sows to the Spirit will of the Spirit reap everlasting life.
// Galatians 6:8 NKJV

APR 11

A tale of dogs

Once a brother in Christ shared with me a tale of two dogs. He said, "There lived a man who owned a black and a white dog. Occasionally, the owner brought the dogs to the city square to fight against each other. And the owner of the dogs would marvel the people with his accuracy in predicting which of the dogs would win on a given day. So, if he said the black dog would win, that would be the case and vise versa – the white dog won when he said it would win".

It was evident that this wasn't a question of one dog being more powerful. For the stronger dog should consistently win. This remained a wonder to the spectators who would gather to watch his game of accurate predictions. So, one day he decided to give away the secret, how he could predict every time with accuracy the winning dog. He told them: "I feed the dog that should win for the day and starve the other. If I want the black dog winning, I feed the black and starve the white before the fight. It's a matter of which dog is better fed".

That's the story of your Spirit and your flesh. The world around us consistently feeds our eyes, ears, and hearts with the lusts of life, ever luring us into unbridled pleasure and sensuality. We see nudity on billboards, in adverts on newspapers and on TV. That's your flesh being fed. So, if you would be victorious over that flesh and let your spirit lead you away from temptation, sin and the consequences, you would have to feed your spirit even better and let it be strong enough to rule that body. Will you sow to the flesh or to the spirit? Like Paul wrote, "Finally, my brethren, be strong in the Lord and in the power of His might". (Ephesians 6:10 NKJV). Sow to your spirit; invest in nourishing and building your spirit. As it is written, "He who sows to the Spirit will of the Spirit reap everlasting life".

> **To be victorious over your flesh, incline your Spirit to the word of God and nourish it to full strength and don't expose yourself to situations that entice you and give you opportunity to sin.**

Prayer

Heavenly Father thank you for the opportunity of another day to glorify you in the earth. Your word we are receiving and hiding in our hearts that we might not sin against You. We receive grace to flee wrong company and occasions that lure us away into sin. We make no room for the devil. In Jesus name.

Bible in one year // **1 Samuel 17-18, Luke 11:1-28**

APR 12

> God made the one who did not know sin to be sin for us, so that in him we would become the righteousness of God. // **2 Corinthians 5:21 NET**

He took our place

It is not uncommon to hear someone say, "There is no one that is righteous, no not one". And that for a good reason, they are quoting the writing of Paul from Romans 3:10-12, As it is written: "There is no one righteous, not even one; there is no one who understands; there is no one who seeks God. All have turned away, they have together become worthless; there is no one who does good, not even one (NIV). Paul was referring to the testimony of David from Psalm 14:3 in correlation with other passages from the Old Testament. However, it is important to follow the discourse to the end and to realize that Paul was not reiterating the declaration of David, he was using those facts to build up his arguments that even though the law was given to Israel, it had not in itself fulfilled the purpose of making anyone righteous.

That saying, "There is no one righteous" was only true until Jesus came and died on the cross. For on the cross, God made him who knew no sin to be the very sin for us, so that we might become the righteousness of God. He took our place as sinners, so that we could take His place as the righteous one. He gave us a clean slate, giving us right-standing with the father and making us blameless. He made righteousness available to us as a gift of grace. Romans 5:17 says: "Those who receive god's abundant provision of grace and of THE GIFT OF RIGHTEOUSNESS will reign in life through the one man, Jesus Christ!"

> **Because Jesus took your place as a sinner, you are righteous if you are in Christ Jesus, for you have been made the righteousness of God.**

It is not uncommon also to hear a Christian stand to pray in the congregation and begin with the words, "We are all sinners". It is a thousand times untrue. While that might echo humility, it is not scriptural. As far as the eyes of the Lord are concerned, He sees us as righteous as Himself. For He made Christ who knew no sin to be sin for us, that we might become His own very righteousness. Today, as many as are in Christ Jesus are righteous. For Jesus took our place as sinners, that we might have His place as the righteousness of God.

Prayer

Gracious Lord, thank you for the sacrifice of Jesus on the cross for our sins. As we commemorate this season, may the verities of His sufferings, death and resurrection be made real in our lives. We pray for as many as have not known you, that they too may find salvation and know this truth. In Jesus' name.

Bible in one year // **1 Samuel 19-21, Luke 11:29-54**

I have fought the good fight, I have finished the race, I have kept the faith.
// 2 Timothy 4:7

APR 13

Live purposefully

These were the words of Paul as he saw his time counting down in the earth. He had lived a purposeful life, doing that which the Lord had called him to do. My biological father went to be with the Lord in March of 2021, he passed on to glory. When I reflect on his life, my comfort remains in the fact that he is with the Lord. It is also refreshing to look at his life and realize what a purposeful person he was and what legacy he left behind. He led us to the Lord before we ever had a chance to taste the world. He was intentional about the values that defined us. His sacrifices and labor of love for us and many who knew him was priceless. Even as his days drew to an end, one of the last things he said to me was this: "Let the name Jesus never depart from your mouth".

> **Live purposefully in the earth, bearing in mind the end of us all when Christ the righteous judge will reward us for all our works.**

I wish we had him longer. But at about 78 years of age, we can only thank God for all the years we were privileged to have had a teacher, a guide and a mentor like him. And we are confident he now has a crown. He is forever glorified. As the bible assures us, "To be absent from the body is to be present with the Lord" –(2 Corinthians 5:8). How the Psalmist reminds us, "Our days may come to seventy years, or eighty, if our strength endures; yet the best of them are but trouble and sorrow, for they quickly pass, and we fly away… Teach us to number our days, that we may gain a heart of wisdom Psalm 90:10-12.

I therefore urge you today to take a moment and ponder on your life and the way you are living it. Living purposefully is the only way you will be able to say like Paul in the end, "I have fought the good fight, I have finished the race, I have kept the faith. Now there is in store for me the crown of righteousness, which the Lord, the righteous Judge, will award to me on that day–and not only to me, but also to all who have longed for his appearing -2 Timothy 4:7-8 NIV.

Prayer

Thank you, Heavenly Father, for you cause all things to work together for the good of those who love you, who have been called according to your purpose. We receive grace to live purposely, laboring to fulfill the purpose for which you have placed each of us in the earth in this time. In Jesus' name.

Bible in one year // 1 Samuel 22-24, Luke 12:1-31

APR 14

Rejoice in the Lord always. I will say it again: Rejoice!
// **Philippians 4:4 NIV**

Rejoice always

The above instruction was written by Paul while serving a prison term, not for committing a crime but for being a messenger of Christ, called and commissioned by God. He had every reason to feel angry, sad, or even feel misled by the Lord for calling him into a life that until now seemed to leave him with more troubles and beatings than when he went about his own affairs. But Paul had come to know this truth in Christ Jesus, that the wellbeing of a person does not consist in the abundance of their life (Luke 12:15). You could be joyful no matter what was going on and no matter what circumstances prevail about you.

Irrespective of the things happening about us, in Christ Jesus we always have the capacity and reasons to rejoice and be exceedingly glad.

The Psalmist knew this when he wrote, "You have put joy in my heart, More than [others know] when their wheat and new wine have yielded abundantly" – Psalm 4:7 Amp. He knew a joy that was independent of circumstances and events, a joy that was from the Lord. In Psalm 46:1-5, he wrote, "God is our refuge and strength, an ever-present help in trouble. Therefore, we will not fear, though the earth gives way and the mountains fall into the heart of the sea, though its waters roar and foam and the mountains quake with their surging. There is a river whose streams make glad the city of God, the holy place where the Most High dwells. God is within her, she will not fall; God will help her at break of day."

David wrote about a river whose streams make glad the city of God. But what is that river and how does that apply to us today? That river is the person of the Holy Spirit. Just as it is written, "On the last and greatest day of the festival, Jesus stood and said in a loud voice, 'Let anyone who is thirsty come to me and drink. Whoever believes in me, as Scripture has said, rivers of living water will flow from within them.' By this he meant the Spirit, whom those who believed in him were later to receive" (John 7:37-39). And as Mathew wrote, "You are the light of the world, a city set on a hill cannot be hidden" (Matthew 5:14). So you are that city of God. And so long the Holy Spirit lives in you, He is that river bringing to you everlasting and unconditional joy, enabling you to rejoice in the Lord always.

Prayer

Heavenly Father thank you for the gift of the Holy Spirit who brings your joy into our lives and floods our hearts with peace that surpasses all understanding. We receive grace to fix our gaze on you irrespective of the things about us, that we will overflow with joy and burst out in praise to you. In Jesus' name.

Bible in one year // **1 Samuel 25-26, Luke 12:32-59**

> I pray that the eyes of your heart may be enlightened in order that you may know the hope to which he has called you, the riches of his glorious inheritance in his holy people. // **Ephesians 1:18 NIV**

APR 15

For this very purpose

Paul's prayer for the Ephesians was this, that the eyes of their understanding might be flooded with light, that they might be illuminated to know the hope of their calling. That they would also know the riches of the glorious inheritance to which they had been called with other saints. Another bible translation has this rendition of the verse, "My prayer is that light will flood your hearts and you will understand the hope given to you when God chose you. Then you will discover the glorious blessings that will be yours together with all God's people" (CEV).

Your Daily Light has the singular vision of bringing to men and women in the world, illumination through the word of God, that they might know the hope of His calling, discover their inheritance in Christ and take full procession of it. It brings to them the daily light for their walk in God, an understanding of scriptures to make them effective and fully equipped for their respective assignments. Like a lighthouse shining the light out to a sailor at sea, helping them navigate their way through turbulent waters, so is Your Daily Light to a soul in the world. It shines the light of God's word to help you find your path and ponder your way to your glorious destiny in Christ.

For this very purpose, I was called, and for this one I live, the Lord Himself enabling me daily as I reach you with the word of illumination, praying also like Paul, that the eyes of your understanding will be flooded with light. That you might know the hope of God's call for your life, what He had in mind when He called you. I also pray always that you will know who you are in Christ Jesus, where you are in His Kingdom, and all that has been made available for you. That you might appropriate all for your enjoyment and the fulfillment of divine purpose. I also invite you to join this movement to sponsor distribution of copies of this devotional to others and bring the Light of God's word to their doorsteps.

> **Your Daily Light comes to you for this very purpose, that the eyes of your understanding will be flooded with light, that you may discover and appropriate your inheritance in Christ.**

Prayer

Heavenly Father thank you for the daily illumination that I receive through your word, being enlightened to know the hope of your calling and my glorious inheritance in Christ. Thank you for those laboring daily for my Spiritual well-being, that I might be nourished and equipped for your glory. In Jesus' name.

Bible in one year // **1 Samuel 27-29, Luke 13:1-22**

APR 16

He chose our inheritance for us, the pride of Jacob, whom he loved.
// **Psalm 47:3 NIV**

A divine positioning

One great truth of scripture is that your inheritance was chosen for you by the Lord himself – your placement in God. This was the Psalmist acknowledgement in the verse of the day: "He chose our inheritance for us". Abraham was only told where to go, Canaan was the Lord's choice for Him. Even so the partitioning of the land later was with divine inspiration, to settle the different tribes of Israel in their respective territories.

Paul writing to the Corinthian church echoes this truth in the body of Christ. "Just as a body, though one, has many parts, but all its many parts form one body, so it is with Christ. For we were all baptized by one Spirit so as to form one body… Even so the body is not made up of one part but of many. Now if the foot should say, "Because I am not a hand, I do not belong to the body," it would not for that reason stop being part of the body. And if the ear should say, "Because I am not an eye, I do not belong to the body," it would not for that reason stop being part of the body. If the whole body were an eye, where would the sense of hearing be? If the whole body were an ear, where would the sense of smell be? But in fact God has placed the parts in the body, every one of them, just as he wanted them to be (1 Corinthians 12:12-18 NIV).

> **Your placement in God was a sovereign choice by God, and you will do well to discover and fully take your place in the body of Christ.**

Paul goes on to add in verse 27 of the above passage, „Now you are the body of Christ, and each one of you is a part of it". And in Ephesians 4:16, he wrote, "He makes the whole body fit together perfectly. As each part does its own special work, it helps the other parts grow, so that the whole body is healthy and growing and full of love (NLT). There is a place for you in God, where you are much needed, and your proper working is necessary for the wellbeing of the whole. He placed each part where He wanted them, for His purpose and according to His will. And what a blessing that is, to find your place in the body of Christ and to be committed there, knowing that God Himself is the one who positioned you.

Prayer

Heavenly Father, thank you for choosing my inheritance in Christ Jesus, and strategically positioning me for the revelation of your glory in the earth. This season I receive grace to recognize my place and to be effective in the discharge of my services for the good of the whole body. In Jesus' name.

Bible in one year // **1 Samuel 30-31, Luke 13:23-35**

We then, as workers together with Him also plead with you not to receive the grace of God in vain. // **2 Corinthians 6:1**

APR 17

Workers together with Him

The vision the Lord has laid on my heart to light our world with His word through the publication and distribution of divinely inspired content is a great one. As He calls me to greater commitment, it becomes more evident how much we need people to identify with what God is doing in our days on the earth so we can accomplish more together as fellow workers with Him.

And as I race along with all that God is calling me to do, I am reminded of a fact too: Those who continually look out for our spiritual wellbeing, don't necessarily do it always from the comfort of life. Just like Paul wrote, "Now he who plants and he who waters are one, and each one will receive his own reward according to his own labor. For we are God's fellow workers; you are God's field, you are God's building" (1 Cor 3:8-9). Indeed, we are laborers together with the Lord in His vineyard, and you are that precious vine. Even greater is the truth that you too are called to join the laborers, for indeed the fields are white but the laborers are few.

> We are workers together with God. Not just us who labor in ministry, but you too who has been called to join the workforce.

There is opportunity for you to also be part of the lighthouse team that seeks to light our world with the word. Through financial partnership, through prayers and active participation in this call. If ever the Lord lays on your heart to join me on this vision, don't hesitate to get in touch. For together, we can be workers with the Lord. It is our vision to distribute millions of copies of Your Daily Light around the globe. You can join us to make this a reality by getting copies for friends and family. We will be sharing testimonies and pictures of such outreaches on the website. Your picture can be one of them. You can also find all the information needed to partner with us financially as we bring this word to many more people around the world. Together, we are workers with the Lord in His field, bringing salvation to men and leading them into their inheritance in Christ.

Prayer

Heavenly Father, thank you for calling us to be laborers with you in your vineyard. We pray today that you will continue to grace, strengthen, keep, and supply all our needs. Help us, that we might recognize the selflessness in their service and the opportunities to join them in them. In Jesus' name.

Bible in one year // **2 Samuel 1-2, Luke 14:1-24**

APR 18

> He chose to give us birth through the word of truth, that we might be a kind of first fruits of all he created. // **James 1:18**

God's prized creation

There is so much to cherish in creation when you look around. The wonders thereof are endless, from the deepest ocean depths to the furthest explored ends in space. So many awe-inspiring creatures and things. But it is even more amazing to stop a moment and realize that man was the ultimate reason for all that was created. For in all creation, God was preparing an environment to host his most prized work – the human race. Just like an expectant mother prepares a room for a baby in her womb, so God was in all creation, preparing an environment for man. So though the baby's room might contain a gold cradle with diamond beads, no matter how costly it was for the mother, it will never measure in worth to the baby. In fact, all the investment in the room only echoes how much value was placed on the baby.

> You are God's jewel of inestimable worth, the most prized of all His creation. Know your worth and don't accept a price tag on your life from the world. And don't devalue yourself but see yourself as God does.

And after the fall of man, God traded Jesus as the sacrifice for your sins. You are God's jewel of inestimable value, the priciest of all He created. Don't let the world give you a price tag by how much you earn or the car you drive, or where your name falls on Forbes list of the richest or the most influential. You are so valuable, the world in its entirety would not measure to your worth in value. That is why Jesus said, "What will it profit a man to gain the world and lose his soul". In other words, you would be trading at a loss if you gave up your soul in exchange for the whole world.

Sin came into the picture and devalued man. The prophet declared, "All flesh is grass, and all its beauty is like the flower of the field. The grass withers, the flower fades when the breath of the LORD blows on it; surely the people are grass" (Isaiah 40:6-8). What a contrast in value and how low humanity fell. But thank God for second chances, that in Christ Jesus, he gave us new birth through the word of truth, that we might once again be His most-prized possession in all of creation. The NLT reads, "He chose to give birth to us by giving us his true word. And we, out of all creation, became his prized possession".

Prayer

Thank you, Heavenly Father, that you have given us new birth and by it made us your most prized possession. We receive grace to see ourselves just as you see us. We pray for those with identity crises, that you would open their eyes to see themselves, just as you see them. In Jesus' name.

Bible in one year // **2 Samuel 3-5, Luke 14:25-35**

For this cause I bow my knees unto the Father of our Lord Jesus Christ.
// **Ephesians 3:14 NIV**

APR 19

For this cause

For what cause was Paul writing about? It is clearer from the preceding verses. He wrote, "Unto me, who am less than the least of all saints, is this grace given, that I should preach among the Gentiles the unsearchable riches of Christ; And to make all men see what is the fellowship of the mystery, which from the beginning of the world hath been hid in God, who created all things by Jesus Christ: To the intent that now unto the principalities and powers in heavenly places might be known by the church the manifold wisdom of God, According to the eternal purpose which he purposed in Christ Jesus our Lord: In whom we have boldness and access with confidence by the faith of him" (Ephesians 3:8-12 NIV).

The question for you today is this: What drives you? Why do you do the things you do? What is your motivation. It is a vital question to answer. It is one reason many people give up in life. Sometimes, because the very thing that drives them was for a moment taken. For Paul, it was His call. He recognized his call as an apostle and the commission from the Lord to preach among the gentiles the unsearchable reaches of Christ. And to make all men see... This resonates with me very much as one called to shine the light of God's word to make all men see and appropriate their glorious inheritance in Christ. And that was Paul's driving force. He wrote, "For this cause, I bow my knees".

> When you find your purpose in God, you will have a true drive for life, finding the and motivation each day to fulfill God's plan for your life.

Take a moment today and evaluate your use of time, your priorities and way of life. What is it like to you? Are you just busying with activities, or have you found a cause to live for? There is a place for you in God, and a reason for your life, there is a purpose for you. And that ought to be the driving force of your life, renewing your zeal every morning to do the things you are called to do. Paul had found his purpose and a drive for life. This is my prayer for you too today, that you would be able to say, "For this cause" and be committed to a heavenly vision. For therein is your fulfillment and eternal reward.

Prayer

Heavenly Father, thank you for today. Thank you for working in us to will and to do of your good pleasure. We receive grace to know and understand your purpose for us. Restore strength and zeal to them that are discouraged and help them run their race with endurance. In Jesus name.

Bible in one year // **2 Samuel 6-8, Luke 15:1-10**

APR 20

*He was the burning and shining lamp, and you were willing for a time to rejoice in his light. // **John 5:35***

Your season to shine

Jesus described John as, "A burning and shining lamp". While John kept shining, he only had a season for it. Even so now is your season and window of opportunity to be a light to your world. Be an example to someone, preach Christ to someone and share the truths of the gospel and scriptures you have received while you have the opportunity today. This is your season to shine as a burning and a shining light to those in your world – your friends, colleagues, family, and community. They can all rejoice in your light.

It wasn't long before John was arrested, and his life taken from him. We might not be arrested but we will soon age and be gone. Even so, the people around us will not always be there. You only have a window of opportunity to shine the light of God to your world, it will not last forever. But your light that shines today might have an eternal impact on others. Just as Jesus said, "You are the light of the world. A city that is set on a hill cannot be hidden. Nor do they light a lamp and put it under a basket, but on a lampstand, and it gives light to all who are in the house. Let your light so shine before men, that they may see your good works and glorify your Father in heaven (Matthew 5:14 - 16).

> **You have been given a window of opportunity to be a light to your world. Use it while it lasts!**

It might be as simple as sharing this devotional today, and you will be participating in impacting a life somewhere. Remember, this isn't about Simon Mungwa. It's for the Lord and His glory. It is for the edification of the saints. Once my sister shared with me feedback from her contact who received the message she her forwarded to the contact. It read, "Receiving just at the right time". It is a joint task! Don't wait for special occasions. Don't wait until it is too late, now is your season to be part of a world illumination movement. Just shine!

Prayer

Thank You Heavenly Father for your word today. As it goes forth, it illuminates and empowers your saints, emboldening them to rise to the respective tasks you have entrusted into their hands. Until together, we flood the earth with the light of the gospel. In Jesus' name!

Bible in one year // **2 Samuel 9-11, Luke 15:11-32**

> No one lights a lamp and then puts it under a basket. Instead, a lamp is placed on a stand, where it gives light to everyone in the house.
> // **Matthew 5:15 NLT**

APR 21

The stage is yours

In John chapter 1, the writer refers to Jesus as "The true Light which gives light to every man". When you receive Jesus, you are lit. And He did not light you to hide you but to position you on a stage where your light can be seen by all. Now you might be quick to think you don'tyet have a stage. No! You have a stage, wherever you are is a stage, wherever you work is a stage and wherever you live is a stage. Whatever brings you into interaction with men is a stage. And even to the least, the social media provides a stage for the most timid person to hide behind a keyboard with internet connection and boldly write or post anything.

> **Wherever you are and whatever brings you into interaction with others is a stage of life for you to shine and show forth the light of God's glory.**

Don't wait till the masses are gathered. Realize in every passing day that you are on a stage and let your light shine. For in this is the father glorified. He lit you and set you on the stage to give light to others. Jesus said, "You are the light of the world. A city that is set on a hill cannot be hidden. Nor do they light a lamp and put it under a basket, but on a lampstand, and it gives light to all who are in the house" (Matthew 5:14-15).

With or without your knowledge, someone is watching. Someone is taking note, someone is reading. Your light is getting noticed. The bigger question is if you are shining the light of God, the light of His word or at worst, a misrepresentation of His light. You are on a stage in life and that stage positions you to shine the light of God to certain people, a light that might never reach them by another person. You might be God's only hope to someone. Don't take it lightly what little opportunities you have to be a light to others. It is the Father's delight to see your light shine.

Prayer

Lord, I thank you for where I am. I can be a light for you to my world. I have a stage and a platform to shine today and always. Bringing men into your glorious light. As I am illuminated in the word daily, your glory is increased over my life and the brightness of it intensified daily. In Jesus' name. Amen!

Bible in one year // **2 Samuel 12-13, Luke 16**

APR 22

> There is one glory of the sun, another glory of the moon, and another glory of the stars; for one star differs from another star in glory.
> // 1 Corinthians 15:41

Your light is unique

Someone once said, "No two persons lights can shine in the exact same way. Use yours as a signature wherever you go and in whatever you do. That would help in making the world a better place". How true! When you look at the night sky on a clear night, the overall beauty of it is the result of the combined lights of the countless stars. What's also true is that each star in their unique sizes, distance from the earth and position, gives off a unique light. The uniqueness of a star's position and its light is actually used by astronomers to name individual stars. What a wonder, that the billions of stars can be distin-guished one from another by their lights.

There is a unique light only you can shine forth, don't be intimidated by the light of another.

Even so it is true for us. No one can shine and reflect the light of God you were sent to show forth just like you. Many times, we end up doing nothing or little for the Lord because we are intimidated by how much others are accomplishing. Our opening verse is true, one star differs in glory from the other. But the light of one star doesn't prevent the other from shining. Like Paul puts it, "There is one glory of the sun, another glory of the moon, and another glory of the stars; for one star differs from another star in glory".

You are uniquely positioned in the earth to reach a set of people I will never meet or get to know. You have a network of persons you connect with in a specific way no one else can. Like a constellation of stars, each of us is well positioned to give off a unique light that comes to others in different ways. And it is only together that we all bring God's light to different people. Together let's indeed light the world. Paul wrote, "Live clean, innocent lives as children of God, shining like bright lights in a world full of crooked and perverse people" (Philippians 2:15 NLT)

Prayer

Thank you, Heavenly Father, that even with over billions in the world, I am not lost in the number. Like the celestial stars, there is a uniqueness in the light you have given me. I therefore shine with confidence, knowing that together with others, we are fulfilling your dream in the earth. In Jesus' name!

Bible in one year // 2 Samuel 14-15, Luke 17:1-19

He makes the whole body fit together perfectly. As each part does its own special work, it helps the other parts grow, so that the whole body is healthy and growing and full of love. // **Ephesians 4:16 NLT**

APR 23

We complement each other

In yesterday's devotional, we were called upon to let our lights shine in their uniqueness without being intimidated by the lights of others. Like the song says, this little light of mine, I am gonna let it shine. I like to replace the "little" with "great". Because when Jesus came, it fulfilled the prophecy, "The people who sat (dwelt enveloped) in darkness have seen a great Light, and for those who sat in the land and shadow of death Light has dawned". (Matthew 4:16 AMP). Jesus is the great light in you. Maybe we should sing, "This great light of mine".

Back to today's focus, we complement each other. As several candles in a large hall light away the darkness, as billions of stars illuminate the night sky, so is the combined effect of our lights. When it came to me to initiate Your Daily Light, for a moment I wrestled with the idea because there are countless devotionals out there from reputable ministers of the gospel. And it was easy to settle for the idea that it wasn't needed. It was easy to think that Your Daily Light was not necessary when there are already many others. But it was a lie.

> We complement each other. Discover your place and stay at it, even if others are doing a similar thing and even seem to do it better.

Your Daily Light is not here to compete with others, it is here to complement them. It also has an audience that the others might never reach. And there are people who now use this as their devotional, people who before now never found the need to use one. They have come to connect with the unique light of my work and ministry. That's why we read, "As each part does its own special work, it helps the other parts grow, so that the whole body is healthy and growing". Find your place and stay at it. We complement each other for the glory of God. Don't fail to do your part because you say others are doing a similar thing already.

Prayer

Father thank you for the uniqueness in my and the task you have entrusted into my hands. Wherever I go today and whatever I do, let your light be seen and your glory be revealed. Together, let our combined lights indeed illuminate the world for your glory. In Jesus name.

Bible in one year // **2 Samuel 16-18, Luke 17:20-37**

APR 24

> God said, "Let the earth bring forth grass, the herb that yields seed, and the fruit tree that yields fruit according to its kind, whose seed is in itself, on the earth"; and it was so. // **Genesis 1:11**

After your own kind

There is a law of reproduction: A species bears fruit after its own kind. Same is expected of you as a disciple of Jesus Christ, that you will bear fruit after your own kind. That is what Jesus really meant when He said in John 15:13, "You did not choose Me, but I chose you and appointed you that you should go and bear fruit, and that your fruit should remain" (John 15:16). He commands us to bear fruits that will remain. It is in line with the word of God to all creation, "Let the earth bring forth grass, the herb that yields seed, and the fruit tree that yields fruit according to its kind, whose seed is in itself, on the earth"; and it was so" (Genesis 1:11).

No doubt when He rose from the death He said to His disciples, "Go therefore and make disciples of all the nations, baptizing them in the name of the Father and of the Son and of the Holy Spirit, "teaching them to observe all things that I have commanded you; and lo, I am with you always, even to the end of the age." (Matthew 28:19 - 20). He sent them to reproduce themselves in the world, making others disciples of Jesus Christ Just as they themselves had become.

> **When you win souls and teach them the things you have known of the Lord, you are making disciples and fulfilling your call to bear fruit after your kind.**

That same task is yours today, to bring forth fruit after your kind. To make disciples for the Lord. When Jesus said, "Make disciples of all nations", He literally meant "Of people from all works of life". And that's what you should be all about. You are God's representative in your world, sent to evangelize, win souls, and raise them up to a minimum of your status. They should grow up in the faith to be at minimum, where you have yourself reached. For in that you will be fulfilling your call, to be fruitful, bringing fruit after your kind -reproducing yourself in the world as a disciple.(Ephesians 6:13). Remember, "Resist the devil, and he will flee from you" (James 4:7 NIV). Satan the opportunist has no alternatives but to flee if you will stand your ground. You have the victory over him.

Prayer

Thank You Heavenly Father because I am not insignificant in your kingdom. There is an addition that comes from me. As I go through my day's activities today, I am conscious of my responsibility to win souls and train them in your ways, making disciples of my world. In Jesus' name.

Bible in one year // **2 Samuel 19-20, Luke 18:1-23**

He who is faithful in what is least is faithful also in much; and he who is unjust in what is least is unjust also in much. // **Luke 16:10**

APR 25

The Multiplier-Effect

Jesus shared this parable, "Again, the Kingdom of Heaven can be illustrated by the story of a man going on a long trip. He called together his servants and entrusted his money to them while he was gone. He gave five bags of silver to one, two bags of silver to another, and one bag of silver to the last – dividing it in proportion to their abilities. He then left on his trip" (Matthew 25:14 - 15 NLT). Like these servants, we are individual entrusted with spiritual gifts and talents in proportion to our abilities. "But to each one of us grace was given according to the measure of Christ's gift" (Ephesians 4:7). Another version says, "However, he has given each one of us a special gift through the generosity of Christ (NLT).

> To each one of us grace was given according to the measure of Christ's gift. When we invest it, we become perfected in that area and God raises us to reach even more people for His glory.

It is called the multiplier effect, when what you have multiplies itself with time, making you ever better and more relevant to your world. But you must at least start. Some are great singers, but because no one ever heard them sing, that's how they never got sponsorship to release the songs God has planted in their spirit through the years. Some are great writers, with several poems no one has ever read, poems as good as some of the classic hymns we have been singing for centuries.

Think of the songs! What if they never wrote them? We might never know the name of the author of "Amazing grace"; but think of what a blessing the song has been to the world. Like the servants in our opening verse, we shall all be called to account for the little duties we were called to do for the good of the kingdom. Even by distributing a devotional like this one to your contacts, you are playing a role in multiplying what God has put in your hands today. And God will reward us all for being faithful in little things by entrusting us with more – that is the multiplier effect!

Prayer

Heavenly Father thank you for gracing me with virtues and talents with which I can participate in the great work you are doing in saving souls, making disciples, and commissioning them to the world. Today, I receive grace to be committed to my call and be effective in it. In Jesus name!

Bible in one year // **2 Samuel 21-22, Luke 18:24-43**

APR 26

You are the light of the world. A city that is set on a hill cannot be hidden. // **Matthew 5:14**

Even for the one

A lot of times, many end up doing nothing for the Lord because they are waiting for the occasion they will stand before a multitude or have the platform to reach the world. But it isn't supposed to be so. And many times, those even doing some little work quit because they feel their efforts seemed not to reach as many people as they would love. The motivation to quit is even greater when your efforts meet unappreciative critics or indifferent persons.

> **Even for the one individual, keep shining as a light. You never know what chain impact it might have.**

It is time to do it like John. The Amplified Bible "John was the lamp that kept on burning and shining [to show you the way], and you were willing for a while to delight yourselves in his light" (John 5:35 AMP). That's your true duty – to keep shining, even for just one person. You never know what chain effect it might have down the line. Once I spent some time in Douala, Cameroon around 2008, I got to share Christ with a younger neighbor, now a friend and brother. That holiday, I spent quite some evenings nurturing him in scriptures.

It was several months later while I was at university in another city that I received an email from him. He informed me of the family Bible study time he had initiated at his home with the whole family joining, and how he was sharing Christ at his secondary school. I particularly loved a line in his email that read, "I am now lighting other lights". My light to one teenage boy, was producing a chain effect. Remember, "You are the light of the world" (Matthew 5:14). Keep shining, even for the one person that sees your light. Don't quit shining for any reason.

Prayer

Heavenly Father I thank you for the privilege to be a light in my world, illuminating the paths of men and bringing glory to your name. Even today as I go about my day, I learn not to despise the opportunities around me, knowing in it you can set in motion chain-effect of transformation in my community and the world at large. In Jesus name!

Bible in one year // **2 Samuel 23-24, Luke 19:1-27**

To each one of us grace was given according to the measure of Christ's gift. // **Ephesians 4:7**

APR 27

Esteem each other

We are admonished, "Walk worthy of the calling with which you were called, with all lowliness and gentleness, with longsuffering, bearing with one another in love, endeavoring to keep the unity of the Spirit in the bond of peace. There is one body and one Spirit, just as you were called in one hope of your calling; one Lord, one faith, one baptism; one God and Father of all, who is above all, and through all, and in you all" (Ephesians 4:1-6).

The reason some people leave church is because they are turned off by others who seem to act as if they own the show or are the most gifted. Although this sometimes results from only a few available person making themselves available for all that has to be done. For same reason, some people never get the courage enough to bring their gifts to serve the church and other believers. They have come to think they are the negligible ones with little to offer. Never let yourself be someone in a position to turn others away from the house of God because someday the Lord will call you to account for the soul you pushed away. On the other hand, never let another person in the house of God make you leave. Remember: That is also your Father's house.

> **Esteem each other in the house of God and accommodate one another despite differences. That together we might share in the blessings of God through fellowship.**

So long as we are together in this world, we are bound to step on each other's toes. Learning to accommodate each other despite our differences is the emphasis for today, esteeming each other and giving them opportunity to bless us with the spiritual gifts God has invested in us all. A more contemporary version puts the verses this way: "Always be humble and gentle. Be patient with each other, making allowance for each other's faults because of your love. Make every effort to keep yourselves united in the Spirit, binding yourselves together with peace. For there is one body and one Spirit, just as you have been called to one glorious hope for the future" (Ephesians 4:2 - 4 NLT).

Prayer

Heavenly Lord you are great and worthy of praise. Search our hearts and take away resentment towards each other. Let love fill our hearts for one another as we receive grace to keep the bond of unity and create an accommodating home for all in your house. In Jesus' name.

Bible in one year // **1 Kings 1-2, Luke 19:28-48**

APR 28

> They devoted themselves to the apostles' teaching and to fellowship, to the breaking of bread and to prayer. // **Acts 2:42**

Better together

Look! How good and how pleasant it is when brothers live together! It is like fine oil poured on the head which flows down the beard – Aaron's beard, and then flows down his garments. It is like the dew of Hermon, which flows down upon the hills of Zion. Indeed, that is where the Lord has decreed a blessing will be available – eternal life (Psalms 133:1

It is great to have personal fellowship with the Lord. But it is even greater when we fellowship one with another in God's presence. We need not let our personal spiritual well-being bring us to a place where we find the assembly with brethren dispensable. Of the early Church it is written, „The group of those who believed were of one heart and mind, and no one said that any of his possessions was his own, but everything was held in common. With great power the apostles were giving testimony to the resurrection of the Lord Jesus, and great grace was on them all" (Acts 4:32).

> **No matter how great your personal fellowship with the Lord, it only gets better in the presence of the brethren.**

As much as the Lord desires us to grow to a place of spiritual independence where we can on our own take responsibility for our growth and development, He has so established a Church or body that only functions better in togetherness. Ephesians 4:16 tells us, "He makes the whole body fit together perfectly. As each part does its own special work, it helps the other parts grow, so that the whole body is healthy and growing and full of love" (NLT)

Just like our opening passage says, "How pleasant it is when brethren live together". The Psalmist goes on to emphasize, "There the Lord commands His blessings". Not only are we better together, there in fellowship, the Lord causes great grace to rest upon us all.

Prayer

Thank you, Father, for the fellowship of the spirit, the communion of the saints and a family of believers with whom to identify. For those who are still searching, direct them to the right church fitting to their needs. That we all may continue to grow into Christ in the appropriate atmosphere. In Jesus' name!

Bible in one year // **1 Kings 3-5, Luke 20:1-26**

According to the grace of God which was given to me, as a wise master builder I have laid the foundation, and another builds on it. But let each one take heed how he builds on it. // **1 Corinthians 3:10**

APR 29

Building together

When you see a great building standing, no matter how skilled an individual is, it is often the result of collaborative work by many builders. An architect might have conceived the plan. You will need electricians, engineers, plumbers, and many other subspecialties to have a complete functional structure. This is the picture Paul paints as He considers the Church of Christ andthe respective tasks we might have to do as individuals, contributing to the whole structure.

"According to the grace of God which was given to me, as a wise master builder I have laid the foundation,and another builds on it. But let each one take heed how he builds on it. For no other foundation can anyone lay than that which is laid, which is Jesus Christ. Now if anyone builds on this foundation with gold, silver, precious stones, wood, hay, straw, each one's work will become clear; for the Day will declare it, because it will be revealed by fire; and the fire will test each one's work, of what sort it is. If anyone's work which he has built on it endures, he will receive a reward. If anyone's work is burned, he will suffer loss; but he himself will be saved, yet so as through fire" (1 Corinthians 3:10 - 15).

> **We were born together into the divine family and each endowed with special abilities so we can build together. Get actively involved!**

We were born together into the divine family and each endowed with special abilities so we can build together. Until you find your place in the body of Christ and actively get involved, you are missing out. It is not for the overly zealous. It is with this awareness that I write daily for the edification of saints around the world as God gives the grace. I am answering duties call to illuminate the saints with the Word. Find your place wherever you sense God's call to duty for your life. Get involved and do it for the reward!

Prayer

Heavenly Lord you are wonderful, you are excellent, you are beautiful. Thank you for entrusting us with the world that we might together build a heavenly family that represents and glorifies you in the earth. In Jesus' name.

Bible in one year // **1 Kings 6-7, Luke 20:27-47**

APR 30

Then Jesus said to them, "Follow Me, and I will make you become fishers of men". // **Mark 1:17**

Fishers of men

That is really what He made us – Fishers of men. God has had one main agenda from the foundations of the Earth. He has been looking for a people to call His own. He started off with Adam and Eve, giving them a mandate to multiply and fill the earth, but they sold out to the devil. Then God picked Noah, the one righteous Man with His family, with a strategy to start all over with a few. But sin was a seed in the flesh. Though the sinful generation died, Noah's descendants were bound by the same law of sin.

> **God is looking for a people to call His own, and as His Child, He has entrusted you with the task to seek and save those around you. You are a fisher of Men.**

Paul puts it this way, "So I am not the one doing wrong; it is sin living in me that does it. And I know that nothing good lives in me, that is, in my sinful nature. I want to do what is right, but I can't. I want to do what is good, but I don't. I don't want to do what is wrong, but I do it anyway. But if I do what I don't want to do, I am not really the one doing wrong; it is sin living in me that does it" (Romans 7:17 - 20 NLT)

God picked Abraham with same vision, called him out and established the nation of Israel. He was looking for a Holy breed, set apart for himself. But all this was impossible until Jesus came and dealt with the issue of sin. Romans 8:2 tells us, "For what the law could not do in that it was weak through the flesh, God did by sending His own Son in the likeness of sinful flesh, on account of sin: He condemned sin in the flesh" (Romans 8:3 NKJV). Then He gave us the great commission: Go and make disciples of all the nations, baptizing them in the name of the Father and the Son and the Holy Spirit. Teach these new disciples to obey all the commands I have given you. And be sure of this: I am with you always, even to the end of the age (Matthew 28:19 - 20 NLT). He made us fishers of men, sending us out to fish men out of the waters of sin in the world and bring them into His glorious light.

Prayer

Lord God almighty, thank you for making me a fisher of men. I receive grace to see the opportunities around me to win souls and make disciples for you, sharing with them the truths I have received. Plow the hearts of men and prepare them as ready grounds for the word. In Jesus' name.

Bible in one year // **1 Kings 8-9, Luke 21:1-19**

MAY

„Be careful," Jesus said to them. „Be on your guard against the yeast of the Pharisees and Sadducees." // **Matt 16:6 NIV**

MAY 1

The yeast of the pharisees

Several times Jesus spoke to His disciples in parables, coding spiritual truths in practical daily life stories. On this occasion like many others, his disciples didn't get it all clear in the first place. Then they later caught the point – beware of the erroneous teachings of the Pharisees and the Sadducees.

These were two groups of Jewish religious cliques who had established different sets of beliefs based on their twisted understanding of the laws of Moses and the writings of the prophets. They had become the voices of doctrines and the models for many. That situation is even worse today with the multiplicity of denomnations and churches. While there are many founded on sound teachings of scriptures,we have also seen more trash and misguiding doctrines and will only see more as the years go by. They have a form of truth and sound spiritual. But they are misleading teachings, deviating from God's truth.

> In the end, after all the teachings you receive, it is your responsibility to guard your heart against falsehood and misguided doctrines by personal verification from scriptures.

The responsibility remains yours to guard your mind and heart against false teachings and wrong doctrines. Like the Berean Christians, don't just embrace and believe anything because someone quoted the Bible. Go back and evaluate all by scriptures, taking into consideration the totality of God's word to be sure verses are not being used out of context. It is written, "Now the Berean Jews were of more noble character than those in Thessalonica, for they received the message with great eagerness and examined the Scriptures every day to see if what Paul said was true" (Acts 17:11 NIV).

Prayer

Thank You Lord for preserving and granting me access to your word. Thank you for our dependable teacher, The Holy Spirit. Today we receive grace to separate form from truth. Continue to raise and inspire ministers of the gospel with accurate knowledge of the word that your sheep might be preserved. In Jesus name!

Bible in one year // **1 Kings 10-11, Luke 21:20-38**

MAY 2

> Therefore, if anyone is IN CHRIST, he is a new creation; old things have passed away; behold, all things have become new.
> // **2 Corinthians 5:17**

In Christ

Christ means "Anointed" or "The Messiah". While that refers to Jesus as a person, it is also used in scripture in several ways to mean a spiritual place of existence. It is a mystery! Jesus the Christ, prayed a prayer for his disciples saying, "I do not pray for these alone, but also for those who will believe in Me through their word; "That they all may be one, as You, Father, are in Me, and I in You; that they also may be one in Us, that the world may believe that You sent Me (John 17:20 - 17:21).

> **Christ is The Messiah and the person of Jesus, The Anointed One. But Christ is also the new spiritual environment of our existence into which we are brought at salvation.**

This was a repetition of similar words in John 14 when He said, "At that day you will know that I am in My Father, and you in Me, and I in you (John 14:20). So even as the Bible talks about Christ in you, with the same emphasis, it talks about you IN CHRIST. But this time, it is much more than talking about His person. It is talking about the new spiritual environment in which you exist. It was in this context of having such a spiritual environment of existence that Paul addressed a people and said to them about the Lord, "For in him we live and move and exist" (Acts 17:28 NLT).

In like manner, to be IN CHRIST is to be brought into a new spiritual environment different from the natural world in which we live. And this has great implications regarding who we have become, what has been made available to us, and our position in relation to other persons, principalities or spiritual authorities and things in every realm of life, both spiritual and physical. That is why Paul wrote, "Therefore, if anyone is in Christ, he is a new creation; old things have passed away; behold, all things have become new" (2 Corinthians 5:17). Join me through this month on a Journey to discover what it really means to be IN CHRIST and the glorious implications thereof!

Prayer

Heavenly Father thank you for your grace and mercies keeping and sustaining us at a time as this. Thank you for guaranteeing our wellbeing in Christ. We rejoice in the blessings for us who are numbered IN CHRIST. We receive grace to understand these truths and their implications. In Jesus' name.

Bible in one year // **1 Kings 12-13, Luke 22:1-20**

For you are all sons of God through faith in Christ Jesus. For as many of you as were baptized into Christ have put on Christ.
// Galatians 3:26 - 3:27 NKJV

MAY 3

Baptized into Christ

Yesterday we saw that as much as the person of Christ is in you, with same emphasis the Bible talks about you IN CHRIST. We went on to see that Christ in the second instance is the spiritual environment of existence into which you were brought at the moment of salvation. We read in Paul's letter to the Corinthians, „For by one Spirit we were all baptized into one body" (1 Corinthians 12:13). Just as it is written, "For as many of you as were baptized into Christ have put on Christ" (Galatians 3:26 - 3:27).

The word baptism is translated from a Greek word "Baptizo" and literally means "To immerse or submerge something totally". Now note that the opening verse is not talking about water baptism but the spiritual translation from the dominion of darkness into the kingdom of God at the point of new birth when you are brought into Christ. As Colossians 1:13 says, „He has delivered us from the power of darkness and conveyed us into the kingdom of the Son of His love".

When that verse says we were baptized by one spirit into Christ, it is the picture of a sea diver who is plunged into the ocean by his team. He is taken from one environment and immersed into another. He is totally in a new environment of existence, surrounded and submerged in water. Even though he has water as a natural part of his blood and body fluids, he is now fully immersed in water, and is for a season existing in a totally different environment. In same manner, when you received Christ as your Lord and savior, you were immersed into Christ as your new environment of existence, and He literally envelops you like a wrapping over a gift. That's why it is written, „For as many of you as were baptized into Christ have put on Christ". Therefore, you are in Christ, as a place of existence – a spiritual environment.

> **The Holy Spirit immersed us into Christ as our place of existence. And just like a fish in water, we have a new spiritual environment for life even though we are in this world.**

Prayer

Heavenly Father, we are thankful for a new day and the blessings it announces. The opportunity for a walk with you and the grace to improve ourselves. Help us to make the most of the things you have entrusted us with as you unveil to us the realities of life in our new environment – Christ. In Jesus' name.

Bible in one year // **1 Kings 14-15, Luke 22:21-46**

MAY 4

You died, and your life is hidden with Christ in God. // **Colossians 3:3**

Secured in Christ

In a world of insecurity and uncertainty, it is important to know that your life is secured in Christ. And this security knows no bounds. There are many who trust the security of their souls, they know it is saved and preserved. However, when it comes to physical security from wicked men or sicknesses and diseases that threaten our lives and wellbeing, it is not the case. There is a security in Christ that goes beyond the preservation of your soul. Jesus said to His disciples, "Are not two sparrows sold for a copper coin? And not one of them falls to the ground apart from your Father's will. But the very hairs of your head are all numbered. Do not fear therefore; you are of more value than many sparrows" (Matthew 10:29 - 31).

Jesus assured us, no physical harm will befall us without the Father's permission as he sends us forth into the world. Oure lives are secured in Christ. Paul wrote, "If then you were raised with Christ, seek those things which are above, where Christ is, sitting at the right hand of God. Set your mind on things above, not on things on the earth. For you died, and your life is hidden with Christ in God" (Colossians 3:1-3).

When you read Psalm 91, it talks of the secret place of the Most High. In essence, that secret place is Christ, the spiritual place of existence where you have been brought into. And this familiar Psalm continues to declare, "Surely He shall deliver you from the snare of the fowler and from the perilous pestilence. He shall cover you with His feathers, and under His wings you shall take refuge; His truth shall be your shield and buckler. You shall not be afraid of the terror by night, nor of the arrow that flies by day, nor of the pestilence that walks in darkness, nor of the destruction that lays waste at noonday. A thousand may fall at your side, and ten thousand at your right hand; but it shall not come near you (Psalm 91:3 - 91:7).

> **You are secured in Christ because your life is hidden in God, far from the reach of demonic influence or earthly plagues and diseases. Rest assured in this security even when the world is insecure.**

Prayer

LORD, you are the strong tower of my life. Though an army may encamp against me, my heart shall not fear; Though war may rise against me, in this I am confident. For in the time of trouble you shall hide me in the secret place of your tabernacle, in Christ where I belong. In Jesus name. (Psalm 27:1 - 5)

Bible in one year // **1 Kings 16-18, Luke 22:47-71**

The inhabitant will not say, "I am sick"; The people who dwell in it will be forgiven their iniquity. // **Isaiah 33:24**

MAY 5

Healed in Christ

We established in the days passed beyond question that to be in Christ is to be brought into a new spiritual place of existence. And these thoughts are coherent with the lessons from January that emphasized you were brought into Zion – the place of your inheritance. As the writer of Hebrews puts it, "You have come to Mount Zion, to the city of the living God, the heavenly Jerusalem, and to countless thousands of angels in a joyful gathering. You have come to the assembly of God's firstborn children, whose names are written in heaven" (Hebrews 12:22 - 12:22 NLT).

He saw us as a people who had come into a new place of habitation. When you regard the tenses in his writing, you can confirm this is not about heaven but about our present-day location – where we exist in Christ. And one thing that is true about this location was prophesied by Isaiah. He said they that dwell in there, referring to us, would not say they are sick. Why? Because they were healed and given divine health. As it is written, "Who Himself bore our sins in His own body on the tree, that we, having died to sins, might live for righteousness – by whose stripes you WERE healed" (1 Peter 2:24)

> In Christ you were healed and given divine health for life so that you would no say "I am sick". You are the healed of the Lord and by His Spirit, He sustains you in health as you continue speaking words of life.

Once again according to the tenses, it is accomplished. You were healed and given divine health. So, what happens when you feel sick or medical diagnosis show you are sick? That happens because nature or the Devil tries to put a question on a divine truth and bring you into doubts regarding who you are and what God has accomplished for you in Christ Jesus. Don't endorse or approve the report no matter the name of the disease. Even while you get medical attention, it is time to rise in faith, proclaim the word and hold fast to the testimony: „I am the healed of the Lord". Believe it, say it and act like it until you see the full manifestation. For in Christ, you were healed and should not say "I am sick"! You were healed!

Prayer

Heavenly Father thank you for the graces in Christ Jesus and the boundless blessings we live. We will not say we are sick, for by the stripes of our Lord Jesus we were healed. Thank you for Your life-giving spirit living in us, vitalizing, rejuvenating, and restoring our mortal bodies to health. In Jesus' name.

Bible in one year // **1 Kings 19-20, Luke 23:1-25**

MAY 6

> His divine power has given to us all things that pertain to life and godliness, through the knowledge of Him who called us by glory and virtue.
> // **2 Peter 1:3**

Blessed with all things

In Christ Jesus, we have been given all things that pertain to life and godliness. That literally means everything we need to live the life God has called us to live and fulfill our purpose has been made available to us. And this is no myth. In Romans, we are encouraged with these words: "What then shall we say to these things? If God is for us, who can be against us? He who did not spare His own Son, but delivered Him up for us all, how shall He not with Him also freely give us all things?" (Romans 8:31 -32).

In Christ Jesus, God has made abundant provisions for all we need to live a godly life and to fulfill our respective callings. What you need is to find access to all that has been made available to you.

This was the story of Abraham, "Now Abraham was old, well advanced in age; and the LORD had blessed Abraham in all things." (Genesis 24:1). For Isaac it was no different. For "Isaac sowed in that land and reaped in the same year a hundredfold; and the LORD blessed him. The man began to prosper and continued prospering until he became very prosperous" (Genesis 26:12 - 13). Even David understood this when he said, "The Lord is my Shepherd, I have everything I need" (Psalm 23:1). And to bring this home to us, Paul wrote, "And this same God who takes care of me will supply all your needs from his glorious riches, which have been given to us in Christ Jesus" (Philippians 4:19 NLT).

At any point in time in our lives, God has made sufficient supplies for the season. The problem often is that we miss out on the heavenly portals that have been opened for us by God for supplies in our lives. Sometimes these portals are job or business opportunities, ministry avenues, business ideas or even key persons God has placed in our lives. If we will look keenly at all points in time, like Abraham, we will always find a ram caught by its horns in the thicket just when we need it most. Remember, "God... richly gives us all we need for our enjoyment" (1 Timothy 6:17 NLT).

Prayer

Thank you, Heavenly Father for your love for us. You are our sufficiency. From you, we have received all things that pertain to life and godliness. We are richly supplied with every heavenly and earthly resource to do your will. We receive ideas for wealth and a discerning heart to recognize our portals. In Jesus' name.

Bible in one year // **1 Kings 21-22, Luke 23:26-56**

For if when we were enemies we were reconciled to God through the death of His Son, much more, having been reconciled, we shall be saved by His life. // **Romans 5:10**

MAY 7

Forever and unconditionally loved

It is ok to doubt if a friend, a family member or even a spouse still loves us. Sometimes we have good reasons to question their love for us. And it would not be surprising to find out that such fears are true. And if that happened to you, don't worry. It only justifies the wide gap between human love and God's love for us. This you might remember was one of the lessons in the previous months. Human love fails. However, in Christ Jesus, you are forever and unconditionally loved by God. Paul even argues like this, "God demonstrates His own love toward us, in that while we were still sinners, Christ died for us. Much more then, having now been justified by His blood, we shall be saved from wrath through Him. For if when we were enemies we were reconciled to God through the death of His Son, much more, having been reconciled, we shall be saved by His life" (Romans 5:8-10).

Paul goes on to write, "What then shall we say to these things? If God is for us, who can be against us? He who did not spare His own Son, but delivered Him up for us all, how shall He not with Him also freely give us all things?... Who shall separate us from the love of Christ? Shall tribulation, or distress, or persecution, or famine, or nakedness, or peril, or sword? ...Yet in all these things we are more than conquerors through Him who loved us" (Romans 8:31)

And to crown it all, Paul wrote, "For I am persuaded that neither death nor life, nor angels nor principalities nor powers, nor things present nor things to come, nor height nor depth, nor any other created thing, shall be able to separate us from the love of God which is in Christ Jesus our Lord (Romans 8:38).

> Sometimes when circumstances of life and personal guilt bring doubts about God's love for you, remember that in Christ Jesus, you are forever and unconditionally loved!

Prayer

Gracious and everlasting Father, thank you for loving us and saving us from the sin, making us your beloved children in Christ. Much more, you have loved us with an everlasting love. We rest assured in Your love for us In Christ Jesus that causes all things to work together for our good. In Jesus' name.

Bible in one year // **2 Kings 1-3, Luke 24:1-35**

MAY 8

And be kind to one another, tenderhearted, forgiving one another, even as God in Christ forgave you. // **Ephesians 4:32**

Forgiven in Christ

Lots of times as Christians, the thought or doubt about being forgiven often cheats us in different ways. I have been down that road a few times particularly when we are young in the faith. The lack of confidence in the forgiveness of our sins cripple's faith. Particularly, when we pray, we will lack the confidence that we are heard and therefore the assurance of the answers thereof. Secondly, we will feel unfit and unqualified to render service unto the Lord.

Sometimes, as I grew up in the faith, and it happened that I had done something wrong, I would feel so terrible about it that I would think I was unqualified to pray or not good enough to serve the Lord. In such instances, people would decline a call to serve in the choir or teach God's word because they feel unfit. And in some churches, they even walk out during the communion. Never fall for that lie, you have been forgiven in Christ Jesus. God is not holding your sins against you.

> You are forgiven in Christ Jesus. Let that consciousness stir faith in you to be confident in the father's presence and inspire you toalways serve the Lord.

One misleading verse for many people is this: "For if you forgive men their trespasses, your heavenly Father will also forgive you. "But if you do not forgive men their trespasses, neither will your Father forgive your trespasses (Matthew 6:14 - 15). Many people have never recognized the fact that Jesus was speaking here to people before His sacrifice on the cross, people under the old covenant. But we are of another class. We do not forgive so that God should forgive us. No! We are called to forgive because we have been forgiven. In Christ Jesus, if you don't forgive someone, you are simply failing to be an imitator of the Father who is a forgiving God (Eph 5:1). You are simply creating an atmosphere for bitterness in your heart which corrupts your service for men and to God (Heb 12:15). God is not holding up your sins against you and waiting for you to forgive another. You are totally forgiven in Christ!

Prayer

Heavenly Father, I thank you for your grace and mercies that are new every morning. Like the psalmist says, you do not deal with us according to our iniquities. But as far as the East is from the west, so you have taken our sins far from us. Therefore, we are confident in your presence and find grace in times of need. In Jesus' name.

Bible in one year // **2 Kings 4-6, Luke 24:36-53**

He has delivered us from the power of darkness and conveyed us into the kingdom of the Son of His love, in whom we have redemption through His blood, the forgiveness of sins. // **Colossians 1:13 - 14**

MAY 9

Redeemed in Christ

Our opening passage for today brings us once again to the fact that we were brought into a new place of existence through salvation. We have been brought into Christ. And there are facts and truths that imply. Over the last days, we have seen that we are secured, blessed, and forgiven in Christ. One more truth is the fact that we are redeemed in Him, as it is written, "He has delivered us from the power of darkness and conveyed us into the kingdom of the Son of His love, in whom we have redemption through His blood, the forgiveness of sins" (Colossians 1:13 - 14).

To redeem means to rescue by paying a price. We were redeemed from the slavery of sin and the dominion of darkness, and that at the cost of the life of Jesus. 1 Corinthians 6:20 echoes that truth. It says, "You do not belong to yourself, for God bought you with a high price" (1 Corinthians 6:19 -20 NLT). That has great implications! First it means the devil has no legal right over you, and therefore has no say in your affairs.

> **You are redeemed in Christ and belong to the Lord. Much more, He has taken upon himself the responsibility to ensure what becomes of you because your life is his own.**

One second truth is this: You are not your own. There is a name in Bambalang, a village in the Northwest Region of Cameroon where I was born. The name literally means "A person's life is in his hands". In other words, the person possessing a life has the responsibility of what becomes of that life. That is also a spiritual truth. Because you were bought with a price and your life now belongs to the Lord, it is his responsibility what becomes of you. No doubt He said to Jacob, "Behold, I am with you and will keep you wherever you go and will bring you back to this land; for I will not leave you until I have done what I have spoken to you." (Genesis 28:15). He says to you today, „For I know the plans I have for you, they are plans for good and not for disaster, to give you a future and a hope" (Jeremiah 29:11 NLT).

Prayer

Gracious Father, blessed be your name. Thank you for rescuing us from the consequences of sin and from the clutches of darkness. The Devil has no say over the affairs of my life. For my life is in your hands. To you be all the glory in Jesus' name!

Bible in one year // **2 Kings 7-9, John 1:1-28**

MAY 10

Therefore, having been justified by faith, we have peace with God through our Lord Jesus Christ. // **Romans 5:1**

Justified in Christ

The Psalmist pondered on the blessedness of the man whose sins are forgiven. He wrote, "Blessed is he whose transgression is forgiven, whose sin is covered. Blessed is the man to whom the LORD does not impute iniquity, and in whose spirit there is no deceit (Psalm 32:1 - 2). He counted himself blessed for being forgiven, for his sin being covered. As great as that is, it is nothing close to what we have in Christ Jesus – it is nothing close to justification!

> In Christ, we are more than forgiven. We have been declared totally innocent because Jesus took our place of guilt so we could take his place of untainted righteousness!

We already saw that we are forgiven in Christ. More than being forgiven, we were redeemed and bought out of the consequences of sin. As if that was not enough, we were justified in Christ. No doubt the Gospel is called the Good News. It truly announces the love and goodness of God towards us. Sometimes, too good to seem true. But this is the reality and truth of the Spirit, the testimony of God regarding what He has done or made available to mankind in Christ. Paul wrote about us, "Therefore, having been justified by faith, we have peace with God through our Lord Jesus Christ" (Romans 5:1).

But what does it really mean to be justified? To be justified means to be declared "Not guilty". This is more than being forgiven. To be forgiven means you are recognized as the criminal; however, the charges against you are cleared. It means it is written that you did wrong on your record. But to be justified means you have been examined and found innocent with no need for forgiveness. Because as far as heaven is concerned, your slate is clean, you didn't do it, you are not guilty! How is that possible? Because Jesus took our place, and "The Lord laid on him the sins of us all". (Isaiah 53:6 NLT). so "God made Him who knew no sin to be sin for us, that we might become the righteousness of God in Him" (2 Corinthians 5:21).

Prayer

Thank You Heavenly Father for your love for me that has acquitted me in Christ Jesus, justifying me and declaring me "Not guilty", despite my wrongs. That I can stand in your presence with no sense of guilt or feeling of condemnation because of the sacrifice of Jesus Christ who took my place and was condemned on my behalf. I receive grace to walk in righteousness. In Jesus' name.

Bible in one year // **2 Kings 10-12, John 1:29-51**

That I may gain Christ and be found in Him, not having my own righteousness, which is from the law, but that which is through faith in Christ, the righteousness which is from God by faith. // **Philippians 3:8**

MAY 11

You are righteous Pt. 1

It is still common to be in a Christian gathering and hear someone pray and say "We are all sinners", actually referring to the congregation of God's people. And these are people who profess Jesus as their Lord. It is not a mark of humility when you pray as a believer or teach other believers and say „We are all sinners". It echoes an ignorance! For in Christ Jesus, you received Righteousness as a gift (Romans 5:17). Some even take it a step further to quote scripture saying there is none that does good, there is none righteous, no not one! They are quoting the words of David from Psalm 14, which Paul used in his letter to show that we were helpless without Christ and could never attain righteousness by our own efforts (Romans 3:10-12).

When you read the bible, you should learn to separate the things that applied to humanity before the sacrifice of Jesus and the things that apply to us believing in Him. For all who are born again are righteous, made righteous in Christ Jesus. We are not sinners. Like Paul wrote, "That I may gain Christ and be found in Him, not having my own righteousness, which is from the law, but that which is through faith in Christ, the righteousness which is from God by faith" (Philippians 3:8

> **You are righteous in Christ Jesus; as righteous as God Himself because your righteousness is not your own, but God's righteousness imputed to you.**

Never say again, there is no one that is righteous. Because now it has been made possible and there are many that are righteous, including YOU, if only you are in Christ. As we saw yesterday, "God made Him who knew no sin to be sin for us, that we might become the righteousness of God in Christ" (2 Corinthians 5:21). In other words, we have the very righteousness of God. We are as righteous as God himself. It is a status given to us in Christ Jesus. That is why Paul will write, "Not having my own righteousness, which is from the law, but the righteousness, which is through faith in Christ, the righteousness which is from God by faith". For in Christ Jesus, were all made righteous.

Prayer

    Heavenly Father, Thank you for Your love and mercies towards us. You have made us righteous in Christ Jesus and given us the Holy Spirit who enables us to live for you. Even when we stumble and fall, you are ever calling us to repentance and inviting us to walk above sin. Thank you for such grace. In Jesus' name!

Bible in one year // **2 Kings 13-14, John 2**

MAY 12

> I, therefore, the prisoner of the Lord, beseech you to walk worthy of the calling with which you were called. // **Ephesians 4:1**

You are righteous Pt. 2

Yesterday, examining from several scriptures, we established a fact that is true for those in Christ Jesus: We are righteous! But as I wrote, seemed I could hear someone reading and justifying their reasons for praying like that. And their reason is this: "We all are likely to sin in some way. We are all sinners for all have sinned and fallen short of the glory of God". It is a deception from the devil. Because if you continue to see yourself as a sinner, you will feel unqualified to pray and have answers, and unqualified to serve the Lord. And that is the true goal of Satan, to make you ineffective in your walk of faith.

Such a person is missing out on two things. First, they don't understand what it means to be righteous or to be a sinner. It is about what nature an individual has. To be righteous does not mean you never stumble. It simply means, at all times, "You have the freedom to stand in the presence of God without guilt or condemnation because God has given you his RIGHTEOUS NATURE" (2 Corinthians 5:21). On the contrary, you are not a sinner because you sin. A sinner is someone who has not been born again. They still have in them a SIN NATURE, which is rebellious and cannot submit to God (Ephesians 2:1-3).

> **Don't let an old and twisted understanding of scripture blind you from the truth in Christ Jesus. You are righteous and not a sinner if you are born again. Therefore, reflect that righteousness in all you do.**

The second group of people who find problems with this kind of truth are sometimes ministers. They think telling people they are righteous because of the finished work of Christ will give Christians an open ticket to sin. It is another lie from the Devil. Instead, this truth gives you a consciousness to reflect the righteousness in you. That's why Paul wrote, "Walk worthy of the calling with which you were called". In other words, reflect the life of righteousness you have been given. He goes on to add, „You should no longer walk as the rest of the Gentiles walk, in the futility of their mind, having their understanding darkened, being alienated from the life of God, because of the ignorance that is in them, because of the blindness of their heart" (Eph 4:17-18).

Prayer

Heavenly Father, thank you for delivering us from the lies of the devil and misconceptions of men. For giving us truth and empowering us to live accordingly, that men might see our good works and glorify our father who is in heaven. In Jesus name.

Bible in one year // **2 Kings 15-16, John 3:1-18**

We have been made holy through the sacrifice of the body of Jesus
Christ once for all. // **Hebrews 10:10 NIV**

MAY 13

You are holy

You are holy if you are in Christ Jesus. This is very true for every one of us. You are Holy! Many don't know or understand this. The writer of Hebrews understood that he was writing to a people who had been sanctified by the blood of Jesus, they had been made Holy. He wrote to them, "Therefore, holy brothers and sisters, who share in the heavenly calling, fix your thoughts on Jesus, whom we acknowledge as our apostle and high priest" (Hebrews 3:1 NIV). And what does it mean to be holy? It means to be set apart by God and for His purpose. It means to be hand-picked by God and separated unto Himself for His glory. That is what it means to be holy.

> You are holy if you are in Christ Jesus. Stop trying to be Holy and start living the life that reflects your holiness. And that is in your ability to do through the Holy Spirit who lives in you.

Paul writing his letters would often address the readersas saints – people who are holy. For example, he addresses the Corinthians saints in his first letter in the first chapter. The second verse reads, „To the church of God in Corinth, to those sanctified in Christ Jesus and called to be his holy people, together with all those everywhere who call on the name of our Lord Jesus Christ – their Lord and ours!". In the second letter, he wrote, "Paul, an apostle of Christ Jesus by the will of God, and Timothy our brother, to the church of God in Corinth, together with all his holy people throughout Achaia" (2 Corinthians 1:1 NIV).

Now it is interesting to follow the letter and realize that it was not a perfect Church. They had real moral issues such as Paul said wasn't even heard among the nonbelievers. But he recognized that these were a people washed by the blood of Jesus, despite their weaknesses. Like Hebrews says, „We have been made holy through the sacrifice of the body of Jesus Christ once for all" (Hebrews 10:10 NIV). You are also Holy in Christ Jesus, even while you strive to overcome your weak-nesses by the power of the Holy Spirit.

Prayer

Gracious and Everlasting Father, glory be to your holy name. You have given us more than we might ever grasp in Christ Jesus, making us holy and acceptable in your presence all because of the finished work of Christ Jesus. We receive grace today to live lives holy and consecrated for you. In Jesus' name!

Bible in one year // **2 Kings 17-18, John 3:19-36**

MAY 14

For you are all sons of God through faith in Christ Jesus.
// Galatians 3:26

You are a son

This passage speaks for itself. You are a son of God. It doesn't matter whether you are male or female. If you are in Christ Jesus, you are a son. Once in a while, you will come across Bible versions that say "Sons and daughters". It is just to appease feminists who feel otherwise despised or ignored if the translation is maintained as „Sons". Just as the scripture says, "For you are all sons of God through faith in Christ Jesus. For as many of you as were baptized into Christ have put on Christ. There is neither Jew nor Greek, there is neither slave nor free, there is neither male nor female; for you are all one in Christ Jesus" (Galatians 3:26 - 28).

> You are a son in Christ Jesus, and this has nothing to do with your gender. Rather, it's implications are greater and to your advantage.

A good example is in Hebrews 3:1 which we came across yesterday. In the NIV translation, the verse reads. "Therefore, holy brothers and sisters, who share in the heavenly calling, fix your thoughts on Jesus, whom we acknowledge as our apostle and high priest." However, in many versions that are more literal than contemporary, same passage reads, "Therefore, holy brothers, you who share in a heavenly calling...". These include versions like the KJV and ESV. The word translated to mean brothers, actually only means brothers. It does not mean brothers and sisters. Because he was writing to sons of God, both male and female.

Even in Romans 8:14, The verse reads, „For as many as are led by the Spirit of God, these are sons of God". That was the New King James Version (NKJV). In some versions, to make it more inclusive of the female gender, it is translated: "For all who are led by the Spirit of God are children of God" (NLT). Now there are even those questioning why God is always referred to with the masculine pronoun and not the female. They don't understand this has nothing to do with masculinity or femininity. This is spiritual truth. You are a son in Christ Jesus, even though God might have given you a female body for your earthly purpose! You are a son, and that has implications as you will understand later.

Prayer

Thank You Heavenly Father that I am called a son in Christ Jesus. Born by your Spirit into Your big family. Thank you for revealing truth to me. I receive grace to understand the implications of this sonship and to walk in the light of the duties, authority, and freedom it entails. In Jesus' name!

Bible in one year // **2 Kings 19-21, John 4:1-30**

If children, then heirs – heirs of God and joint heirs with Christ, if indeed we suffer with Him, that we may also be glorified together.
// **Romans 8:17**

MAY 15

You are an heir

Many times, we have failed to grasp what it means to be an heir of God. An heir can be defined as a person legally entitled to the property or rank of another following the death of that person. It usually has to do with the death of the person to be succeeded. And that is what you are – a joint heir with Christ to the throne of God. In other words, God is the one to be succeeded. However, in His will, He has chosen to not be succeeded by Christ alone, but rather to make you a joint heir with Christ. As Paul wrote, "The Spirit Himself bears witness with our spirit that we are children of God, and if children, then heirs – heirs of God and joint heirs with Christ" (Romans 8:16 - 17).

If God was not eternal, you would succeed Him in joint administration with Christ to function in His office and manage all that God has – His wealth. But that is not the case. God lives forever. So what then does it mean to be heirs to someone who will never die? It simply means God has made you a legal administrator of His wealth, giving you the authority to act on His behalf even while He is alive. When He sent Moses, He told Moses "See, I have made you as God to Pharaoh". (Exodus 7:1). What a proclamation! He gave Moses the legal authority to represent Him as God, to act on His behalf.

> You are an heir to the throne of God, His legal representative among men and the administrator of His resources in the Kingdom.

Finally, when they approached the Red Sea, Moses had a word of encouragement for the Israelites. And Moses said to the people, "Do not be afraid. Stand still, and see the salvation of the LORD, which He will accomplish for you today. For the Egyptians whom you see today, you shall see again no more forever. "The LORD will fight for you, and you shall hold your peace (Exodus 14:13 - 14). Good word! But when Moses turned to call on the Lord, He asked Moses, "Why do you cry to Me? Tell the children of Israel to go forward. (Exodus 14:15). The Lord had expected Moses to take responsibility and act on His behalf. He had expected Him to part the waters because He made Moses a legal representative of Himself.

Prayer

Gracious and Everlasting father, maker of heaven and earth and possessor of everything therein, blessed be Your Holy Name. For all we are and all we have in Christ Jesus, we say thank you. We receive grace to walk in authority and knowledge to appropriate all that has been made available to us. In Jesus' name!

Bible in one year // **2 Kings 22:23, John 4:31-54**

MAY 16

> Therefore let no one boast in men. For all things are yours.
> // 1 Corinthians 3:21

All things are yours

Sometimes I say there is no way to preach the full gospel without sounding like what some have termed "prosperity preacher". I get they are going after those who try to use the gospel as the gateway to financial freedom, often abusing the sowing and reaping teachings. While that is scripturally true, the abuse of it is totally bad. It stains the work of the Father and misrepresents His servants who are genuinely and correctly dividing the word of truth. The fact that there are counterfeit currencies have not stopped us from using bank notes. We just learn to separate fake from real.

Even so has God given us all things in Christ Jesus. Yes, prosperity is part of the salvation package. Prosperity is God's idea. The problem is that many want to measure prosperity by the wrong standards, by the cars and mansions and material possessions only. That is wrong! It simply means having sufficient in season to accomplish the purpose of God for your life. Like the Psalmist would say, "The Lord is my Shepherd, I have everything I need" (Psalm 23:1). The bible tells us, "Therefore let no one boast in men. For all things are yours: whether Paul or Apollos or Cephas, or the world or life or death, or things present or things to come – all are yours. And you are Christ's, and Christ is God's (1 Cor 3:21-23).

> **All things are yours: whether people or things, or the world or life or death, or things present or things to come – all are yours in Christ Jesus!**

The heaven, even the heavens, are the LORD's; But the earth He has given to the children of men. (Psalm 115:16). That was written by the Psalmist. He was echoing a truth from creation that God had entrusted the earth to us (Genesis 2:15). However, in Christ Jesus, we have received more – both things in heaven and on earth. Because all that God owns has been entrusted to us as heirs to His throne. Remember, "The earth is the Lord 's, and everything in it. The world and all its people belong to him (Psalm 24:1). That's why He says to us, "All things are yours".

Prayer

Thank you, Father, for you have given me all things that pertain to life and Godliness. You will supply all my needs according to the riches of your glory in Christ Jesus. You have surrounded me with the right people to hold my hand and support my cause for your glory. All things are mine. In Jesus name.

Bible in one year // **2 Kings 24-25, John 5:1-24**

> For if by the one man's offense death reigned through the one, much more those who receive abundance of grace and of the gift of righteousness will REIGN IN LIFE through the one, Jesus Christ. // **Romans 5:17**

MAY 17

You are enthroned

To be enthroned means to be installed in in a place associated with a position of authority or influence, especially during a ceremony to mark the beginning of their rule. And this is true for you in Christ Jesus. Over the past days, we saw that you are righteous. We also saw that you are an heir to the throne of God. That didn't mean you are waiting by the side like Prince Charles of the United Kingdom for a throne you might never seat on. No! Your case is different. You are not just an heir, you are enthroned and positioned to reign. Your rule is already on! Paul writes, "Those who receive abundance of grace and of the gift of righteousness will REIGN IN LIFE through the one, Jesus Christ (Romans 5:17).

No doubt Jesus said, "Behold, I give you the authority to trample on serpents and scorpions, and over all the power of the enemy, and nothing shall by any means hurt you (Luke 10:19). Our reign is now, our hour of authority is on. You are enthroned. You can take authority in your life over circumstances, over the devil and his agents. You and exercise lordship because you have been enthroned. You are a man or a woman in authority. Learn to use it and not make yourself a victim of circumstances or the devil.

> **You have been made a king in Christ Jesus, enthroned with him on a heavenly throne and given the authority to rule and reign in life, to be the master of your destiny and an influence in your world.**

John wrote, "To Him who loved us and washed us from our sins in His own blood, AND HAS MADE US KINGS and priests to His God and Father (Revelation 1:5 - 6). And to make this even clearer, Paul writes, "For he raised us from the dead along with Christ and seated us with him in the heavenly realms because we are united with Christ Jesus (Ephesians 2:6). You are an enthroned King, male or female. Remember? You are a son. That is why the Bible didn't say kings and queens. Even as a female, you are a king in Christ, and this is the hour of your reign. Walk with your head up and exercise your authority in Christ.

Prayer

Heavenly Father, thank you for blessing us with every spiritual blessing in Christ, positioning us to rule above principalities and powers, and granting us grace to influence our world through the gospel and the power of the spirit. Today we walk in dominion over darkness, sicknesses and all that is not of you in our lives. In Jesus name.

Bible in one year // **1 Chronicles 1-3, John 5:25-47**

> Therefore, submit to God. Resist the devil and he will flee from you.
> // James 4:7

MAY 18

You are above the Devil and his cohorts

Paul wrote, "This is the same mighty power that raised Christ from the dead and seated him in the place of honor at God's right hand in the heavenly realms. Now he is far above any ruler or authority or power or leader or anything else – not only in this world but also in the world to come. God has put all things under the authority of Christ and has made him head over all things for the benefit of the church" (Ephesians 1:19 - 22 NLT).

> **You are enthroned above the devil and his cohorts. Do not live in fear of them. Rather exercise your authority in Christ and put them where they belong – under your feet!**

We have been on a journey of understanding what it means to be in Christ and the implications thereof. Today we want to take that truth one step further and remind or enlighten you, that you are enthroned over the devil and His cohorts. Remember, you are seated with Christ above all other powers. Some Christians are so Devil-conscious that it seems the only reason they are in Christ is because they are hiding from the devil. Their first prayer point is often against demons, before they can remember to offer words of praise to our God. Instead of welcoming the Holy Spirit to do great things, they focus on binding the devil and chasing him out of the meeting. Now, there is time to cast and bind. It is important.

However, you must realize that you are not in a power tussle with the devil or demons – Satan and his cohort. They are subject to you. You are enthroned far above their reach. Now that doesn't mean they won't try to raise up their ugly heads. If they should, you have all authority and power to bring them to subjection. The Bible says, "Resist the devil and he will flee from you". (James 4:7). It is a law. He has no option but to flee. However, you must convince him that you understand your spiritual placement and know your rights in Christ. Else you will stand with him in a tug of war. You might even get whipped by the devil. It is not because he is over you but because you are failing to walk in the authority and dominion given to you over him. That is why we are admonished, "Leave no [such] room or foothold for the devil [give no opportunity to him]" (Ephesians 4:27 AMP).

Prayer

Heavenly Father, blessed be your holy name for you daily load us with benefits. Thank you for giving us authority over the devil and his Cohorts. Today we take responsibility and command them off our health, off our paths, off our finances, off our territories and off our communities. In Jesus' name.

Bible in one year // **1 Chronicles 4-6, John 6:1-21**

The Father has delivered and drawn us to Himself out of the control and the dominion of darkness and has transferred us into the kingdom of the Son of His love. // **Colossians 1:13 AMP**

MAY 19

You are not under Satans jurisdication

Jurisdiction means in many terms, the legal right to exercise power, or authority and control over a people, a system or a given territory. It principally refers to the extent of the territory over which that authority is exercised. It defines the boundaries of control for an authority. In legal terms, it is forbidden for an authority to act outside their jurisdiction. That is why when political fugitives cross international borders, their hunters stop the pursuit unless they are willing to start an international conflict with that nation in which the fugitives are. If anything, they will need permission from the new jurisdiction.

Spiritually, there are also jurisdictions. The Kingdom of darkness is a jurisdiction under the dominion and authority of the Devil. He is lord in that territory and over all who are not born again. Really? Yes! Because when Adam sinned, sin entered the world, and by that transaction, he sold human sovereignty over the earth to the Devil (Romans 5:12-14). He gave over humanity and their territory as a colony to the Kingdom of darkness. Remember, "The Heaven is the Lord's but the earth He gave to man" (Psalm 115:16). That's how come Satan has a free pass in the earth and the lives of those who are not born again. Even Jesus said to some people, "You are of your father the devil" (John 8:44).

And Paul adds, "You He made alive, who were dead in trespasses and sins, in which you once walked according to the course of this world, according to the prince of the power of the air, the spirit who now works in the sons of disobedience" (Ephesians 2:1 - 2). Did you see that? The person who is not born again is under the dominionof darkness. But that is different for you if you are in Christ. The Kingdom of God is now the Jurisdiction under which you exist. Our opening verse says, "The Father has delivered and drawn us to Himself out of the authority of darkness and has transferred us into the kingdom of His beloved Son". You are no longer under Satan's jurisdiction. Satan no longer has a say in your life!

> **You were transferred out of the Jurisdiction of Darkness into the Kingdom of God when you received Jesus as Lord. Satan no longer has a say in your life.**

Prayer

> Heavenly Lord, thank you for a new day and the privilege to walk in dominion over him who once had authority over me. As it is written, there is no enchantment against Jacob and no divination against Israel. I am free and above demonic oppressions. In Jesus' name.

Bible in one year // **1 Chronicles 7-9, John 6:22-44**

> No evil shall befall you, nor shall any plague come near your dwelling.
> // **Psalm 91:10**

This is true in Christ

HE WHO dwells in the secret place of the Most High shall remain stable and fixed under the shadow of the Almighty [Whose power no foe can withstand]. I will say of the Lord, He is my Refuge and my Fortress, my God; on Him I lean and rely, and in Him I [confidently] trust! For [then] He will deliver you from the snare of the fowler and from the deadly pestilence. [Then] He will cover you with His pinions, and under His wings shall you trust and find refuge; His truth and His faithfulness are a shield and a buckler.

You shall not be afraid of the terror of the night, nor of the arrow (the evil plots and slanders of the wicked) that flies by day, Nor of the pestilence that stalks in darkness, nor of the destruction and sudden death that surprise and lay waste at noonday. A thousand may fall at your side, and ten thousand at your right hand, but it shall not come near you. Only a spectator shall you be [yourself inaccessible in the secret place of the Most High] as you witness the reward of the wicked.

Because you have made the Lord your refuge, and the Most High your dwelling place, there shall no evil befall you, nor any plague or calamity come near your tent. For He will give His angels [especial] charge over you to accompany and defend and preserve you in all your ways [of obedience and service]. They shall bear you up on their hands, lest you dash your foot against a stone (Heb. 1:14). You shall tread upon the lion and adder; the young lion and the serpent shall you trample underfoot. (Luke 10:19) Because he has set his love upon Me, therefore will I deliver him; I will set him on high, because he knows and understands My name. He shall call upon Me, and I will answer him; I will be with him in trouble, I will deliver him and honor him. With long life will I satisfy him and show him My salvation (Psalm 91:1).

> **The secret place of the Most High is CHRIST! As we saw over the last days, you now understand why this Psalm is true for you – Satan lost his jurisdiction over you. And evil shall not prevail in your life.**

Prayer

Thank You Heavenly Father for bringing me into your secret place in Christ, where I live, I move and have my being. In I him I am secured from the fiery darts of the devil and the schemes of the wicked. In Christ I am restored, my health renewed, and my life filled with good things. In Jesus' name!

Bible in one year // **1 Chronicles 10-12, John 6:45-71**

He made us accepted in the beloved. // **Ephesians 1:6**

MAY 21

You are forever accepted

There is a place where you belong, where you are always loved, where you will always be received – a place where you don't have to measure up or qualify for acceptance. That is in Christ! He chose us in Him before the foundation of the world, that we should be holy and without blame before Him in love, having predestined us to adoption as sons by Jesus Christ to Himself, according to the good pleasure of His will, to the praise of the glory of His grace, by which He made us accepted in the Beloved (Ephesians 1:4 - 6). You were made accepted in the beloved, that is in Christ.

> You are forever accepted in the presence of the father in Christ. Even if you deal with rejection in the world or from people, know there is a place where you fully belong.

It is puzzling sometimes to know how many people deal with rejection. Be it from their natural families, spouses, friends, employers, in-laws, or peers. In their minds, such people don't measure up and will never do. And that's the world we live in. It was not programmed for everyone or every circle to accept you. Even as Christians, when you truly hold firm to Christian values, you will not be accepted by some people in some circles. One question I have heard a lot as a scientist is this, "How can you be a scientist and believe in God?". You see, in their minds, you don't fit in. Talking about Jesus, it is written, "He was despised (looked down upon) and rejected (thought unqualified) by men" (Isaiah 53:3). But they never knew that was the Chief corner stone (Psalm 118:22). Even the builders missed it!

The prodigal son had gone away from home with his share of the inheritance. In his wastefulness, he squandered everything. It finally dawned on him he had a home to go back to, even as a servant. To His surprise, the father was standing at the gates with arms wide open. Didn't ask him about the wealth, didn't question what he had done, but welcomed him home with a great feast. And while the feast was on, it was the other son in anger, questioning the father's actions. This is your story in Christ, you can always run into the arms of the father no matter what you have done or where you have been, you are forever accepted in His presence!

Prayer

Heavenly Father, blessed be your name for the great love you have lavished on us that we should be called your sons. Thank you for making us forever accepted in Christ Jesus. Thank you that we can always run to your warm embrace from the rejection and hatred in the world. In Jesus' name.

Bible in one year // **1 Chronicles 13-15, John 7:1-27**

MAY 22

Giving thanks to the Father who has qualified us to be partakers of the inheritance of the saints in the light. // **Colossians 1:12**

You have an inheritance

We saw at the very beginning that you are a joint-heir with Christ Jesus. That really does imply you have an inheritance. Just Peter highlights, "Blessed be the God and Father of our Lord Jesus Christ, who according to His abundant mercy has begotten us again to a living hope through the resurrection of Jesus Christ from the dead, to an inheritance incorruptible and undefiled and that does not fade away, reserved in heaven for you" (1 Peter 1:3 - 1:4). A lot can be said or written about your inheritance in Christ and how to obtain it.

> You have an inheritance in Christ and through the word of God, you are built up and taught how to appropriate your full package of the inheritance.

My older sister, Beatrice Mbapah, wrote a book titled INHERITANCE, a book I got to contribute in. This subject is very much examined to every detail. There you have everything to discover about your inheritance in Christ and how to take full possession of it. Your inheritance in Christ has to do with all that is rightfully yours in Christ Jesus, things willed for you by the Father. And it is your responsibility to discover what these things are and know how you can be positioned to receive them all – a part in the earth and the rest in eternity.

Paul wrote about how he prayed for the saints, "Giving thanks to the Father who has qualified us to be partakers of the inheritance of the saints in the light" (Colossians 1:12). Yes, we each have an inheritance in Christ. That is why same Paul said, "So now, brethren, I commend you to God and to the word of His grace, which is able to build you up and give you an inheritance among all those who are sanctified (Acts 20:32).

Prayer

Almighty God, maker of heaven and earth, possessor of everything therein, to you be all the praise and adoration. Thank you for qualifying me as an heir and apportioning to me an inheritance in Christ. I receive grace to discover, appropriate and enjoy all the blessings you have lavished on me in this new life. And the wisdom to glorify you in all things. In Jesus' name!

Bible in one year // **1 Chronicles 16-18, John 7:28-53**

If children, then heirs–heirs of God and joint heirs with Christ, if indeed we suffer with Him, that we may also be glorified together.
// **Romans 8:17**

MAY 23

Persecution is yours

We are in the world, but we are not of this world. We live by a set of rules and hold firm to a set of precepts that surpass the laws and standards of men. In this setting, there is bound to be misunderstandings, misjudgment, and misrepresentation of who we are. To its worst, we will always be misfits in certain places. And if some people have the authority and opportunity to stop us, they will try to go at any length to archive that. That is persecution, to be maltreated because of your faith.

Jesus said, "Blessed are you when they revile and persecute you and say all kinds of evil against you falsely for My sake. Rejoice and be exceedingly glad, for great is your reward in heaven, for so they persecuted the prophets who were before you" (Matthew 5:11 - 12). You are blessed to be persecuted. We live in a world with atheists continuously pushing an agenda to see Christianity out of government establishments and public influence. That's persecution. Once in the US, a Christian couple almost lost their bakery in a court case because they refused to make a wedding cake for a lesbian couple. The court judge fined the business with a hundred thousand dollars. That is persecution.

All these are yours in Christ Jesus: The misjudgment, the misrepresentation, and the resentment from people who neither know God nor understand your faith. The apostles were killed for this. Once after being beaten, "The apostles left the high council rejoicing that God had counted them worthy to suffer disgrace for the name of Jesus (Acts 5:41 NLT). All around the world, there are many Christians who can't openly practice their faith, particularly in Asia. China has had a crackdown on churches for having a cross on the buildings. They don't want any cross. Jesus says rejoice when you are persecuted. For exceedingly great is you reward. Don't give in, don't give up. Romans 8:17 says, "If we are to share his glory, we must also share his suffering (NLT).

> **The life in Christ is not all a bed of roses. You also signed up to suffer for his course, knowing that greater is your reward in heaven.**

Prayer

Heavenly Father thank you for the privilege to endure oppositions in the name of Jesus, knowing that greater is my reward in heaven. For what will it profit a me to gain this world and lose my soul? I pray you keep your children across the globe and preserve us from the persecutions of men. In Jesus name.

Bible in one year // **1 Chronicles 19-21, John 8:1-27**

MAY 24

My people are destroyed for lack of knowledge. // **Hosea 4:6**

If these things are true

One reason many people, even ministers criticize "Prosperity preachers" is because they are not able to reconcile their lack with the riches promised in Christ, their poor health with the verse that says „By His stripes you were healed"; they don't connect abundance with the life in Christ because they have known financial and material lack for too long. Their experiences do not reconcile with scriptures. So they settle for the idea that Jesus only brought freedom from sin. But Jesus did more. He said Himself, "I have come that you might have life, and have it to overflowing" (John 10:10). One version puts it this way: "My purpose is to give them a rich and satisfying life" (NLT).

If these things be true of scripture, why does the reality of many people deviate so far from the promises of God? How can this be true? So many people have settled in a position that accepts the defeats of life and denies the truth of the promises of God. In some way, they are shunning the „Prosperity Gospel". This question we will answer in the days ahead, and in the process, show you how to make these great truths a reality in your life. One of the reasons is spiritual immaturity! Paul wrote, "Now I say that the heir, as long as he is a child, does not differ at all from a slave, though he is master of all, but is under guardians and stewards until the time appointed by the father" (Galatians 4:1-2). Another reason is ignorance. As the prophet mourned, "My people are destroyed for lack of knowledge" (Hosea 4:6).

These declarations about you in Christ are true, and there is a way to make them a reality in your life as you grow in your knowledge of God and the principles of this Kingdom life.

Now, while there is an abuse of these teachings of prosperity, and the marketing of the Gospel by some false persons seeking personal gain, it does not change the truth. The Gospel means good news, and that includes the prosperity and wellbeing of the saints. Without prosperity, the message of the Gospel is incomplete. Remember this, „Beloved, I pray that in every way you may succeed and prosper and be in good health [physically], just as [I know] your soul prospers [spiritually]" (3 John 1:2 AMP).

Prayer

Thank You Heavenly Father for another day, knowing you have called me by name and brought me into your great family for a purpose. I receive your promises for me today and the knowledge to make them a reality in my life. And your glory seen through me will draw men to you. In Jesus' name.

Bible in one year // **1 Chronicles 22-24, John 8:28-59**

So now, brethren, I commend you to God and to the word of His grace, which is able to build you up and give you an inheritance among all those who are sanctified. // **Acts 20:32**

MAY 25

Grow into your inheritance

Yesterday we asked a vital question: If these things are true for us in Christ, why does our reality seem far from some of these truths? One reason we said was spiritual immaturity. That therefore presents us with a solution – grow into your inheritance. Even Jesus grew. And until he was an adult, He was subject to His parents, as tutors (Gal 4:1-2). The Bible even says He learned obedience by the things He suffered. As is written, "He was a Son, yet He learned obedience by the things which He suffered. And having been perfected, He became the author of eternal salvation to all who obey Him, called by God as High Priest" (Hebrews 5:8-10).

There are things which are rightfully yours in Christ, but you will need to mature to possess them and live in the reality of some truths. Even though David was anointed king, it was not until several years later that he was officially king over Israel. He had to grow into what was his own. Sometimes, we are not ready to manage the blessings. Other times, it is because we lack the spiritual knowledge of how to make a blessing manifest in our lives.

> **Spiritual maturity prepares you and makes you ready to manage the blessings of God. It also brings with it the knowledge you need to make them manifest in your life.**

But growing up spiritually will position us where we are supposed to be, it brings us into the knowledge of how to take full possession of what is rightfully ours in Christ. That's why Paul could say, "I commend you to God and to the word of His grace, which is able to BUILD YOU UP AND GIVE YOU AN INHERITANCE among all those who are sanctified" (Acts 20:32). Commit yourself to spiritual growth and development. It does not just happen by chance. It comes as you grow in the knowledge of God's word and mature in the understanding of how to obtain results through faith. Then you will grow into all that God has for you as you put His word to work.

Prayer

Heavenly Father thank you for the blessing of a new day. Today we receive grace to grow in our walk with you, to increase in knowledge of you and to understand our responsibility in making manifest your word and promises in our lives. That we might appropriate our inheritance. In Jesus' name.

Bible in one year // **1 Chronicles 25-27, John 9:1-23**

MAY 26

*Blessed is she who believed, for there will be a fulfillment of those things which were told her from the Lord. // **Luke 1:45***

Believe the word

One simple secret in experiencing the blessings of God in Christ Jesus is to believe that they are yours, here and now. Stop arguing with the word and justifying your condition with human philosophies and reasoning. Stop arguing and opposing the blessings you want to see. Don't justify your sickness and why it will continue. If He said you are healed, it doesn't matter what name the disease is called, accept, and believe that you are healed. Stop opposing the prosperity message. Declare prosperity and believe to experience it. Don't justify poverty. Jesus said, "Did I not tell you that if you believe, you will see the glory of God?" (John 11:40 NIV). That is a law of the Spirit. You must believe it in order to experience it.

> **Believe the promises of God to you in Christ and He will cause it to manifest in your life. Don't oppose them or justify your situation that is contrary to the word of promise. Believe the word.**

Is it not funny that we say, "God shall supply all my needs according to His riches in Christ Jesus", but we turn around to say a person declaring financial blessings in Christ is a prosperity preacher? Like I have always indicated, there are those who abuse the message. But the fact that some people abuse truth does not invalidate that truth. The truth remains. Don't oppose truth because it has been abused. Believe the word. As it is written, "Blessed is she who believed, for there will be a fulfillment of those things which were told her from the Lord" (Luke 1:45).

Remember, „For no matter how many promises God has made, they are 'Yes' in Christ. And so, through him the 'Amen' is spoken by us to the glory of God" (2 Corinthians 1:20 NIV). If God says it is yours, just accept it to be so. That is the meaning of believing. Zachariah had a problem receiving because he was focused on justifying his circumstance with Elisabeth the wife. But all he had to do was say like Mary, „Be it unto me according to your word Lord" (Luke 1:38).

Prayer

Thank You Everlasting God for all your promises in Christ are guaranteed to me based on His finished work on the cross. Today I receive health, strength, glory, wealth, virtues and every good thing that you have purposed for me in Christ Jesus. Help me to share this good news to my world. In Jesus' name.

Bible in one year // **1 Chronicles 28-29, John 9:24-41**

His mother said to the servants, "Whatever He says to you, do it".
// John 2:5

MAY 27

Do the word

John records, "On the third day there was a wedding in Cana of Galilee, and the mother of Jesus was there. Now both Jesus and His disciples were invited to the wedding. And when they ran out of wine, the mother of Jesus said to Him, 'They have no wine.' Jesus said to her, 'Woman, what does your concern have to do with Me? My hour has not yet come.' His mother said to the servants, 'Whatever He says to you, do it'" (John 2:1 - 5). The question I sometimes ask is this: Was Jesus the host of this occasion or was He the one who invited the Guests? What was His mother doing when she came to tell Jesus the people were out of wine? Well, that's what good mothers do. They always carry the world's concerns on their shoulders and in the end they make it your own. I have a mother like that. But much more, Mary probably had seen the son turning water into oil or sand into salt – many possibilities.

What is more interesting is that the mother ignored Jesus' taunting question and talked to the servants. She said, "Whatever He says to you, do it". That's the other law of the Spirit. For every blessing in Christ, you would have to find and learn the principles that govern that blessing. And when you know them, do it without questioning.

Leprous men came to Jesus for Healing. Jesus said to them, "Go show yourselves to the priest". Now they could have stood there and argued with Jesus how the priest was not supposed to touch the unclean. They could have asked why He didn't just touch them and heal them, but they went. And behold, on the way, they were made whole. Stop arguing with divine principles. The word says Humble yourself and you will be exalted. That

There are principles that govern different blessings in Christ. Learn them, put the word to practice and you will see the manifestations.

tells you what to do if you want a lifting. It says give and it shall be given to you, sow and you will harvest. But that is where some Christians take offense. For some, you are a good preacher until the day you call them to give. They want the harvest but not the sowing. Do as the Word says, and you will see the manifestations of the blessings.

Prayer

Heavenly Father we acknowledge you today for all you are to us. We rejoice in your love and hope in your promises. As we understand your word, we put them to practice and see the manifestation of your blessings in our lives. We walk in peace, health, wealth and are fully graced to serve you. In Jesus' name.

Bible in one year // **2 Chronicles 1-3, John 10:1-23**

MAY 28

> Do not become sluggish, but imitate those who through faith and patience inherit the promises. // **Hebrews 6:12**

Live by faith

Our experience as believers in Christ is very much anchored on the quality and size of our faith. Even so, appropriating and enjoying all that God has for you in Christ Jesus will be impossible without faith. You must fully understand the concept of faith and how to make it work in other to get godly proves. For the word of God is indeed profitable, there are results to be obtained by the word. Like we saw already, all the promises of God are as good as fulfilled. It is our responsibility to bring them to manifestation through our faith. The writer of Hebrews exhorts us, "Do not become sluggish, but imitate those who through faith and patience inherit the promises" (Hebrews 6:12).

The examples abound throughout scriptures of men who through faith, changed difficult situations that were contrary to God's promise or purpose. This is the reason we are here, to establish the will of God in the earth through partnership with Him. And it is through our faith that we come into partnership with God to make manifest His promises and plans in our lives. Even as it is written, "For we walk by faith, not by sight" (2 Corinthians 5:7).

> **Like believing and doing the word are acts of faith, even so your faith will be responsible for your Christian experience. Refuse to settle for any thing less than God's best for your life. Live by faith.**

It is written of Sarah, "By faith Sarah herself also received strength to conceive seed, and she[d] bore a child when she was past the age, because she judged Him faithful who had promised. Therefore from one man, and him as good as dead, were born as many as the stars of the sky in multitude – innumerable as the sand which is by the seashore" (Hebrews 11:11-12). It was already promised her by God, it was always part of His plan. But without faith, it seemingly would have ended as mere wishes. The Spirit expressly says, "By faith, Sarah received strength to conceive seed". Her faith brought to manifestation the blessings of God in her life. This is what we must do. We must imitate those who through faith and patience, obtained the promises.

Prayer

Heavenly Father, thank you for your grace in my life. That I am enabled to walk by faith and not by sight; to imitate those who through faith and patience inherit the promises you have. I receive grace to see every opportunity to put faith to work for supernatural results. In Jesus' name.

Bible in one year // **2 Chronicles 4-6, John 10:24-42**

The testimony about Christ was confirmed among you, so that you do not lack any spiritual gift as you eagerly wait for the revelation of our Lord Jesus Christ. // **1 Cor 1:6-7 HCSB**

MAY 29

Fully equiped for service

One reason many Christians shy away from positions of responsibility in the house of God is because they often feel inadequate and unprepared. They are waiting and praying for a spiritual gift so they can serve the Lord with it. This is an error! Our opening verse says that „You do not lack any spiritual gift". Now while that was with regards to the body of Christ in Corinth, it does highlight a truth. You have been fully endowed with spiritual gifts with which you should be serving the Lord. Stop waiting for anothe gift and start using the gifts of the Spirit in your life ifyou are not yet doing so. He will add other gifts when the need arises. Sometimes, even the gifts you are praying for are already in you. But you will not see them until you step out in faith.

Paul wrote, "I always thank my God for you because of God's grace given to you in Christ Jesus, that by Him you were enriched in everything – in all speech and all knowledge. In this way, the testimony about Christ was confirmed among you, so that you do not lack any spiritual gift as you eagerly wait for the revelation of our Lord Jesus Christ" (1 Corinthians 1:4

> In Christ, you are endowed with every Spiritual grace and virtue for service, and you can always grow while on the task. Stop waiting and start serving!

Don't be cheated or deceived by the whispers of the devil asking you if you are good enough, if you are qualified or if there isn't someone better to do the task. You are the one for the task! If it came to your heart, then jump out for it. You might never know who is waiting just for you. Someone recently shared their testimony of how Your Daily Light devotional inspired them to start writing a new devotional that is reaching many others. How amazing! There is a world of people only you can reach and while we wait for the coming of the Lord, you are fully equipped with the gifts you need to serve Him in season and reach those in your world. Now that does not mean you don't need training. Go for training if you have to. But don't idly wait for spiritual virtues the Lord has already bestowed upon you for service in His Kingdom.

Prayer

Thank You Heavenly Father for I am equipped with the gifts of the Spirit for service to you and for men. I receive more grace to do more. I receive the courage to stay at it in the face of opposition. I pray that my works will be acceptable in your sight as I show forth your praise. In Jesus' name.

Bible in one year // **2 Chronicles 7-9, John 11:1-29**

MAY 30

> You have given me greater joy than those who have abundant harvests of grain and new wine. // **Psalm 4:7 NLT**

Unspeakable joy

Of all the things we have received in Christ Jesus, unspeakable joy is one of the most important. And this for many reasons we would not be able to consider today. That is one reason there is such an attack on the joys of men, every effort by the enemy to keep them depressed. For a depressed person can hardly glorify God. They are easily overwhelmed with all that is not where it should be that they will hardly focus on the blessings of God that inspires thanksgiving. Depression will also make a person ineffective in anything they have to do for others or for the Lord. At its worst, its impact on those who love us can be overwhelming. It becomes contagious if those around it do not really mount guards on their own hearts.

> If you are born again, then you have received the Holy Spirit who brings into your spirit the joy of the Lord – joy unspeakable. Therefore, choose to be joyful and let nothing steal your joy.

But that is not the life God has called us to. We have better in Christ Jesus – unspeakable joy through the Holy Spirit. It is first a fruit of the spirit, one of the many things which are naturally present in an individual because of the presence of the Holy Spirit. "But the Holy Spirit produces this kind of fruit in our lives: love, joy, peace, patience, kindness, goodness, faithfulness, gentleness, and self-control" (Galatians 5:22-23 NLT). This implies if you are born-again, unspeakable joy is fully yours.

This joy is not a joy that comes because all things are going well in your life. It is a joy that is of the Lord. It is the joy of the Lord flowing out of us. Jesus said this with reference to the Holy Spirit, "Anyone who is thirsty may come to me! Anyone who believes in me may come and drink! For the Scriptures declare, 'Rivers of living water will flow from his heart.'" (When he said, "living water," he was speaking of the Spirit, who would be given to everyone believing in him" (John 7:37-39 NLT). If you have the Holy Spirit, you don't even need to pray and ask God to give you joy. He already gave you all the joy you could ever get by putting His Spirit in you. What you need to do is to learn how to manage that joy and make it a reality in your life every day. For example, meditating on the great blessings that are yours in Christ.

Prayer

Heavenly Father, thank you for the joy of the Holy Spirit poured out in my heart and giving me the capacity to experience unspeakable joy in every day. Even through challenging times, I will rejoice in you always, knowing that all things will work together for my good. In Jesus' name.

Bible in one year // **2 Chronicles 10-12, John 11:30-57**

Yet you are holy, enthroned on the praises of Israel.
// **Psalm 22:3 NLT**

MAY 31

Praise led the way

There is a profound truth hidden in the order of procession of the Israelites when they journeyed from Sinai as they headed for the promised land. God gave Moses an order by which the tribes ought to proceed with Judah leading the way (Numbers 10:13-28). If it were according to birth order, the tribe of Reuben should have led. If it were by responsibility, the priestly tribe of Levi should have led; but that was not the case. It was Judah who led the way. When the people set out for the first time, following the instructions the Lord had given through Moses, Judah's troops led the way (Numbers 10:13 - 14 NLT)

But why Judah? The name Judah literally means praise (Genesis 29:35). And as it is written, "Yet you are holy, enthroned on the praises of Israel" (Psalm 22:3 NLT), God inhabits the praise of his people. That is why Psalm 114 reads, "When Israel went out of Egypt, the house of Jacob from a people of strange language; JUDAH WAS HIS SANCTUARY, and Israel his dominion". In other words, the tribe of Judah, which was symbolic of praise, became God's dwelling, the place of His habitation. Then the effect of God's presence inhabiting Judah was seen as dominion over Israel, giving them the victory everywhere.

> God inhabits the praise of His people, and His presence guarantees the victory. Therefore, go with praise on your lips and you will always see God's presence manifested in victory.

As a consequence, "The sea saw it, and fled: Jordan was driven back. The mountains skipped like rams, and the little hills like lambs"...Then the Psalmist continues to testify, "What's wrong, Red Sea, that made you hurry out of their way? What happened, Jordan River, that you turned away? Why, mountains, did you skip like rams? Why, hills, like lambs? Tremble, O earth, at the presence of the Lord, at the presence of the God of Jacob" (Psalm 114:5 - 7 NLT). In that procession with praise leading the way, they became unstoppable. God's presence was with them, giving them the victory all because praise led the way.

Prayer

Gracious and Almighty God, blessed be your holy name. For you daily bear us up, keeping us from the fowler's snares, instructing us in the way we should go, surrounding us with support systems to help us in times of need. For all you are and all you do, we give you praise in Jesus' name.

Bible in one year // **2 Chronicles 13-14, John 12:1-26**

JUNE

The blessing of the LORD makes one rich, And He adds no sorrow with it.
// **Proverbs 10:22**

JUN 1

Understand the blessing

It is sometimes common that the definition of the words we use the most elude us. We have probably mastered the usage of the words with only a partial understanding of their meaning. This is even more true when it comes to spiritual vocabulary; partly because our understanding of certain words or concepts can be clouded by the world's perspective from where we are coming. That is why the bible admonishes us, "Do not conform to the pattern of this world, but be transformed by the renewing of your mind" (Romans 12:2 NIV). And that is one reason for Your Daily Light, to give us divine perspectives.

One such spiritual word that I bring to your attention today is "Blessing". In some form, this word probably does not escape your lips in the day as we all commonly tell people, "God bless you". A clear understanding will help us use the word with more intentionality, understanding the implications thereof. Importantly, it is worth noting that often, English dictionaries cannot help you with accurate definitions of some spiritual words such as the word blessing, because it is beyond their scope.

> The blessing is a supernatural divine endowment upon your life that creates an enabling atmosphere for success and progress; an atmosphere in which negatives do not thrive.

Thank God for our teacher the Holy Spirit who leads us into all truths. And with His help, I will give you a definition. The blessing is a supernatural endowment or spiritual deposit by God upon a life, which creates for the individual, an atmosphere that enables and enhances their success and progress in all things; an atmosphere in which nothing negative can thrive. That is the blessing. Just like our opening passage puts it, "The blessing of the Lord makes a man rich and with it, He adds no sorrow". It is written of Isaac at a time of famine, "Isaac planted crops in that land and the same year reaped a hundredfold, because the Lord blessed him. The man became rich, and his wealth continued to grow until he became very wealthy" (Genesis 26:). Isaac was supernaturally endowed to prosper in all things. And this is your story too. You are blessed if you are in Christ.

Prayer

Gracious and everlasting father, thank you for daily loading us with benefits. Thank you for your blessing that makes rich and with it comes no sorrow. This season, we rejoice in your goodness and reject every cause for sorrow, that only your will and purpose will be established in our lives. In Jesus name.

Bible in one year // **2 Chronicles 15-16, John 12:27-50**

> The Lord went before them by day in a pillar of cloud to lead the way, and by night in a pillar of fire to give them light, so as to go by day and night.
> // **Exodus 13:21**

JUN 2

Understand the blessing Pt. 2

We defined the blessing yesterday as a supernatural endowment or spiritual deposit by God upon a life, which creates for the individual an atmosphere that enables and enhances their success and progress in all things; an atmosphere in which nothing negative can thrive. That is clearly echoed in Proverbs 10:22 when it says, "The blessing of the Lord makes rich and with it, He adds no sorrow". To paint a better picture of what this definition means, we will relate to the journey of the Israelites as the Lord moved them from Egypt to the promised land.

> **The blessing of the Lord upon a life is like a measure of the cloud of His presence that rests over that person and creates a conducive and favorable atmosphere for their wellbeing and prosperity.**

You can think of the blessing to be a cloud that permanently rests above a person, creating an atmosphere for success, progress, and wellbeing about them, irrespective of their natural environment or the prevailing circumstances where they are. They carry over them their own divine atmosphere, enabling them to thrive against natural circumstances. And under that cloud, nothing that should work in opposition to their wellbeing is allowed to thrive; anything negative only diminishes away if by some means they came under that cloud. We are talking of a spiritual invisible cloud. This is not just an illustration but the reality of what it means to be blessed. It is to have the lord measure out a cloud of His presence upon your life.

It was written of Joseph even as a slave, "The Lord was with Joseph so that he prospered, and he lived in the house of his Egyptian master. When his master saw that the Lord was with him and that the Lord gave him success in everything he did, Joseph found favor in his eyes and became his attendant. Potiphar put him in charge of his household, and he entrusted to his care everything he owned. From the time he put him in charge of his household and of all that he owned, the Lord blessed the household of the Egyptian because of Joseph. The blessing of the Lord was on everything Potiphar had, both in the house and in the field (Genesis 39:2-5 NIV). Do you notice that? The blessing of the Lord was ON EVERYTHING, causing the estate to flourish".

Prayer

Heavenly Father thank you for the cloud of your presence upon my life that creates about me an atmosphere for success irrespective of what is happening in my surrounding or the prevailing circumstances in the world. And I will see your goodness in the land of the living. In Jesus' name.

Bible in one year // **2 Chronicles 17-18, John 13:1-20**

For all of God's promises have been fulfilled in Christ with a resounding "Yes!" And through Christ, our "Amen" (which means "Yes") ascends to God for his glory. // **2 Corinthians 1:20 NLT**

JUN 3

The choice is yours

Blessed is the man who walks not in the counsel of the ungodly, nor stands in the path of sinners, nor sits in the seat of the scornful; but his delight is in the law of the LORD, and in His law he meditates day and night. He shall be like a tree planted by the rivers of water, that brings forth its fruit in its season, whose leaf also shall not wither; and whatever he does shall prosper. The ungodly are not so but are like the chaff which the wind drives away. Therefore, the ungodly shall not stand in the judgment, nor sinners in the congregation of the righteous. For the LORD knows the way of the righteous, but the way of the ungodly shall perish. (Psalm 1:1 - 6)

It is very much the case that God has given us the liberty to choose, even on things that can be our own destruction. That is one thing He gave us and would not take away - our will. Moses told the Israelites, "I call heaven and earth as witnesses today against you, that I have set before you life and death, blessing and cursing; therefore, choose life, that both you and your descendants may live (Deuteronomy 30:19). He made known to them options and counseled them on what was beneficial. However it was not going to be imposed on anyone what to do. You choose what outcome you are ready to experience and act accordingly. That is the summary of the Psalm above.

> **The Choice is yours to make in many things, it is yours to choose to be the blessed one.**

You can choose to be the blessed one by doing what it says. And you can also choose away from the paths of blessing. The choice is made even easier for us in this generation. For the blessing is far beyond words of instructions of dos and don'ts. The choice really is the decision to chose Jesus. For He is the Heir to all the blessings and promises of God. And when you accept Jesus, you receive Him with all the blessings of God. Just as it is written, "For all the promises of God in Him are Yes, and in Him Amen, to the glory of God through us" (2 Corinthians 1:20). To choose the blessing is to choose Jesus as Lord.

Prayer

> Gracious Lord thank you for making plain your ways to us, giving us Light for every day that we might know your ways and walk in your paths. Today I choose to be the blessed one, rightly positioned for all the good things you have purposed for them that love you. In Jesus name.

Bible in one year // **2 Chronicles 19-20, John 13:21-38**

JUN 4

> For if by the one man's offense death reigned through the one, much more those who receive abundance of grace and of the gift of righteousness will reign in life through the One, Jesus Christ. // **Romans 5:17**

By the one man

One great blessing we would have as individuals in our walk with Christ and even as a Church, will be the full understanding of the covenants of God, particularly the Old and the New testaments. To know what was before and what is now, being able to separate the two in their application to our dispensation. Yesterday we exhorted you on the need to choose right, to choose to be the blessed one by choosing Jesus.

Under the Law, according to the Old Testament, you were blessed by doing the things you were commanded to do and cursed by doing the contrary. Making the choice to be the blessed one was about choosing to walk in the ways of the Lord. As good as that is, and still applies today, there is a new dispensation. The choice to make is really about Jesus. If you would choose Him or not. If you received Him or not. That is truly where the blessing is, the blessing is in Christ. For Jesus is the heir of all things and to him has been conferred all the blessings of God.

> **To choose to be the blessed one is about the choice to be in Christ. For that is where all the blessings of God have been richly made available to all humanity.**

On the contrary, we all by our natural descend from Adam, partook of his sin and by it, the consequences thereof. But God through Jesus offered us another opportunity to a blessed life, far from every curse. In fact, you could not even be cursed. It is written, "All praise to God, the Father of our Lord Jesus Christ, who has blessed us with every spiritual blessing in the heavenly realms because we are united with Christ" (Ephesians 1:3 NLT). By the one man, sin and all its associated negatives came into the world, but even much more were the blessings made available to us by the one man, Jesus Christ. And in this present dispensation, to choose to be the blessed one is to choose to be in Christ.

Prayer

Heavenly Father thank you for blessing me with every spiritual blessing in Christ Jesus. For by Him I have been delivered from the dominion of sin and its curse and brought into the Kingdom of Light. Thank you for blessing me and making me a blessing in Jesus' name.

Bible in one year // **2 Chronicles 21-22, John 14**

So all who put their faith in Christ share the same blessing Abraham received because of his faith. // **Galatians 3:9 NLT**

JUN 5

It is of faith

Paul writes a letter to the Galatians with an open rebuke. These were a people who had begun a walk of faith with the Lord but had become caught in the prevailing teachings of the Jews. They were trying to obtain by works, their own efforts and merits, the things God had freely given to them in Christ Jesus. He asks them a very bold and seemingly derogatory question: "You foolish Galatians! Who has bewitched you? Before your very eyes Jesus Christ was clearly portrayed as crucified" (Galatians 3:1 NIV). Then he goes on with reference to the law to help them realize they were blessed because they had put their faith in Jesus, not because of the works of the law they could fulfill.

> The blessing of God for us is first of faith, for by the law shall no one measure up or qualify for all that God has for us in Christ Jesus.

Paul wrote, "Therefore know that only those who are of faith are sons of Abraham. And the Scripture, foreseeing that God would justify the Gentiles by faith, preached the gospel to Abraham beforehand, saying, 'In you all the nations shall be blessed.' So then those who are of faith are blessed with believing Abraham. For as many as are of the works of the law are under the curse; for it is written, 'Cursed is everyone who does not continue in all things which are written in the book of the law, to do them'" (Galatians 3:7-10).

It is a likelihood for us today to quickly shift from a place of faith and total reliance on the finished work of Christ to obtain the blessings, and to become caught up in a legalistic life where we try to do certain things so that we would not be cursed but will receive the blessing. That does not apply to us. You could not be cursed in Christ Jesus, not even for failing for doing certain things. For a blessing only is what you were called to inherit. And it is of faith that we are blessed, that faith that you had to receive and accept Jesus as Lord. He redeemed us in order that the blessing promised to Abraham would come to the Gentiles in Christ Jesus, so that by faith we might receive the promise of the Spirit (Galatians 3:14).

Prayer
> Heavenly Father, thank you for taking the burden of ever trying to qualify for your blessings in Christ Jesus off our shoulders. For in our own abilities, even our best of righteous acts would be like filthy rags in your sight. But you have qualified us to partake in the inheritance of the saints. In Jesus' name.

Bible in one year // **2 Chronicles 23-24, John 15**

> No curse can touch Jacob; no magic has any power against Israel. For now it will be said of Jacob, "What wonders God has done for Israel!"
> // **Numbers 23:23 NLT**

JUN 6

No room for a curse

The above verse were the words of the Prophet Balaam to Balack, the Moabite king. It had happened that as God led the Children of Israel from Egypt towards the land of Canaan, He made them victorious in every battle, except in seasons when they failed to follow His counsel or wisdom. They were one blessed people programmed to succeed and overcome every obstacle in their path. You might remember what it means to be blessed from previous days lessons. On this Occasion, as the Israelites approached the Moabite territory, their King Balack sought to be victorious over them in battle, and for this he had a strategy.

> **There is no room for a curse in your life, you were called to inherit a blessing and a blessing only. And whom God has blessed cannot be cursed.**

The Bible records, "The king of Moab said to the elders of Midian, 'This mob will devour everything in sight, like an ox devours grass in the field!' So Balak, king of Moab, sent messengers to call Balaam son of Beor... His message said: 'Look, a vast horde of people has arrived from Egypt. They cover the face of the earth and are threatening me. Please come and curse these people for me because they are too powerful for me. Then perhaps I will be able to conquer them and drive them from the land. I know that blessings fall on any people you bless, and curses fall on people you curse'" (Numbers 22:4 - 6 NLT).

Balack understood the power of a curse – the very opposite of a blessing. As you might remember, we defined a blessing to be a supernatural endowment or spiritual deposit upon a life, which creates for the individual an atmosphere that enables and enhances their success and progress in all things; an atmosphere in which nothing negative can thrive. In contrast, a curse is a spell upon an individual that programs them to fail and be unsuccessful in an aspect or all areas of life. Balack, the King hired Balaam that he might pronounce a curse upon Israel and make them vincible in battle. But there was no room for a curse for Israel, no opportunity for one to thrive. And this is your story in Christ Jesus. Just like it was for Israel, there is no room for a curse in your life if you are born again. You cannot be cursed, neither can any proclaimed words of curse prevail in your life if you have this knowledge of truth.

Prayer

Heavenly Father, thank you for the surpassing power of your blessing upon my life which leaves no room for a curse. We are blessed in our going out and in our coming in. The negative utterances and words of others, such as do not conform to your purpose for us cannot prevail in our lives. In Jesus name.

Bible in one year // **2 Chronicles 25-27, John 16**

It is like the dew of Hermon, descending upon the mountains of Zion;
for there the Lord commanded the blessing – Life forevermore.
// **Psalm 133:3**

JUN 7

Be rightly positioned

Sometimes we can be wrongly positioned, and the consequence will be a failure in the manifestation of divine blessings in our lives. It matters where you are, where you live and where you fellowship. These can have such a great play on the manifestation of God's blessings in your life. This has to do with both physical location at a season in time as well as your spiritual placement in God. The Psalmist wrote, "How good and pleasant it is when brothers live together in unity! It is like precious oil poured on the head, running down on the beard, running down on Aaron's beard, down upon the collar of his robes. It is as if the dew of Hermon were falling on Mount Zion. For THERE the Lord bestows his blessing, even life forevermore (Psalm 133:1-3 NIV).

In a time of drought and famine, the Lord spoke to the prophet Elijah, „Leave here, turn eastward and hide in the Kerith Ravine, east of the Jordan. You will drink from the brook, and I have ordered the ravens to feed you there" (1 Kings 17:3-4). His blessings of supplies were guaranteed in that place where the Lord led him to be positioned in season. In a parallel story, Isaac was going to go down to Egypt at a time of famine, but the Lord stopped him from doing so. He became rightly position for the manifestation of God's blessings (Gen 26:12-13).

We read of the early Church in Acts 4:33, "With great power the apostles continued to testify to the resurrection of the Lord Jesus, and much grace was upon them all" (NIV). Just like the Psalmist wrote, there the Lord bestows His blessing, even so He bestowed His grace in great measure upon the believers as they gathered in fellowship. This is one reason it is important to belong to a local church and meet with other saints. For in that meeting and fellowship, the Lord commands His blessing. Also give attention to the Lord to guide and lead your steps in life, for in His paths he has laid up everything you need for life. There indeed the Lord has commanded the blessing.

> Make sure you are part of a church family where you meet with other saints and be in God's will for your life. For THERE, He commands the blessings.

Prayer

Thank you, Heavenly Father, for the blessing of the Holy Spirit, that by Him you can lead us in the way we should go and bring us into the places where the things you have for us are prepared. Even in this season, help us to be rightly positioned in the church in the atmosphere of your grace. In Jesus' name.

Bible in one year // **2 Chronicles 28-29, John 17**

> The Lord bless you and keep you; the Lord make His face shine upon you and be gracious to you; the Lord lift up His countenance upon you and give you peace. // **Numbers 6:24-26**

JUN 8

The priestly blessing

Growing up at a Baptist Church before my teenage years, I often sat with my dad together at the back of the Church. It was traditional and is still the case in most Baptist Churches in Cameroon to have on the service program a section termed "Benediction", usually the last on the agenda just before the service officially comes to an end. As I sat behind with my dad, on multiple occasions, I observed people would leave immediately after the sermon. In my mind as a kid, it planted in me the thought that the most important aspects of the service was done. So as I grew up into the teenage years, I came to practice the same. It was as good for me to be late and as well leave before the benediction.

> **Never make light the blessings proclaimed upon you by your pastor or spiritual leader, these are words the Lord expects and looks to honor.**

However, this changed as I found out in scripture when I was about 19 years old. It was a command from the Lord to the priests to bless his people as they went away after a holy gathering and time of communion. It was this passage: The Lord said to Moses, "Tell Aaron and his sons, 'This is how you are to bless the Israelites. Say to them: 'The Lord bless you and keep you; the Lord make his face shine on you and be gracious to you; the Lord turn his face toward you and give you peace.'" "So they will put my name on the Israelites, and I will bless them" (Numbers 6:22-27 NIV).

This was a very biblical practice and principle, the ministers were placing in some sense, divine words upon the people, words the Lord himself looked forward to honor. I learned I was every time excluding myself from the priestly blessings by walking out earlier. This could be you too. Or maybe you never realized before today the potency of the words from a minister or your pastor when they say to you, "God bless you". Those words are indeed potent and command upon your life priestly blessings you will live to experience when you receive them with faith.

Prayer

Heavenly Father, thank you for the ministers and shepherds you have given to us, shepherds after your own hearts. Inspired by your Spirit, give them utterance always to proclaim the right words of blessings upon your flock. And as they do, cause the full manifestation for your glory. In Jesus' name.

Bible in one year // **2 Chronicles 30-31, John 18:1-18**

The generous soul will be made rich, and he who waters will also be watered himself. // **Proverbs 11:25**

JUN 9

Be a blessing

The very promise of God to Abraham is the same promise to which you are an heir. It is also to you today the words written: I will bless you and you will be a blessing (Genesis 12:2). You are blessed so you can yourself be a blessing to another person. Be it your spiritual giftings, material resources or knowledge in a given area. You have been blessed with that of God so that someone will have reasons to glorify him because of you as you consciously make yourself an available blessing to others.

> Be the blessing you are called to be to those around you and you will be enriched.

James shares with us a practical example. What good is it, my brothers and sisters, if someone claims to have faith but has no deeds? Can such faith save them? Suppose a brother or a sister is without clothes and daily food. 16If one of you says to them, "Go in peace; keep warm and well fed," but does nothing about their physical needs, what good is it? (James 2:14-16).

Remember the wise words of proverbs 11:25, Whoever brings blessing will be enriched, and one who waters will himself be watered (ESV). You only make room for more in your life when you make yourself an available channel for the blessings of the Lord to flow unto others. Don't be a selfish and self-centered person whose focus is to see how he look out only for his own wellbeing and care less about those you have an opportunity to bless. Be a blessing to someone and you will be enriched. Just as scripture commands us, "Therefore, whenever we have the opportunity, we should do good to everyone–especially to those in the family of faith" (Galatians 6:10 NLT).

Prayer

Heavenly Father, thank you for blessing me and making me a blessing to my world that I might be the reason for many smiles. Even today, open my eyes to the opportunities to be a blessing to others that they might overflow in thanksgiving towards you. And I will not be any means miss my reward in Jesus' name.

Bible in one year // **2 Chronicles 32-33, John 18:19-40**

JUN 10

"Anyone who receives you receives me, and anyone who receives me receives the Father who sent me" // **Matthew 10:40 NLT**

Receive a sent one

It is interesting to look at Israel sometimes and to see that some people are still waiting for the first coming of Christ. They are looking forward to receiving the Messiah as was promised to them through the prophets of old. They are looking forward to what happed already, just it did not happen as they expected. They missed out on the hour of their visitation. To some, Jesus was just another prophet. To others, he was even a false prophet. And by their failure to receive the one whom God sent, they miss out on all He brought for them.

> God has appointed and sent out people into his vineyard with a mantle to distribute his blessings, and it is in our interest to recognize and receive them in the name of the Lord, for therein lies for us a blessing.

Jesus said to His disciples when he sent them out: "Whenever you enter a city or village, search for a worthy person and stay in his home until you leave town. When you enter the home, give it your blessing. If it turns out to be a worthy home, let your blessing stand; if it is not, take back the blessing. If any house-hold or town refuses to welcome you or listen to your message, shake its dust from your feet as you leave. I tell you the truth, the wicked cities of Sodom and Gomorrah will be better off than such a town on the judgment day" (Matthew 10:11-15 NLT). Then Jesus added, "Anyone who receives you receives me, and anyone who receives me receives the Father who sent me" (Matthew 10:40 NLT).

This is true also today. God has blessed the Church with ministers, people He has sent out into His vineyard to bring good tidings to His people. Ephesians 4:11 tells us, Christ chose some of us to be apostles, prophets, evangelists, pastors, and teachers. These positions come along with a divine mantle as distributors of divine blessings. We who are called into these special offices come with divine blessings. It is in the interest of an individual to recognize and receive a sent one. Just like Jesus said in our passage above, they bring to you blessings that you can receive or forfeit. Never fall in the error of joining others to deny someone as a minister without a sure discerning word from the Lord. For many in so doing, have pushed away their own heavenly blessings by not receiving the one God has sent to them.

Prayer

Heavenly Father, thank you for your daily illumination in the word as you lead us to take hold of all that you have in store for us. We receive grace to recognize those you have sent to us that we might receive them rightly, and with it, receive the blessings you have entrusted to them for our good. In Jesus name.

Bible in one year // **2 Chronicles 34-36, John 19:1-22**

Whoever gives one of these little ones only a cup of cold water in the name of a disciple, assuredly, I say to you, he shall by no means lose his reward. // **Romans 10:42**

JUN 11

Seize the opportunities

We must search the scriptures and know the mind of God on a subject and not be carried away by unnecessary arguments between people with conflicting opinions. There are those who have made it their goal to promote an agenda that discourages giving to the Church or to ministers. It is not that we do not recognize there could be abuse by some people. You must not let such persons who tarnish the work of the Lord, cheat you out of the knowledge of the truth. It is indeed your opportunity for a blessing always to give to one sent by the Lord, an opportunity you should seize.

Just as Jesus said, "Whoever welcomes a prophet as a prophet will receive a prophet's reward, and whoever welcomes a righteous person as a righteous person will receive a righteous person's reward. And if anyone gives even a cup of cold water to one of these little ones who is my disciple, truly I tell you, that person will certainly not lose their reward" (Matthew 10:41-42 NIV). This word is valid and true, and will remain true until Jesus comes. It is important to note that in context, these little ones referred to the disciples he was sending out to preach.

The story is written of Elijah who was sent off to the widow of Zeraphat (1 Kings 17:7-16). It was for the widow's sake that the brook dried up. And the widow responding in obedience to a opportunity to attend to the minister's need, was together with her son sustained with abundant supply in a time of famine. Ministers sure feel refreshed and are thankful to be received by those they are sent to. However, it is important for you as an individual to recognize that it is to your advantage to give to them who labor for you spiritually. Know that you guarantee for yourself heavenly blessings in doing so – such as money cannot buy.

> **Seize the opportunities that come your way to give to them that labor for you in the Lord, for it guarantees divine blessings.**

Prayer

Heavenly Father, thank you for them that labor for us in the kingdom, who daily bear our burdens in prayer, nourish us with the word and make themselves available as listening ears and counselors when we need it most. Help us to recognize their sacrifices and labor of love that we might appreciate them in our giving. In Jesus name.

Bible in one year // **Ezra 1-2, John 19:23-42**

JUN 12

> He who looks into the perfect law of liberty and continues in it, and is not a forgetful hearer but a doer of the work, this one will be blessed in what he does. // **James 1:25**

Be a doer of the Word

James writes to his readers, "But be doers of the word, and not hearers only, deceiving yourselves. For if anyone is a hearer of the word and not a doer, he is like a man observing his natural face in a mirror; for he observes himself, goes away, and immediately forgets what kind of man he was. But he who looks into the perfect law of liberty and continues in it, and is not a forgetful hearer but a doer of the work, this one will be blessed in what he does" (James 1:22-25).

James highlighted that the person who is a doer and not just a reader will be blessed in what he does. And that is where the power of God's word lies. It is not in the hearing only, although just hearing the word of God accomplishes something. For faith comes by hearing and hearing by the word of God (Romans 10:17). However, it does not profit you just to listen and know in your heart what the bible says. The blessing is in the doing of the word. Even as Your Daily Light comes to you, don't just read and nod your head in agreement and say to yourself this is good. Let it inspire you to action.

> **In every regard, don't be a listener or a reader of the word only, be a doer of the word of God. For therein lies the blessing.**

The word of God is a mirror that shows us who we are and how we are called to live. Like the psalmist puts it, "Blessed is the man who doesn't walk in the counsel of the wicked… Instead, he finds pleasure in obeying the Lord's commands; he meditates on his commands day and night." (Psalm 1:1-2). And because he does this, David adds, "That person is like a tree planted by streams of water, which yields its fruit in season and whose leaf does not wither– whatever they do prospers". Like James puts it, you deceive your own self if you are only a hearer. For example, you were exhorted in the last days to consciously make yourself a blessing to someone as well as bless those who invest in you spiritually. That was a call to action. And as you respond to that word in action, you will be blessed in all you do.

Prayer

Heavenly Father, thank you for your Holy Spirit in us who enables us to do your word as you work in us, causing us to will and to do according to your good pleasure.
We receive grace to be doers of the word and not hearers only, that we might prosper in all our ways as you cause us to flourish in our endeavors. In Jesus' name.

Bible in one year // **Ezra 3-5**, John 20

Jesus asked them, "When I sent you without purse, bag or sandals, did you lack anything?" "Nothing," they answered. // **Luke 22:35**

JUN 13

An example to emulate

As much as there is so much controversy about giving to ministers, sometimes because of the ignorance of many believers or their experiences with wolves in sheep clothing who rubbed them in the past, it is important that you do not in your own way fuel the misconception that you are serving the Lord for material gain. Choose to give dignity to your ministry and deprive people without understanding from boastings that will not help your work in the Lord. Follow Paul's example. He wrote of himself:

Was it a sin for me to lower myself in order to elevate you by preaching the gospel of God to you free of charge? I robbed other churches by receiving support from them so as to serve you. And when I was with you and needed something, I was not a burden to anyone, for the brothers who came from Macedonia supplied what I needed. I have kept myself from being a burden to you in any way, and will continue to do so. As surely as the truth of Christ is in me, nobody in the regions of Achaia will stop this boasting of mine (2 Corinthians 11:7-10).

> As one who ministers to others, never give the impression of desperation as if God who called you fails in his responsibility to care for you. Give your ministry the dignity that comes with the call.

God who called us is too big to supply our every need in diverse ways (Luke 22:35). Never set your eyes on the pockets of those you minister to, set your eyes on God for your supplies, knowing that He can use anyone from anywhere to bless you. And if the Lord leads you, establish independent sources of finance so that your life and family will not seem to depend on the mercy of those you minister to. Though you need ministry partners, it is not everyone you should welcome in that capacity or share financial burdens with. Let God lead you to people who recognize the privilege it is to take part in sponsoring a heavenly vision. For such people give gladly and themselves count it a privilege to do so. They give knowing that their reward from the Lord is sure.

Prayer

Father thank you who called us to your service. Thank you for daily bearing our burdens and supplying all our needs according to your riches in Christ Jesus. We receive wisdom to deal diligently in dealing with material things that we will not misrepresent you. In Jesus' name.

Bible in one year // **Ezra 6-8, John 21**

JUN 14

> Obey those who rule over you, and be submissive, for they watch out for your souls, as those who must give account. // **Hebrews 13:17**

The order of blessing

The writer of Hebrews takes on a discourse to show that Abraham who is the father of faith was lesser than Melchizedek. He wrote, And without question, the person who has the power to give a blessing is greater than the one who is blessed (Hebrews 7:7 NLT). It is a spiritual law, that the blessing only flows from the one that is spiritually positioned above someone to that individual. Don't get distracted from today's focus. There is a direction of flow of blessings. Blessings are commanded from top to bottom, not to say that others are less valued than some, but because God has structures set in place by which he runs and governs his body – the Church.

> *There is a direction of flow of spiritual blessings from the greater to the lesser, make sure you are rightly positioned in God's structure.*

But because of the ignorance of some believers, they would say things like, "Are we not all children of God? Sure, we all are, but he has chosen and placed certain persons over us as watchmen for our souls, people who are answerable to him. Like Hebrews 13:17 says, "Obey those who rule over you, and be submissive, for they watch out for your souls, as those who must give account. Let them do so with joy and not with grief, for that would be unprofitable for you".

And that is also a privileged position to be in, when someone looks out for your spiritual wellbeing. In this regard, you are called to recognize those placed over you spiritually and be positioned for them to speak blessings in your life. Sometimes, it is by reason of their calling and the surpassing grace given to them for your good, sometimes by reason of their age and longevity in the faith ahead of you, and sometimes by reason of the nurturing role over your life. And you are also cautioned to not express spiritual ignorance in going about blessing those who have been positioned over you. To such people, you rather say "God bless you". You pray a blessing over them. It is different from commanding a blessing upon them, when you say, "I bless you".

Prayer

Heavenly Father, thank you for making us part of your big family, the Church. Help us to recognize our place that we might be rightly positioned in service, in submission and in taking responsibility. Let the flow of your blessings never be interrupted in our lives as we regard your principles. In Jesus' name.

Bible in one year // **Ezra 9-10, Acts 1**

I have set the Lord always before me; because He is at my right hand I shall not be moved. // **Psalm 16:8**

JUN 15

All I see is you

This is a song title from the gospel musician, Sinach. Among many songs, it is one of the songs on my playlist particularly in seasons when lots of things seem to get my attention, when the pressures of life come rushing in like a flood and I am tempted to get desperate and sound overwhelmed. It has proven each time to have such power to help me keep my eyes on the Lord even as we are commanded in Hebrews 12:2.

The amplified Bible has a better rendition of the verse: "Looking away from all that will distract us and focusing our eyes on Jesus, who is the Author and Perfecter of faith". This is what the Psalmist was doing when He said, in Psalm 16:8, "I keep my eyes always on the LORD. With him at my right hand, I will not be shaken" (NIV). You will have to make a resolve and say to the Lord like Sinach, "All I see is you", irrespective of what is going on about you. You might want to find that song and listen to it today, particularly if lots of challenges seem to impose themselves on you to cripple your faith. Use a song like that and let your heart be set upon the Lord. A similar song is by Don Moen when he sings, "When the oceans rise and thunders roar, I will soar with You above the storm".

> When all you see is the Lord, all your challenges and distractions will fade away in the shadows. In the end, you will look around to realize He indeed had it all figured out.

Here goes some lines from the song, All I See is you. Sinach sings, "All I see is You as I worship and adore You. I yield myself to You, This is where I want to be In Your Presence oh God". Do set you heart upon the Lord today and fix your gaze on Him, and you will be surprised how quickly all your giants will fade away in the shadow of His presence – when all you see is him.

Prayer

Heavenly Father, today like the psalmist, I lift my eyes to you from where my help comes, from you the maker of heaven and earth. You are at my right hand, and I will not be moved. You will never leave nor forsake me but will watch over your words until they are fulfilled in my life. In Jesus' name.

Bible in one year // **Nehemiah 1-3, Acts 2:1-21**

JUN 16

> We do not look at the things which are seen, but at the things which are not seen. For the things which are seen are temporary, but the things which are not seen are eternal. // **2 Corinthians 4:18**

Invisible but real

There is a paradox in this amazing verse when it says, "We look not at the things which are seen but at the things which are unseen". If they are unseen (invisible), how then do you look at them. You look at them with the eyes of the spirit. For these things are only invisible to the natural eyes. However, they are real. To a nonbeliever and atheist, they say there is nothing. They speak by their natural understanding limited to their natural senses. Their logic is this: If I can't see it, I can't touch it or appreciate it with my natural five senses, then it does not exist. But it is helpful to consider the world of telecommunications.

The technology in the world has so much developed through the decades, going from cable phones to mobile phones. And today, wireless communication with the internet, Wi-Fi, Bluetooth and other technologies. All these things that have become a real part of our daily lives function and operate because of an invisible world of radiations that facilitate transmission of signals. At the speed of light, you can now have direct calls with video images across the globe. There is an invisible but real connection. The radiations are invisible to the natural eyes, but they impact our lives daily – knowingly, or unknowingly. Today, radiotherapy is a strategy to treat cancer when a regulated dose of invisible X-ray is used to kill cancerous cells.

> **The invisible world of angels and demons is so real. But it is good to know that those that are with us are more powerful and outnumber them that are against us.**

Humanity has learned to explore, manipulate, and control an invisible world of radiations, harnessing all that knowledge to their advantage. Even so is the spiritual world. It is invisible but real. And like information technologies, we can understand it, explore it and be able to harness our knowledge of it for our good. Just as God is spirit, even so is the real world with spiritual entities of angels and demons, invisible to the natural eyes but real. When the King of sent an army to capture the prophet Elisha, the prophet was aware: "Those who are with us are more than those who are with them." There was an unseen world of angels ready to fight for them (2 Kings 6:15-17).

Prayer

Thank you Heavenly Father for enlightening us that we might understand life and stand up in victory against the forces that seek to oppose your purpose and works in our lives. Thank you for giving us the victory in Christ Jesus. Let the eyes of our spirits be open to these realities. In Jesus' name.

Bible in one year // **Nehemiah 4-6, Acts 2:22-47**

We do not wrestle against flesh and blood, but against principalities, against powers, against the rulers of the darkness of this age, against spiritual hosts of wickedness in the heavenly places. // **Ephesians 6:12**

The invisible world of demons

It is not unusual that as one called on the frontline spiritually, it is the norm to face demonic entities because we are continuously in their paths, working against all that they are out to do. And you should be aware of demonic activity. You also need enlightening on where you stand in the inevitable spiritual battles and how to take responsibility for a victorious life in Christ. It is only spiritual blindness that makes a person think the spiritual world is a fantasy. The spirit world rules and controls the natural. One will be missing out on life itself to think that all that we see is all that there is.

> There is more to life than catches the eyes, including a world of invisible demons that are determined to wreak havoc in your life. So we must be aware and prevent it.

If you have followed Your Daily Light for a while now, you might have noticed that we've hardly had a focus on the demonic world and their activities. That for a good reason. In ministering to the saints, it is my call to let them know who they are in Christ Jesus, what they have received, where they have been positioned and what they are called to do. Like a Lighthouse to a sailor at sea, so I am called to shine the Light of God's word to help men and women navigate their way to their God-ordained destinies. In this light, there is a lot more to focus on in building up people spiritually that we might not easily invest much time over a defeated foe and his kingdom. For if we focus on growing spiritually, we will always know how to deal with him when he shows up. But a strong emphasis on demons and their works without us getting to know who we are in Christ will only breath fear in our lives.

When you think of the illustration above of your life as a sailor at sea, you can think of demons as the pirates of life on the open sea. While you, like a sailor set your gaze towards your destination at sea, there are these entities on the open sea, armed and equipped to terrorize whoever they meet, rob them of their belongings, take them hostage or captive, interrupt their joy and prevent them from reaching their destination. As scripture says, we are wrestling against principalities, against powers, against the rulers of the darkness of this age, against spiritual hosts of wickedness in the heavenly places.

Prayer

Heavenly Father, thank you for illuminating us with the realities of life. Thank you for opening our eyes to see the invisible world and harness such knowledge for a victorious life in Christ. In Jesus' name.

Bible in one year // **Nehemiah 7-9, Acts 3**

JUN 18

This is the message which we have heard from Him and declare to you, that God is light and in Him is no darkness at all. // 1 John 1:5

The origin of demons Pt.1

It is good to know the origin of demons if you will understand certain aspects of their existence, their mission, and how to deal with them. It is also justifying for the Lord who created all things to know that He is not the author of the evil in the world. For many have questioned why a good God created such evil entities, in other words, blaming God for the havoc they wreak in the world. And the series of questions that these thoughts inspire are endless, such questions with very strong implications that if not careful, can turn a believer who hasn't experienced spiritual realities to embrace the idea that there is no God.

> God is Light and in Him there is no darkness at all. He is not the author of evil and is not responsible for the sufferings in the world.

We are assured, "God is light and in him there is not darkness at all" (1 John 1:5). God is not the author of evil. Don't be misled by some verses from the bible that suggest God authored evil. For example, we read of Saul: Now the Spirit of the LORD departed from Saul, and an evil spirit from the Lord tormented and terrified him (1 Samuel 16:14). If you don't evaluate this verse in the context of the totality of God's revelations of His person and Character, you would wrongly conclude that indeed God sent an evil Spirit to torment Saul. But in effect, what really happened is this: When the Holy Spirit left and God withdrew His presence from Saul, it created room for an evil spirit to come in, an evil spirit not sent by God. God doesn't commission evil spirits. What fellowship has light with darkness? (2 Corinthians 6:14).

Remember what Jesus said about casting out a demon. When the demon goes about and finds no other place, it returns to check the house it had left. If that person has not been filled with the Holy Spirit, then the demon goes away and brings seven more wicked spirits so that the person's later condition is worse than it was at the beginning (Matthew 12:43-45). I personally made this mistake once with an Indian lady who practiced Hinduism. After delivering her by the Spirit of God from a crippling back ache, I did not immediately lead her to Christ. She was fine the whole week. But one week later, the pain was back with greater intensity. Sadly, she was unwilling again to be prayed for because I we touched on the need for her to receive Jesus. It is what evil spirits do. They are not of God but seek vacant dwellings.

Prayer

Heavenly father, thank you for you are a good God. You know the plans you have for us, plans to prosper us. Thank you for filling our lives with your presence and leaving no room for the devil. In Jesus' name.

Bible in one year // **Nehemiah 10-11, Acts 4:1-22**

For indeed He does not give aid to angels, but He does give aid to the seed of Abraham. // **Hebrews 2:16**

JUN 19

The origin of demons Pt.2

Demons are fallen angels. God never created demons. He created angels, supernatural beings who serve his purpose. Like a nation's work force, so are angels to God. Angels constitute God's work force created long before humanity. Just as Psalm 103:20-21 says, "Praise the Lord, you his angels, you mighty ones who do his bidding, who obey his word. Praise the Lord, all his heavenly hosts, you his servants who do his will". Angels were created to serve God's purpose. And among them, the Chief demon, the Devil. Yes, Satan was not always Satan, he was created an Angel of great authority.

The prophet Ezekiel wrote of the circumstances that made him the devil. "You were the sealer of perfection, full of wisdom, and perfect in beauty. You were in Eden, the garden of God. Every precious stone was your covering… On the day you were created they were prepared. I placed you there with an anointed guardian cherub; you were on the holy mountain of God; you walked about amidst fiery stones. You were blameless in your behavior from the day you were created, until sin was discovered in you. In the abundance of your trade you were filled with violence, and you sinned; so I defiled you and banished you from the mountain of God" (Ezekiel 28:12-17). Satan was an anointed Cherub, an angel of high standing. But he became corrupt. And along with him, long before human creation, he was cast out of heaven with a third of angels (Revelation 12:7-9).

> **Demons are fallen angels who in anger over their loss have set themselves together with the devil to work against every divine plan and purpose.**

Satan the leading rebel, together with his click of angels were cast out of heaven. And that was the birth of evil. For Satan and the fallen angels knowing they had lost their place in heaven, set themselves to work against every divine agenda. Demons are fallen angels who lost their place and would not let others enjoy what they will never get. For they are eternally condemned. Just like fallen man, they too needed salvation, a salvation God decided never to give. That is why the author of Hebrew writes, "He (Christ) does not take hold of [the fallen] angels [to give them a helping hand], but He does take hold of [the fallen] descendants of Abraham [extending to them His hand of deliverance] (Hebrews 2:16 Amp).

Prayer

> Heavenly Father, Like the Psalmist says, "What is man that You are mindful of him, and the son of man that You visit him? Thank you for choosing us in Christ Jesus and making us heirs of salvation, giving us a second chance to have a place in your Kingdom. In Jesus' name.

Bible in one year // **Nehemiah 12-13, Acts 4:23-37**

JUN 20

> These signs will follow those who believe: In My name they will cast out demons. // **Mark 16:17**

A united front

Jesus dealt with demons during his earthly ministry and left us with the task of completing His work in the earth. Among his instructions to us, the very first he mentioned according to Marks account was to "Cast out demons". Jesus said, These signs will accompany those who believe: In my name they will drive out demons (Mark 16:17 NET). Jesus was himself accused to be of the devil because of His work against demonic activity. And to this, he had a response that tells us demons operate on a united front. Jesus said, "How can Satan drive out Satan? If a kingdom is divided against itself, that kingdom cannot stand. (Mark 3:23-24 NIV).

When you read from Revelation 12, you realize somethings about this united front of fallen angels. After the devil was cast down, he went out to make war on earth. The earth is the only ground for his work and humanity is the only thing He seeks to destroy, for that is the only thing close the heart of God with which he can toy. "The great dragon was hurled down—that ancient serpent called the devil, or Satan, who leads the whole world astray. He was hurled to the earth, and his angels with him... Then the dragon was enraged at the woman and went off to wage war against the rest of her offspring—those who keep God's commands and hold fast their testimony about Jesus" (Revelation 12:9 & 17).

> **The devil and his cohort of demons are on a united front to work havoc in the lives of men. But we have been given the authority to interrupt their works and put them out.**

Satan like an army general together with every angel that was cast out of heaven form a united front against humanity, particularly the children of God. They are enraged because we are privileged to be part of what they once enjoyed, much more, we are children of God. And for the person who is not a child of God, they are already in Satan's grip. That is the reason we are sent to set the captives free. And the devil and his cohort know they have little time. In anger, they are on a mission to work as much havoc as they can in the time left until their day of condemnation (Revelation 12:12). But the good thing is that we have been commissioned to cast them out.

Prayer

Heavenly Father, thank you for the authority we have in the name of Jesus to cast out demons and to arrest demonic activities. We frustrate every plan of darkness and raise up a shield against every attack on our health, finance, family, career, joy and all that concerns us. In Jesus' name.

Bible in one year // Esther 1-2, Acts 5:1-21

Be sober, be vigilant; because your adversary the devil walks about like a roaring lion, seeking whom he may devour. // **1 Peter 5:8**

JUN 21

Spiritual warfare is no choice

There are people who ignorantly say they don't want to have anything to do with demons. What they fail to know is that believe it or not, spiritual warfare is not a choice. You don't have to go looking for battles. Be sure they will come to you. The actual question is if you will stand up to fight and take your place or let yourself become victim of demonic activity. Peter cautioned his readers, "Stay alert! Watch out for your great enemy, the devil. He prowls around like a roaring lion, looking for someone to devour. Stand firm against him and be strong in your faith. Remember that your family of believers all over the world is going through the same kind of suffering you are" (1 Peter 5:8-9 NLT).

> **Spiritual warfare is not a choice, it is standing up to the forces of darkness who are constantly pressing on to frustrate God's plans in your life and in the world.**

Satan is friend to none. It doesn't matter if they believe in God or not. In fact, if you don't believe in God and in the reality of the spiritual world, you are already a victim of the devil. The bible puts it this way, Satan, who is the god of this world, has blinded the minds of those who don't believe. They are unable to see the glorious light of the Good News. They don't understand this message about the glory of Christ, who is the exact likeness of God (2 Corinthians 4:4 NLT). Then Jesus gives us more understanding to why the devil blindfolds people: So that 'Seeing they may see and not perceive and hearing they may hear and not understand; lest they should turn, and their sins be forgiven them (Mark 4:12).

Indeed no one is a friend to the devil. He has made humanity his enemy and is willing to keep as many people as possible out of the plans and purposes of God. The greatest aim is to have people reject God so they can find themselves together with him in hell at the end. It is important to know that hell was not created for man. Hell was created for the devil. People will only go to hell because they rejected the paths to life. Particularly for a child of God, the day you made Jesus Lord of your life, the devil made you a target in his mission. Just as Jesus said to Peter, Satan has asked to sift each of you like wheat. But I have pleaded in prayer for you, Simon, that your faith should not fail (Luke 22:31-32 NIV).

Prayer

> Heavenly Father, thank you for the word that we might not be ignorant of the devil and his schemes. Thank you for the victory we have in Christ Jesus, for Satan has no power over us. In Jesus' name.

Bible in one year // **Esther 3-5, Acts 5:22-42**

JUN 22

In all these things we are more than conquerors through Him who loved us. // **Romans 8:37**

More than conquerors

What then shall we say to these things? If God is for us, who can be against us? He who did not spare His own Son, but delivered Him up for us all, how shall He not with Him also freely give us all things? Who shall bring a charge against God's elect? It is God who justifies. Who is he who condemns? It is Christ who died, and furthermore is also risen, who is even at the right hand of God, who also makes intercession for us. Who shall separate us from the love of Christ? Shall tribulation, or distress, or persecution, or famine, or nakedness, or peril, or sword? As it is written: "For Your sake we are killed all day long; We are accounted as sheep for the slaughter."

> We are more than conquerors in Christ Jesus. Our victory was long secured. The call to spiritual warfare is actually a call to continue living in the proceeds of our victory through Christ Jesus.

Yet in all these things we are more than conquerors through Him who loved us. For I am persuaded that neither death nor life, nor angels nor principalities nor powers, nor things present nor things to come, nor height nor depth, nor any other created thing, shall be able to separate us from the love of God which is in Christ Jesus our Lord (Romans 8:31

A conqueror is one who conquers. To be more than conquerors means to have gone pass the place of people conquering to conquerors living the joys of the victories. They have gone pass trying to win a battle. They already won the battle and now looking at their victory in the past. And this is what we have in Christ Jesus. We are not as much in a thug-of-war with the devil and His cohorts. We are a people whose victory over the devil was long established. As it is written, "Having disarmed principalities and powers, He made a public spectacle of them, triumphing over them in it" (Colossians 2:15). NLT says, "He shamed them publicly by his victory over them on the cross".

Prayer

Heavenly Father, thank you for giving us the victory in Christ Jesus. We are more than conquerors through the power of the Spirit over every opposition, situation, and demonic agenda. In Jesus name.

Bible in one year // **Esther 6-8, Acts 6**

I remain confident of this: I will see the goodness of the Lord in the land of the living. // **Psalm 27:13 NIV**

JUN 23

Be confident in the Lord

The Lord is my light and my salvation; whom shall I fear? The Lord is the strength of my life; of whom shall I be afraid? When the wicked came against me to eat up my flesh, my enemies and foes, they stumbled and fell. Though an army may encamp against me, my heart shall not fear; though war may rise against me, in this I will be confident (Psalm 27:1-3). In essence, this is faith. When you have unshakable confidence in the Lord based on His word and His ability that has been revealed to you through the scriptures.

This was the confidence David had in the Lord. You can see his confidence displayed in all of scripture in the accounts of his life or the Psalms he wrote. He declared the Lord to be his refuge, his strength, his shepherd, the stronghold of His life. David was confident in the Lord. This should be our story too. For God who proved true in the life of David, giving him victory over all his adversaries, has not changed. He is the same yesterday, today, and forever.

> **Just like David, be confident in the Lord at all times and do not let even the fear of demons rise in your heart.**

David goes on to boast, "For in the time of trouble He shall hide me in His pavilion; in the secret place of His tabernacle, He shall hide me; He shall set me high upon a rock. And now my head shall be lifted up above my enemies all around me; therefore, I will offer sacrifices of joy in His tabernacle; I will sing, yes, I will sing praises to the Lord... When my father and my mother forsake me, then the Lord will take care of me... I would have lost heart, unless I had believed that I would see the goodness of the Lord In the land of the living" (27:1).

Prayer

Heavenly Father, thank you for being my light and my salvation, an ever-present help in trouble. So that we will not fear, though the mountains tremble, the ocean roars and the earth quakes. Though a mighty army of darkness arise against us. We are confident we have the victory in you. And we will live to see your goodness in the land of the living. In Jesus name.

Bible in one year // **Esther 9-10, Acts 7:1-21**

JUN 24

> In this way, he disarmed the spiritual rulers and authorities. He shamed them publicly by his victory over them on the cross.
> // Colossians 2:15 NLT

A vanquished foe

"Stay alert! Watch out for your great enemy, the devil. He prowls around like a roaring lion, looking for someone to devour" (1 Peter 5:8 NLT). Peter informed us about our enemy, an adversary – that is the devil who always lurks around looking for an opportunity to strike. Jesus had to deal with him too. The bible expressly says, "When the devil had finished tempting Jesus, he left him until the next opportunity came" (Luke 4:13 NLT). If there is one thing to learn from the devil, it is his quality to endure and not give up, though he fails a thousand times. He never quits trying to distract you, steal your joy, and make you question God' love. But here is the good news: Satan is a vanquished foe. He was defeated for you.

Paul wrote to the Colossians about what Jesus accomplished on the cross, "Having disarmed principalities and powers, He made a public spectacle of them, triumphing over them in it" (Colossians 2:15). The amplified bible has a more explicit rendition of the same verse when it says, "When He had disarmed the rulers and authorities [those supernatural forces of evil operating against us], He made a public example of them [exhibiting them as captives in His triumphal procession], having triumphed over them through the cross".

> **The devil is a defeated foe. Together with his cohorts, they do not stand a chance to prevail over a child of God who knows who they are and take their stand.**

Three things to note. The first is that the devil and his cohorts were disarmed. They have no weapon of war against you, they don't have the capacity for war with you. The second thing is that they were defeated totally through the cross. And finally, it was an open victory recorded in the journals of eternity. All this just means one thing: The call to spiritual warfare is not really a call to fight to obtain a victory, it is really the call to stand your ground and hold the devil where he belongs, under your feet as a defeated foe. You are called to keep him down, so he does not show up in your affairs and in your world. You are called to war from a vantage point, to keep a defeated foe in subjection to the will of God.

Prayer

Heavenly Father, we give you praise for the victory we have in Christ Jesus through the cross by which he disarmed principalities and power, making an open show of His victory over them. Thank you for we are partakers together with Christ in this victory. In Jesus' name.

Bible in one year // Job 1-2, Acts 7:22-43

He has delivered us from the power of darkness and [a]conveyed us into the kingdom of the Son of His love. // **Colossians 1:13**

JUN 25

A matter of jurisdications

National boundaries define the limit of a nation's jurisdiction, the limit to which a government has control and influence. It is a violation of international laws for another country to cross international boundaries to take a person away as prisoner without permission or authorization from the host country. This is how come journalists and opposition leaders can find a haven in foreign countries from where they live freely and carry out their agenda against their governments. With all their tyranny, a ruling authority has no authority over that person in a foreign nation. It is a matter of jurisdictions.

The same is true spiritually. There are really two spiritual jurisdictions. These are the Kingdom of Light and the Kingdom of darkness. Paul wrote to the Colossians, "Giving thanks to the Father who has qualified us to be partakers of the inheritance of the saints in the light. He has delivered us from the dominion of darkness and conveyed us into the kingdom of the Son of His love" (Colossians 1:12-13). What a profound passage that enlightens us about our present-day spiritual location. That we were delivered from the control and influence of darkness and brought into the Kingdom of the Son He loves, that is the Kingdom of Light.

> As one who is born again, you were delivered from the dominion of darkness and brought into the Kingdom of light. The devil has no legal authority over you because you are out of his jurisdiction.

We were delivered out of the devil's jurisdiction and translated into a new spiritual territory over which the devil has no legal control or influence. We are outside His jurisdiction, free to live for God and His purpose. What is even more fascinating is that when we were delivered from the dominion of darkness, not only were we brought into the Kingdom of God. We were also given authority and dominion over the one who once had control over us. Now we can exercise authority over the devil, forbidding him where we don't want him to be and kicking him out of any place where we find him. It is indeed a matter of Jurisdictions. We were brought out of the devil's jurisdiction into the Kingdom of God which has authority even over the Kingdom of darkness.

Prayer

Heavenly Father, thank you for delivering us from the dominion of darkness and for bringing us into the Kingdom of the son you love. Thank you for giving us authority over the one who once had control over us. Today we take authority over the forces of darkness and limit their works in our lives. In Jesus name.

Bible in one year // **Job 3-4, Acts 7:44-60**

JUN 26

> Behold, I give you the authority to trample on serpents and scorpions, and over all the power of the enemy, and nothing shall by any means hurt you. // **Luke 10:19**

Forget about ranks

When it comes to spiritual warfare, one thing that remains true is the fact that the Kingdom of darkness is highly structured with Satan as its lord. And from him follows a structured organization with demons organized under sub-commanders in different camps as their destructive mission might necessitate. And of course, just as an angel is sent on a mission, you often have a demon in operation as a loner. Or even as many as thousands. We find all these scenarios in scriptures. For example, we read from Luke 8:2 that Jesus cast out 7 demons from Mary Magdalene. Jesus also encountered the demon who called himself Legion (Mark 5:1-15).

> You were given authority over all the power of the enemy. There is not one demon that is too high ranking for you to deal with as a child of God when you know who you are in Christ Jesus.

Now there are those who try to build in the minds of believers, through inaccurate teachings, that some demons because they are higher in rank might not be at their level to cast out. Such knowledge is not from sound bible understanding. Never border about the rank of a demon. No matter how high the rank, starting with the devil, they have all been placed under our feet in Christ Jesus. All you need as a child of God is to know who you are and have some faith in your heart. And with the name of Jesus on your lips, there is no demon that can stand up to you. Ignore their ranks. Jesus said: "Behold, I give you the authority to trample on serpents and scorpions, and over all the power of the enemy, and nothing shall by any means hurt you" (Luke 10:19).

You have been given authority over ALL THE POWER of the enemy, not over some power. Such teachings about some demons being too powerful comes from their failed encounters when they were not able to cast out a certain evil spirit. Reminds us of David and Goliath. Before David came to the battlefield, the whole army with King Saul on the lead had been going back and forth, saying Goliath was too big for them to tackle. This is what is happening in the Church today when you have a minister saying some high-ranking demons are not for you to tackle. But David proved them wrong (1 Samuel 17). The same is true for you. No demon is too high ranking for you – not even Satan. Ignore their ranks.

Prayer

Heavenly Father, thank you for giving me authority over unclean spirits and all their powers. Thank you for the additional assurance that NOTHING shall by ANY MEANS harm me. In Jesus' name.

Bible in one year // Job 5-7, Acts 8:1-25

God raised us up with Christ and seated us with him in the heavenly realms in Christ Jesus. // **Ephesians 2:6 NIV**

JUN 27

Seated in heavenly places

One reason many are fearful of demons is because like Goliath, they have been magnified in their minds to be these mighty supernatural wicked beings. And that is a great aspect of truth. They are mighty, strong, and cunning. It is important to know that they have been around the world long before the first man, Adam. In terms of age and experience, they also know a million ways to trick and trouble humanity. However, it is important to have the right perspective as a child of God, to know that you are indeed above them. Your positioning is above that of the devil and his team of fallen angels.

Ephesians 2:6 informs us, God raised us up with Christ and seated us with him in the heavenly realms in Christ Jesus (NIV). And it doesn't end there. In another place he wrote, "He (God) raised Christ from the dead and seated him at his right hand in the heavenly realms, far above all rule and authority, power and dominion, and every name that is invoked, not only in the present age but also in the one to come. And God placed all things under his feet and appointed him to be head over everything for the church, which is his body, the fullness of him who fills everything in every way (Ephesians 1:20-23).

> **Because you are seated in heavenly places with Christ Jesus, every other authority and name has been made subject to you, including Satan and all other demonic authorities.**

Now if you connect those two verses, it gives you a clear picture of your placement in Christ with regards to the devil and his cohorts. God has raised us up to seat together with Christ in heavenly places and He has placed all things under our feet, for our benefit as the church, that is the body of Christ. What a privilege! We are seated together with Christ in authority over and above every other title or name that any demon could assume. Be it the prince of the air, queen of the coast, prince of Persia, or Legion. Whatever name a demon might go by or authority they might assume, it is all in subjection to you who are in Christ Jesus, because you are seated in heavenly places with him.

Prayer

Heavenly Father, thank you for delivering me from the dominion of darkness and bringing me into the Kingdom of light, for raising me up and seating me in heavenly places with Christ, far above all principalities and powers. I have authority over the devil and his cohorts. In Jesus' name.

Bible in one year // **Job 8-10, Acts 8:26-40**

JUN 28

Be strong in the Lord and in the power of His might.
// **Ephesians 6:10**

Be strong in the Lord

Be strong in the Lord! This was the profound instruction from Paul to us in Ephesians 6:10. He wrote, "Finally, my brethren, be strong in the Lord and in the power of His might. Put on the whole armor of God, that you may be able to stand against the wiles of the devil. For we do not wrestle against flesh and blood, but against principalities, against powers, against the rulers of the darkness of this age, against spiritual hosts of wickedness in the heavenly places" (Ephesians 6:10-12). Having been informed and enlightened on the Kingdom of darkness and the ongoing spiritual warfare to which we must respond, the final word is this: Be strong in the Lord and in the power of His might. Paul rightly guarantees that with the full armor of God on you, you will be able to stand against the devil and his schemes.

> Be strong in the Lord and in His mighty power. Put on the whole armor that you might be able to stand against the forces of darkness and their agenda.

He goes on to emphasize that our battle is not against flesh and blood but against spiritual forces and authorities in dark places, forces in heavenly realms. There are those who are always focused on praying for the death of their enemies. And on that subject, we can have such a huge debate. The greater truth is that this is uncalled for. Such people who advocate such teachings have as anchor, the verse that says, "Suffer not the witch to live" (Exodus 22:18). They fail to recognize the dispensation in which we live. In the Old Testament, the Israelites did not have the authority to cast out demons.

When the apostles angered by the rejection from a city wanted to call down fire and destroy the people, Jesus said to them, "You do not know what manner of spirit you are of. For the Son of Man did not come to destroy men's lives but to save them" (Luke 9:55-56). To the people under the old covenant, they were given a task of annihilation, a commission to war against the enemies of God and to get out of the way anyone that seemed an opposition (1 Samuel 15:1-9). But to us was given a ministry of reconciliation, to seek and to save the lost so that the blood of Christ might not be in vain (2 Corinthians 5:20). Our fight is not against humans. We war against spiritual forces of wickedness.

Prayer

Heavenly Father, thank you for giving us all things that pertain to life and godliness, including the whole armor to be victorious in our wrestling in spiritual warfare. Help us to fix our gaze on the right target even at war. As wrestle not against humans but against the forces of darkness. In Jesus' name.

Bible in one year // **Job 11-13, Acts 9:1-21**

Take up the whole armor of God, that you may be able to withstand in the evil day, and having done all, to stand. // **Ephesians 6:13**

JUN 29

Stand therefore

Stand therefore, having girded your waist with truth, having put on the breastplate of righteousness, and having shod your feet with the preparation of the gospel of peace; above all, taking the shield of faith with which you will be able to quench all the fiery darts of the wicked one. And take the helmet of salvation, and the sword of the Spirit, which is the word of God, praying always with all prayer and supplication in the Spirit, being watchful to this end with all perseverance and supplication for all the saints (Ephesians 6:14-18 NKJV)

> **Stand therefore, fully prepared for the day of evil, with the full armor of God.**

Paul was building on with the thoughts we considered yesterday, when he wrote, "Finally, my brethren, be strong in the Lord and in the power of His might. Put on the whole armor of God, that you may be able to stand against the wiles of the devil. For we do not wrestle against flesh and blood, but against principalities, against powers, against the rulers of the darkness of this age, against spiritual hosts of wickedness in the heavenly places. Therefore, take up the whole armor of God, that you may be able to withstand in the evil day, and having done all, to stand (Ephesians 6:10-13).

In summary, Paul was saying, "Given we have this warfare that is inevitable, stand therefore fully armed and ready for the day of evil with the full armor of God. Indeed, God has given us all things we need for life (2 Peter 1:3). You were never intended to be a victim of the devil as a child of God. In fact, the author of Ecclesiastes calls it "An error that proceeds from the ruler" (Ecclesiastes 10:5-7). An error because the one who ought to be holding the devil down is the one being held down, such an error that comes because the ruler, the one in authority failed in some sense. This is one reason Your Daily Light comes to you, to enlighten you concerning your true placement in Christ and help you lead a fulfilling and a victorious life in Him. You have all it takes to be victorious against the devil and his cohorts. Stand therefore and put on the whole armor of God!

Prayer

> Heavenly Father, thank you for giving us all things that pertain to life and godliness, that being fully armed, we are well able to stand in the day of evil. And having done all to stand, we will stand. We receive grace to be discerning of spirits and effective in warfare. In Jesus' name.

Bible in one year // **Job 14-16, Acts 9:22-43**

JUN 30

Submit to God. Resist the devil and he will flee from you. // **James 4:7**

No retreat, no surrender

This is the title of a Jean-Claude Van Damme movie from the 1980s. The very title highlights the attitude we should have as believers, particularly towards demonic activity. Do not retreat, do not surrender, for you have all it takes to be victorious in Christ Jesus. In little digestible bits for a devotional, we have share on contents that are better treated and covered in a book. We have examined the origin of demons, emphasized their mission, and highlighted among many things: your victory in Christ Jesus.

> Never retreat nor surrender on your journey with God but stand your ground against demonic activity, for the victory is yours in Christ Jesus.

And it is my prayer for you that these truths will take root in your heart and inspire in you the faith to be fearless towards demons and their activity, being ready to sanction their disobedience and trespassing at all times. Even as Paul wrote, "For though we walk in the flesh, we do not war according to the flesh. For the weapons of our warfare are not carnal but mighty in God for pulling down strongholds, casting down arguments and every high thing that exalts itself against the knowledge of God, bringing every thought into captivity to the obedience of Christ, and being ready to punish all disobedience when your obedience is fulfilled (2 Corinthians 10:3-6).

The weapons you have are indeed mighty through God to topple any wall of defense. In the old testament, it was said of the Israelite: "One person can chase a thousand of them, and two people put ten thousand to flight" (Deuteronomy 32:30). But to us, in the name of Jesus, even as a one-man army, you can put the whole band of demons to flight. This is what David meant when He said, "Indeed, with your help I can charge against an army" (Psalm 18:29). I leave you with a final word on this subject like Paul. Never retreat nor surrender. "Put on every piece of God's armor so you will be able to resist the enemy in the time of evil. Then after the battle you will still be standing firm" (Ephesians 6:13). For the devil has no option but to flee, if you do not surrender (James 4:7).

Prayer

Father, let your word take root in my heart, that I will be illuminated by the Spirit to understand with the saints what is the riches of my glorious inheritance in Christ. I declare an end to the works of darkness in my life and all that concerns me. And I call forth a restoration of all things. In Jesus' name.

Bible in one year // **Job 17-19, Acts 10:1-23**

JULY

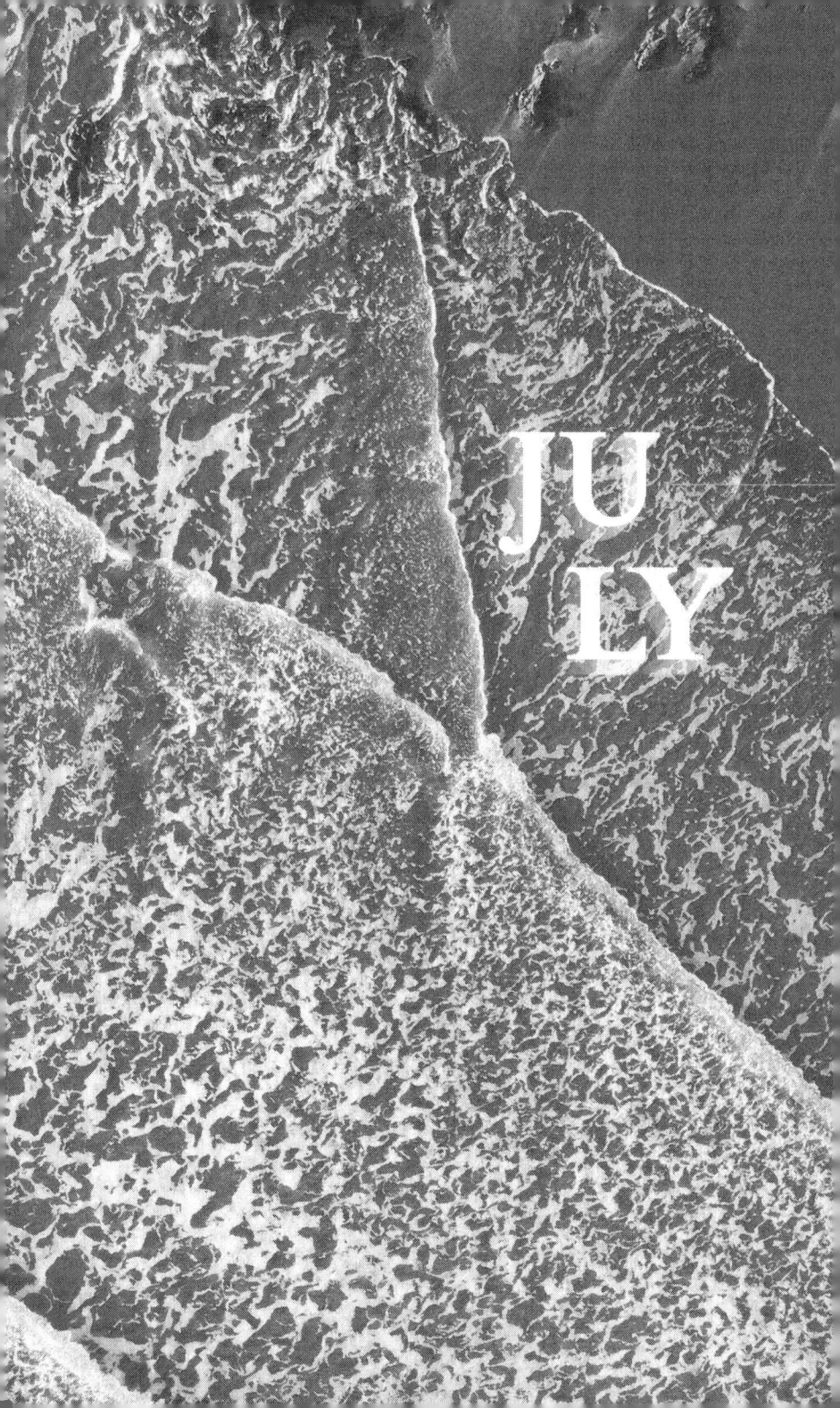

You are of God, little children, and have overcome them, because He who is in you is greater than he who is in the world. // **1 John 4:4**

JUL 1

Do not be afraid

Last month, among other things, there was a focus on demonic activity and the call to spiritual warfare. True to the outline of the introduction, we had illumination from the scriptures on our placement in Christ and the call to stand our ground and maintain the victory He wrought on the cross for us. Just as Colossians 2:15 makes it plain: "He disarmed the spiritual rulers and authorities. He shamed them publicly by his victory over them on the cross". The goal of this lesson was not to inspire fear in you through the consciousness of demonic activity, but rather to inspire faith as you recognize who you are and understand the weapons you have been given to use in battle.

> Do not be afraid. You have no reason to fear. He has said He will never leave you nor forsake you so you can boldly say, the Lord is my shepherd, I will not be afraid.

Therefore, do not be afraid of demons and their works, neither be intimidated by Satan their boss. For they all together are not able to successfully stand against you if you would take your rightful place. Jesus said it as a matter of fact, "I will build my church, and all the powers of hell WILL NOT conquer it" (Matthew 16:18 NLT). More so, it is written, "Ye are of God, little children, and have overcome them: because greater is he that is in you, than he that is in the world" (1 John 4:4). It is also worthy of note, that as there be demons, there are far more angels assigned to you by God. The Psalmist declared, "For He shall give His angels charge over you, to keep you in all your ways. In their hands they shall bear you up, lest you dash your foot against a stone" (Psalm 91:11-12).

God cares for you that much, he doesn't want even your feet to be hurt against a stone as you journey in destiny. Indeed, you have no reason to fear. Even as you face this new month, do so with confidence in God, walk with the consciousness of angels on guard and have no fear for the devil and his activities. Put on the whole amour of God and be ready at all times to emerge victorious in all things. Even so you shall find reasons to celebrate as you take steps with God. And it is my prayer for you, that the Lord will keep you, be gracious to you and cause His face to shine upon you in all your endeavors – In Jesus' name.

Prayer

> Heavenly Father, thank you for you have not given us a spirit of fear but of boldness and a sound mind. Like a Lion that doesn't retreat from its prey, so we face a new month in the confidence of your presence, guidance, and provisions, knowing that all things work together for our good. In Jesus' name.

Bible in one year // **Job 20-21, Acts 10:24-48**

JUL 2

> Above all, taking the shield of faith with which you will be able to quench all the fiery darts of the wicked one. // **Ephesians 6:16**

Your shield of faith

Sometimes, a great and well-armed army can be taken into captivity not because they were not armed, but because they were not skilled in the use of their artillery. And this is the condition of many Christians who end up needing deliverance. It is not supposed to be so. But because of ignorance, as the bible says, God's people are destroyed. In the next few days, I would highlight a few aspects of God's armor given to us. As it is written, "Take up the shield of faith, with which you can extinguish all the flaming arrows of the evil one" (Ephesians 6:16 NIV).

With the shield of faith in place, no weapon of darkness shall prevail in your life. Give therefore attention to the word of God, for faith comes by hearing His word.

What a potent shield we have – one that extinguishes every arrow of the devil. It is not some arrows. This just really says so long faith is in place, no weapon fashioned against you will prosper. And this is one reason for Your Daily Light, to inspire your faith daily as you meditate in the word of God. For faith comes by hearing and hearing by the word of God. But what is faith? Faith is such a big topic with many aspects that can't be exhausted in a day's writing. But I'll leave you with a definition for today. Faith is the full conviction of the reality of spiritual things that gets you, talking and acting like it, even when the circumstances do not necessarily match those convictions. Read that definition again and ponder over it.

That is what makes the shield, when you have become so conscious of the reality that the devil has no say in your affairs to the extent that no fear cripples you over the thoughts of demonic activity, when you can speak words of authority commanding the devil and demons to stay clear, knowing they have no choice but to obey. That is holding up the shield of faith. Talking and acting in the consciousness of who you are in Christ Jesus. Have the audacity of faith that turns away from nothing; but takes every challenge head on like a bull. For such faith is indeed a shield, impenetrable to every dart of the devil.

Prayer

Gracious Father, we rejoice in your love and hope in your promises, being confident that you who has started the good work in our lives will bring it to completion. We receive grace to be strong in faith, holding it up as a shield with which we quench every fiery dart of the evil one. In Jesus' name.

Bible in one year // **Job 22-24, Acts 11**

For the word of God is living and powerful, and sharper than any two-edged sword, piercing even to the division of soul and spirit, and of joints and marrow, and is a discerner of the thoughts and intents of the heart. // **Hebrews 4:12**

JUL 3

A sword like no other

When you consider the whole amor of God, you realize Paul in writing, had a fully armed Roman soldier of his days in mind. And of all the weapons that Paul listed, the only offensive weapon was the sword of the Spirit – a sword like no other. He admonished his readers, "Take the sword of the Spirit, which is the word of God" (Ephesians 6:17 NLT). In another place, we are enlightened even more on what makes the word of God such a sword. We read in Hebrews 4:12, "The word of God is alive and active. Sharper than any double-edged sword, it penetrates even to dividing soul and spirit, joints and marrow; it judges the thoughts and attitudes of the heart" (NLT).

Jesus demonstrated how to use this sword in spiritual warfare when He was himself visited and tempted of the devil. Jesus responded with the word; He spoke in unison with God the things He had said. For example, when the tempter came to him, he said, "If thou be the Son of God, command that these stones be made bread". But Jesus answered and said, "It is written, Man shall not live by bread alone, but by every word that proceeds out of the mouth of God". Jesus was quoting from Deuteronomy 8:3. It was with the word that Jesus was able to stand the devil and ward him off.

> The word of God is an offensive weapon, like a sword, it is potent to wade off every attack and put any demon to flight, even Satan the chief commander.

This is how you use the word as a sword, by speaking it in response to the attacks of the devil. It must not be an attack from darkness even. The word of God is indeed a sword like no other, sharper than any two-edged sword, potent both in the material and spiritual world. Take it up therefore and stand your ground against the devil and his cohorts. Chase them off with the word until they recognize their boundaries in your life.

Prayer

Heavenly Father, thank you for the word that is potent on our lips to produce results by the Spirit. As we speak your word, demons obey, situations align, authorities submit and your will and purpose is established in our lives and in the land. In Jesus name.

Bible in one year // **Job 25-27, Acts 12**

JUL 4

Those who know your name trust in you, for you, LORD, have never forsaken those who seek you. // **Psalm 9:10**

Understand the name Jesus

This verse birth a curiosity in me years ago. Just the first part said it all: "Those who know your name will put their trust in you". This meant more than just knowing how someone is called, there is something about the knowledge and understanding of the name that translates to faith and trust in the Lord. It is more than knowing the name of the Lord. And this is a major crisis in the body of Christ. There are many who call the name Jesus but do not understand the name or its use, sadly, even among ministers. So, as I will share with you over the next days some thoughts in this regard.

This lack of understanding of the name of the Lord is the reason a wrong doctrine has taken root in certain Christian settings, the teaching that certain demons are above your authority as a believer. They say you need a higher authority or many ministers to deal with such a demon. It is a lie from men. Reminds me of Jesus rebukes to the religious teachers of his days. Jesus said of them: "They teach man-made ideas as commands from God" (Matthew 15:9 NLT).

> **The name Jesus is your most potent weapon in spiritual warfare. You must therefore understand the name and its usage.**

It is a lie to embrace that certain demons are above your authority. The devil is also happy with such teachings circulating. Because while you believe it and fold your arms saying some demons are above your control, such demons can have their freedom to continue wreaking havoc. But such ideologies will fade away in the shadows when we turn on the light of God's word and examine things from scripture. Now, this subject is not content for a devotional, we couldn't richly explore the topic as a devotional content. This is content for a book. To uproot such age-long doctrines and give you a full understanding of the name of Jesus and its use, we'll need a lot more time and details. Regarding spiritual warfare, understanding the name of Jesus and its use is so vital, for it is your most potent weapon against the devil and his cohorts. As it is written, "At the name of Jesus every knee should bow, of things in heaven, and things in earth, and things under the earth" (Philippians 2:10).

Prayer

Heavenly Father thank you for the word of illumination that comes to us daily, shining your light on our paths that we might walk in your ways, do your will and become all that you have intended us to be. Thank you for the name of Jesus that has been given unto us for results in the earth. In Jesus' name.

Bible in one year // Job 28-29, Acts 13:1-25

> In that day you will ask Me nothing. Most assuredly, I say to you, whatever you ask the Father in My name He will give you. // **John 16:23**

JUL 5

More than a cliché

To say "In the name of Jesus" is more than a cliché. A cliché can be defined as a phrase or sentence, usually expressing a popular or common thought or idea, that has lost originality and impact by long overuse. And for some, that is really what it means to say "In the name of Jesus"; it is just the usage of a phrase because they heard it used in prayer, in church or in proclamations of blessings. But they have never taken a moment to think through what it really means to say "In the name of Jesus". If you are keen, you would even hear people pray to Jesus and end the prayer saying, In the name of Jesus. An example for such prayer could go something like this: "Lord Jesus, thank you for today... Thank you for answering our prayer in Jesus' name".

> The phrase "In the name of Jesus" is more than a spiritual cliché in prayer, it is a phrase that spells out that we are talking and acting on behalf of Jesus, we are saying Jesus himself is the one talking.

Now that is not only spiritually wrong, but in terms of language, also very incorrect. You cannot pray to Jesus in the name of Jesus. If you say such a prayer, it is just an indication that you have not understood the meaning and use of the name Jesus. It has everything to do with delegated authority or the right of attorney when you say "In the name of Jesus". This we will make clearer in the days ahead. Like I mentioned already, some teachings are too extensive to richly address in a few days of devotional. Like now, it would not be strange if someone is saying with regards to the example above, "But Jesus is God, so I can pray to Jesus". Now if the person pauses there, it might be a little more correct. But to pray to Jesus in the name of Jesus makes no sense in terms of language and spiritual knowledge.

Jesus said: In that day you will no longer ask me anything. Very truly I tell you, my Father will give you whatever you ask in my name. Until now you have not asked for anything in my name. Ask and you will receive, and your joy will be complete (John 16:23-24). Jesus said, ask The Father in my Name. So when you pray and say "In the name of Jesus", it is not just a cliché or a formal way to put a full stop in the prayer. It is using delegated authority, standing in the place of Jesus, and speaking to the Father on his behalf. You are literally acting and speaking as Jesus himself.

Prayer

> Almighty Father, we receive with thanksgiving all you have for us. As we understand and use the name Jesus, we rejoice in the results we see and the victories we have over Satan and situations. In Jesus name.

Bible in one year // **Job 30-31, Acts 13:26-52**

JUL 6

> These signs will follow those who believe: In My name they will cast out demons. // **Mark 16:17**

The power of attorney

When Jesus spoke to us saying, "These signs will accompany those who believe: In my name they will drive out demons", He gave us the power of attorney to use his name. It is in the same light that He said to us, "Most assuredly, I say to you, whatever you ask the Father in My name He will give you" (John 16:23). It has every-thing to do with delegated authority. In legal terms, the power of attorney is a legal document given by a person to another which authorizes them to speak or act on their behalf in specific matters. In this case, the person who receives the power of attorney is fully considered to be the person who gave it, and their words and actions are as binding as it were the original person. In other words, the power of attorney makes you the legal representative of the one who gave it.

> *Jesus gave you the power of attorney to use His name, He gave you the legal right to stand in His place and act on His behalf. So that it is no longer you talking, but Jesus himself speaking when you talk.*

For a practical example, if I were invited to a book launch occasion to which I could not go because of other commitments, I can choose to send you. Now the invitation I received has my name on it. When you reach the gates, you will not present your name, because it is not on the list of invitees. You are not there on your own account – you are there in my name. Therefore, when the host receives you, they are not seeing you, they are seeing the one that was invited. On that account, you will be taken to the seat that bears my name and served the food I had to eat. This is what it means to pray in the name of Jesus. It means you are Jesus on the scene.

This is what Jesus meant when He said, "In my name". He really meant, "Standing as my legal representative, fully representing me with all my authority to act on my behalf, you stand in my place to cast out demons or to talk to the Father". If you don't get this, go back, and read over and over until it makes sense. When you understand this, you will understand the believer's authority and your placement in God. You will understand why no demon is above any believer. You will understand what foolishness there is to pray to Jesus in the name of Jesus. You will understand what authority has been entrusted to you, such understanding that would strengthen your faith in dealing with demons and put more meaning to your prayer.

Prayer

Heavenly Father, the eyes of our understanding are flooded with light that we might comprehend with all the saints what is the glorious riches for us in Christ Jesus. Thank you that we are growing in the knowledge of who we are and what ye have received for a victorious life with you. In Jesus' name.

Bible in one year // Job 32-33, Acts 14

In that day you will ask in My name, and I do not say to you that I shall pray the Father for you. // John 16:26

JUL 7

Should you pray to Jesus?

This question was the wake-up call that drew my attention to the need for a personal study on understanding and using the name of Jesus. I had been visiting my older sister for a weekend. At this time, I would sometimes pray to Jesus and end the prayer saying, "In the name of Jesus". Something just did not seem right about that construction. I asked my sister Prisca, "Should we pray to Jesus in the name of Jesus?" It turned out she had been having a similar question. However, because we both did not know any better at that time, we ended up concluding it did not matter because Jesus is God. What an error that was! You might be in the same error today. If you think there is no problem with it, then you are in the same situation I was.

If you followed yesterday's devotional, this was made quite plain what it means to pray in the name of Jesus. "You are indeed Jesus on the scene", I wrote. If that really makes sense to you, you will realize you cannot be standing as Jesus and yet talk to Jesus. You stand as Jesus to talk to the Father. And when it comes to using the name to cast out demons, you stand as Jesus to talk to the demons. That is what it really means "In the name of Jesus". This also should now make sense why there is no demon above a believer (This point I will expatiate on tomorrow).

> **We do not pray to Jesus. We pray to the Father in the name of Jesus. We cannot pray to Jesus in the name of Jesus because we are standing in His place.**

We don't pray to Jesus. We pray to the Father in the name of Jesus even though we can talk to Jesus and fellowship with Jesus. But we ask the Father in the name of Jesus. Jesus himself said, "In that day you will no longer ask me anything" (John 16:23). Now another person will argue, "We ask Jesus and Jesus asks the father". Incorrect! Jesus himself said he won't do that. He told the disciples, "In that day you will ask in my name. I am not saying that I will ask the Father on your behalf. No, the Father himself loves you because you have loved me and have believed that I came from God" (John 16:26-27). This is also the reason it is as wrong to pray through Jesus. Like some people say, "This we ask through Jesus".

Prayer

Heavenly Father, Thank you for illumination by the word. That we do not remain ignorant but continue to grow in the knowledge of truth as you unveil scripture to us day by day. Thank you for making us more effective in our spiritual walk for greater results in all things. In Jesus name.

Bible in one year // Job 34-35, Acts 15:1-21

JUL 8

The name of the Lord is a strong tower; the righteous run to it and are safe.
// **Proverbs 18:10**

Trust in the name

David wrote, "May the Lord answer you when you are in distress; may the name of the God of Jacob protect you. May he send you help from the sanctuary and grant you support from Zion. May he remember all your sacrifices and accept your burnt offerings. May he give you the desire of your heart and make all your plans succeed. May we shout for joy over your victory and lift up our banners in the name of our God. May the Lord grant all your requests. Now this I know: The Lord gives victory to his anointed. He answers him from his heavenly sanctuary with the victorious power of his right hand. Some trust in chariots and some in horses, but we trust in the name of the Lord our God. They are brought to their knees and fall, but we rise up and stand firm (Psalms 20:1).

> **Trust in the name of the Lord Jesus, it is a dependable weapon at war and a secured shelter from the enemy.**

David was a man ahead of His generation. He understood spiritual truths beyond His time. He saw the Lord and knew the power in His name ahead of his day. But it was not given to that generation to understand the full implications of its use. Even as it is written: For "Whoever calls on the name of the Lord shall be saved" (Romans 10:13).

The name of the Lord is more than an appellation as a word by which He is identified and recognized. His name is a weapon of war, a shelter of refuge, a cheque for provision and a seal of ownership on those who are His own. Even as Paul wrote to Timothy, "Let everyone who names the name of Christ depart from iniquity" (2 Timothy 2:9). You can trust in the name of the Lord. As it is written, "The name of the Lord is a strong tower; the righteous run to it and are safe" (Proverbs 18:10).

Prayer

Heavenly Father, let your name be glorified today and always. As we walk in the victory guaranteed to us, in the name of Jesus.

Bible in one year // Job 36-37, Acts 15:22-41

Jesus came up and said to them, "All authority (all power of absolute rule) in heaven and on earth has been given to Me. // **Matthew 28:18 Amp**

JUL 9

The authority of Jesus

There are those who teach and believe that certain demons are above the authority of a believer. Always, I have one response for such persons or anyone who has embraced such an erroneous doctrine: They have not understood the name of Jesus and its use. Now we have in some details, explained over the days gone, what it means to use the name of Jesus. However, without knowledge of the authority of Jesus, that name is as good on your lips like the name of a popular rockstar in the world. The name will hardly work for you because you would lack the faith in its use. For the name of Jesus is not a magical word you enchant in the face of adversity. It is a weapon you use with understanding to get results.

When Jesus rose from the death, He came to His disciples and declared, "All authority in heaven and on earth has been given to me" (Matthew 28:18). All authority! That's the authority Jesus has. Not some authority. Jesus is the overall boss, the authority to which every authority in all creation submits as a law. When Jesus speaks, it is final. In another place, Jesus himself said, "I am the Living One; I was dead, and now look, I am alive for ever and ever! And I hold the keys of death and Hades" (Revelation 1:18). Paul added, "Jesus is the head of all principality and power, all authority and rule" (Colossians 2:10).

> Jesus is the head of every authority that exists or could ever exist. And that is the authority by which you speak when you stand and say, "In the name of Jesus". Every other authority is bound to submit.

To shed more light, Paul writes about the extent of Jesus authority. We read, "God raised Christ from the dead and seated him at his right hand in the heavenly realms, far above all rule and authority, power and dominion, and every name that is invoked, not only in the present age but also in the one to come. And God placed all things under his feet and appointed him to be head over everything for the church (Ephesians 1:20-22). As if that were not enough, Paul wrote in Philippians 2:9-11, Therefore God also has highly exalted Him and given Him the name which is above every name, that at the name of Jesus every knee should bow, of those in heaven, and of those on earth, and of those under the earth, and that every tongue should confess that Jesus Christ is Lord, to the glory of God the Father. Just look at that!

Prayer

Heavenly Father, thank you for the privilege to stand and speak with the highest authority there is in this age and in the age to come. We receive grace this season, that as we speak in that name, situations will align, demons will flee, and things will be established in Jesus' name.

Bible in one year // **Job 38-40, Acts 16:1-21**

JUL 10

> Behold, I give you the authority to trample on serpents and scorpions, and over all the power of the enemy, and nothing shall by any means hurt you. // **Luke 10:19**

The believer's authority

We shared on the authority of Jesus in yesterday's writing. In summary, we could show clearly from Scripture that Jesus is the greatest authority there exist in all creation, whose dominion encompasses every territory possible – of things in heaven, of things on the earth and of things underneath (Philippians 2:9-11). Jesus is Lord even over the Kingdom of darkness. And we are privileged to have the power of attorney to use his name. (Refer to the devotionals from previous days).

> You have the same authority Jesus has over the forces of darkness, including their boss, the devil himself. Only add to that authority, faith. And nothing will be impossible.

The believer's authority is the same authority Jesus has. These emphases I make for one main reason: That you would realize that there is no demon hatched out of hell that is above your authority, no demon that you cannot prevail over. When Jesus sent out 72 of his disciples, they returned to him with these words as feedback, "Lord, even the demons are subject to us in Your name" (Luke 10:17). Then Jesus responded saying, "I saw Satan fall like lightning from heaven. Behold, I have given you authority to tread on serpents and scorpions, and over all the power of the enemy, and nothing shall hurt you. Nevertheless, do not rejoice in this, that the spirits are subject to you, but rejoice that your names are written in heaven" (Luke 10:18-20).

When Jesus said I give you authority, he used the Greek word, "Exousia" which means delegated authority – the right to act on his behalf. He even specified that the authority he gave was over all the power of the enemy. I really ask the question: which part of this English is not clear to those who say your authority is limited to certain demons and some demons are above you as a believer? Such is not from a clear understanding of scripture but a communication of their experiences in instances where they failed to cast out a demon. On one occasion, the disciples were unable to cast out a demon. The Bible tells us, Afterward the disciples asked Jesus privately, "Why couldn't we cast out that demon?". "You don't have enough faith," Jesus told them. "I tell you the truth, if you had faith even as small as a mustard seed... Nothing would be impossible" (Matthew 17:19-20).

Prayer

Heavenly Father, thank you for giving us authority over every unclean spirit, that what we bind in the earth is bound in heaven and what we loose in the earth will be loose in heaven. With this authority therefore, we take our place against all the works of darkness. In Jesus' name.

Bible in one year // Job 41-42, Acts 16:22-40

The heaven, even the heavens, are the Lord's; but the earth He has given to the children of men. // **Psalm 115:16**

JUL 11

Forget territorial demons

When I write, "Forget territorial demons", that is not to say they don't exist. It is to say that even though a demon might be territorial, they have no authority over that territory, at least not above you as a believer. Some Christians have been misguided to think that because they came from some other physical location, they lack spiritual authority to deal with demonic activity in another country. That is another lie from the devil. To begin with, no demon was ever given a territory by God. The bible tells us, "The highest heavens belong to the LORD, but the earth he has given to mankind" (Psalm 115:16 NIV).

It was to humanity that God gave the earth. No demon was ever given the earth. Adam only lost authority to the devil through sin. However, that authority has been restored to us in Christ Jesus. Like the Prince of Persia, the demon with whom Angel Michael wrestled with, there are demons that have taken residence over different nations and claim authority over it as they seek to keep the people in bondage and blind them from the love of God (Daniel 10:10-14). Another record of territorial demons is in the Gospels when Jesus entered the region of the Gerasenes (Mark 5:1-20). Mark specifically records this about the demon, "He begged Jesus repeatedly not to send them out of the region" (Mark 5:10).

> No demon has right over any territory. We only have demons resident in places and claiming authority over it. You have the authority in the name of Jesus to address any demon anywhere, any day.

The reason the demon begged to not be kicked out of that region was because it was familiar territory where he had become resident and was comfortable in operation. There are really no such thing as territorial demons, there are just demons who have settled in specific locations and there, claim authority. But as Jesus said, "All authority in heaven and on earth has been given to me" (Matthew 28:18). Then Jesus said to us, "Go in my name, for as the father has sent me, so send I you". Now with same authority, anywhere, any day, any time in any location, you can stand up against any demon and cast them out. Forget about territorialdemons. We are lords over every territory in Jesus' name. Just like the Lord said unto Joshua, "I will give you every place where you set your foot" (Joshua 1:3).

Prayer

Heavenly Father, thank you for delivering us from the dominion of darkness and bringing us into the Kingdom of light where we have authority over every unclean spirit in all places in the name of Jesus. Today we limit their works and activities in our lives and cities. In Jesus' name.

Bible in one year // **Psalms 1-3, Acts 17:1-15**

JUL 12

> My brethren, count it all joy when you fall into various trials, knowing that the testing of your faith produces patience. // **James 1:2-3**

Count it all joy

Trials are never fun but they are needful. And what are trials? These are the uncomfortable situations in which we find ourselves, sometimes, as a result of our steps of faith, or just circumstances that put our faith to test and make us question the things we have believed. They are usually difficult moments that bring us to a place where we question the promises of God, or His commitment to make them manifest in our lives. In all, they bring us to crossroads where we ponder doing things God's way or finding outside alternatives; holding on to our faith or quitting. Sometimes, it might mean for some people, a total rejection of God because they feel disappointed in Him.

Our text of the day lets us know there is a benefit – it produces patience. They are never meant to break you but to make you; molding you into the person God wants you to be. In fact, the writer of Hebrews says your legitimacy as a son is questionable if you do not have trials at some point on your journey. He wrote, "As you endure this divine discipline, remember that God is treating you as his own children. Who ever heard of a child who is never disciplined by its father? If God doesn't discipline you as he does all of his children, it means that you are illegitimate and are not really his children at all (Hebrews 12:7 - 8 NLT).

> **Count it all joy when you fall into various trials, knowing that the testing of your faith is a confirmation of your sonship and an attestation that God is at work in you, bringing you to an expected end.**

Even of Jesus, it is written, "Though Jesus was God's Son, he learned obedience from the things he suffered. In this way, God qualified him as a perfect High Priest, and he became the source of eternal salvation for all those who obey him (Hebrews 5:8 - 9 NLT). And of Joseph, "Until the time came to fulfill his dreams, the Lord tested Joseph's character (Psalm 105:19 NLT). So, count it all joy during your trials, it is a confirmation of your sonship and an attestation that God is at work in you, bringing you to an expected end.

Prayer

Thank you Lord for being the good Shepherd, who calls me by name and leads me in paths of righteousness. You bring me through the valley of the shadow of death and shield me from the hands of those too strong for me. You anoint my head with oil and fill my mouth with songs of victory even in stormy weather. I rest assured in your faithfulness today and always. In Jesus' name.

Bible in one year // **Psalm 4-6, Acts 17:16-34**

We know that all things work together for good to those who love God, to those who are the called according to His purpose. // **Romans 8:28**

JUL 13

We´ll look back in thanksgiving

"But I want you to know, brethren, that the things which happened to me have actually turned out for the furtherance of the gospel, so that it has become evident to the whole palace guard, and to all the rest, that my chains are in Christ; and most of the brethren in the Lord, having become confident by my chains, are much more bold to speak the word without fear (Philippians 1:12 - 14 NKJV).

This was Paul looking back in thanksgiving and testifying to how all things had worked out for good. His imprisonment and chains had resulted in the spread of the gospel and the emboldening of the saints to do more for the advancement of the Kingdom of God. It was a similar thing when Joseph's brothers who sold him into slavery finally met him in Egypt as governor. Joseph said to them, "But as for you, you meant evil against me; but God meant it for good, in order to bring it about as it is this day, to save many people alive. "Now therefore, do not be afraid; I will provide for you and your little ones." (Genesis 50:20 - 21 NKJV). They all looked back in thanksgiving to God for all the difficulties they had faced. The same will be our story in the end. We'll look back in thanksgiving to God.

> Someday soon, we will look back in thanksgiving for the challenges that come our way. Some of us can already do so because it turned out right.

This we can be sure of that if the Lord lets us go through certain situations, that we will look back in thanksgiving if we will trust Him and stay in His path. Romans 8:28 says, "We know that all things work together for good to those who love God, to those who are the called according to His purpose". It assures us that ALL THINGS work together for our good if we love the Lord and are called according to His purpose. The question is this: Do you love the Lord and are you doing your most to be on course with Him? If the answer is yes, then relax. All things will work for your good.

Prayer

Thank you, Heavenly Father, for you cause all things to work for the good of us who love you and are called according to your purpose. Thank you for the plans you have for us, to prosper us and to bring us to an expected end. We give you all the glory now and always in Jesus' name.

Bible in one year // **Psalms 7-9, Acts 18**

JUL 14

> Whoever hears these sayings of Mine, and does them, I will liken him to a wise man who built his house on the rock. // **Matthew 7:24**

Build on the word

We are all builders, building our lives by the way we go about things. The outlook of your life, your attitude towards others, the value you place on certain things all reflect and show the underlying principles that rule and lead you. Like a house that is seen, the principles by which you live form the foundation on which you build. This is what Jesus meant when He shared with the disciples the parable of the wise and the foolish builders.

Let the word of God and the principles of Christ form the foundation of your life – build your life on the word.

Jesus taught, "Therefore, whoever hears these sayings of Mine, and does them, I will liken him to a wise man who built his house on the rock: and the rain descended, the floods came, and the winds blew and beat on that house; and it did not fall, for it was founded on the rock. But everyone who hears these sayings of Mine, and does not do them, will be like a foolish man who built his house on the sand: and the rain descended, the floods came, and the winds blew and beat on that house; and it fell. And great was its fall" (Matthew 7:24-27).

Choose to be the wise builder, the one who structures and shapes their life according to the word of God. Let the word of God guide and rule your life. Let the principles of Christ shape and influence you. Proverbs 26:12 says, "Do you see a person wise in their own eyes? There is more hope for a fool than for them". Human wisdom is good and a gift from God. But when such wisdom and foundational principle is in opposition to the word of God, drop it off. Let the word of God be your standard for living. Then you will be a wise builder, who builds on a sure foundation able to stand the strongest storms of life. Do not find yourself justifying why you should do things contrary to what the word of God teaches. That is not only being wise in your own eyes, it is much more, being stupid to think you could know better than God. Indeed, there is more hope for a fool than for a person who is wise in their own eyes. Even as it is written, "The foolishness of God is wiser than men" (1 Corinthians 1:25).

Prayer

Heavenly Father, thank you for the word preserved for us through the ages that we might know your ways and walk in them. Thank you for the light that shines on our paths, making plain your ways before us. We receive grace to mold our lives based on your time-tested principles. In Jesus' name.

Bible in one year // **Psalm 10-12, Acts 19:1-20**

Lay up for yourselves treasures in heaven, where neither moth nor rust destroys and where thieves do not break in and steal. // **Matthew 6:20**

JUL 15

Make eternal investments

Do not lay up for yourselves treasures on earth, where moth and rust destroy and where thieves break in and steal; but lay up for yourselves treasures in heaven, where neither moth nor rust destroys and where thieves do not break in and steal. For where your treasure is, there your heart will be also (Matthew 6:19-21 NKJV). These were the words of Jesus in his lengthiest recorded sermon. Summarily, He said, "Make eternal investments". How do you use your time and resources? What are your priorities in life and how do they connect with God's eternal plan? How are you actively contributing to the spread of the gospel, the salvation of souls, the growth of the church and the expansion of the Kingdom of God?

Sooner or later, we would all be gone from here and all that will be left of us in the earth, no matter how much wealth we amass, might be squandered if it finds the wrong hands. Even if well preserved, the most expensive cars are soon deteriorated, the most expensive homes needing demolition and all that once glittered becomes worn with use and age. Indeed, these are all earthly investments where moth and rust will over time, bring them to nothing. That is not to say we should not invest in these things if we are blessed with them. The bible is clear on this, God gives us richly all things to enjoy.

> **Make eternal investments through your sacrifice of time, service, and resources for the fulfilment of God's purpose in the earth for a sure reward.**

However, your services, your time invested in the things of God, your acts of compassion to the needy, your care for God's servants, your contribution to the spread of the gospel and expansion of the Kingdom of God are all timeless investments into heaven's treasure store. And when the time is due, you will join the Lord only to be amazed with how much heavenly wealth you amassed by your earthly sacrifices. Peter had become concerned about his sacrifices. Peter said to Jesus, "We have left all we had to follow you!" "Truly I tell you," Jesus said to them, "No one who has left home or wife or brothers or sisters or parents or children for the sake of the kingdom of God will fail to receive many times as much in this age, and in the age to come eternal life" (Luke 18:28-30).

Prayer

Heavenly Father, thank you for choosing me and calling me to be part of the household of faith. This season, I receive grace to make the right investments that will echo through eternity. In Jesus' name.

Bible in one year // **Psalm 13-15, Acts 19:21-41**

JUL 16

> Assuredly, I say to you, in as much as you did it to one of the least of these My brethren, you did it to Me. // **Matthew 25:40**

Don't look too far

"Now an expert in religious law stood up to test Jesus, saying, "Teacher, what must I do to inherit eternal life?" He said to him, "What is written in the law? How do you understand it?" The expert answered, "Love the Lord your God with all your heart, with all your soul, with all your strength, and with all your mind, and love your neighbor as yourself." Jesus said to him, "You have answered correctly; do this, and you will live." But the expert, wanting to justify himself, said to Jesus, "And who is my neighbor?" (Luke 10:25-37).

Jesus gave a parable saying, "A man was going down from Jerusalem to Jericho, and fell into the hands of robbers, who stripped him, beat him up, and went off, leaving him half dead. Now by chance a priest was going down that road, but when he saw the injured man, he passed by on the other side. So too a Levite... But a Samaritan who was traveling came to where the injured man was, and when he saw him, he felt compassion for him. He went up to him and bandaged his wounds, pouring olive oil and wine on them. Then he put him on his own animal, brought him to an inn, and took care of him... Which of these three do you think became a neighbor to the man who fell into the hands of the robbers?" The expert in religious law said, "The one who showed mercy to him." So, Jesus said to him, "Go and do the same".

> **To make eternal investments, you don't need to look too far, you can start with the person next to you who needs a helping hand.**

In this story, Jesus made it clear who your neighbor is. It is not just someone living next to you in the neighborhood. Your neighbor is the person next to you needing your assistance, wherever that might be. You don't have to look too far. And that could likewise be an absolute stranger. It became clearer as well that when God commanded the Israelites to love their neighbor as they did themselves, he wasn't just talking of having feelings for affection. He meant love that demonstrates itself in action, reaching out to those around you who need your hand. This is the true essence of life and an investment into eternity. Jesus will someday say, "When you did it to one of the least of these my brothers and sisters, you were doing it to me!" (Matthew 25:40).

Prayer

Heavenly Father thank you for choosing us as ambassadors of goodwill in the world. We receive grace to reach out to the one next to us needing the assistance we can offer. That just as you give us richly all things, we ourselves will be true channels of your blessings. In Jesus' name.

Bible in one year // **Psalms 16-17, Acts 20:1-16**

> The lamp of the body is the eye. If therefore your eye is good, your whole body will be full of light. // **Matthew 6:22**

JUL 17

Take off the shades

These were the words of Jesus, "If therefore your eye is good, your whole body will be full of light. But if your eye is bad, your whole body will be full of darkness. If therefore the light that is in you is darkness, how great is that darkness!" (Matthew 6:22-23). Though Jesus explained many parables later, this is one of those parables that remained unexplained in scripture. However, when you read in context, you would realize it can be summarized in the words, "Take off the shades". The amplified reads, "The eye is the lamp of the body; so if your eye is clear [spiritually perceptive], your whole body will be full of light [benefiting from God's precepts]".

Paul prayed, "I pray that the eyes of your heart may be enlightened in order that you may know the hope to which he has called you, the riches of his glorious inheritance" (Ephesians 1:18). Above, Jesus was talking about the eyes of the spirit, which provides the window of entrance of information into your soul. This has nothing to do with physical sight. It has to do with the capacity to perceive and grasp the right spiritual truth. He called the Pharisees blind, and it had nothing to do with physical blindness (Matthew 23:24). He said to them, "Because you claim to see, your guilt remains" (John 9:41).

> **Be sure to verify the truths to which you cling, because if they are wrong, they will become a shade on your eyes, depriving you of the true illumination that comes through the unadulterated word of God.**

Jesus also makes comparison to the one who has light, but the light is darkness. They hold on to what they call "Truth", but it is in reality, a lie. And because of these "Truths" they have, it puts a shade of darkness on every other information coming their way, even the information that might have value to save their souls. It is like the scientist, who because of the notion of evolution cannot embrace the accounts of the bible. We all could easily fall into a place of prejudice where we have embraced partially wrong doctrines and ideas in the past from erroneous biblical teachings which have left us with shades that make embracing the true knowledge difficult. If we will receive divine truth, we would have to take of the shades when we approach the word of God by putting aside our opinions and pre-conceptions and let the word of God speak for itself.

Prayer

Heavenly Father, thank you for your Light that shines and illumines us in every day. Our spiritual eyes are open, that we may see with clarity as you bring to us enlightenment through the word. In Jesus name.

Bible in one year // **Psalms 18-19, Acts 20:17-38**

JUL 18

> Do not be conformed to this world, but be transformed by the renewing of your mind, that you may prove what is that good and acceptable and perfect will of God. // **Romans 12:2**

Change your way of thinking

One easy way to become stagnated when you move into a new environment is to continue doing things they way you are familiar with from your old environment, particular when these two places are very much different in structure, policies and level of economic development. The same is true spiritually. When one becomes born again, they are brought into a new environment where different rules apply (Colossians 1:13). It is different from life in the world, though you continue to live in the world. And unless the mind be renewed, your way of thinking changed, your spiritual progress will be hampered, and your experience of divine realities will be limited.

> **Mind renewal is the acceptance of new information that replaces your old way of thinking and that is what happens when you receive the word of God and accept His perspective.**

That is why Paul admonished his readers, "Do not be conformed to this world, but be transformed by the renewing of your mind, that you may prove what is that good and acceptable and perfect will of God (Rom 12:2). Mind renewal is simply a change in our way of thinking as we learn to receive the word of God and accept the divine perspective it communicates. Never be such a person who says, "I know the bible says..... BUT I personally think that". In this context, such a person goes ahead to make a contradicting proposition to the word of God. In their minds, the word is in error, they have a better opinion than what the Lord communicates through his word.

Learn to receive the word of God and let it give you perspective for life; let it become the lenses through which you filter everything else. This is not being brain-washed as some people call it. This is living by the greatest standards of truth and reality. Remember, even if you will choose to hold on to your own contradicting opinions, that someday you will stand before the Lord to answer for your way of life. And that day you will be called to account based on his standards and perspective, not according to what you thought was a better opinion. You will be doing yourself much good to accept God's perspective.

Prayer

Thank you Heavenly Father for your word that is conforming me daily to the image of Christ as I receive it and embrace your perspective. Thank you for eyes that see, ears that hear and a heart that understands your ways because of the enabling of the Holy Spirit who is at work in me. In Jesus' name.

Bible in one year // **Psalms 20-22, Acts 21:1-17**

Keep your heart with all diligence, for out of it spring the issues of life.
// **Proverbs 4:23**

JUL 19

Some fell among the thorns

This was Jesus sharing a parable to illustrate why the word of God might prove fruitless in some lives. You must understand that the word of God is for results, it is intended to cause and produce a change in your life. And this is not just a change with regards to character and way of life. While all that is good and commended, the word of God is more than a moral code for life. It has creative power to bring about the manifestation of the very thing it talks about in your life. The word works. Nonetheless, it must meet the right ground, it must reach the right heart. For the ground in the parable of Jesus, is the heart of man.

Jesus narrated, "A sower went out to sow. And as he sowed, some seed fell by the wayside; and the birds came and devoured them. Some fell on stony places, where they did not have much earth; and they immediately sprang up because they had no depth of earth. But when the sun was up they were scorched, and because they had no root they withered away. And some fell among thorns, and the thorns sprang up and choked them. But others fell on good ground and yielded a crop: some a hundredfold, some sixty, some thirty. He who has ears to hear, let him hear!" (Matthew 13:3-9).

While you can see the full explanation of this parable, I will call your attention to the seed that fell among thorns. Jesus explained, "He who received seed among the thorns is he who hears the word, and the cares of this world and the deceitfulness of riches choke the word, and he becomes unfruitful" (Matthew 13:22). The word was meant to produce fruit, but the person's heart was filled with other things that choked the word and made it unfruitful. No doubt the writer of provers admonishes us, "Keep your heart with all diligence, for out of it spring the issues of life" (Proverbs 4:23). You must rid your heart of things that are not supportive for results by the word of God: lust, the love of the world, bitterness, unforgiveness, jealousy and all these things which are unbecoming for God's people. These are all thorns that take up residence in the heart, causing the word to fail to produce its fruits.

> **Guard your heart with all diligence, get rid of anything that could take rook and make the word of God unfruitful in your life.**

Prayer

Father thank you for the word of illumination to me daily. My heart is plowed, and like fallowed ground, it brings forth fruit bountifully, producing the very things it talks about in my life. I am transformed daily, more and more into the image of Christ by the Spirit as I receive your word in my heart. In Jesus' name.

Bible in one year // **Psalms 23-25, Acts 21:18-40**

JUL 20

They are life to those who find them, and healing and health to all their flesh. // Proverbs 4:22 Amp

It is health to your flesh

"My son, give attention to my words; incline your ear to my sayings. Do not let them depart from your eyes; Keep them in the midst of your heart; For they are life to those who find them, And health to all their flesh (Proverbs 4:20-22)". The writer of Proverbs calls us to give attention to the word of God and to not let it depart from our hearts. Yesterday's devotional, you would remember, was a call to guard your heart above all else. Just as Jesus shared why the word becomes unfruitful in some lives. He said the word like a seed, is choked by other things.

But much more a reason to celebrate is what happens when we retain that word in our hearts. It is life to all who find it, and health to all their flesh. These are not mere words; these are the words of the one who created and sustains all things. It carries in it the same power of creation and rejuvenation. It will indeed impact even your health if you will receive it and store it up in your heart. Yes, the word of God has an effect even on your physical body. Psalm 107:20 says, "He sent out his word and healed them, snatching them from the door of death".

> The word of God you receive and store in your heart can impact even your health. For in it is life-giving power. The word also inspires your faith to take hold of the divine health which is yours in Christ Jesus.

Give the word of God attention, and guard in your heart jealously the truths you receive. For it has the power to impact even your health. This is accomplished in many ways. First, the word itself by its very entrance communicates divine virtues into your spirit and body. This includes health. Just as it is written, "The entrance of Your words gives light; it gives understanding to the simple" (Psalm 119:130). The second means by which it accomplishes health in you is by building your faith into the experience of the promises of God. For anything we will ever receive and experience of God is of faith. The word of God is indeed health to your body, renewing your flesh and inspiring your faith for the experience of divine health.

Prayer

Heavenly Father, thank you for your word that gives life and renews health. As I meditate on it daily, it renews my youth like the eagle's and brings healing to all my flesh. My heart is open as a receptacle for your word, where it is stored and brings forth fruit in due season visible to all. In Jesus name.

Bible in one year // **Psalms 26-28, Acts 22**

For indeed the gospel was preached to us as well as to them; but the word which they heard did not profit them, not being mixed with faith in those who heard it. // **Hebrews 4:2**

JUL 21

Mix it with faith

The writer of Hebrews highlights to us one other reason why the word of God might fail in a life. He wrote, "For indeed the gospel was preached to us as well as to them; but the word which they heard did not profit them, not being mixed with faith in those who heard it" (Hebrews 4:2 NKJV). It is not strange to meet someone who said, "I used to be a Christian" or "I used to go to Church but it did not help me". In summary, they are saying it did not profit them, they never saw an outcome for which they could continue. The problem was never the word, the problem was their hearts. Either they never received the right message, or they failed to mix the message they received with faith in their hearts. For the word of God brings profit, it brings results when it falls on the right ground.

> The word of God has capacity to produce the results it talks about; all you have to do is mix the word you receive with faith and it will produce for your what it talks about in due season.

As Jesus said, "He who received seed on the good ground is he who hears the word and understands it, who indeed bears fruit and produces: some a hundredfold, some sixty, some thirty" (Matthew 13:23). Paul wrote to the Colossians, "Indeed, just as in the whole world the gospel is constantly bearing fruit and spreading [by God's power], just as it has been doing among you ever since the day you first heard of it and understood the grace of God in truth [becoming thoroughly and deeply acquainted with it] (Col 1:6). The word of God was bringing forth fruit among these people as it was in the rest of the world.

As far as the word of God is concerned, its potency in your life depends on your faith. It is your faith that gives the word of God expression. On the contrary, unbelief is its greatest opposition. In fact, the word of God will fail in a life that refuses to believe it. Even Jesus was unable to help his people because of their lack of faith. "He did not do many miracles there because of their lack of faith" (Matthew 13:58). So, as you read and meditate on the word of God, believe it and let your acceptance of the word be evident through your words and action. That is faith! And this kind of faith always gets a harvest of results from the word of God in due season, for the word has been mixed with faith in the heart.

Prayer

Heavenly Father, thank you for your word is alive and powerful, sharper than any two-edged sword. Thank you for the power of the Holy Spirit at work in us to make manifest the results assured in your word, that our lives will reflect its potency, now and always. In Jesus' name.

Bible in one year // **Psalms 29-30, Acts 23:1-15**

JUL 22

> How sweet are Your words to my taste, sweeter than honey to my mouth! // **Psalm 119:103**

Two tastes of the Word

How the Psalmist declared, "How sweet are your words to my taste, sweeter than honey to my mouth!" (Psalm 119:103 NIV). It wasn't the first time someone was likening the Word to something of sweet taste. The prophet Ezekiel wrote, "He said to me, 'Son of man, eat what is before you, eat this scroll; then go and speak to the people of Israel.' So, I opened my mouth, and he gave me the scroll to eat. Then he said to me, 'Son of man, eat this scroll I am giving you and fill your stomach with it.' So I ate it, and it tasted as sweet as honey in my mouth" (Ezekiel 3:3 NIV).

Akin to Ezekiel's encounter, is the experience of John. He writes, "Then the voice that I had heard from heaven spoke to me once more: 'Go, take the scroll that lies open in the hand of the angel who is standing on the sea and on the land.' So I went to the angel and asked him to give me the little scroll. He said to me, 'Take it and eat it. It will turn your stomach sour, but 'in your mouth it will be as sweet as honey.' I took the little scroll from the angel's hand and ate it. It tasted as sweet as honey in my mouth, but when I had eaten it, my stomach turned sour. Then I was told, "You must prophesy again about many peoples, nations, languages and kings." (Revelation 10:8-11).

> **If you sufficiently take in the word of God, it will become impossible to hold it in. Your words will be filled with wonder-working scriptures, not for a show but because from the abundance of the heart, the mouth speaks.**

The word tasted sweet in the mouth but sour in the stomach. That simply meant, it could not be contained in the stomach, unpleasant to stay there. This explains a simple law of the Spirit. If you take the word into you long enough, and much of it like one eating a scroll, it will well up out of you in words. Before both servants of God went out to prophesy, they were given the scroll to eat. Just as Jesus said, out of the abundance of the heart, the mouth speaks. The Lord said to Joshua. "This book of the law shall not depart from your MOUTH. You shall meditate on it day and night, and so you shall make your way prosperous and have good success". You see, one reason for meditating on God's word is not just so you can know the truths therein. You are like a soldier loading his gun with bullets. Jemiah testified, Then I said, "I will not make mention of Him, nor speak anymore in His name." But His word was in my heart like a burning fire shut up in my bones; I was weary of holding it back, and I could not" (Jeremiah 20:9).

Prayer

Heavenly Father, Thank you for the illumination in your word. As I receive the word, it abides in me and I speak accordingly, releasing words with creative power, words that edify, words that encourage and impart grace to the hearers. In Jesus name.

Bible in one year // **Psalms 31-32, Acts 23:16-35**

Do you not say, 'There are still four months and then comes the harvest'? Behold, I say to you, lift up your eyes and look at the fields, for they are already white for harvest! // **John 4:35**

JUL 23

Be such an ox

Where there are no oxen, the manger is empty, but from the strength of an ox come abundant harvests (Proverbs 14:4). This verse highlights the difference a single ox can make in the store house by the harvest they bring in. I remember several years ago when I first understood this verse and its application. It dawned on me that I could bring in such a harvest for the Lord that will make an obvious difference. Yes, it is a blessing when we have oxen, for even then the harvest is greater. But it is also very important to see yourself as able to cause a change and make a difference, even as a lone ox in the manger.

Be such an ox, which by its great strength brings in a great harvest. That is what Jesus was all about in his earthly ministry, and that is one reason for which He took hold of you, that you might continue the task and join force in the harvest. Jesus spoke these words to his disciples, "My food is to do the will of Him who sent Me, and to finish His work. Do you not say, 'There are still four months and then comes the harvest'? Behold, I say to you, lift up your eyes and look at the fields, for they are already white for harvest! And he who reaps receives wages, and gathers fruit for eternal life, that both he who sows and he who reaps may rejoice together (John 4:34-36).

> You can make a significant difference in the harvest of souls in the world as an individual, and our combined effort will have an amplified outcome.

Some people are concerned by the multiplicity of churches and the increasing new ministries that are born daily. While it is true that some are uncalled for because of the damage and misrepresentation of Christ they exhibit, it is also the joy of the Lord that many soldiers are responding to the urgent need for harvest. For even then, the laborers are still few with regards to the great harvest in the world. And you can truly be like that ox in our opening passage, seeing yourself as one called to bring in the sheaves into the master's store house. The fields are indeed white, the harvest is plentiful, and your hands are needed on the field. Therefore, be such an ox which brings in a great harvest for the Lord.

Prayer

Heavenly Father, thank You for the blessing of a new day and the privilege to be part of your end-time harvesters. In this season we receive grace to be more effective, as you open our eyes to the opportunities that abound to bring the lost home. In Jesus name.

Bible in one year // **Psalms 33-34, Acts 24**

JUL 24

Jesus said to them, "My food is to do the will of Him who sent Me, and to finish His work". // **John 4:34**

Be about His business

It is a sad reality that some believers think that those who are bold in their faith and continuously get involved with winning souls or establishing them through follow up and the committed distribution of edifying content such as this devotional, are just being overzealous. Such have not understood the urgency of the hour and the task committed to their charge. Neither are they conscious of the limited window of time allotted us to do what has to be done. Jesus, even as a boy, was about the Father's business. The boy Jesus had stayed behind after the feast as the family left for Nazareth, his hometown. The parents journeyed for three days before realizing Jesus wasn't with them.

Returning to Jerusalem and finding him, the boy had rather a question for them in response to their search. For they had been worried about his whereabout. Jesus asked, "Why did you seek Me? Did you not know that I must be about My Father's business?" But they did not understand the statement which He spoke to them (Luke 2:49-50). It was same mindset Jesus had even as His time for departure drew close – He was always about the Father's business. In John 4, when the disciples brought him food, He wasn't as moved by it though He was hungry. "My food," said Jesus, "is to do the will of him who sent me and to finish his work" (John 4:34).

> Don't make assumptions regarding how much time you have to do the things the Lord is calling you to do. It will be good he meets you busy about His business, that is where your true reward lies.

If the Lord has placed on your heart a vision, don't make assumptions regarding the time you have ahead of you. Jesus shared this parable, "Who then is the faithful and wise manager, whom the master puts in charge of his servants to give them their food allowance at the proper time? It will be good for that servant whom the master finds doing so when he returns. Truly I tell you, he will put him in charge of all his possessions. But if that servant says in his heart, 'My master is delaying his coming,' and begins to beat the male and female servants, and to eat and drink and be drunk, the master of that servant will come on a day when he is not looking for him, and at an hour when he is not aware, and will cut him in two and appoint him his portion with the unbelievers (Luke 12:41-46). If ever there was a time to be about the things the Lord has called you to do, it is now. We must be about His business.

Prayer

Heavenly Father thank you for the gift of life and the opportunity to serve you in the earth for a reward that is guaranteed. I receive grace this season to know that which you would have me do and the discipline to be about my task. Thank you for the grace to stay true till the end. In Jesus' name.

Bible in one year // **Psalms 35-36, Acts 25**

Oh, magnify the Lord with me, and let us exalt His name together.
// **Psalm 34:3**

JUL 25

Magnify the Lord with me

"Oh, magnify the Lord with me". This was the call of David, as he looked back to all the Lord had been to him and what things the Lord had done. It is my very call to you today as we start a new day. Come on and magnify the Lord with me; and let us exalt His name together. It doesn't matter what is currently going on in your life and what things you wish could be better. If only you will look about you, you will find reasons to magnify the Lord today and exalt His holy name.

For David, he had a lot to say always. Reading about his life and considering his plethora of heavenly poetry and songs, you will find countless reasons he gives for magnifying the name of the Lord. We read, "I will bless the Lord at all times; His praise shall continually be in my mouth. My soul shall make its boast in the Lord; the humble shall hear of it and be glad. Oh, magnify the Lord with me, and let us exalt His name together. I sought the Lord, and He heard me, and delivered me from all my fears" (Psalm 34:1-4). David could look back and thank God for answered prayers.

> **Look back in your life and you will see many reasons to magnify the name of the Lord and let his praises be on your lips – at least for the things which are now a reality, things that were once prayer points.**

Pause today for a moment and look back on your life. Remember all the things you now enjoy that was once a prayer point. You might now be a mother, a house owner, a car owner, might have completed a training program, met a life partner, moved into a new house, or recovered from a time of sickness. You might have overcome depression; you might have been released from prison or survived an accident. If you will look back, though there might be failed dreams, you sure have come to live some imaginations that once seemed far off. Even for the grace to still be firm in the Lord and to not have given up on your faith after all you have been through, if you say your own life has been totally difficult – that is itself a great call to exalt the Lord today and magnify His name with me. For God kept you, and you did not give up.

Prayer

> Heavenly Lord, you are indeed beautiful beyond description. Too marvelous for words, too wonderful comprehension. Who can grasp the depth of your love or fathom the breath of your wisdom? We stand in awe of you to whom all praise is due. You cause all things to work for our good. In Jesus' name.

Bible in one year // **Psalms 37-39, Acts 26**

JUL 26

Bless the Lord, O my soul, and forget not all His benefits.
// **Psalm 103:2**

Forget not His benefits

When we read these words of David from the Psalm, we can easily connect the dots and realize indeed he had benefitted much from walking with the Lord. The Lord Himself sending words to David through the prophet Nathan had this to say, "Now then, tell my servant David, 'This is what the LORD Almighty says: I took you from the pasture, from tending the flock, and appointed you ruler over my people Israel" (2 Samuel 7:8). No doubt David could say to himself, "Bless the Lord, O my soul, and forget not all His benefits" (Psalm 103:2).

> An intentional recall to mind of the goodness of God in your life will inspire praise for today and faith for tomorrow. Ponder on what things the Lord has done and forget not His benefits.

And when you read all of that Psalm 103, you will realize David did a good job to list some of them, benefits which are true to us even today. He wrote, „Bless the Lord, O my soul; and all that is within me, bless His holy name! Bless the Lord, O my soul, and forget not all His benefits: Who forgives all your iniquities, Who heals all your diseases, Who redeems your life from destruction, Who crowns you with lovingkindness and tender mercies, Who satisfies your mouth with good things, so your youth is renewed like the eagle's... The Lord is merciful and gracious, slow to anger, and abounding in mercy. (Psalm 103:1-8).

Without going through the whole Psalm, we see how intentional David was in recalling the benefits he had received from the Lord. It is easy to become familiar with the Lord's goodness, when we don't recognize the privilege to be alive, but get caught up complaining about all that is not where we would like them to be, forgetting the benefits we already have. The call to you today is to "Forget not His benefits". Like David, remembering the things the Lord has done for you will inspire praise even in the darkest nights and renew your faith for the things yet to come. Let us with grateful hearts sing his praises and indeed forget not the good things He has done.

Prayer

Heavenly Father, thank you for a new day and the privilege to be numbered among the living. Thank you for salvation of our souls, for illumination through the word, for freedom from the oppressions of darkness and for giving us a hope in Christ that cannot disappoint. We give you praise in Jesus' name.

Bible in one year // **Psalms 40-42, Acts 27:1-26**

This is the day the Lord has made; we will rejoice and be glad in it.
// **Psalm 118:24**

JUL 27

Choose to be joyful

To me, David is one who lived ahead of His times. When you consider his rich walk with God even as a teenage boy, it was something to greatly commend. By the time he served King Saul or faced goliath, he already had a rich accumulation of faith lessons for someone at his age – slaying wild animals who came after the sheep. If you consider his many battles and woes, you will realize even how much he had reasons to live a depressive life. But not David. He understood the Joy of the Lord (Psalm 46:1-5). He was not going to let others and things define his mood. He was not going to give them the upper hand. He had an attitude even in facing his days. He wrote, "This is the day the Lord has made; we will rejoice and be glad in it" (Psalm 118:24).

And when depression came knocking on the door, He was quick to shut it out. In Psalm 42:11, David wrote, "Why, my soul, are you downcast? Why so disturbed within me? Put your hope in God, for I will yet praise him, my Savior and my God". He wasn't going to continue in a pity party until someone else came to his support. This is not to play down on the value of support and the need. For there is a place for it. You don't have to shy away from help if you need it, meeting professionals or spiritual authorities who can support you.

> **Choose to be joyful in every day and not let your joy depend on happenstances or other persons. In fact, it is a setup for depression to let your joy depend on others or happenings.**

Sometimes depression is spiritual, like King Saul's depression. It was an evil spirit that tormented him the bibles says. So, you might need more than words of a comedian to cheer you up. You will need the prayers of the saints. Be open and talk to someone, particularly if you have suicidal thoughts. In fact, that is an active role you are playing in the choice to be joyful, by seeking the help you need. The good thing is this: if you are born again, then you have the Holy Spirit in you who brings to you the Joy of the Lord in every situation. Joy is a fruit of the Spirit (Galatians 5:22). It is yours in Christ Jesus. In effect, the true responsibility you have is not to try to be joyful, but to let the joy of the Lord in you get expression despite the challenges that might abound. It is your choice to be joyful. Like David, let us recognize that this is a day the Lord has made. Then rejoice and be glad in it.

Prayer

Heavenly Father, thank you for the gift of the Holy Spirit and the overflowing joy He brings in my life. Thank you for giving us the capacity to be joyful above our circumstances and to rejoice in you always. Let that overflowing joy be our lot today and may it overflow and impact those about us in Jesus' name.

Bible in one year // **Psalms 43-45, Acts 27:27-44**

JUL 28

> Jesus said to him, "If you can believe, all things are possible to him who believes." // **Mark 9:23**

Only believe

Believing is so important. Its power cannot be over emphasized. It impacts not only your life and experience with God, but it also even impacts your eternity. In fact, people will be judged on the last day based on if they believed in Jesus or not. It is that important. People will be eternally condemned for not believing and others forever glorified for believing. Whether you live and experience the glory of God is anchored on believing. Jesus said, "Most assuredly, I say to you, he who hears My word and believes in Him who sent Me has everlasting life, and shall not come into judgment, but has passed from death into life" (John 5:24).

ust think about that! That the salvation of men is anchored on this simple responsibility of believing. Someone once rightly said: "When I read the bible, I pay double attention to what Jesus himself said". How important that is today to realize that Jesus is the one speaking. On another occasion Jesus said, For God did not send His Son into the world to condemn the world, but that the world through Him might be saved. "He who believes in Him is not condemned; but he who does not believe is condemned already, because he has not believed in the name of the only begotten Son of God. And this is the condemnation, that the light has come into the world, and men loved darkness rather than light, because their deeds were evil (John 3:17-19). And to the apostles, Jesus said: "He who believes and is baptized will be saved; but he who does not believe will be condemned" (Mark 16:16).

> Believing is so important. Your life experiences, your walk with God and your eternity all anchor on your beliefs. Therefore, don't take it lightly what you believe or choose not to believe.

And when it came to the working of miracles, once again the capacity of the people to believe was in play and responsible for the results seen or their absence thereof. It is written of Jesus on one of the visits to His hometown, „He did not do many mighty works there because of their unbelief" (Matthew 13:57-58). And when it came to the resurrection of the daughter of Jairus from the dead, even for such a miracle, all Jesus said to the synagogue ruler was "Do not be afraid; only believe" (Mark 5:36). Even today, be it regarding your health, job, finance or family, anything is possible for you if only you will believe. For „All things are possible to him who believes!" (Mark 9:23).

Prayer

Heavenly Father, thank you for opening my eyes to truth that I do not walk in ignorance regarding your existence, the salvation you offer in Christ Jesus and the pending judgement that is coming to the world. Therefore, I do not walk in the dark but walk according to the truths I now know. In Jesus' name.

Bible in one year // **Psalms 46-48, Acts 28**

You shall know the truth, and the truth shall make you free.
// John 8:32

JUL 29

You can know the truth

Now the term believer can be misleading. While we often use it to mean a believer in Christ when we share from a Christian perspective, it is important to know that even the supposed nonbeliever is also a believer, they just believe something else. Even the atheist is a believer – they believe God does not exist. The agnostic is also a believer – they believe if there is a God or not, it is not in our capacity to know. And we of course have those who believe in other deities or practice the worship of the dead. Truth is this, everyone in the world is a believer somewhere, they just believe differently. While some have the truth, others hold on to a lie. While some believe right, others believe wrong.

To many, we will all find out what was right in the next life. That is another bone of contention. Some don't even believe there is a life beyond this. As far as they are concerned, it all ends here – that is what they believe. However, you don't have to bargain on such a risk, to only find out in the afterlife what was true. For the price will be too costly if you believed wrong. Don't say it doesn't matter what you believe. It does. And as a Christian, never be one who thinks it is not their business what others believe; it absolutely is. Because you have come to the light and are sent out to shine that light to the lost, the confused and the ignorant, to save their souls, help them experience the love of God and deliver them from the coming judgement.

> In Christ Jesus, you can know the truth and ascertain the things you believe. And in the process, you get to know also what beliefs are wrong. Just as Jesus guaranteed, you shall know the truth.

What do you believe? You should verify what you believe and be sure you are believing the truth. For what you accept as true will influence your actions. Don't wait to find out in the afterlife. That is the blessing of Christianity – that it offers to you the opportunity to ascertain on this side of life the reality of the spiritual truths it professes. You can know the truth. Jesus Himself said, "Those who accept my commandments and obey them are the ones who love me. And because they love me, my Father will love them. And I will love them and reveal myself to each of them." (John 14:21 NLT). Jesus is alive and gives us the opportunity to experience him beyond a shadow of doubt, an experience that authenticates the things we believe. We go beyond believing to knowing as Jesus said, "You shall know the truth".

Prayer

> Heavenly Father, thank you for the Holy Spirit who has been given to us to guide us into all truth that we might not walk in darkness but have the light of life. Therefore, we believe right and make decisions in line with the truth, even as you continue to manifest yourself to us daily in diverse ways. In Jesus' name.

Bible in one year // **Psalm 49-50, Romans 1**

JUL 30

> Therefore let no one boast in men. For all things are yours.
> // 1 Corinthians 3:21

Don't settle there

I have often pondered over the story of Abram's biological father. Not much is written of him in the scripture. But in the few lines where we read of him, it is difficult to not notice one thing. He seemed a quitter, one who would settle for less if he got comfortable enough. It is recorded of Abram's father: "Terah took his son Abram, his grandson Lot son of Haran, and his daughter-in-law Sarai, the wife of his son Abram, and together they set out from Ur of the Chaldeans to go to Canaan. But when they came to Harran, they settled there. Terah lived 205 years, and he died in Harran (Genesis 11:31-32).

Terah did not follow up on His visions till the end. He settled for something else. Whatever was the motivation and reason, we cannot tell. But one thing strikes me – the fact that God called Abram to move to Canaan. It is plausible that for the destiny of His family, Terah had been drawn out already to move to Canaan. It is plausible that God was in it and might have failed to get the Generation before Abram to where He really wanted the family tree to go. While that is my opinion, it is no dispute however that Terah gave up on a life dream initiated. He settled on the way. And sadly, there is sometimes a mediocre mindset with some people who are contented to just have enough. Just a life of trying to barely survive until Jesus comes. No! That is failing the Father.

> What visions did you have, on which you are giving up or quitting? Settle for nothing less! Become all God wants you to be, get all God wants you to have and live life to the fullest like God has given you in Christ Jesus – Life in abundance.

And while some rest on their laurels with such a mentality, men and women of the world who give no sleep to their eyes set seemingly impossible goals and achieve them. These people who don't know the Lord, careless about the welfare of humanity and seek nothing but sheer pleasure become the law makers of our days, presidents of nations, members of parliaments, the rich and influential while some people of faith sit back and watch. But I am glad God is raising a new generation of men and women who will not accept mediocrity nor settle for less when He has given us the whole world. Just as it is written, "All things are yours" (1 Cor 3:21-23).

Prayer

Heavenly Father, thank you for the life given us in Christ Jesus, life overflowing. Today we expand our visions to see the world through your eyes, we open our minds for visions that will bring us to realms of great wealth and influential positions of society. In Jesus' name.

Bible in one year // **Psalm 51-53, Romans 2**

But you are a chosen generation, a royal priesthood, a holy nation,
His own special people, that you may proclaim the praises of Him
who called you out of darkness into His marvelous light. // **1 Peter 2:9**

JUL 31

It is the Father's delight

These were the words once came to me: "It is the Father's delight that you shine and make a show of His glory". You know, it is not uncommon to hear a minister, be it a preacher or a worship leader go up the stage in the congregation and start with the words, "That I might decrease that Jesus may increase, that I might not be seen but only Jesus will be seen". And this I did myself say, when I started off ministering. However, I have come to know better. It is the Father's delight to make a show-off with you. He is not all about showing off Jesus although that is prime. He wants you to shine forth a glory that only you can reflect, and this is his delight. He wants you to increase, He wants you to be seen.

Someone may ask, "But what is wrong with that?" It is everything wrong. The very first is that it is a negative confession, one that is born out of humility and not a full understanding of the context of this. When John said those words, "He must increase so I must decrease" (John 3:30), He was referring to His fading ministry and the fact that His purpose had been fulfilled. He was referring to the fact that the multitudes were now drawn to Jesus and his crowds at the meetings were thinning out. Everyone was going to Jesus (John 3:26). More so, it is rather the father's desire that you increase in all things, until you fully are a true representative of Christ. It is written, "Speaking truth in love, we may grow up in all things into him, who is the head, even Christ" (Ephesians 4:15). So, you should increase and manifest Christ.

Now someone says, well it just means that less of me and more of him. Oh no! It is because you have not recognized that you are yourself a son of God, and the "You in you", the new creation man, is not supposed to be hidden, he is not supposed to decrease. He is not of a nature that has to be concealed. For he was recreated in the very image and likeness of God (Ephesians 4:24). You don't have to decrease so that Jesus can increase. You were called to shine along with him. That is the very purpose you were called out of darkness, "That ye may show forth the excellencies of him who called you out of darkness into his marvelous light" (1 Peter 2:9). It is the Father's delight to see you shine and reflect His glories.

> You are a chosen generation, a royal priest, called out of darkness into God's marvelous light. And it is the Father's delight to see you shine forth, showing forth his virtues and perfections in the world.

Prayer

> Heavenly Father, thank you for the virtues and glories in me, that you have lit me up as a light and set me up on a lamp stand to give light to all in the room. Therefore, I shine forth, reflecting the virtues and excellencies of the recreated man, being forever conformed to the image of Christ. In Jesus' name.

Bible in one year // **Psalms 54-56, Romans 3**

AUGUST

Blessed be the Lord, who daily loads us with benefits, The God of our salvation! // **Psalm 68:19**

AUG 1

A daily load of benefits

David the Psalmist had a grateful heart. He was always quick to recognize the goodness of God even in the little things. Even when you read His psalms of complaints, they often end with the twist of hope and confidence in the fact that the good Lord that has seen Him through other challenging situations will also bring him through again victoriously. So he could declare boldly in Psalm 27:13, "I remain confident of this: I will see the goodness of the LORD in the land of the living" (NIV). Jesus talked about the daily load of God's benefits, even upon the non-believing. Jesus said, "For he gives his sunlight to both the evil and the good, and he sends rain on the just and the unjust alike" Matthew 5:45.

> Let us bless the LORD always, for He daily loads us with benefits. Indeed, great is His faithfulness unto us.

Have you ever taken time to consider the full lyrics of the hymn, Great is thy faithfulness written by Thomas Chisholm? You will indeed say, "He daily loads us with benefits. He wrote, "Great is Thy faithfulness, O God my Father, there is no shadow of turning with Thee. Thou changest not, Thy compassions, they fail not. As Thou hast been, Thou forever wilt be. Great is Thy faithfulness, great is Thy faithfulness. Morning by morning new mercies I see. All I have needed Thy hand hath provided. Great is Thy faithfulness, Lord, unto me.

He goes on to add a few more profound stanzas. "Summer and winter, and springtime and harvest; Sun, moon and stars in their courses above, join with all nature in manifold witness to Thy great faithfulness, mercy, and love... Pardon for sin and a peace that endureth. Thine own dear presence to cheer and to guide. Strength for today and bright hope for tomorrow, blessings all mine, with ten thousand beside". Hopefully, you can sing along today as we all testify to his faithfulness unto us. Just like the Prophet writes, "Through the Lord's mercies we are not consumed, Because His compassions fail not. They are new every morning; Great is Your faithfulness" (Lamentation 3:22-23).

Prayer

Gracious and Faithful father, thank you for your love and mercies that are new every morning. That you daily load us with benefits. Thank You for your wonderful works and many blessings in our lives. We give you praise. In Jesus' name.

Bible in one year // **Psalms 57-59, Romans 4**

AUG 2

> For I am confident of this very thing, that He who began a good work in you will perfect it until the day of Christ Jesus. // **Philippians 1:6 NASB**

He perfects His works

The Lord brings to completion that which He initiates, He will not leave it partly done. This was the confidence of the Psalmist when he said, "The LORD will perfect that which concerns me" (Psalm 138:8). This is your story. Just as it is written, "For I know the thoughts that I think toward you, saith the LORD, thoughts of peace, and not of evil, to give you an expected end" (Jeremiah 29:11 KJV). He has it all figured out. Although in the process, you might wonder and be confused about what is currently going on in your life, I am fully persuaded that someday you will look back and say, "I can now connect the dots of what the Lord was doing all this time, He had it all figured out".

> **God will perfect that which concerns you, He will not leave you but will bring to completion His good works in your life.**

Sometimes you have to picture God's work in your life like that of engineers at a construction site. If you ever visited one, particularly at the start of their work, all you see will be machines and building materials. What structure it might ultimately be is hardly apparent from the start. The look of things can be discouraging. Like some of the Israelites after the Babylonian captivity, when they saw the foundation of the second temple in construction, they sat down and wept. In their minds, there was hardly going to be anything good enough to come out of what they were seeing, comparable to the glory of the first temple they knew (Ezra 3:12). But God had a good word for them: "The glory of this present house will be greater than the glory of the former house..., And in this place I will grant peace" (Haggai 2:9).

In the same light, I want you to be encouraged this day, knowing that God will indeed perfect all that concerns you. He says to you today the same thing He said to Jacob, "I will not leave you until I have done what I have promised you" (Genesis 28:15). It is His character to bring His works to perfection. It started in Eden. He did not stop until He saw everything He had made, and it was very good (Genesis 1:31). Then He rested from His works. No doubt Paul could write to the Philippians, "I am confident of this very thing, that He who began a good work in you will perfect it until the day of Christ Jesus" (Philippians 1:6 NASB).

Prayer

Heavenly Father, thank you for the good thoughts you have towards me. I receive grace in season to be patient where I do not understand, to trust where I cannot see, to follow where you lead, and to keep busy in season in your call for me until you perfect all that concerns me. In Jesus' name.

Bible in one year // **Psalms 60-62, Romans 5**

The path of the righteous is like the morning sun, shining ever brighter till the full light of day. // **Proverbs 4:18 NIV**

AUG 3

An ever-glorious path

The path of the righteous only gets better by the day. That is what our opening verse says. And you can trust this to be true even if your experience so far does not seem to echo this truth. That is where faith comes in. When we accept God's word as truth irrespective of what circumstances suggest, then in the confidence of that truth, we enforce and bring into full manifestation that which God's word declared. For the word of God will always prove true. Let no one deceive you with an alternative perspective. It is as the word puts it, "The path of the just is like a shining light that gets brighter unto the perfect day. That doesn't mean challenges will not come nor cloudy days appear. Those will come, but the guarantee is that when the cloud is passed, the light that shines will be even brighter.

It is important to know that the righteous one is the person who has right standing with God, whose slate is clean, not because of how strictly they have been able to follow God's word, but because of the finished work of Christ. For, "God made him who had no sin to be sin for us, so that in him we might become the righteousness of God" (2 Corinthians 5:21 NIV). So if you are in Christ Jesus, you are that righteous one. For righteousness is never attained by the efforts of any man. That is why the prophet Isaiah wrote, "When we display our righteous deeds, they are nothing but filthy rags" (Isaiah 64:6 NLT)

> Our path in Christ is one of ever-increasing glory. It only gets better by the day even if temporarily, there be challenges.

If you are in Christ Jesus, you are that righteous one whose path shines brighter and brighter unto a perfect day. Paul echoed this truth in different ways to the Corinthian Church. He wrote in His letter, "And we all, who with unveiled faces contemplate the Lord's glory, are being transformed into his image with ever-increasing glory, which comes from the Lord, who is the Spirit" (2 Cor 3:18 NIV). And in another place, he wrote, "Therefore we do not lose heart. Even though our outward man is perishing, yet the inward man is being renewed day by day. For our light affliction, which is but for a moment, is working for us a far more exceeding and eternal weight of glory (2 Cor 4:16-17).

Prayer

Thank you, Heavenly Father, for we have been brought out of the dominion of darkness into your glorious light. Even this season, we overcome every obstacle and command all things to align themselves for the manifestation of your glory on our paths. In Jesus' name.

Bible in one year // **Psalms 63-65, Romans 6**

AUG 4

> Since we are surrounded by so great a cloud of witnesses, let us lay aside every weight, and the sin which so easily ensnares us, and let us run with endurance the race that is set before us. // **Hebrews 12:1**

A cloud of witnesses

Whatever we might be dealing with, someone at some point in time faced similar. Even if not in same circumstances or generation, someone has had a similar pinch. You are not the first and you are not going to be the last, even though your situation might have its peculiarity. Don't try to argue how different your situation is. It will only help you to miss out on the way and power to come out victorious. For you will find reasons to yield to defeat. Scripture emphasizes this: "No temptation has overtaken you except such as is common to man; but God is faithful, who will not allow you to be tempted beyond what you are able, but with the temptation will also make the way of escape, that you may be able to bear it" (1 Corinthians 10:13).

For a moment in time, when Elijah found himself on a run, he was convinced he was alone trying to survive the persecution of the queen, Jezebel. But he was reminded that there were as many as 7,000 prophets living the same situation. Sometimes we just have to tune to the news and the devastating situations of others will just remind us of how blessed we are, despite whatever we are dealing with.

> *We have a cloud of witness to look to for renewed hope and strength while we fix our eyes on Jesus.*

More than looking at the news for heart-breaking stories of others that remind us of our better situations, the writer of Hebrews shows us throughout the eleventh Chapter, the amazing overcoming stories of people of faith. These are for us a cloud of witnesses, whose biography stand as a testimonial for us on our faith journey. These men lived diverse situations of trials, hardships, and uncertainties. But one thing they all had in common that made them triumphant was faith. Today, we have the call to look to the cloud of witnesses and be encouraged by their stories. It might be of the biblical patriarch or of great stories in our generation. These testimonies all give us a blessed reassurance as we run our race, fixing our eyes on Jesus, the author and finisher of our faith. These testimonies assure us of a victory that is sure, if we don not compromise our stand of faith.

Prayer

Thank you, Heavenly Father, that there is nothing new under the sun. It might be different in form or time, but it is in some way common to man. I receive grace today to see even in the cloud of witnesses, the testimonials that pertain to my situation. And I remain victorious in all things. In Jesus' name.

Bible in one year // **Psalms 66-67, Romans 7**

I gave them the same glory you gave me, so that they may be one, just as you and I are one. // **John 17:22**

He shared His glory

Growing up in Church, one of the songs we sang often had these lines: "You are the Lord, that is your name. You will never share your glory with anyone". It is evidently a song inspired by the words of the prophet Isaiah when he spoke for the Lord saying, "I am the Lord; that is my name! I will not yield my glory to another or my praise to idols" (Isaiah 42:8). While these words were true and remain valid, it is important to bear in mind in what context this was, so that it does not cheat you of a greater truth – the truth that God has shared His glory with you. To understand better what the Lord meant when He said He will not share His glory with anyone, it will be helpful to consider an incident with King Herod.

"Now Herod had been very angry with the people of Tyre and Sidon; but they came to him with one accord, and having made Blastus the king's personal aide their friend, they asked for peace, because their country was supplied with food by the king's country. So on a set day Herod, arrayed in royal apparel, sat on his throne and gave an oration to them. And the people kept shouting, "The voice of a god and not of a man!" Then immediately an angel of the Lord struck him because he did not give glory to God. And he was eaten by worms and died (Acts 12:20-23). Herod's error was to receive for himself the credits that was due the Lord, He received praises and failed to the Lord who was worthy of it all.

> God has shared His glory with you in Christ Jesus, so you might reflect this to your world. In this also is the Fathers delight even as Jesus said. Let your light so shine that men may see your good works and glorify your Father who is in Heaven.

This is what the Lord meant when He said He will not share His glory with another – He will not let another take credit for the things He has done. However, when it concerns His glory which has to do with the outshining of His beauty and the radiance of His presence, He has shared that with you. God does share His glory, and if you are in Christ, then He has bestowed upon you the same glory He has so you can shine it forth. Just as Jesus prayed to the Father saying, "I gave them the same glory you gave me, so that they may be one, just as you and I are one (John 17:22).

Prayer

> Heavenly Father, thank you for the glory you have shared with us, that we might be one with you. As we shine your light in the earth through our good works, we receive grace to be quick to point to you as the author and source of it all. So that you will be glorified in the earth. In Jesus' name.

Bible in one year // **Psalms 68-69, Romans 8:1-21**

AUG 6

I can do all things through Christ who strengthens me.
// Philippians 4:13

Strengthend with all might

"For this reason we also, since the day we heard it, do not cease to pray for you, and to ask that you may be filled with the knowledge of His will in all wisdom and spiritual understanding; that you may walk worthy of the Lord, fully pleasing Him, being fruitful in every good work and increasing in the knowledge of God; strengthened with all might, according to His glorious power..." (Colossians 1:9-11). This is a prayer I would say for you today. Such a rich prayer with every point having great implications for everyday life. However, I want to call your attention to just this point – strengthened with all might!

In Christ Jesus, you are strengthened with all might through the Holy Spirit to face whatever life throws at you as you continually wait upon the Lord through meditation in the word and time in prayer.

Spiritual strength is a reality and a necessity, and this is something richly made available to you in Christ Jesus. The writer of proverbs had this to say, "If you faint in the day of adversity, your strength is small" (Proverbs 24:10). And this is great truth. Before you give up, it is first because you feel exhausted. And now that is not a word that should be part of the believer's vocabulary – the word exhaustion! And if you should use it, use it as a word to express how you feel and not to declare your state. For example, say "I feel exhausted", don't say "I am exhausted". Even as scripture commands, "Let the weak say, 'I am strong'" (Joel 3:10). Remember, your words have power. In saying I am strong, you are strengthened.

The word "Exhaustion" is not a part of our vocabulary because the source of all divine strength lives in us – the Spirit of God. He is called the strengthener! Paul prayed for the Christians, that they might know "What is the exceeding greatness of His power toward us who believe" (Ephesians 1:9). He wrote of himself, "I can do all things through Christ who strengthens me" (Philippians 4:13). Isaiah understood exhaustion wasn't part of our vocabulary when he wrote, "He gives power to the weak, and to those who have no might He increases strength. Even the youths shall faint and be weary, and the young men shall utterly fall, but those who wait on the Lord shall renew their strength; they shall mount up with wings like eagles, they shall run and not be weary, they shall walk and not faint (Isaiah 40:29-31).

Prayer

Heavenly Father, thank you for the strength at work in me supplied richly by the Spirit. I walk and do not grow faint, I run and do not grow weary, but my strength is renewed day by day, and my youth like the eagle's. Therefor I am strengthened and enabled to serve you all the days of my life. In Jesus' name.

Bible in one year // **Psalms 70-71, Romans 8:22-37**

You are the light of the world. A city that is set on a hill cannot be hidden.
// **Matthew 5:14**

AUG 7

And so are you

Jesus made a declaration of Himself saying, „I am the light of the world. Whoever follows me will never walk in darkness but will have the light of life" (John 8:12). And that is a truth many of us have come to accept and appreciate. That Jesus is the light of the world. However, He did not end there. He also said, "You are the light of the world". And he meant what He said. You are indeed the light of the world if you are in Christ Jesus. For in him, you have received the true light. This is the same truth John echoed in his writing, "The true light that gives light to everyone was coming into the world" (John 1:9).

Jesus is the light of the world, and so are you. It is His desire that you would shine that light to your world as far as it can reach like a city set upon a hill. Jesus went ahead to add, „People do not light a lamp and put it under a basket but on a lampstand, and it gives light to all in the house. In the same way, let your light shine before people, so that they can see your good deeds and give honor to your Father in heaven" (Matthew 5:14-15 NET). When He talked of lighting a lamp and placing it on the lampstand in comparison to us, he meant the light he gave us was not intended to be concealed and enjoyed in solitude. No! He wants to strategically position us as beacons of light in the world to bring that light to all.

> **You are the light of the world. Shine your light for all to see. For someone else depends on the light you have received.**

You might have known about my calling. I have shared how the Lord called me as a lighthouse to my world, to shine this light of the gospel of Jesus Christ, and to bring people into their inheritance in God. However, when you consider this call I received, it is the same thing Jesus assigned us all to do in some way. Like a lighthouse to your world, He has called you to shine that light to as many as you have within your reach. And you should take that as a responsibility. You might not have to preach anything special. At minimum, you can bring the word of God close to others by sharing the one you have received, even by passing on writings like this. You will never know who will be blessed and give glory to God because you did. It is all part of shining the light you have received.

Prayer

> Thank you, Heavenly Father, for your love and mercies that are new every morning. Thank you for the privilege you have given us to be the light of our world. We receive grace today to shine even brighter and reach as many as you have called us to illuminate with your word of truth. In Jesus' name.

Bible in one year // **Psalms 72-73, Romans 9:1-15**

AUG 8

> To this end I also labor, striving according to His working which works in me mightily. // **Colossians 1:29**

It is at work in you

The story of Gideon is one to look at every time you feel challenged with situations that make backing out seem the easiest solution. It is good to be reminded how God sees you, as an overcomer and a victor, one who is totally able and fit to accomplish the things He is calling you to do. It is good to always remember that God is not looking for your ability, He is always looking at your willingness. For it is by Him that you will overcome or accomplish His plans for you. Just as He said to Zerubbabel, "Not by might nor by power, but by my Spirit" (Zechariah 4:6).

Gideon was hiding like many others from the Midianites who were constantly oppressing the Israelites at this time. What is worth noting is the address of the Angel of the Lord when He appeared to Gideon. The Angel of the Lord said to him, "The Lord is with you, you mighty man of valor!" Gideon answered, "O my lord, if the Lord is with us, why then has all this happened to us? And where are all His miracles which our fathers told us about, saying, "Did not the Lord bring us up from Egypt?" But now the Lord has forsaken us and delivered us into the hands of the Midianites". Then the Lord turned to him and said, "Go in this might of yours, and you shall save Israel from the hand of the Midianites. Have I not sent you?" (Judges 6:12-14).

> **God's supernatural strength is at work in you today to do all that He has called you to do without burn out, exhaustion is not ours in Christ Jesus. Walk in the consciousness of this spiritual reality.**

Gideon saw himself weak and incapable, helpless and a victim without strength to overcome the enemy. The Lord didn't even show up saying to him, "I will give you strength". He had it all the while. The Lord said to Him, "Go in this your might". This was the mentality David had. He wasn't looking for strength from outside. He knew it was His every time. No doubt He could write, "In your strength I can crush an army; with my God I can scale any wall" (Psalm 18:29). Because of that strength, David knew he was literally unstoppable. And this is true for you too. Paul also wrote a similar thing: "To this end I also labor, striving with all His energy working powerfully within me" (Colossians 1:29). Just like Gideon, supernatural strength was at work in David and Paul. And the same is at work in you today.

Prayer

Heavenly Father, thank you for your strength at work in me. I declare therefore like David, "In your strength I can crush an army, and with you I will scale any wall". I work daily with the power that works in me through the Holy Spirit as I fulfill my destiny. In Jesus' name.

Bible in one year // **Psalms 74-76, Romans 9:16-33**

Let us lay aside every weight, and the sin which so easily ensnares us, and let us run with endurance the race that is set before us, looking unto Jesus, the author and finisher of our faith. // **Hebrews 12:1-2**

AUG 9

Stay focused

"Let your eyes look straight ahead, and your eyelids look right before you. Ponder the path of your feet and let all your ways be established. Do not turn to the right or the left; remove your foot from evil" (Proverbs 4:25-27). If we summarize these lines from the writer of Proverbs, it will say "Stay focused". And how important that is – not to let yourself be distracted or sidetracked from your path or goal. A great example of how much can go wrong with a little distraction becomes evident when we consider highway accidents and how statistics warn against manipulating the phone while driving.

> You will have to cultivate the discipline of keeping your attention stayed on the things that matter and not let yourself be distracted on your journey in life or from attaining your goals.

Just like staying focus in driving is necessary if you will avoid a crash, staying focused in destiny is as important if you will fulfil your call and do all God has called you to do. There is so much to distract us on our journey. You will have to make a conscious decision to look away from the distractions and be true to your course. Sometimes, your very first solution to overcome a distraction is to not look. You can ask some men with broken homes. They will tell you it was one look at a strange woman, maybe a seductive one, and they could hardly look back in the direction of their wife until their ruin began. For your education, business, ministry, and other areas, you will have to identify distractions and shun them.

Sometimes, distractions are relationships and ties that add nothing to your life except rob you of valuable time that can be invested in making progress. This is one reason you must carefully choose your associations and be sure they are not just time wasters but people with whom you are either growing together, helping them grow, or you are inspired and supported by them to grow. Proverbs says, "Do not turn to the left or to the right". The author of Hebrews wrote, "Let us throw off everything that hinders and the sin that so easily entangles, and let us run with perseverance the race marked out for us. Let us fix our eyes on Jesus, the author and perfecter of our faith, who for the joy set before him endured the cross, scorning its shame, and sat down at the right hand of the throne of God" (Hebrews 12:1-2).

Prayer

> Heavenly Father, thank your for the grace to be focused with undivided attention. As I commit myself to today's task, I receive grace to be focus and effective in all I do, giving attention to You, and to the things and persons that matter the most for your glory. In Jesus name.

Bible in one year // **Psalms 77-78, Romans 10**

AUG 10

The hand of the diligent will rule, but the lazy man will be put to forced labor. // **Proverbs 12:24**

Diligent hands

In the past, many misleading doctrines might have been responsible for some degree of lack of diligence for some believers. Such doctrines will include the likes of "It is difficult for a rich person to enter the kingdom of God, therefore being intentional about wealth creation is like looking for what will hinder your walk with God". A conscious pursuit of wealth for the greater part of time, seemed a taboo for many. The result sometimes is the wrong attitude we have towards work, an attitude void of diligence. But that is not God's desire for us. He has given us hands that can be diligent at work for great benefits. The Bible tells us, "The hand of the diligent will rule, But the lazy man will be put to forced labor" (Proverbs 12:24).

> Whatever your hands find to do, do it with all your might. Be diligent at your work, knowing that the hands of the diligent will make them a master at their task and reward them in due season.

Diligence is careful and persistent work, when you are committed, giving full attention to your work with dedication. This was the reason Jacob grew in wealth as he cared for the flocks of his uncle Laban (Genesis 31:38-42). This was the attitude Joseph had towards work that made him ruler even over other slaves in the house of Potiphar (Genesis 39:2-9). And when Joseph found himself in prison, even without a salary, he worked fully assisting the prison guard and became lord over other prisoners (Genesis 39:20-22). It is true that there is injustice in the world and some employers fail to reward diligence. That should not be reason for you to deal with lazy hands. The bible cautions, "He becomes poor who works with a lazy hand, but the hand of the diligent brings wealth" (Proverbs 10:4).

Even as an employee, Paul paints a beautiful picture of hope for us in Colossians when he writes, "Bondservants, obey in all things your masters according to the flesh, not with eyeservice, as men-pleasers, but in sincerity of heart, fearing God. And whatever you do, do it heartily, as to the Lord and not to men, knowing that from the Lord you will receive the reward of the inheritance; for you serve the Lord Christ" (Colossians 3:22-24). There is an assurance of a reward, even if not from your employer, the Lord who sees your diligent hands at work will not leave you without compensation.

Prayer

Heavenly Father, thank you for giving us the grace and ability to work and be diligent in what we do. And as we work diligently for the Kingdom and in the world, let promotion be our portion; may are barns be full of good things and our harvests multiplied in Jesus' name.

Bible in one year // **Psalms 79-80, Romans 11:1-18**

Better to be a nobody and yet have a servant than pretend to be somebody and have no food. // **Proverbs 12:9 NIV**

AUG 11

Despise not a source of livelihood

Even as economies fail around the world with corresponding exponential increase of job seekers, a lot more people find themselves left to do the jobs that don't measure up with their qualifications. While others are willing for the compromise of a season, to settle lower and have the financial independence they need, sometimes there are those many, like the writer of Proverbs puts it, hold on to their high profiles and would not settle for less, even for a season. In the end, there is dignity in fending for yourself and livelihood, so long it is by godly means.

Never despise any source of livelihood, or the opportunity to independently provide for yourself. You know for sure, this does not in any way encourage mediocrity or call you to give up on bigger dreams. This is a call to recognize the little opportunities that are provided you today to be independent while building for the future, a call to have regard for others who in society seem to be rated as the least among men because of the jobs they do. For there is dignity in labor, no matter the type. Just the very fact that someone puts their own hand in the dirt to fend for themselves should be saluted, and they respected.

And if ever others were to despise you or someone else because of the source of their livelihood, don't join their league. Despise not the source of a livelihood. For indeed it is better to be a nobody and have a servant than to claim to be somebody and have no food. A parallel verse echoes similar thoughts: "One pretends to be rich, yet has nothing; another pretends to be poor, yet has great wealth" (Proverbs 13:7). In the end, every human need provides an opportunity for something to do – an employment and with it earnings. Although not every task has honor attached to it. Whether it seems honorable to others or not, if it offers an opportunity for a livelihood, despise it not. For there is more dignity in fending for yourself than having high standards and yet begging for bread.

> **No labor that brings to a person their livelihood is without dignity. For dignity is first in the fact that they step out to fend for themselves and their loved ones.**

Prayer

Heavenly Father, thank you for the power you give us to make wealth, the opportunities for a livelihood and the provisions that come from it. We receive grace to be thankful in our states, making the most of today's opportunities even as we grow in grace and in wealth. In Jesus' name.

Bible in one year // **Psalms 81-83, Romans 11:19-36**

AUG 12

Never be lazy; but work hard and serve the Lord enthusiastically.
// **Romans 12:11 NLT**

Learn from the ants

The book of proverbs is filled with sayings of wisdom for practical application, wisdom that has the potential to program you for success and give you a mastery over life. One such call is this: "Take a lesson from the ants, you lazybones. Learn from their ways and become wise! Though they have no prince or governor or ruler to make them work, they labor hard all summer, gathering food for the winter" (Proverbs 6:6-8 NLT). They have an attitude towards work that guarantees their supply even for the season when they can't work, they work for more than the present. They are foresighted and save for the unfavorable seasons. The amazing part here is they have no ruler bossing them. They have no meteorologists informing them about the seasons. Instinctively, they labor and save for the winter.

Let us have same attitude towards work, when we don't need someone pushing us to do the things we have to do, getting busy with our duties for the Lord. Jesus had this mindset that a time was coming when you will not be able to do your assignments. He was hungry and his disciples had been away to get food. But when they finally came back to Jesus, His attention was no longer on the food. He had taken the opportunity to minister to a Samaritan woman. And when the disciples urged Him to eat, Jesus answered them, "My food is to do the will of Him who sent Me, and to finish His work" (John 4:34).

> **Learn a lesson from the ants, who without supervision are committed laborers, working hard to guarantee their supplies even in the seasons when work is not possible.**

Hard work is commanded and expected of us, giving our all to see the results we expect. Life doesn't just happen. Like someone rightly said, "Pray as though everything depends on your prayer but work as though everything depends on your effort". Our dependence on the grace of God and His favor is not a passport to laziness. On the contrary, knowing that we are graced and favored to have supernatural results by our little efforts, our attitude towards work should be better than that of the nonbeliever. For we are confident, that our hard work will bring in a rich harvest of results. Let us therefore emulate the ants, even as Paul exhorts: "Never be lazy, but work hard and serve the Lord enthusiastically" (Romans 12:11 NLT).

Prayer

Heavenly Father, thank you for the grace to be a hard worker. I am graced to be fruitful and prosperous. I am committed to hard work, laboring with all my strength to fulfill my purpose. I am enriched by a great harvest and richly supplied through my work. In Jesus' name.

Bible in one year // **Psalms 84-86, Romans 12**

A little sleep, a little slumber, a little folding of the hands to rest and poverty will come on you like a thief and scarcity like an armed man.
// **Proverbs 6:10-11 NIV**

Flee like a gazelle

As much as you are intentional about your spiritual progress, be intentional about your growth in all areas, particularly your finances. Regarding a place of indebtedness, we are admonished, "Flee like a gazelle". Do all you can to come out of such a place and situation as if your life is in danger. But much more, have same attitude towards the pursuit of wealth. You must be intentional about the pursuit of wealth. This is one teaching that the body of Christ has often played down on, raising godly people who are broke and contented with being broke. And the quest of wealth demonized as if it is something bad, but the reverse is true. So long wealth is not pursued at the expense of your soul, it is a commendable and worthy course.

In the end, the focus is not to get rich but to be able to do more with the riches we get for the glory of God... it is about accumulating wealth that gives us greater capacity and influence in our world. Remember, Jesus said do not lay up for yourselves treasures in the earth. However, to layup that treasure in heaven, you will need to get it in the earth and put it to godly use. That is how you accumulate treasure in heaven.

Be intentional about establishing financial stability and growing in wealth. It is a commendable thing to do. Wealth empowers us to do more for God. Like a gazelle, deliver yourself from poverty.

You can read the whole discourse from Proverbs 6:1-11. Some lines worth highlighting are put out for you here. How long will you slumber, O sluggard? When will you rise from your sleep? A little sleep, a little slumber, a little folding of the hands to sleep – So shall your poverty come on you like a prowler, and your need like an armed man (Proverbs 6:9-11). Just as we can come to poverty through wasteful extravagancy and laziness, we can also like a gazelle flee from poverty and strategically pursue wealth. It is a commendable thing to flee from the end of being in debt and becoming a lender. That is the prophecy upon your life as a child of God (Deuteronomy 28:12).

Prayer

Heavenly Father, thank you for giving us all things that pertain to life and godliness. Thank you for delighting in the prosperity of your servants and for the opportunities this season to grow our fortunes. And as we grow in wealth may we be willing to give even more for the Kingdom. In Jesus' name.

Bible in one year // **Psalms 87-88, Romans 13**

AUG 14

> For as the churning of milk produces butter, and wringing the nose produces blood, so the forcing of wrath produces strife.
> // **Proverbs 30:33**

A hallmark of champions

Consistency is a hallmark of champions. And if you will excel in any thing in life and standout, consistency is a trait you must cultivate, even in the little things. It always yields its fruit if you are on the right path and engaged in the right things.

Even Jesus our role model demonstrated Himself consistent in many regards. He was consistent in going to the synagogue. We are informed, "As His custom was, He went into the synagogue on the Sabbath day, and stood up to read (Luke 4:16 NKJV). It was a custom and this wasn't the only routine Jesus had. We also learn, "Coming out, He went to the Mount of Olives, as He was accustomed, and His disciples also followed Him" (Luke 22:39).

> **Consistency is the hallmark of champions, a necessary trait if we will see true and enduring success in our endeavors.**

When it came to prayer, Jesus emphasized the importance of consistency. Using the parable of a judge and a widow, He showed us how being consistent in prayer would bring their results. Because of the woman's persistence, the Judge said to himself, "Even though I don't fear God or care what people think, yet because this widow keeps bothering me, I will see that she gets justice". And the Lord said, "Will not God bring about justice for his chosen ones, who cry out to him day and night? Will he keep putting them off? I tell you; he will see that they get justice, and quickly (Luke 18:1-8).

These all remind us of the words from proverbs, "As the beating of cream yields butter and striking the nose causes bleeding, so stirring up anger causes quarrels" (Proverbs 30:33). This verse simply says there are things if you do and stay at it, there are results you will get. To churn means to mix vigorously. Now the butter might not appear in the first minute of churning cream, it might not appear after the first 30 minutes, and the arms might get weary. But if you will just keep churning, and stay consistent, before long, you will get butter. Same is true for any worthy course, if you will just be consistent and true, you will see results in due season.

Prayer

Heavenly Father, thank you for the grace to be consistent and true on the things you have called me to do, knowing that I will reap a harvest in due season if I faint not. Thank you for renewed strength where there is discouragement and hope where the results seem slow. In Jesus' name.

Bible in one year // **Psalms 89-90, Romans 14**

And this gospel of the kingdom will be preached in all the world as a witness to all the nations, and then the end will come. // **Matthew 24:14**

AUG 15

The good news

God is always interested in your progress, and this is no lie or sweet talking. In fact, that is part of the reason the gospel is called Good News. The word gospel indeed literally means good message, it is a translation of the word "Euaggelion" (yoo-ang-ghel'-ee-on). Jesus said, "This gospel of the kingdom will be preached in all the world as a witness to all the nations, and then the end will come" (Matthew 24:14). He called it "Good news". Never let anyone preach to you another gospel other than that which is made plain to us in scriptures. You can find it as you study the bible.

One nice passage that clearly demonstrates the content of this gospel and makes it good news is from the words of the prophet Isaiah. Jesus himself read from this passage He set the pace for the gospel we are sent out to preach. It is written of Jesus, "He went into the synagogue on the Sabbath day, and stood up to read. And He was handed the book of the prophet Isaiah. And when He had opened the book, He found the place where it was written: The Spirit of the Lord is upon Me, because He has anointed Me To preach the gospel to the poor; He has sent Me to heal the brokenhearted, to proclaim liberty to the captives and recovery of sight to the blind, to set at liberty those who are oppressed; to proclaim the acceptable year of the Lord" (Luke 4:16-19).

The good news is a message of hope, a message of God's goodwill towards humanity. A message that says God wants his people saved, free, blessed, healthy and prosperous. Never accept anything less. Some people like to present a gospel that excludes prosperity, yet they quote with gladness, "The Lord is my shepherd, I shall not be in want" (Psalm 23:1). It is such a paradox and self-contradiction. God wants you well, and that's why He sent us forth with the charge, "Heal the sick and raise the death". This is the gospel. It means good news! It is the good news that Christ paid it all and made available to all humanity. It is now available to all who believe (2 Cor 1:19-20).

The good news Jesus preached, lays the foundation of any true gospel today. It is a message of hope and salvation, a message intended to save you, equip you, and make you effective for kingdom service.

Prayer

Heavenly Father, thank you for the hope offered to us in Christ Jesus, the hope that the lost shall be saved, the sick healed, the captives delivered, the poor blessed, the blind receive sight and the dead raised back to life. We receive with thanksgiving all the promises. In Jesus' name.

Bible in one year // **Psalms 91-93, Romans 15:1-13**

AUG 16

I have come that they may have life, and that they may have it more abundantly. // **John 10:10**

A superior life

Jesus on many occasions defined the reasons for which He came. And this is always helpful for us to point out what was accomplished. On one such occasions, Jesus said, "I have come that they may have life, and that they may have it more abundantly" (John 10:10). And this is the message of the gospel. Jesus came that you may have life and have the life in abundance. It gets even richer when we highlight the meanings of two of the words Jesus used. For as much as we are thankful for all the bible translations, sometimes it is rewarding to take a closer look at original words for an understanding that might have been lost in translation.

Today, we will consider the word "Zoe", the Greek word translated to mean "Life". This is the same word Jesus used when He said, "God so loved the world that He gave His only son that whosoever believes in Him should not perish but have everlasting life" (John 3:16). You must remember that Jesus was talking to people who already had a life. These were living people. They were alive but with a human life. Jesus was talking about a superior life, a life that is of God, a gift from the Father. Even as it is written, "For the wages of sin is death, but the give of God is eternal life in Christ Jesus our Lord" (Romans 6:23 NKJV). Once again, Paul in His writing used the same word, Zoe.

The life offered you by Christ Jesus in the Gospel is a life superior to whatever life you could ever have without him, a life that is divine, perpetual and overflowing to give life to everything about you.

Zoe is the God-kind of life, the life that stems from the divine nature, a life born by the spirit of God. It is superior in quality to the human life and that is what we have in Christ Jesus. This is the life that is immune to disease and superior to sickness. It is a perpetual life, a life that continues beyond death. To have Zoe is more than being alive, it is having a life that gives life to other things and persons, a life that is communicable. It is different from Psuche (Psoo-chay) mentioned in acts 20:24, when Paul says "I do not count my life dear to me". This life is not parallel to the human life, it is superior to it.

Prayer

Heavenly Father, thank you for the superior life offered to me in Christ Jesus. As I grow and walk in the consciousness of this life, the supernatural manifestations that accompany it will be made evident as your life flows through me, bringing life to those in my world. In Jesus' name.

Bible in one year // **Psalms 94-96, Romans 15:14-33**

*Whoever drinks the water I give them will never thirst. Indeed, the water I give them will become in them a spring of water welling up to eternal life. // **John 4:14 NIV***

AUG 17

An overflowing life

When Jesus said, "I have come that they might have life and have it in abundance", he used the second word of emphasis we will consider today. It is the word "Perissos" (Per-is-sos')". This is the word translated to mean abundance. While abundance is in itself good, it tones down a little on the full meaning of the word. It means to have over and beyond in terms of quality and quantity, exceedingly more. The meaning of this word is parallel to the word used in Ephesians 3:20 translated to mean "exceeding abundantly above". It is a life to overflowing.

It reminds us of the words of Jesus when He said, "Whoever drinks of this water will thirst again, but whoever drinks of the water that I shall give him will never thirst. But the water that I shall give him will become in him a fountain of water springing up into everlasting life" (John 4:13-14). The life was going to be a fountain, welling up, overflowing out, a fountain of life, a life that pours out even more life. He was once again talking of the Zoe life we have in Him, a life that gives life. John wrote of Jesus, "In Him was life and the life was the light of men... the true light that lights every man" (John 1:1 & 9).

> **The Zoe we have in Christ Jesus is anoverflowing life that flows into whatever we engage ourselves to do on course with the Lord, and that life brings life and vitality into everything else around you.**

On one occasion Jesus said, "If anyone thirsts, let him come to Me and drink. He who believes in Me, as the Scripture has said, out of his heart will flow rivers of living water" (John 7:37 & 38). This is the life in you if you are born again, a life that overflows to others in blessings, a life that gives life to others, a life that brings life to death things about you. It doesn't matter what that is, if you get involved in it with Zoe in you, that Zoe overflows into your endeavors, into your business, into your education, into your relationships and gives it vitality. It is for such a reason that the Psalmist wrote, "He is like a tree planted beside streams – a tree that produces fruit in season and whose leaves do not wither. He succeeds in every-thing he does" (Psalms 1:3).

Prayer

> Heavenly Father, thank you for making me a life-giving spirit in Christ Jesus, that I bring life into whatever I get involved in, a life that results in visible progress to the praise of your name. Even as the Holy Spirit indwells me and gives life to my mortal body, even so the life overflows to my world. In Jesus name.

Bible in one year // **Psalms 97-99, Romans 16**

AUG 18

There is a river whose streams make glad the city of God, the holy place where the Most High dwells. // **Psalm 46:4**

A river of joy

The psalmist had an understanding of supernatural joy, a joy that is beyond the prevailing circumstances in an individual's life, a joy that is from the Lord. David painted a picture of extreme chaos in one of his writings. It is a picture of all the forces of nature in destructive display – a roaring ocean (think of a Tsunami), an earthquake and a volcanic mountain in eruption pouring out hot lava headed in your direction. Just one of these is enough to destabilize a person. But think of all unfolding at the same time. And this is figuratively the life of someone this season – a state of extreme chaos.

> You have the capacity to be joyful always in Christ Jesus irrespective of what is going on in your life. You are the city of God to which the Holy Spirit, like a river, continually brings joy.

Like David, you can know joy even through the extreme chaos while the Lord perfects that which concerns you, you can rejoice and be glad today, knowing that all things work together for good to them that love God and are called according His purpose (Romans 8:28). David wrote about a river of Joy. "God is our refuge and strength, always ready to help in times of trouble. So, we will not fear when earthquakes come and the mountains crumble into the sea. Let the oceans roar and foam. Let the mountains tremble as the waters surge. A river brings joy to the city of our God, the sacred home of the Most High. God dwells in that city; it cannot be destroyed. From the very break of day, God will protect it" (Psalm 46:1-5 NLT).

David knew of "A river that brings joy to the city of God". It is worth noting that the joy did not depend on what is happening in the city, the joy comes to the city because the river carries and brings joy. And how prophetic this was concerning us. Jesus said, "You are the light of the world, like a city set on a hill". Then He spoke of the Holy Spirit as a river (John 7:37-39). If you connect these dots, you will see one thing: You are that city of God to which a river brings joy independent of what is happening in the city. It can be joyful and glad because its joy is independent of what is happening around. For there is a river that makes glad that city, that is you. No doubt Paul could write, "Rejoice in the Lord always. I will say it again: Rejoice!" (Philippians 4:4).

Prayer

Heavenly Father thank you for the Joy of the Holy Spirit in me, that gladdens my heart and puts a song on my lips even through the darkest nights. As I rejoice in you, may your glory be made manifest as you perfect all that concerns me, in the name of Jesus.

Bible in one year // **Psalms 100-102, 1 Corinthians 1**

All Scripture is given by inspiration of God, and is profitable for doctrine, for reproof, for correction, for instruction in righteousness.
// **2 Timothy 3:16**

AUG 19

Like the extra oil

When this devotional was still mainly distributed by daily publication on social media platforms, I was late on a day with sending out the day's post. Knowing how many people had come to depend on Your Daily Light for their daily nourishment in the word of God, I thought to myself, "Someone is waiting to read from you". While that was true, a greater question was how much longer they were going to wait. This reminded me of the parable of Jesus concerning the five wise and five foolish virgins.

They had been waiting for the bridegroom who was long coming. They waited so long, that their lamps burned out all the oil. But the five wise virgins had thought ahead of time. They had taken with them extra oil for the road. They had planned and made provisions for the unexpected. They had extra oil (Matthew 25:1-13). Sometimes I have had to buy certain things more than was needed, or something I probably did not need. The saying and justification was often, "Better have it and not need it than to need it and not have it". And it often played out that I indeed either needed it, or it later served someone else.

This is also true for the word of God you are learning today. You might not directly see how some knowledge of the word of God you are receiving today might directly serve you later. So, you will be doing yourself much good by building in you a reservoir of God's word. For in due season, it will well up as the need arises. Like extra oil, never find yourself saying regarding some knowledge from God's word, "That portion of the bible is unnecessary". For ALL scripture is inspired of God and no heavenly writing is without relevance. We know, "ALL Scripture is given by inspiration of God, and is profitable for doctrine, for reproof, for correction, for instruction in righteousness, that the man of God may be complete, thoroughly equipped for every good work" (2 Tim 3:16-17).

> Continue to grow your wealth of knowledge in the word of God, like extra oil, it will serve you on a day you least expect. It is a wise thing to do!

Prayer

Heavenly Father, thank you for another day and an opportunity to glorify your name in the earth. Thank you for your works in our lives as you continue to lead us on a perpetual victorious match in Christ, causing your knowledge to spread through us like a sweet, smelling fragrance. In Jesus' name.

Bible in one year // **Psalms 103-104, 1 Corinthians 2**

AUG 20

> For in Christ all the fullness of the Deity lives in bodily form, and in Christ you have been brought to fullness. He is the head over every power and authority. // **Colossians 2:9-10**

The fulness of God

Sometimes spiritual communication can be misleading unless we consider in what context it is used. It was said of Jesus, "For the one whom God has sent speaks the words of God, for God gives the Spirit without limit" (John 3:34). Because until this time, only a measure of God's abilities was made available to an individual through the indwelling of the spirit of God. For Samson, it was might. For Daniel, the spirit of wisdom and of revelation. And for the kings, an anointing to lead, the spirit of lordship, usually, The Spirit of the Lord. But of Jesus, the fullness of God was made manifest in Him. John testifies of Him saying, God gave Him the Spirit without measure.

Paul wrote of Jesus, "He is the head of the body, the church; he is the beginning and the firstborn from among the dead, so that in everything he might have the supremacy. For God was pleased to have all his fullness dwell in him" (Colossians 1: 18-19). Paul emphasized the very thing John had testified of, that Jesus had the fullness of God. Now this does not mean someone can be half full of God, for God dwells in us by His spirit. And the Spirit is either present or absent. He is a person. He can't be half present. Having the fullness of God really means God manifesting all His attributes, virtues, and graces through an individual. And this wasn't limited to Jesus. It was only the beginning of a new era when God will be fully manifested through men.

> **Understanding the boundless, unconditional love of God and being able to demonstrate that love towards others is the secret to being filled with the fullness of God.**

Paul prayed for the Ephesians, that they might "Know the love of Christ which passes knowledge; that they may be filled with all the fullness of God" (Ephesians 3:19). The Amplified bible has a better rendition, "That you may come to know [practically, through personal experience] the love of Christ which far surpasses [mere] knowledge, that you may be filled up [throughout your being] to all the fullness of God [so that you may have the richest experience of God's presence in your lives, completely filled and flooded with God Himself]. You too can experience the fullness of God in your life.

Prayer

Heavenly Father, thank you for your love is shed abroad in our hearts by the Holy Spirit, giving us the capacity to love unconditionally and to love the "unlovables" around us. As we reach out to them with your boundless unconditional love, may we indeed manifest your fullness. In Jesus' name.

Bible in one year // **Psalms 105-106, 1 Corinthians 3**

The fool has said in his heart, "There is no God.". // **Psalm 14:1**

AUG 21

It is unwise Pt. 1

There are many things the bible lets us know are unwise and we will be looking at some of these as they point us to the way of wisdom. For example, to think that there is no God is a very unwise thing. In fact, it is the first definition of a fool. The Psalmist puts it like this, "The fool has said in his heart, "There is no God" (Psalm 14:1). And that for good reason: "The heavens declare the glory of God; the skies proclaim the work of His hands. Day after day, they pour forth speech; night after night, they reveal knowledge. They have no speech, they use no words; no sound is heard from them. Yet their voice goes out into all the earth, their words to the ends of the world" (Psalm 19:1-4).

> **It is unwise to doubt or deny the existence of God when it is all plain in the works of His hands. Much more, He is always close by, willing to reveal himself to anyone that truly seeks Him whole-heartedly.**

To the Psalmist, it is plain and evident by observation that the things which we see, the visible world is a testimonial to a thoughtful work of art. To him, it is unfathomable to look at all of nature, the complexity of life, the organization of the solar system, the wonders of nature, and to think that these things were a product of chance events that had no intentionality in them. To him, it is ridiculous. In fact, you have to look away from facts and evidence to come to such a conclusion. Paul argues in a similar light. "What may be known about God is plain to them because God has made it plain to them. For since the creation of the world, God's invisible qualities – his eternal power and divine nature – have been clearly seen, being understood from what has been made, so that people are without excuse (Romans 1:19-20).

A former atheist recounts his turning point as he sat on a hilltop at nightfall as a teenager. He was fascinated by the night lights of the city. It dawned on him what feat of engineering it was to electrify and light up a city at night, with lights that did not measure to the brightness of the sun, the moon, and the stars. And he said to himself, it is impossible for creation and the heavenly lights to have existed without the orchestration of an intelligent being. This began his journey of quest to know the Lord. And in time, God revealed himself to him. Just as He guarantees in His word, "You will seek me and find me when you seek me with all your heart (Jeremiah 29:13).

Prayer

Heavenly Father, thank you for the privilege to know and walk with you the creator of all things. We pray for those who have not known you, whose eyes have been blinded by the evil one, that the scales on their eyes will fall off so they can see your glory in Christ and come to the light. In Jesus' name.

Bible in one year // **Psalms 107-109, 1 Corinthians 4**

AUG 22

> They, measuring themselves by themselves, and comparing themselves among themselves, are not wise. // **2 Corinthians 10:12**

It is unwise Pt. 2

Paul calls our attention to one unwise thing to do, something we all could easily find ourselves doing in every day, particularly with the pressures of social media appearances. It is the unwise thing of measuring yourselves with others. "For we dare not class ourselves or compare ourselves with those who commend themselves. But they, measuring themselves by themselves, and comparing themselves among themselves, are not wise" (2 Corinthians 10:12). He lets us know it is unwise to compare yourself with others for any reason.

> **It is unwise to compare yourselves with others because your paths in life are unique. Rather, compare your present situation with what God has planned for you and continue reaching forward for it.**

You must understand that you are unique as God's creation. Not just that, your paths through life are unique. Sometimes where you are might not look all glorious in the eyes of many with regards to their seeming high placements. It doesn't mean you are failing. In fact, you might be acclaiming the one who in the sight of the Lord has failed woefully. It reminds me of Esau. He was not in any way a failure by human standards. He became a mighty man, wealthy with servants and his descendants became a great nation called Edom (Genesis 33:1). Sadly, of him we are cautioned in Hebrews, "Make sure that no one is immoral or godless like Esau, who traded his birthright as the firstborn son for a single meal". He is remembered as one of the worst persons you could be like.

A widow was going to be despised for her giving by appearances, but Christ gave her the highest commendation to the surprise of all (Luke 21:1-4). Joseph for a season might have been in a pit, been a slave or in prison, but these were only stages on his unique path to greatness. It is indeed unwise to measure yourself with others. You don't know where God is bringing you or them. You don't have to be under the societal pressure of owning goods of class to look better, nor shy away from your mates who seem more successful. You must recognize your placement in God and the assignment He has called you to do in season. And so long as you are in that position, the only comparison you should make is compare where you are with where God wants you to be, and make every effort to get there.

Prayer

Heavenly Father thank you for the consciousness of my uniqueness in Christ Jesus. I receive grace to see clearly your paths traced out for me that I might walk in them and fulfil my call. In Jesus name.

Bible in one year // **Psalms 110-112, 1 Corinthians 5**

Don't long for "the good old days." This is not wise.
// **Ecclesiastes 7:10 NLT**

AUG 23

It is unwise Pt. 3

It is indeed unwise to long for the good old days as a child of God. For it doesn't matter how glorious your past might have been, it never measures to the glory that lies ahead of you. It is not a lie that sometimes, because of great mistakes we've made, we can clearly see how a wrong move or decision at a point in time shifted things for the worse down an unpleasant path. Even that does not justify one reminiscing of the good old days with the longing to go back to them. If anything, it only cheats you out of the joy of today and blinds you from the hope of tomorrow.

Don't long for the good old days, look forward to greater days to come. If you are in Christ, there are quite many reasons why you should always look forward to better days, no matter what happens. The writer of proverbs assures us, "The path of the just is like a shining light that shines ever brighter unto a perfect day" (Proverbs 4:18). Paul echoes a similar truth when he wrote, "For our light and momentary troubles are achieving for us an eternal glory that far outweighs them all. So, we fix our eyes not on what is seen, but on what is unseen, since what is seen is temporary, but what is unseen is eternal" (2 Corinthians 4:17-18).

Do not be trapped in the past, not in its victories or failures. Only look back to them for the lessons they bring, the thanksgiving they inspire and the reminders they echo regarding the faithfulness of God to you. As great as they might be, the victories of the past can also become our greatest limitations from greater accomplishments if we content ourselves with them. There are people who boast in what they used to do for the Lord, how they used to be on fire for him, and accomplished things in his name but seemingly have retired. Stop glorying in the past while today's opportunities pass you by. "Do not remember the former things, nor consider the things of old. Behold, I will do a new thing, now it shall spring forth; shall you not know it? I will even make a road in the wilderness and rivers in the desert (Isaiah 43:18-19).

> **Don't long for the good old days, it is unwise. No matter the glories of yesterday, the Lord has for you even greater glories ahead, for it only gets better by the day as He brings us from glory to glory.**

Prayer

Heavenly Father, thank you for the paths I have walked this far, its victories and setbacks, its glories, and trials. I remain confident that all things work together for good to them that love you and are called according to your purpose. I look forward in hope to the greater things. In Jesus' name.

Bible in one year // **Psalms 113-115, 1 Corinthians 6**

AUG 24

> Everyone who hears these sayings of Mine, and does not do them, will be like a foolish man who built his house on the sand. // **Matthew 7:26**

It is unwise Pt. 4

The goal of the thoughts we are sharing under this caption of certain things being unwise, is to point us in the way of wisdom so we make a harvest of its benefits. Talking about wisdom, the writer of proverbs had this to say, "My son, let them not depart from your eyes– Keep sound wisdom and discretion; so they will be life to your soul and grace to your neck. Then you will walk safely in your way, and your foot will not stumble. When you lie down, you will not be afraid; yes, you will lie down and your sleep will be sweet" (Proverbs 3:21-24). And indeed, it is guaranteed the quality of life you can have with God when you truly lead a life in the paths of the wisdom He reveals. On the contrary, the only guarantee for being foolish is destruction (Proverbs 1:32).

One thing that is very unwise to do then is to set aside the wisdom of God for human opinions or traditions. This is something Jesus rebuked the Pharisees for. He said to them, "You have a fine way of setting aside the commands of God in order to observe your own traditions!" (Mark 7:9). The word of God is His wisdom to us, it reveals trust-worthy principles for life and guides us in the paths of righteousness. To set it aside for any reason is unwise. It is a foolish thing to do, to set aside the word of God or embrace opposing opinions over what His revealed word suggests.

> **To live by the word of God is to be a wise builder, building on a firm and sure foundation. To live otherwise is unwise.**

Jesus shared a parable as He taught saying, "Therefore whoever hears these sayings of Mine, and does them, I will liken him to a wise man who built his house on the rock: and the rain descended, the floods came, and the winds blew and beat on that house; and it did not fall, for it was founded on the rock. "But everyone who hears these sayings of Mine, and does not do them, will be like a foolish man who built his house on the sand: and the rain descended, the floods came, and the winds blew and beat on that house; and it fell. And great was its fall" (Matt 7:24-27). So, you decide, which are you going to be? It is unwise to set aside the word of God and to act in opposition to His wisdom.

Prayer

Heavenly Father, thank you, for you are working in me to will and to do according to your good pleasure. I meditate in your word daily and conduct my life accordingly. Therefore, I am like the tree planted by the rivers of waters, which brings its fruits in season for your glory. In Jesus' name.

Bible in one year // **Psalms 116-118, 1 Corinthians 7:1-19**

Do not plot harm against your neighbor, who lives trustfully near you. // **Proverbs 3:29**

AUG 25

Don't betray trust

It is unwise to betray trust. This is the fifth unwise thing to do on our list. Unfortunately, without realizing, this is an unfitting thing that happens even among believers in Christ. Sadly, there are persons you can no longer trust on their words because of your experiences with them. Sometimes, these are people we looked up to spiritually. But the little agreements you had with them over something could hardly be honored, they could hardly keep to their words, and probably hardly explained why.

> To betray the trust someone has for you is unwise. You might only hurt yourself in the process or harm your own future in your dealings with others

One practical place of example is borrowing. It is okay to reach out to one another in times of need, but if it is on a borrowing term, do all you can in your ability to honor your words. You might never know how that plays on their willingness to lend you something the next time. In fact, if you owe someone money, which is not encouraged, it is even a wiser thing to do to borrow from another person and honor the date of payment. Like the saying goes, rob Peter and pay Paul. And when the due date for Peter is around the corner, do everything in your power to have had the money. This wasn't to encourage a life in debt, but a practical illustration of how without realizing, even among believers, many betray trust through unpaid debts.

Sometimes someone trusts you with a job, a project to manage. Do not because, they are your brother or sister in the Lord, go about it carelessly. They could likewise have hired a stranger out there who is qualified to deliver even a better outcome. Don't take it lightly and say, "They will understand". You might just be burning the bridges for the future. In whatever way you have to deal with people, demonstrate integrity and do not give them reasons to not trust you; not to your spouse, not to your parents, and not to your employers or friends. As believers in Christ Jesus, we are expected to be trust-worthy. As the writer of proverbs admonishes, "Do not plot harm against your neighbor, who lives trustfully near you" (Proverbs 3:29).

Prayer

Heavenly Father, thank you for the grace to be a person of integrity, one who keeps to their words and honor their promises, one who is without reproach but reflects the integrity cultivated through your word. Even this season, I receive grace to be trust-worthy for your glory. In Jesus' name.

Bible in one year // **Psalms 119:1-88, 1 Corinthians 7:20-40**

AUG 26

> Among you there must not be even a hint of sexual immorality, or of any kind of impurity, or of greed, because these are improper for God's holy people. // **Ephesians 5:3**

Don't be lured away

It is unwise to be lured away into sexual sins. The writer of proverbs paints a picture of what it is like by sharing an observation he made from the window of his home. That writing spoke to me in my days of youthful excitement and inspired me with the wisdom to not be lured away with the seemingly irresistible beauties that crossed my path. In fact, every time I felt pressure in my flesh, to experiment and explore the luring pleasure that enticed me, I would open my bible to this passage and read again and again, to remind myself of the real sting that probably awaits me at the other end of the delusions suggested by sexual cravings. And we all need these reminders and perspective to help us maintain sexual purity as singles or married men and women. No one is immune to sexual temptations.

Sexual sins can be compelling and promise a great deal of pleasure, but in the end, are a snare for the soul. And many have lost their lives, fortunes and missed out on destiny by treading that road.

The author of proverbs wrote, "I noticed among the young men, a youth who had no sense. He was going down the street near her corner... All at once he followed her like an ox going to the slaughter, like a deer stepping into a noose till an arrow pierces his liver; like a bird darting into a snare, little knowing it will cost him his life. Now then, my sons, listen to me; pay attention to what I say. Do not let your heart turn to her ways or stray into her paths. Many are the victims she has brought down; her slain are a mighty throng. Her house is a highway to the grave, leading down to the chambers of death" (Proverbs 7:6-27).

We are admonished, "Among you there must not be even a hint of sexual immorality, or of any kind of impurity, or of greed, because these are improper for God's holy people" (Ephesians 5:3). When you consider the paths to sexual sins, it is often a long slippery road with many stop points. When you look at the story above, you would realize for every step the young man took towards the lady, he could as well have taken that step back away from her. And this is not one-sided. Men like women are tempted and drawn away. But it will be unwise for you to give in. For often, the consequences on us, and sometimes family are irreparable. To let yourself be lured away into sexual sins is the sixth unwise thing to do.

Prayer

Heavenly Father thank you for the Holy Spirit who lives in us and gives us the power to bring our body to submission to your will. And as we walk by the spirit, we shall not fulfill the passions of the flesh in response to unruly sexual cravings outside what is prescribed for us, your holy people. In Jesus' name.

Bible in one year // **Psalms 119:89-176, 1 Corinthians 8**

The waywardness of the simple will kill them, and the complacency of fools will destroy them. // **Proverbs 1:32**

AUG 27

Don't be complecant

As I conclude on this note of unwise things, not because we exhausted the list, it is worth emphasizing a verse from scripture. It tells us what happens to the complacent. The bible lets us know, "The waywardness of the simple will kill them, and the complacency of fools will destroy them" (Proverbs 1:32). "The simple" is one without knowledge, one who is ignorant. And to be complacent means to be marked by self-satisfaction especially when accompanied by unawareness of actual dangers or deficiencies. So in other terms, that verse says: The waywardness of the ignorant will kill them, and fools will be destroyed because of their unwillingness to make changes resulting from their delusional satisfaction with the way things are.

But who is a fool? It is easy to define one from scripture. Jesus told us who a fool is, the one who hears his word but does not do it. That is a fool. A fool is one who ignores divine counsel. A fool is one who does not guide or lead their lives by the precepts of God's word. They might call themselves wise, but they are fools. Proverbs 3:7 warns, "Do not be wise in your own eyes". Proverbs 5:1 says, "My son, pay attention to my wisdom". He calls words inspired of God, wisdom. It is practical wisdom for a fulfilling life, showing you the way of life, its snares, and its secrets. You can live your best life and spare yourself lots of trouble just by living by the word of God. Of course, you can also get into trouble because you did what the Lord led you to do. But then it is good trouble, for He will answer for you and fight for you.

> **The complacency of a person will be their undoing, but commitment to change through the word of God will bring us into ever-increasing measures of glory.**

But to be complacent and fail to make the changes you need in your life to conform with the word of God is a dangerous thing. Is the word of God calling you to change somethings this season? Of the list of unwise things to do, are you guilty of any? Are you consciously practicing a habit that is expressly condemned in scripture? For some, the Lord might just be calling you to do even more for him. Don't be complacent. There is more for you in God. Don't be complacent. It is unwise.

Prayer

Heavenly Father, thank you. For you work in me to will and to do according to your good pleasure. By your zeal in me, I continually make progress by your word, ever conforming to the image of Christ. Therefore, I thrive and make progress in every area of my life by your grace. In Jesus' name.

Bible in one year // **Psalms 120-122, 1 Corinthians 9**

AUG 28

> God has united you with Christ Jesus. For our benefit God made Him to be wisdom itself. // **1 Corinthians 1:32 NLT**

Christ is your wisdom

James wrote, "If any of you lacks wisdom, you should ask God, who gives generously to all without finding fault, and it will be given to you. But when you ask, you must believe and not doubt, because the one who doubts is like a wave of the sea, blown and tossed by the wind. That person should not expect to receive anything from the Lord. Such a person is double-minded and unstable in all they do" (James 1:5-8). That was an open ticket to his readers, letting them know they could get all the wisdom they needed just by asking. However, as great as this is, what is even greater is the truth that there is no believer in Christ who lacks wisdom, and this I will show you.

As you study the bible, you must recognize the things that were written for the naïve and inexperienced in Christ and the things that were written for the mature. There is the milk for the babies and the meat for the adults, who can digest and accept greater truths. Here is one such. Just as the writer of Hebrews wrote, "Anyone who lives on milk, being still an infant, is not acquainted with the teaching about righteousness. But solid food is for the mature, who by constant use have trained themselves to distinguish good from evil" (Hebrews 5:13-14).

> **You have wisdom if you are in Christ. For Christ is the embodiment of divine wisdom. However, that wisdom is fully made manifest in you as you meditate in the Word and commune with the Holy Spirit.**

In this light, James could write saying, "If anyone lacks wisdom, let him ask of God". But when you read 1 Corinthians 1:32, you will realize that if you are in Christ, then you do not lack wisdom. That verse says, "God has united you with Christ Jesus. For our benefit God made Him to be wisdom itself" (NLT). You see, if you have Christ, then you have the embodiment and epitome of wisdom in you. You do not lack wisdom. Christ has been made unto you your wisdom, a wisdom that is greater than the wisdom Solomon possessed. What you need now is continues meditation in the word of God and communion with the Holy Spirit to stir up that wisdom to full manifestation.

Prayer

Heavenly Father, thank you for your wisdom at work in me. As I meditate in the word daily, I and inspired in the way I should go, finding the wisdom I need in complex situations. Therefore, I make wise decisions and continually make progress that brings glory to you. In Jesus name.

Bible in one year // **Psalms 123-125, 1 Corinthians 10:1-18**

Let us therefore come boldly to the throne of grace, that we may obtain mercy and find grace to help in time of need. // **Hebrews 4:16**

AUG 29

His grace is sufficient

God's grace is sufficient for you this season. He has made it richly available to you in Christ Jesus. You don't even need to pray for grace, you appropriate it. It is yours to take hold of. For God in Christ Jesus already extended to you all the grace you could ever need. Paul informs us, "If by the one man's offense death reigned through the one, much more those who receive abundance of grace and of the gift of righteousness will reign in life through the One, Jesus Christ" (Romans 5:17).

It is important to note Paul's construction when he says, "Those who receive abundance of grace". He says this because God's grace is already richly extended towards you – grace in abundance. It is the picture of an outstretched arm giving you something, it is yours to take. It is not for you to ask to be given. That is al-ready done, it is already given in abundance. This was God's response to Paul at a time he felt he really needed a divine intervention. Paul recounts, "Concerning this thing I pleaded with the Lord three times that it might depart from me. And He said to me, 'My grace is sufficient for you, for My strength is made perfect in weakness.'" (2 Corinthians 12:8-9).

> God's grace is sufficient for you in Christ Jesus, enabling you to live the life He has called you to, and accomplish all that He has laid as dreams in your heart this season and beyond.

Even when the word encourages us to come to the throne room, it does not ask us to come ask for grace; it calls us to come and find it. Why? Because it is already richly made available. That verse says, "Let us therefore come boldly to the throne of grace, that we may obtain mercy and find grace to help in time of need" (Hebrews 4:16). It doesn't matter the challenges you are facing this season or the projects you have at hand. His grace is indeed sufficient for you. Never think you can't take it no more, never think you are not able to carry on, never think you reached your end, so long as you are walking in the path He has called you to take. His grace is more than sufficient to see you through. Appropriate the grace of God and activate it by confessing that grace is yours and is at work in your life.

Prayer

Heavenly Father, thank you for the abundance of grace given us in Christ Jesus. That grace is sufficient for me today, to walk in righteousness and live Holy, to do mighty things and fulfill your purpose for my life. I am enabled by grace in Jesus' name.

Bible in one year // **Psalms 126-128, 1 Corinthians 10:19-33**

AUG 30

Grow in the grace and knowledge of our Lord and Savior Jesus Christ.
// 2 Peter 3:18

Grow in grace

That is this very clear instruction given to us in scripture, we are instructed to grow in grace. I like such an instruction because it puts the ball right into our own hands. It lets us know we have something to do about it. And this is one area of concern in the body of Christ, that many times we are waiting on the Lord for things He has shown us how to get, praying for things that have been given and believing to get to where we have already been positioned. This is one reason we must go into the word of God to know His thoughts and see what ours in Christ Jesus is. This is the purpose of Your Daily Light, bringing you illumination from the word of God and helping you appropriate your inheritance in Christ.

Continue to meditate in God's word, and His grace will be multiplied in your life.

2 Peter 3:18 tells us, "Grow in the grace and knowledge of our Lord and Savior Jesus Christ". It is an instruction. And in another place, we are told how that growth in grace will come. The grace of God in our lives is multiplied as we grow in the Knowledge of God and His Son, Jesus Christ. As it is written, "Grace and peace be multiplied unto you through the knowledge of God, and of Jesus our Lord" (2 Peter 1:2). So, you can multiply the grace of God in your life just by growing in the knowledge of His word.

Even Jesus, during His earthly life, grew in grace. The bible records of Him, "The child grew and became strong; he was filled with wisdom, and the grace of God was on him". And in another place, Luke adds, "Jesus increased in wisdom and stature, and in favor with God and men" (Luke 2:40 & 52). There is room for growth in the grace of God in your life, and there are avenues by which this increase in grace comes. One such is by growing in the knowledge of God, and of His son Jesus Christ. Suddenly you realize you are stronger, wiser, and able to accomplish more. For the grace of God has been multiplied in your life through the knowledge you are receiving. So, even Your Daily Light is a dispenser of God's grace, as it brings you the word of God daily.

Prayer

Thank you, Heavenly Father for your word that comes to me daily, by it, your grace in my life is multiplied. I grow in favor with you and with men. My ability is increased, and my output multiplied. I walk and not faint, I run and do not grow weary. For your grace in my life is sufficient. In Jesus' name.

Bible in one year // **Psalms 129-131, 1 Corinthians 11:1-16**

God resists the proud but gives more grace to the humble.
// James 4:6

AUG 31

Like two sides of a coin

With regards to grace, humility and pride are like the two sides of a coin. Like in a football game, what side of the coin faces up, determines who is going to have the ball first. Even so, being proud or humble determines how much of God's grace you will experience. James 4:6 tells us, "God resists the proud but gives more grace to the humble". You can decide what side of the coin you want and the experience thereof.

If you are one who is proud, one who exalts himself above others because of what they have or who they are, you are making God your opposer. God will resist you and stop you in your tracks. And you will be surprised that all those you once boasted to be above might gradually overtake you and you will find yourself looking up to them. That is when you are humbled against your will. This explains sometimes why some people who started off so well end so badly. The enemy might not have been the Devil, maybe God stopped them because of the pride in their hearts. But if you want to experience more of God's grace, clothe yourself with humility as Colossians 3:12 tells us.

> True to scripture, the humble will receive more grace, in the end they will be exalted. But the proud will be brought low, as God Himself resists them.

Humility is the character of putting aside your accolades, certificates, status, or education and relating with others for who they are as God's creation. Humility is when you do not lift yourself above others because God has exalted or favored you over them. Humility is when despite the lesser position of others, you can bring yourself to their level and relate with them as if you were at the same. This is what the bible encourages us to do. It tells us how Christ humbled himself and encourages us to do likewise. "Let this mind be in you which was also in Christ Jesus, who, being in the form of God, did not consider it robbery to be equal with God, but made Himself of no reputation, taking the form of a bondservant, and coming in the likeness of men" (Philippians 2:5-7). And in the end, Christ was exalted and given a name above every other name (Philippians 2:9-11). Be therefore humble, that you might receive more grace from the Lord.

Prayer

Heavenly Father, thank you for giving us the mind of Christ and the capacity to act like him. We are humbled in your presence and in our relationship with others. We, therefore, grow from grace to grace as you lift us up in season. In Jesus name.

Bible in one year // **Psalms 132-134, 1 Corinthians 11:17-34**

SEP TEM BER

With great power the apostles gave witness to the resurrection of the Lord Jesus. And great grace was upon them all. // **Acts 4:33**

SEP 1

Be rightly positioned

A lot of things can go well or wrong in life because of positioning. This is no lie when you think of life in the physical world. No matter in which nation you live, there are cities or neighborhoods that are by nature dangerous or safe. And being positioned in one of them could mean everything for your well-being. Positioning has something to do. This is also true with our experience of God's grace. You must be rightly positioned in the body of Christ. Where you fellowship matters and who ministers to you matters. For grace can be dispensed by one to another. And the grace over a fellowship of believers can vary, one from another. This is a scriptural reality.

> **Be rightly positioned in the body of Christ. Belong to a living Church and abide where the Lord leads you, for there, He has bestowed a grace for your life.**

Remember, grace as we saw recently, can be a function of our depth of knowledge of God and His son Jesus Christ as growth in grace comes through knowledge. This explains the difference we sometimes observe from one denomination to another, that one is more prophetic, others are sound in knowledge, others living daily miracles, and yet, there are those denominations wondering if any of such things like miracles and prophecies still exist. It all has to do with the grace at work in the fellowship and what is being dispensed to the people. We read of the early Church, "With great power the apostles gave witness to the resurrection of the Lord Jesus. And great grace was upon them all" (Acts 4:33).

There was great grace upon that assembly of believers. No doubt when persecution broke out and the believers scattered, they rather went on to multiply the works of the apostles (Acts 6-8). They carried along with them the great grace that was upon the assembly, a grace that came through their rich fellowship, the teachings of the apostles and the Lord blessing their gathering. Do not be mistaken. Because it is called grace, does not mean you have nothing to do with its increase and growth in your life. That will be erroneous. One thing that matters is your positioning in the body of Christ, where you fellowship. For the grace of God over that assembly will have a rub-off on our lives.

Prayer

Heavenly Father, thank you for the Holy Spirit given us to lead us into all truths and to guide us in our choices. Help us to see where to be positioned in the body for the fullness of your grace. In Jesus name.

Bible in one year // **Psalms 135-136, 1 Corinthians 12**

> Let us not neglect our meeting together, as some people do, but encourage one another, especially now that the day of his return is drawing near.
> // **Hebrews 10:25**

SEP 2

Finding a living church Pt. 1

Generally, the question of finding a living church comes for two main reasons: First, because of relocation to a new environment where continued fellowship with our old church family is practically impossible or will be ineffective. The second reason often is because someone is new to the Faith and looking for a place where they can grow. Outside these two reasons, there can be many other commendable reasons for needing to move to a new place of fellowship, of course a living Church. Whether you should belong to a Church is not a question. Hebrews 10:25 tells us, "Let us not neglect our meeting together, as some people do, but encourage one another, especially now that the day of his return is drawing near".

> **When finding a living Church, the goal is to have a suitable environment where you can grow together with other believers, where you can serve the Lord in faith.**

Now, the phrase "Living church" is not a spiritual construction. Spiritually, "Living Church" will be tautology. For it is inherent for the Church to be living and life-giving. However, the phrase "Living Church" is to emphasize that it is a Church living up to its purpose, founded on the word of God, a Church where God's presence is evidently at work and the Holy Spirit is acknowledged, a church where your spiritual gifts can be identified, nurtured, and maximized for the good of the whole. A living Church is one where spiritual growth is eminent and your spiritual development and well-being are guaranteed.

Finding a living Church is therefore of utmost importance. Sometimes, moving to a new Church is also encouraged. However, you must be sure it is necessary. Now don't look for a perfect Church. There is hardly any, so long as we are on the earth, and we are a people being perfected. Our imperfections while we meet with other believers can always cause some degree of nuisance. And that is why we are commanded, "Make allowance for each other's faults, and forgive anyone who offends you. Remember, the Lord forgave you, so you must forgive others" (Colossians 3:13). We share with you a practical guide on making such a decision about finding a living Church in the pages ahead.

Prayer

Heavenly Father, thank you for we are made partakers of the glorious inheritance in Christ and members of His body which is the Church. As we seek to grow in our relationship with you and commitment in service, we pray that we will be rightly positioned in a living Church. In Jesus' name.

Bible in one year // **Psalms 137-139, 1 Corinthians 13**

Your ears shall hear a word behind you, saying, "This is the way, walk in it;" Whenever you turn to the right hand or whenever you turn to the left.
// **Isaiah 30:21**

Finding a living church Pt. 2

The thought of the day yesterday highlighted the main goal in finding a living Church. It is to have a suitable environment where you can grow together with other believers, serving the Lord in faith. However, making this decision can be challenging, particularly if we do not get a clear word from the Lord or are not in the disposition to hear him. However, if we are truly open and prayerful, He will lead us to a living Church. Just as scripture echoes, "Whether you turn to the right or to the left, your ears will hear a voice behind you, saying, 'This is the way; walk in it.'" (Isaiah 30:21). In another place we are told, "Seek his will in all you do, and he will show you which path to take" (Proverbs 3:6).

Besides having a clear leading from the Lord, there are practical steps to take. In today's world of technology, particularly if a Church is living up to the times in which we are, they will have a webpage or at minimum, be on a social media platform that makes them visible on the internet space. This is particularly helpful when people move into a new environment and are looking for a new Church. Find the Churches in your area on the internet, visit the webpage and check out the mission statement. Also check out their statement of faith. These two pages are usually sufficient to communicate to you a summary of what they believe and teach, helping you to already judge from a distance if they are sound in bible doctrines and based on God's revealed truth.

Take the next step and attend a meeting. Watch out for a witness of the Lord in your heart. For He will affirm to you when you find one, "This is the place". Above all, remember, we walk by faith not by sight. Now, a Church might not necessarily meet all our expectations, but will meet our needs in season according to God's purpose. It is a blessing when the Lord brings you to a place where you can grow, but sometimes, He brings you to a place where you have responsibility to make it grow, to improve things and be a strength to them. Sometimes He brings you to that Church because there was a vacancy, and the He needs you there. Don't only think of what you get belonging to a Church, also think of what you bring that the Church needs, for God has graced you with something for His Church.

> **Take practical steps towards finding a living Church. While you do, don't only think of what you can get by belonging there. God might be bringing you in because of a vacancy that exists, a vacancy you will fill.**

Prayer

Heavenly Father, thank you that I have something to offer in your house and a place to serve. I receive grace to be well-positioned and to serve with greater effectiveness in Jesus' name.

Bible in one year // **Psalms 140-142, 1 Corinthians 14:1-20**

SEP 4

I was glad when they said to me, "Let us go into the house of the Lord."
// **Psalm 122:1**

Finding a living church Pt. 3

Another practical way to find a new living Church is by recommendation – the suggestion of others based on experience. Talk to someone about your search for a living Church. Someone might invite you, don't hesitate, check it out. What is the worst that can happen if the invitation is truly to a Church? The worst that might happen is that you endure an hour or two of service in a place that can't be a spiritual home to you. On the other hand, you might truly just find yourself a new home. Like David rejoiced, I was glad when they said to me, "Let us go into the house of the LORD" (Psalm 122:1)

Sometimes, you can consider a popular denomination of Churches. If you already belong to one such denomination that has other Churches in another location, it is always the easiest way to just locate another branch of that Church in your new city. You must think of it like prospecting a new flat or house you are considering moving into. You pay prospective visits, and in the end decide, hopefully led by God or at minimum, according to your needs in season. It is ok to prospect Churches. It is not a bad thing to do. It is your destiny you are shaping, it is your future you are deciding, so it is ok to check out what options you have. And if you are new to the faith, the best way to find your first Church is to follow the one who led you to Christ or ask them for guidance.

> **Take practical steps and be open for newness; find a living church and abide there. Don't look for a perfect Church, look for a spiritual home.**

Whatever step you take, however you go, it is more important to be open to newness. Don't be trapped in your mind with how things were done from where you are coming. That is why it is called a new Church to you, because it is new. Therefore, expect newness, be it positive or negative. Like families, no two churches are identical. No matter how similar the structure, it is an assembly of new persons with new personalities. Even if all the churches use the same guiding principles, they will go about it in different ways. Even if the ministers were to preach on the same Topic, they would approach it differently. Therefore, be open to newness. Lookout to see that the spirit of God is present and that you can serve the Lord in that place. For unless you are open, you will be on an endless journey of finding a living Church and live like a "Spiritually homeless" Christian who finds fault with every place.

Prayer

Heavenly Father, thank you for situating a spiritual home for me where I can grow, serve you and be blessed. Thank you for ordering my steps to the place of blessing and progress. In Jesus' name.

Bible in one year // **Psalms 143-145, 1 Corinthians 14:21-40**

Stay alert! Watch out for your great enemy, the devil. He prowls around like a roaring lion, looking for someone to devour. // **1 Peter 5:8 NLT**

SEP 5

A stratagem of darkness

Sadly, it is the case that some Christians for sometimes seemingly understandable reasons, have resorted to not belong to a Christian fellowship. They choose to have nothing to do with a Church and to be independent. Some commonly say it is a matter of the heart. Sure, it is a matter of the heart, nonetheless, belonging to a fellowship of believers is prime for your spiritual wellbeing. Sometimes, such decisions came out of hurt or abuse when someone had a bad experience at a Church. You don't have to stay there if that is you, it is like deciding never to go to the hospital because you met one bad doctor. It is parallel to deciding never to use money again because you were cheated with a counterfeit note.

No! Never let a fake thing cheat you out of experiencing the genuine and the joy it brings. Never let a bad experience from one Church cheat you from finding a new place of fellowship. Whatever the reason might be, never resort to not belonging to a fellowship of believers and to be on your own. It is a stratagem of darkness to keep you away from fellowship with other believers. It is the devil luring you away for your destruction.

> It is a stratagem of darkness to lure away a believer as a loner to a vulnerable place for destruction. Don't fall for his scheme. Belong to a fellowship.

The bible tells us, "Stay alert! Watch out for your great enemy, the devil. He prowls around like a roaring lion, looking for someone to devour" (1 Peter 5:8 NLT). We are called to watch out against the devil. We are called to be alert, "So that Satan will not outsmart us. For we are familiar with his evil schemes" (2 Corinthians 2:11 NLT). Now if you think of how lions and other animals of prey hunt, you will realize they often go for the lone prey. That is an easy target. Even if the animal of prey was in a herd, their first goal will be to isolate it from the group. It is the same thing spiritually. The devil starts by trying to lure away a believer from the rest, for on their own, they are most vulnerable and an easy target. Never fall for this stratagem of darkness. Find a living church or community of believers with whom you can fellowship. Don't be a loner. It is dangerous.

Prayer

> Heavenly Father, thank you for making us wiser than our enemy the devil, that we are not ignorant of his strategies. Therefore, we are alert and watchful, abiding in your house and in fellowship with other believers where we grow and thrive spiritually for your glory. In Jesus name.

Bible in one year // **Psalms 146-147, 1 Corinthians 15:1-28**

SEP 6

> If by the one man's offense death reigned through the one, much more those who receive abundance of grace and of the gift of righteousness will reign in life through the One, Jesus Christ. // **Romans 5:17**

Called to reign

When God made the first man, he made him a king. He gave him authority and dominion to rule over the earth. He said to the couple, "Be fruitful and multiply; fill the earth and subdue it; have dominion over the fish of the sea, over the birds of the air, and over every living thing that moves on the earth" (Genesis 1:28). They were called to reign. However, that dominion and authority was lost to the devil. But God had a better plan, another occasion. Jesus came to deliver us from the dominion of darkness. Paul wrote, "He has delivered us from the power of darkness and conveyed us into the kingdom of the Son of His love, in whom we have redemption through His blood, the forgiveness of sins" (Colossians 1:13-14).

> **In Christ Jesus, we have been made kings and called to reign in life, taking our place and living in authority and dominion.**

Much more, not only were we freed from the dominion of darkness, but we were also once again given dominion through Christ Jesus. Romans 5:17 tells us, "For if by the one man's offense death reigned through the one, much more those who receive abundance of grace and of the gift of righteousness will reign in life through the One, Jesus Christ" (Romans 5:17). The bible makes it plain that those who have received of the gift of righteousness will reign in life through Christ Jesus. Now that is talking about you, if you have received Christ. You are called to reign in life.

It is written for us in Revelation 1:5-6, "From Jesus Christ, the faithful witness, the firstborn from the dead, and the ruler over the kings of the earth. To Him who loved us and washed us from our sins in His own blood, and has made us kings and priests to His God and Father, to Him be glory and dominion forever and ever". We are kings and we are priests in Christ Jesus. Sadly, many have only understood the priestly ministry and call. They have not understood the kingly placement and call to reign, and that will be our focus over the next days. You are called to reign; you are called to be in charge. God wants you to be in control and not live life as a victim. He has made you a king and you are called to reign in life through the one, Jesus Christ.

Prayer

Heavenly Father, thank you for the blessing of a new day and the privileges we have in Christ Jesus. Thank you for making us kings and priests and calling us to reign in life by Jesus Christ. We receive the call gladly and stand up to the responsibility for your glory. In Jesus' name.

Bible in one year // **Psalms 148-150, 1 Corinthians 15:29-58**

God raised us up with Christ and seated us with him in the heavenly realms.
// **Ephesians 2:6**

SEP 7

Enthroned

Not only were you made king, but you were also enthroned. And it is also important to know, that Paul was not just referring to the afterlife when he wrote, „They that have received of the abundance of grace and of the gift of righteousness will reign in life by the one man, Jesus Christ" (Romans 5:17). Paul was talking about this life, the one we are living presently. Just as Jesus said, „I have come that they might have life and life, more abundantly " (John 10:10). It is a guarantee of reigning in this present life, and a promise in the life to come. You were not only made king, you were also enthroned in this life.

Now to enthrone means to install one on a throne or in a royal office to mark the beginning of their reign. And that is what God did for you. You were enthroned in Christ Jesus. You were put in office to take charge over circumstances, over principalities and over the world. You were installed in office to reign. Paul writes, "God raised us up with Christ and seated us with him in the heavenly realms" (Ephesians 2:6). You are seated together with Christ, you are enthroned. This was not just a seating on a chair, it was a seating on a throne, a joint seating with Christ from where He reigns. It was in that position that the Psalmist prophetically said, "The LORD said to my Lord, "Sit in the place of honor at my right hand until I humble your enemies, making them a footstool under your feet" (Psalm 110:1).

Paul echoes this heavenly seating again: "God demonstrated this power in Christ by raising Him from the dead and seating Him at His right hand in the heavens far above every ruler and authority, power and dominion, and every title given, not only in this age but also in the one to come. And He put everything under His feet and appointed Him as head over everything for the church" (Ephesians 1:20-22). This is the same seating we had, a joint seating with Christ. No doubt Jesus said to us, "I tell you the truth, whatever you forbid on earth will be forbidden in heaven, and whatever you permit on earth will be permitted in heaven (Matthew 18:18). He was saying we have been given the command. Hallelujah!

> **Not only were you made a king in Christ Jesus, you were also enthroned, seated together with Him in heavenly places and positioned to take charge of things in the world.**

Prayer

> Heavenly father, thank you for the authority and power bestowed upon me in Christ Jesus, to forbid what is not in line with your purposes and to command into establishment your will in the earth. Today therefore I take authority and set things as they should be wherever I am. In Jesus' name.

Bible in one year // **Proverbs 1-2, 1 Corinthians 16**

My people are destroyed for lack of knowledge. // **Hosea 4:6**

SEP 8

Why many are not reigning

The word of God was not given us to use in justifying our failures and limitations, but to help us see how through God, indeed nothing is impossible. While there are seasons of trials that might subject us to undesirable circumstances and situations, it is important to not justify why things must be difficult, why it is ok to be poor, why sickness is a part of life. No, and a thousand times no! And this is not what some term, prosperity Gospel. This is the Gospel. When Jesus defined the purpose of his coming, He declared healing for the sick, freedom for the oppressed, wellbeing for the poor and liberation for the captive. That is what makes it good news, it offers hope for today, in this life and in eternity.

The reverse is only true for the one who is not born again because they are under the dominion of the devil. The devil is still their legal master and therefore has right of way to afflict, harass and abuse them. This is what the Psalmist makes clear. He shows us two classes of people and their life experiences (Psalm 1:1-6). He shows us of the blessed one who meditates in the word of the Lord daily, who is like a tree planted by the rivers of water and fears not concerning drought. He prospers in all he does and bring forth his fruits in season. But the wicked he says, they will not stand in the congregation of the righteous, they are like chaff blown by the wind.

> We must grow up spiritually to take our full position of authority in Christ and to gain the knowledge by which we can reign in life through Christ, living above circumstances, the world and the devil.

We have a responsibility to make the promises of God a reality in our lives. And the lack of spiritual understanding and the knowledge of how to make it a reality is the reason many Christians are not reigning and are still subject to the devil. Paul explains this in Galatians 4:1-2, "As long as an heir is underage, he is no different from a slave, although he owns the whole estate. The heir is subject to guardians and trustees until the time set by his father". Unless we grow up spiritually, we will not be able to take our full positions as heirs. This is in line with the words of the prophet when he declared, "My people are destroyed for the lack of knowledge" (Hosea 4:6). This is the reason for Your Daily Light, bringing to you knowledge through the word of God for a victorious and a fulfilling life in Christ.

Prayer

Heavenly Father thank you for the grace to continue in the word as I am instructed daily in the way I should go. As I mature and take my place as an heir, I live above circumstances and the challenges of life, fulfilling the call you have for me and bringing glory to you. In Jesus' name.

Bible in one year // Proverbs 3-5, 2 Corinthians 1

Whoever says to this mountain, 'Be removed and be cast into the sea', and does not doubt in his heart, but believes that those things he says will be done, he will have whatever he says. // **Mark 11:23**

SEP 9

We reign with words

We reign with words, that is a spiritual law of the Kingdom of God. Just as Ecclesiastes 8:4 puts it, "Where the word of a king is, there is power". Because you were made a king (Revelation 1:5-6), your words carry power. This was the kind of authority the centurion understood when he met Jesus. He had approached Jesus regarding the servant who was sick and at home saying, "Lord, my servant is lying at home paralyzed, dreadfully tormented." And Jesus said to him, "I will come and heal him." The centurion answered and said, "Lord, I am not worthy that You should come under my roof. But only speak a word, and my servant will be healed. For I also am a man under authority, having soldiers under me. And I say to this one, 'Go,' and he goes; and to another, 'Come,' and he comes; and to my servant, 'Do this,' and he does it." (Luke 8:5-9).

The centurion was simply saying to Jesus, "Your words are enough as one in authority to cause the change I desire". And that is the spiritual reality that applies to you too. That is why Jesus assured us, "For assuredly, I say to you, whoever says to this mountain, 'Be removed and be cast into the sea,' and does not doubt in his heart, but believes that those things he says will be done, he will have whatever he says Mark 11:23). When Jesus said "Assuredly", he meant "Guaranteed", he meant, "On a serious note", he meant, "You don't have to doubt this truth".

> **Where the word of the king is, there is power. It is a spiritual law that will work for you or against you. Learn to talk right, speaking to situations, commanding things to conform to the will of God.**

If you will learn to live the kingly life in Christ Jesus and walk in the blessedness and the dominion of this office, you will have to learn to use your words. For indeed, where the word of the king is, there is power. God himself is back that word, watching it to make it a reality (Numbers 14:28). Angels are on assignment on your behalf, standing by for the right proclamations from your lips to effectuate them (Hebrews 1:14). That is why you must talk right. Remember, "All things were made by the word and without the word was nothing made" (John 1:1-3).

Prayer

Almighty God, thank you for the privilege and blessing to be a king in Christ Jesus and called to rule over circumstances and the devil. Today I walk in this consciousness, knowing my words are powerful to effect changes by the Holy Spirit. In Jesus' name.

Bible in one year // **Proverbs 6-7, 2 Corinthians 2**

SEP 10

> When you pray, go into your room, and when you have shut your door, pray to your Father who is in the secret place; and your Father who sees in secret will reward you openly. // **Matthew 6:6**

Enter your closet

I once read a book on payer. One instruction I have never forgotten from this book was the instruction to turn the closet into a courtroom. In this book, the author explained the prayer of supplication, emphasizing that if ever you came out of the closet without a response, it simply meant "Case adjourned". You are going to get back into that closet and continue in prayer. Talking about reigning in life, there are avenues given to us by which we effect our influence and control, so that we are not just victims of circumstances. Rather, we are the force behind the events, shaping things as we enforce the will of God on the earth. And prayer provides us one such avenue.

> **Prayer is one of the avenues given to us by God through which we reign in life, for by it we can influence the course of events as God inspires us.**

Jesus said about prayer, "When you pray, go into your room, and when you have shut your door, pray to your Father who is in the secret place; and your Father who sees in secret will reward you openly" (Matthew 6:6). There is a lot we can change on our knees, there is a lot we can change in the place of prayer. A great example of scripture should encourage us today. This is the story of Elijah. He was a man in authority, even influencing the weather. But this was not mere wishful proclamation of words. In fact, before he prophesied, he camefrom the place of prayer. And this is the missing link and the frustration we have often, that people proclaim words that are not inspired of God.

Elijah understood the place of prayer. Six times he sent his servant to observe the clouds if there was anything happening. And six times the servant came back to say "Nothing". Elijah stayed on his knees until the seventh time when the servant came saying, Seven times Elijah told him to go and look. Finally the seventh time, his servant told him, "I saw a little cloud about the size of a man's hand rising from the sea". Then Elijah shouted, "Hurry to Ahab and tell him, 'Climb into your chariot and go back home. If you don't hurry, the rain will stop you!'" (1 Kings 18:43-44). James recounts, "Elias was a man subject to like passions as we are, and he prayed earnestly that it might not rain: and it rained not on the earth by the space of three years and six months" (James 5:17)

Prayer

Thank you, heavenly Father, that we can come boldly to the throne of grace to find mercy and obtain grace in times of need. As we make our requests known to you, we rest assured in your faithfulness to answer and cause all things to work together for our good. In Jesus' name.

Bible in one year // **Proverbs 8-9, 2 Corinthians 3**

By me princes rule, and nobles, all the judges of the earth.
// **Proverbs 8:16**

SEP 11

Wisdom is necessary

Proverbs 8 is an amazing chapter where wisdom is personified. And if you would carefully examine this portion of the Bible in the light of who Jesus is, you will indeed confirm that Christ is wisdom personified. That the Bible clearly echoes that Christ is the wisdom of God. As it is written, "But unto them which are called, both Jews and Greeks, Christ the power of God, and the wisdom of God" (1 Corinthians 1:24). Indeed, Christ is the wisdom of God.

With this understanding, Wisdom personified speaks for Himself saying, "Counsel is mine, and sound wisdom: I am understanding; I have strength. By me kings reign, and princes decree justice. By me princes rule, and nobles, even all the judges of the earth" (Proverbs 8:14 - 16). Wisdom says, "By me, kings reign". How profound. If you will reign as one made king in Christ, you will have to live by the wisdom of God. This is a wisdom that helps you to master and manage complex situations. By this wisdom, even with limited resources, you will know how to get yourself out and over. Solomon understood his need for wisdom to reign as King after his enthronement. After he had offered up sacrifices to the Lord, such a sacrifice that moved God to offer him an open check, Solomon was quick to ask for wisdom (1 Kings 3:10-11 NLT).

> The word of God is His wisdom for life to us to enable us live victoriously above circumstances, the world's systems and the devil, totally reigning in life.

And because Solomon made the right request, God was pleased to grant it to him, and with that wisdom, wealth, and long life. Now this does not call you to start praying for wisdom. For if you are in Christ, you have the fullness of God's wisdom personified. More so, you have the word of God that gives you God's perspective and wisdom for life. You are better placed than Solomon to live by the wisdom of God, and as you meditate and live by the word of God and the guidance of the Holy Spirit, He will make you victorious in all things.

Prayer

Lord God almighty, I give you praise and Glory for your boundless love towards us. Thank You for your wisdom at work in me, by which I can maneuver my way through life, emerging victorious in all circumstances as I put your Word to work. In Jesus name

Bible in one year // **Proverbs 10-12, 2 Corinthians 4**

SEP 12

And do not be drunk with wine, in which is dissipation; but be filled with the Spirit. // **Ephesians 5:18**

Be filled with the Spirit

My friend had been called to lead a youth fellowship over central and west Africa as I remember. As a youth himself, this was a new challenge. While he prayed, the Lord gave him a vision. In that vision, He saw a ball afloat in a bucket of water. Then the ball was taken and placed upon the ocean. And the ball remained afloat. Then the word of the Lord came to him saying, I paraphrase, "So long as the ball is filled with air, it doesn't matter where you place it and the amount of water there is, the ball will stay afloat. Same it is with you if you will remain filled with the Spirit. You will stay afloat and be on top of things anywhere". What a word!

As we consider the ways in which you can position yourself to reign in life as the king you have been made in Christ, this is one thing you have need of. Not just once, but always. You must be continually filled with the Spirit. Like Paul wrote to the Church in Ephesians, "Be filled with the Spirit" (Ephesians 5:18). And that for good reason. When you read about the Seven Spirits of God, you will understand one of the seven spirits of God is the Spirit of Lordship, the spirit of dominion. Throughout the Old Testament, this was referred to as the Spirit of the Lord in certain situations. Now don't get mistaken with terminology. That is a subject for a book, The seven spirits of God. And the Spirit of Lordship is one of the seven.

> **Be filled with the Spirit. He is also the Spirit of dominion, and when he overwhelms you, you are set above and positioned to take charge of things for good outcomes.**

Whenever someone was overtaken by the Spirit of the Lord, they took command and became in charge, they rose above situations and circumstances, even the most fearful like Gideon. We read in Judges, "The Spirit of the Lord came upon Gideon; then he blew the trumpet, and the Abiezrites gathered behind him" (Judges 6:34). He rose above his fears and became a leader, because he was overtaken by the spirit of dominion. Same will be your story if you are continually filled with the Spirit.

Prayer

Heavenly Father, thank you for giving us the Holy Spirit our dependable helper. As we spend time in your presence and become filled with your Spirit daily, we rise above our human limitations and inabilities to overcome all challenges that we face as we live and fulfil your call for us in Christ. In Jesus name.

Bible in one year // **Proverbs 13-15, 2 Corinthians 5**

As many as are led by the Spirit of God, these are sons of God.
// **Romans 8:14**

Be led by the Spirit

When you examine the successes and victories in the life of David as a king, one thing stands out. David was a man led by the Spirit of God. Even in the most evident situations, he was careful to consult with the Lord and take the right steps. And in this way, his Kingdom was established, and his reign sustained. This we all need today. Many times, at the root of our failures and defeats, is a straying from divine paths. For where the Lord leads, he makes provisions, protects, sustains, and guarantees well-being. Isaiah wrote about Israel, "They did not thirst When He led them through the deserts; He caused the waters to flow from the rock for them; He also split the rock, and the waters gushed out (Isaiah 48:21).

It is God's desire to lead us through life, ordering our steps in the paths prearranged for us. How the Amplified version of the bible nicely renders Ephesians 2:10: For we are His workmanship [His own master work, a work of art], created in Christ Jesus [reborn from above–spiritually transformed, renewed, ready to be used] for good works, which God prepared [for us] beforehand [taking paths which He set], so that we would walk in them [living the good life which He prearranged and made ready for us]. There are prearranged paths traced out for you.

> The Lord makes a way where He leads us by His spirit, providing, sustaining, protecting and causing us to triumph for the glory of his name. Therefore, be led by the Spirit.

What we all need is to be guided into God's paths for our lives, for on that course, he makes us indomitable and victorious, He causes us to reign. We can be led by God as He instructs and guides us by His Spirit. As His children, it is his commitment. However, he will not break our will. That is why you will have to learn to seek his counsel. Proverbs 3:6 tells us, "Seek his will in all you do, and he will show you which path to take. God wants to lead us always, guiding us away from snares, inspiring us with wisdom in the most complex situations, and causing us to triumph in all things. Remember, "As many as are led by the Spirit of God, these are sons of God" (Romans 8:14).

Prayer

> Heavenly Father, thank you for a new day and the opportunities it brings to glorify you in the earth. Our ears are open to hear you, our eyes are open to see what you are showing us, and our hearts are willing to walk in your paths as you lead. Be our guide by Your Spirit, now and always. In Jesus name.

Bible in one year // **Proverbs 16-18, 2 Corinthians 6**

> He has delivered us from the power of darkness and [a]conveyed us into the kingdom of the Son of His love. // **Colossians 1:13**

Find your place

To reign in life, you will need to find your place in Christ, where God has called you to be and what He has called you to do. It is a spiritual law of life. You cannot beat a person who is in their God-given place. You cannot be victimized in your God-given place, at least not for long. He carved out for you a portion before creation, a place for you to live and function. Even if it doesn't look all glorious in the eyes of men, you can be sure it is the best you could have. When it comes to purpose and assignment, the grass is never greener on the other side. There is no place where you would thrive better and succeed better than the place you were designed to operate and function in.

> **When you find your God-given place in life, both spiritually and geographically, thriving and reigning in life will be a natural outcome.**

God's call for your life is first a spiritual placement. This is the easiest way to shine and stand out. Have you found your place? Do you know what the Lord has called you to do? And are you about that business? Someone once asked a question, "Why is it that many Christians have to suffer so long before their breakthrough?" And a minister of the Gospel answered saying, "Because many Christians are head-strong in the wrong direction". That does make sense when we remember the fact that where the Lord leads, He makes the way. If things are so difficult, and the whole teaching about reigning in life seems a myth, it might be time to check if you are on the right track. Now it is also true that we can be on course with God and come into trials and challenging times. In such a case, faith is commanded.

At a time of famine, God forbade Isaac from moving to Egypt and at a time of drought, caused him to flourish where it was practically impossible (Genesis 26:1-13). When Elijah settled at the brook by divine instructions, even ravens were sent with deliveries (1 Kings 17:1-6). These men all thrived because they were positioned where God would have them be in season. Even spiritually, God had to reposition us before anything. As the bible says, "He has delivered us from the power of darkness and conveyed us into the kingdom of the Son of his love" (Colossians 1:13).

Prayer

Heavenly Father, thank you for where you have positioned me this season. Help me to be alert to your move that I will be rightly positioned always, where you want me to be, doing what you have called me to do. In Jesus' name.

Bible in one year // **Proverbs 19-21, 2 Corinthians 7**

Above all, taking the shield of faith with which, you will be able to quench all the fiery darts of the wicked one. // **Ephesians 6:16**

SEP 15

Exercise your faith

About reigning in life, it will be incomplete without calling you to exercise your faith. For that is the commanding force. In fact, these series of lessons generally do not go without meeting some defeated mindsets who have come to accept that they are victims in life, that life is very difficult, that the devil is too powerful and reigning in this life is an impossibility. If anything, a heretic teaching. But glory to God, there are a people who are rising to the knowledge of who they are in Christ, the knowledge of what they have received in Christ and are learning to put that knowledge to work for real life results.

Regarding faith, one of my favorite bible portions is from Hebrews 11:32-34 where the writer climaxes his account on the life of faith. This is a good day to read the whole chapter. But I draw your attention to these few verses: "And what shall I more say? for the time would fail me to tell of Gedeon, and of Barak, and of Samson, and of Jephthah; of David also, and Samuel, and of the prophets: Who through faith subdued kingdoms, wrought righteousness, obtained promises, stopped the mouths of lions. Quenched the violence of fire, escaped the edge of the sword, out of weakness were made strong, waxed valiant in fight, turned to flight the armies of the aliens".

> **Faith is essential to see the manifestation of the word of God in our lives as we talk and act in accordance with the things that are written concerning us.**

It talks of men who through faith, reigned in life, men who dominated circumstances, subdued kingdoms, overturned natural laws, made manifest the supernatural power of God in the face of adversity. Men who through faith turned around tables of death to banquets of festivity. Where it was all evident that their lives were on the line and would be snuffed from them, there they prevailed and became victorious, all through faith. And it all begins with accepting the truth of God's word for what it says. Then learn to talk and act like it for the results it assures us. Through our faith, we can indeed reign in life. Even as Ephesians 6:16 admonishes, "Above all, taking the shield of faith with which, you will be able to quench all the fiery darts of the wicked one."

Prayer

Heavenly Father, thank you for faith and the gift of the word that daily inspires even more faith. We are victorious in all things as we exercise our faith in your word. Thank you for your power made available to work wonders, angels commissioned for supernatural interventions through all things. In Jesus' name.

Bible in one year // **Proverbs 22-24, 2 Corinthians 8**

SEP 16

> Yet in all these things we are more than conquerors through Him who loved us. // **Romans 8:37**

More than conquerors

The sum of the series of lessons over the last days have been anchored on this very fact: In Christ, we are more than conquerors in all things; therefore, live like it. That is really what it means to reign in life. To live as one who is above everything, above circumstances, above systems, and above the devil and his schemes. This is not a call to ignore the realities of this life and the challenges thereof, but a call to live life from the Kingdom of God, superimposing its victory and authority on the natural world and enforcing the will of God in the earth. This is the faith life, a victorious life, and the reality in Christ.

Paul sums this all with this amazing writing to the Romans, "What then shall we say to these things? If God is for us, who can be against us? He who did not spare His own Son, but delivered Him up for us all, how shall He not with Him also freely give us all things? Who shall bring a charge against God's elect? It is God who justifies. Who is he who condemns? It is Christ who died, and furthermore is also risen, who is even at the right hand of God, who also makes intercession for us. Who shall separate us from the love of Christ? Shall tribulation, or distress, or persecution, or famine, or nakedness, or peril, or sword? As it is written: "For Your sake we are killed all day long; We are accounted as sheep for the slaughter." Yet in all these things we are more than conquerors through Him who loved us" (Romans 8:31-37).

> *In all things, not some things. In all things, we are more than conquerors through Jesus who loved us and gave His life for us. Let us therefore live like it.*

This was Paul's mindset, he was never defeated. It did not matter the situation, he looked pass the circumstances. In fact he even boasted in his ability to live independent of circumstances. He wrote to the Philippians, "Not that I speak from [any personal] need, for I have learned to be content [and self-sufficient through Christ, satisfied to the point where I am not disturbed or uneasy] regardless of my circumstances (Phil 4:11). And what was his secret? He wrote of this in 2 Cor 4:18: „So we fix our eyes not on what is seen, but on what is unseen, since what is seen is temporary, but what is unseen is eternal". Paul had learned to see and live life from the Kingdom of God and not as a natural man.

Prayer

Heavenly Father, thank you for the life prearranged and made ready for us in Christ Jesus, paths traced out that we might walk in them. As we take our place, walking in knowledge and exercising our faith, we reign in life to the praise of your glory. In Jesus name.

Bible in one year // **Proverbs 25-26, 2 Corinthians 9**

Thanks be to God, who always leads us as captives in Christ's triumphal procession and uses us to spread the aroma of the knowledge of him everywhere. // **2 Corinthians 2:14 NIV**

SEP 17

One victorious parade

Together in Christ, we make one victorious parade. Have this picture in mind, the picture of being a part of a parade on a perpetual victorious match. This is the actual picture of who we are together in Christ Jesus, we make one victorious parade. This is nicely coined in 2 Corinthians 2:14. It says, "Thanks be to God, who always leads us as captives in Christ's triumphal procession and uses us to spread the aroma of the knowledge of him everywhere" (NIV). It talks of a triumphal procession, a victorious parade. A procession is several people moving forward in an orderly fashion. And a parade is specifically a public procession, generally one celebration, a people showcasing themselves as they pass.

> As people reigning in life, we make one victorious parade in Christ Jesus, a people on a triumphal match, showcasing the virtues and glories of God as we bring the knowledge of Him to every place.

It reminds me of the old song with lines, "We are matching to Zion, Beautiful, beautiful, Zion: We're marching upward to Zion, The beautiful city of God". The author of this song understood the procession of God's people. He understood together we are like a people on a match. However, the author missed out on one truth. We are not matching to Zion. We are in Zion already. Hebrews 12:22 tells us, "But you have come to Mount Zion and to the city of the living God, the heavenly Jerusalem, to an innumerable company of angels" (NKJV). We are in Zion, the city of the great King. We are there now. We were translated out of the dominion of darkness and brought into the Kingdom of the son He loves (Colossians 1:13). However, there is a heaven to go to.

You must understand, there is a big difference between heaven and Zion, the city of the great king. But that's not our focus. The point of emphasis is this, there is a procession, a victorious parade, it is the assembly of God's people on the earthly mission to spread the knowledge of Him in all places like a sweet, smelling aroma everywhere. Paul wrote of the procession, seeming to lament on our position in the parade as ministers: "For it seems to me that God has put us apostles on display at the end of the procession, like those condemned to die in the arena. We have been made a spectacle to the whole universe, to angels as well as to human beings" (1 Corinthians 4:9). We are part of a victorious parade.

Prayer

> Almighty God, thank you for calling us out of darkness into your marvelous light that we might display the virtues and excellences thereof. Thank you for the victories and testimonies we have on our journey through diverse challenges that all echo your works in our lives. In Jesus' name.

Bible in one year // **Proverbs 27-29, 2 Corinthians 10**

SEP 18

> You shall receive power when the Holy Spirit has come upon you; and you shall be witnesses to Me in Jerusalem, and in all Judea and Samaria, and to the end of the earth. // **Acts 1:8**

A night of horror

I had been leading a home cell in Buea, Cameroon while I pursued a Master of Science degree in Biochemistry. This was every Tuesday during the semester. After completing my experiments for the day at the laboratory, I will end the evening at a home across the University campus, joining some precious saints to lead a time of bible study and home fellowship. On one such days, I had to leave the laboratory before a friend to be in time for my meeting. Not being able to wait and have the keys to the lab, my friend would have to bring them to the venue. And that he did, he brought to me the keys at the home. I went to the door and received the keys but did not invite him in to join for fellowship.

> You are God's watchman in your world, and he has charged you with a responsibility to bring the light to others, a responsibility for which you would be held accountable.

I stayed back and had a great meeting with the saints, a time of glory with God's presence manifested fully. We had instant healings, deliverance and diverse manifestations of the power and presence of God. The meeting ended and I went home. That night, I had a dream, it was a night of horror. In the dream, I was with this friend. The next thing I saw was that I had killed him and abandoned the body in a pit and his blood was on my hands. I was overwhelmed with dread of what the justice was going to do to me. I could not conceal the crime; I was fully guilty and would be called to give an account. Then I woke up. You would not imagine the joy of realizing that was a dream. The message was clear. The Lord was saying to me same thing he said to Ezekiel and says to you today.

The Lord said to Ezekiel, "I have made you a watchman for the house of Israel; therefore, you shall hear a word from My mouth and warn them for Me. When I say to the wicked, 'O wicked man, you shall surely die!' and you do not speak to warn the wicked from his way, that wicked man shall die in his iniquity; but his blood I will require at your hand. Nevertheless, if you warn the wicked to turn from his way, and he does not turn from his way, he shall die in his iniquity; but you have delivered your soul" (Ezekiel 33:7-9). So, I woke up realizing I had missed an opportunity to witness to my friend in a special way by not letting him join us that evening. Learn from my lesson today and be more intentional about your contribution for the salvation of others for He has made us His witnesses (Acts 1:8).

Prayer

Heavenly Father, thank you for the opportunity to be your witness to bring salvation to our families, friends, communities, and the world. We receive grace to use every opportunity. In Jesus' name.

Bible in one year // **Proverbs 30-31, 2 Corinthians 11:1-15**

Behold, I say to you, lift up your eyes and look at the fields, for they are already white for harvest! // **John 4:35**

SEP 19

A harvest season

This is a season of great harvest – the harvest of souls. Jesus said, "Do you not say, 'There are still four months and then comes the harvest'? Behold, I say to you, lift up your eyes and look at the fields, for they are already white for harvest!" (John 4:35). The fields are ready for harvest. And the Lord is counting on you and me to bring in the harvest. That is why he sent us out to the world to share the good news. It is not the task for a selected Christians, or those that are overzealous. It is a task for everyone. You have friends and family whose hearts the Lord has already prepared to accept the truth. They just need someone to clearly present to them the gospel. That is what Jesus meant when He said the fields are white for harvest. It is because the hearts of men are prepared and ready to turn to God.

There are many who are looking for the truth you have found in Christ, and with willing hearts will turn to the message when you share it. Soul winning is God's number one priority. And you cannot make it your priority without yourself becoming God's priority. When you become intentionally involved with the propagation of the gospel through your time, money, and efforts, you will be positioning yourself for great blessings. Then will this saying prove true in your life, "Seek first the kingdom of God and His righteousness, and all these things shall be added to you" (Matthew 6:33). The writer of Proverbs tells us, "He who wins souls is wise" (Proverbs 11:30).

> This is a season of great harvest, and you will be doing a wise thing to be part of those actively involved with the spread of the gospel and the salvation of souls.

On the other hand, there is another verse for those who do nothing this season towards the spread of the gospel. The writer of Proverbs tells us, "He who gathers crops in summer is a prudent son, but he who sleeps during harvest is a disgraceful son" (Proverbs 10:5). Such a one who is a child of God but does nothing about the spread of the gospel at this season of great harvest is indeed what the writer refers to as a disgraceful son. I pray that will not be you. Be a wise son or daughter of the Most High, participating in the joy of heaven by contributing to the spread of the gospel.

Prayer

> Heavenly Father, thank you for the wisdom in your word that inspires me to right actions. Thank you for making me a soul winner and worker in your Kingdom. I receive grace for greater effectiveness as a wise child who gathers in this season of great harvest through soul winning. In Jesus' name.

Bible in one year // **Ecclesiastes 1-3, 2 Corinthians 11:16-33**

SEP 20

> How beautiful are the feet of those who preach the gospel of peace, who bring glad tidings of good things! // **Romans 10:15**

Find a connection

When it comes to evangelism, a lot of wisdom could be required for the diverse opportunities we will have to share Christ with others. You don't always have to walk up to someone with a big bible in your hand and tell them, "I want to share the gospel with you". While the Lord will often create an opening and position people who are ready to receive you like this, there are a lot many people who are im-mediately turned off. In fact, when some people see you are about to start in that direction, they already look the other way. But there can also be a seeming effortless way to bring in the subject, when you are intending to share the gospel with someone you have been able to strike a conversation with, an acquaintance, a colleague, or a family member. It could even be a stranger seating next to you on a bus.

One easy way is always to strike a conversation on a totally different subject. You can start off with the political situation in the country, the current tournaments on TV, fashion trends, the weather, or whatever brought you two into contact. And while in that conversation, you are consciously searching a link to drift the conversation towards sharing the gospel. You intentionally look out for an opportunity to drive the conversation in the direction that will permit you discover if they are Christian or not, an opening to present to them the gospel. Sometimes you will discover they rather have questions that are standing in the way like stumbling blocks, preventing them from believing the truth and accepting Jesus as Lord. Then you might find the opportunity to demolish those strongholds by providing answers.

> Be intentional about spreading the good news and learn to find the connecting point in conversations. Remember, "How beautiful are the feet of those who bring good news"!

This is how the Lord led Philip to the Ethiopian Eunuch for the salvation of his soul (Acts 8:26-40). He was zealous for God but had not known Jesus, who is the only mediator able to reconcile God and man. Philip found a link and started off a conversation with Him. He then invited Philip to come up and sit with him. The bible tells us, "Then Philip began with that very passage of Scripture and told him the good news about Jesus". Philip found the connection with a stranger and starting with that, drove a conversation that led to the salvation of the Eunuch.

Prayer

Heavenly Father, thank you for wisdom to make the most of opportunities when in interaction with others as we bring the good news to our families and acquaintances. In Jesus' name.

Bible in one year // Ecclesiastes 4-6, 2 Corinthians 12

Many of the Samaritans of that city believed in Him because of the word of the woman who testified, "He told me all that I ever did".
// John 4:39

SEP 21

Preach Jesus

One wrong step you can take which is commonly made in soul winning is to approach people with a condemnation of their character and person. Though that might work, a lot more times, people are turned off. You must understand the content of the gospel if you are going to bring that message to others. It is called good news not bad news. It is the good news that the way is now open for personal relationship with God through Jesus. It is the good news that Jesus paid the price for our wrongs, and we can now come into a fellowship with God. It is the good news that it is possible to live righteously through the power of the Holy Spirit when you accept Jesus as Lord.

> Preach Jesus, bearing witness of His person, what He has done and will do for an individual. For when they experience Jesus, He will himself work in them the repentance.

Preach Jesus. That is what we are really sent out to do, to present Jesus to the world as the way out of sin and its consequences. For when they receive Jesus, He will work in them the fruit of repentance. I know John the Baptist and Jesus both preached saying, "Repent, for the Kingdom of God is at hand". But you must understand they both preached to a people who could not receive the Holy Spirit, for Christ was not yet glorified. Jesus and John preached to a people who had to live by the law of Moses through their own efforts, a people who understood the law and were familiar with the dos and don'ts of God. That is the reason they had this approach.

Jesus said: You shall receive power when the Holy Spirit has come upon you. And you shall be my witnesses (Acts 1:8). We are witnesses! But who is a witness? A witness is one who testifies about something, they testify for or against someone, they bear testimony of what they saw, heard, or experienced. And that is what we are sent to do, to testify of Jesus, who He is, what He has accomplished for humanity, and what life we have with him. We preach Jesus and present him to the world like a marketer sells a product, testifying to what it will do to them. Just like the Samaritan woman testified and brought her whole city to Christ, "He told me all that I ever did". This is our true calling.

Prayer

Heavenly Father, thank you for the illumination from your word that makes us wise and effective witnesses for Christ. Today we are empowered for the mission as we go about our activities. In Jesus name.

Bible in one year // **Ecclesiastes 7-9, 2 Corinthians 13**

> The wages of sin is death, but the free gift of God is eternal life through Christ Jesus our Lord. // **Romans 6:23 NLT**

Avoid controversial subjects

The Bible is plain on many things, but on certain issues, you will have to examine many scriptures to see God's viewpoint on such. However, the missing connections often result in a diversity of opinions on some subjects among Christians. This is the source of controversy when there are many opposing views on a subject. An example of a subject of controversy among believers in some places is alcohol, some declaring as a taboo while others endorse its consumption. This should not be a subject of Controversy if we would clearly examine scripture. Moreover, "The kingdom of God is not a matter of eating and drinking, but of righteousness, peace and joy in the Holy Spirit" (Romans 14:17).

> *In sharing Christ with others, avoid arguments of what is right or wrong, focus on showing them man's need for Jesus and the gift of eternal life in Christ.*

What is termed controversial even gets worse when we extend the situation to the circular world and our interaction with nonbelievers. It will be counter-productive often to try to evangelize to someone by debating over what is sin or not. Sadly, this touches on subjects that ought to be clear like homosexuality. Nonetheless, remember they are first in that state of mind because of the rebellious nature at work in them, making them a slave to sin. "They are darkened in their under-standing, being alienated from the life of God because of the ignorance that is in them" (Ephesians 4:18).

The spiritual condition of the non-Christian gives them a terrible judgment of what is wrong or right. Therefore, instead of spending time arguing with them about what way of life is right, simply let them understand that humanity was separated from God because of the initial sin. Just as Romans 5:12 tells us, "When Adam sinned, sin entered the world. Adam's sin brought death, so death spread to everyone, foreveryone sinned (Romans 5:12 NLT). So when the Bible says all have sinned, it is first because of the sin inherited in Adam. Our message is simple, "Because of Adam, everyone has sinned and fall short of God's glorious standard (Romans 3:23 NLT). But good news, "The wages of sin is death, but the free gift of God is eternal life through Christ Jesus our Lord" (Romans 6:23 NLT).

Prayer

Heavenly Father, we thank you for the privilege to know the truth, that the eyes of our understanding have been opened to see the glory in Jesus in whom we have found salvation. We break the hold of darkness over minds in the world as we bring the word of life to the lost. In Jesus name.

Bible in one year // Ecclesiastes 10-12, Galatians 2

Let your good deeds shine out for all to see, so that everyone will praise your heavenly Father. // **Matthew 5:16**

SEP 23

Be a living epistle

No matter how much of the gospel you preach to others, in the end, no message speaks louder than your life. Like it or not, someone is watching you, someone is taking notes, and someone is making conclusions about you. And if you fail to live a life that reflects the gospel you have received, it will discredit even the message you preach. Paul informed the Corinthians, "You are our epistle written in our hearts, known and read by all men; clearly you are an epistle of Christ, ministered by us, written not with ink but by the Spirit of the living God, not on tablets of stone but on tablets of flesh, that is, of the heart (2 Corinthians 3:2-3).

Jesus said, let your light so shine before men that they might see your good works and glorify your father in heaven (Matthew 5:16). He was saying the same thing as Paul, your life is a letter from the Lord to the world. And while you go about sharing the gospel, there is no louder message than the life you live. Before long, someone will get inquisitive about your exemplary lifestyle. They will want to know why you are the way you are, why you live the life you live, they will want to identify with such virtues and character that is rare to find in a corrupt world today. Then you can point them to Christ, the author and finisher of our faith.

> Your life is an open book to the world, a living epistle of Christ to others. Therefore, let your life reflect the life of God that draws men to Christ.

We are instructed, "Live no longer as the Gentiles do, for they are hopelessly confused. Their minds are full of darkness; they wander far from the life God gives because they have closed their minds and hardened their hearts against him. They have no sense of shame. They live for lustful pleasure and eagerly practice every kind of impurity. But that isn't what you learned about Christ. Since you have heard about Jesus and have learned the truth that comes from him, throw off your old sinful nature and your former way of life, which is corrupted by lust and deception. Instead, let the Spirit renew your thoughts and attitudes. Put on your new nature, created to be like God—truly righteous and holy (Ephesians 4:17-24 NLT).

Prayer

Heavenly Father, thank you for the life we have in Christ Jesus, a life that radiates your glory and echoes your goodness to our world. As others watch us, they will be drawn to you because of us. In Jesus name.

Bible in one year // **Song of Solomon 1-3, Galatians 2**

SEP 24

Make the most of every opportunity in these evil days.
// **Ephesians 5:16**

A window of opportunity

We might have an opportunity of a lifetime, but that opportunity will not forever be there. We must therefore take advantage of the opportunity while it lasts. You might even be one who looks back to see how a single opportunity you took has shaped your life for the better, or you might be on the other side, living with the regrets of a life opportunity you failed to take. Such will only go to emphasize to us the value of today's thoughts and serve as a lesson so we can maximize the opportunities of this season. And it is my prayer for you, that the Lord will open for you doors of opportunity in every regard.

A window of opportunity is the timeframe for which an opportunity is available. And God has given us such a window of opportunity to spread the knowledge of His word, to preach Christ to the world and to see His Kingdom come. These opportunities to witness will not forever be, we have a limited time. The time we have is the years of our lives left with us in the earth. If not that, Jesus is coming again. And when that final trumpet will sound, the last soul would have been won, the last message would have been preached and no other message will have value. A time of judgement and retribution is what will be at hand. The opportunity to be involved in the increase of the Kingdom would have ended.

> We must make the most of the opportunities we have, for they will not always be there. Time is of the essence, particularly for the spread of the gospel and the knowledge of God's word.

Jesus was conscious of the window of opportunity He had. He said, "I must work the works of Him who sent Me while it is day; the night is coming when no one can work" (John 9:4). Let this be your consciousness; that time is of the essence, and we must make the most of the opportunities we have. As we are admonished, "Be very careful, then, how you live–not as unwise but as wise, making the most of every opportunity, because the days are evil" (Ephesians 5:15-16 NLT). Be sensitive to opportunities and make the most of them. You can only use an opportunity while it lasts. One opportunity we all have is to advance the agenda of God's kingdom, reaching the world with salvation even as we are doing through Your Daily Light. You can be part of this move too in partnership.

Prayer

Heavenly Father, thank you for the window of opportunity given us to be part of the great commission, to reach the lost with your word and to bring them to your saving knowledge. We are graced to discern divine opportunities for our lives so that we will not miss the blessings due. In Jesus' name.

Bible in one year // **Song of Solomon 4-5, Galatians 3**

> Blessed is that servant whom the master finds doing his job when he comes. // **Matthew 24:46 CSB**

SEP 25

Where are you?

I believe this is the question the Lord is asking us today. The Lord is asking me just as He is asking you, where are you? It will not be the first time He asks such a question. He asked Adam the same question in the beginning. Genesis 3:9 tells us: "The LORD God called to Adam and said to him, 'Where are you?'". That's His question to you today. It is not a question he asks because He does not know where we are. He knows that. And this was true for Adam. The questions He asked about Adam's whereabouts or if he ate the forbidden fruit was not because He was uninformed. These were questions to help Adam evaluate his placement or position with regards to God's plan. That's the call to us today. To examine where you are and adjust if need be.

> **God is calling us to evaluate our positioning and work for him and make necessary adjustments to guarantee a maximum reward.**

Jesus talked about a master who gave talents to three of his servants, each according to their capacity (Matthew 24:14-30). On his return, they were called to account. Two of the servants put their talents to profitable use. But the third servant who received just a talent had a justification to why He had not invested the talent. The bigger question today is this: What kept him busy, to what did he give his attention, and what profit did he make of it? Whatever justifications he had, was not going to spare him from the master's punishment. He was going to receive his lot among the wicked.

So, when the Lord is asking us the question today, "Where are you", it isn't because He is uninformed of our position or activities. He is all knowing! It is a call to evaluate where we are, and what we are doing with the resources entrusted to us regarding His call for our lives. If you can answer the question with the words, " Right here, doing what you called me to do", then glory. If not, make the necessary adjustments. Think of your placement in the body of Christ, the resources and opportunities God has given you and how you are using them for His Kingdom. How Jesus declared, "Blessed is that servant whom the master finds doing his job when he comes" (Matthew 24:46 CSB).

Prayer

Heavenly Father, thank you for life and the opportunity to adjust, to improve on ourselves and be more committed and effective in our service for you. Open our eyes to areas of need, that we might not be found wanting on the day of reward. In Jesus' name.

Bible in one year // **Song of Solomon 6-8, Galatians 4**

SEP 26

> No temptation has overtaken you except such as is common to man; but God is faithful, who will not allow you to be tempted beyond what you are able, but with the temptation will also make the way of escape, that you may be able to bear it. // **1 Corinthians 10:13**

You can stand

This is a statement of fact. There is nothing we are dealing with at any point in time that is all new to humanity, nothing that we cannot find a parallel to, from the word of God. Indeed, there is nothing new under the sun, and that includes the trials and temptations we could be facing. But much more comforting is the assurance, "God is faithful. He will not allow the temptation to be more than you can stand. When you are tempted, he will show you a way out so that you can endure" (NLT).

> **You can stand, if you do not give up but put on the whole armor of God made available to you in Christ Jesus.**

Therefore, no matter how hard pressed you feel, don't say "I can't take no more". No matter how great the challenge life throws at you, know that you can stand. And this is not just motivational writing, it is a statement of fact. The verse above says so, God will not let you be tempted beyond what you can stand. So, if it came your way, it is because He evaluated the situation and knows you can handle this. You can stand whatever comes your way if you are in Christ and walking in His paths for you.

If you are so challenged and think of quitting, the one question you should seek to answer is whether you are where the Lord would have you be. For sometimes, the challenges in our lives could be a product of paths chosen away from the Lord's leading. Proverbs 19:3 tells us, "The foolishness of a man ruins his life, but he blames God for it". Like the prodigal son in this case, we will have to find our way back to the Father and away from whatever heat we might have exposed ourselves to. But if you are doing your best, seeking the Lord, and learning to live by His will, you can be sure nothing can break you on that journey. You can stand if you will take on the whole armor and do your part. Just as we are commanded, "Put on the full armor of God, so that when the day of evil comes, you may be able to stand your ground, and after you have done everything, to stand" (Ephesians 6:13 NIV).

Prayer

Heavenly Father, thank you for making me more than a conqueror, that I can stand the challenges of life and be victorious in all things. My eyes are open to see the way you have made for my escape out of any challenging situation. I overcome in all situations and remain standing for your glory. In Jesus' name.

Bible in one year // **Isaiah 1-2, Galatians 5**

His divine power has given to us all things that pertain to life and godliness, through the knowledge of Him who called us by glory and virtue. // **2 Peter 1:3**

SEP 27

Be supply-conscious

There is a mindset we are to have in Christ Jesus, a mindset shaped by the word of God. We should have a consciousness that reflects itself in our words and actions. One of them is being supply conscious. Don't be need-conscious. Be the one who recognizes that God has given them all things in Christ – all things required for life. Then you will not say, "Lord give me strength". Even if you feel weak, scripture tells you what to do. It says, "Let the weak say I am strong". Be conscious of the strength you have been supplied in Christ and speak like it.

The more you understand scriptures, the more you will realize you have all things already supplied to you in Christ Jesus. God already gave you all things. As it is written, "His divine power has granted to us everything pertaining to life" (2 Peter 1:3). Paul writes in another place, "All things are yours" (1 Corinthians 3:21). Therefore, talk as a possessor, talk as one who has even when you don't see it. That is faith! Remember, "You shall have whatever you say" (Mark 11:23). Be more conscious that God has made things available to you, than being conscious of what he is yet to do. For indeed He did so already.

Establish a consciousness based on the word of God. And when you quote scriptures, don't just say words but understand the implications. You cannot declare "The Lord is my shepherd; I have everything I need" then turn around to say how poor you are. Such a paradox, a bundle of contradiction. I once saw a post that read, "Lord give us the strength to quench every fiery dart of the devil". Honest request. But these are the kind of prayers we makesometimes, requests that show our lack of understanding of scriptures. Ephesians 6:16 tells us, "Take with you the shield of faith with which you will quench all the fiery darts of the wicked one. A few verses earlier, it already admonished us, "Be strong in the Lord and in the power of His might" (Ephesians 6:10). That person wasn't supply-conscious but need-conscious. That person's communication overlooked what has been made available to them.

> Be supply conscious, and let your communication echo the fact that you have a God who has not forsaken you. He has given you all things that pertain to life and godliness.

Prayer

Heavenly Father, thank you for giving me all things that I need for life. I am richly supplied as you cause all things to abound in my life for the fulfilment of my destiny. Thank you for all our needs are supplied according to your riches in glory, and we shall lack nothing. In Jesus' name.

Bible in one year // **Isaiah 3-4, Galatians 6**

SEP 28

> When you were dead in your trespasses and in the uncircumcision of your sinful nature, God made you alive with Christ.
> // **Colossians 2:13 NIV**

The living dead

If you are a movie enthusiast, this caption will bring to your mind a horror movie and its sequels from the past. But far from it, we have our focus on a real-life situation. The living dead describes a true spiritual condition of many people, persons, who though alive, are dead. They are the true living dead, a group of people who lack life but are living. For there is more to being alive than just the capacity to breath and live like other living things. As a statement of fact, scriptures declare, "God has given us eternal life, and this life is in his Son. Whoever has the Son has life; whoever does not have the Son of God does not have life" (1 John 5:11-12). It is a sovereign declaration. It is not up for arguments or baseless human opinions. We all will be living-dead without Jesus.

The living dead defines a true spiritual condition of the human who is alive but is not united with God through His son Christ Jesus. Though they are alive, they are dead spiritually.

But how is this possible? This is so because there are two types of deaths. There is spiritual death, which is the separation from God, the disconnect from the source and sustainer of all life. This death came into the world through sin and spread to all men. And there is none that could escape its reach. Romans 5:12 tells us, "When Adam sinned, sin entered the world. Adam's sin brought death, so death spread to everyone, for everyone sinned" (NLT). So, it is the natural fate of every human, to be spiritually dead because of the sinful nature inherited all the way from the first man. But there is a second death, which is what the world is more familiar with, the cessation of life on earth.

So is the condition of any human who lacks Christ, they are cut off from life though they are living. However, there is hope, and that is why we bring the good news. You will know true life when you receive Jesus as Lord and savior if you have not done that yet. For those of us who have received him, it is written, "When you were dead in your trespasses and in the uncircumcision of your sinful nature, God made you alive with Christ" (Colossians 2:13 NIV). We were made alive, so we can be living and alive. And while we enjoy that, bring that life to others in the world.

Prayer

Heavenly Father, thank you for making me alive in Christ Jesus, delivering me from the bondage of sin and death and giving me life in abundance. Because I have the Son, I have life. And death has no power over me. Receive all the praise. In Jesus' name.

Bible in one year // **Isaiah 5-6, Ephesians 1**

Be anxious for nothing, but in everything by prayer and supplication, with thanksgiving, let your requests be made known to God.
// **Philippians 4:6**

SEP 29

Let your heart not be troubled

This is one of the profound instructions Jesus gave us. He said, "Let not your heart be troubled: ye believe in God, believe also in me" (John 14:1). The very reason Jesus said that was because He knew we would have reasons for our hearts to be troubled, He was aware of the challenges of life that come our way and would call for concern. In fact, He guaranteed us that such will happen. He said, "I have told you these things, so that in me you may have peace. In this world you will have trouble. But take heart! I have overcome the world" (John 16:33). He assured us of troubled times so long as we are in this world. However, much more was the assurance that no matter what happens, it would turn out right (Romans 8:28). Therefore, we need not let our hearts be troubled.

> Let not your heart be troubled but be confident in the Lord no matter what comes your way. For He will neither leave you nor forsake you.

Let not your heart be troubled is a command; it means we have something to do about it. It means it is our responsibility to keep our hearts from getting troubled. It is like handing over a dog to you that is on a leash and telling you: "Don't let the dog run off". So, we must mount guard over our hearts; hold it still and be calm, even in the face of adversity. Don't give your heart the room to be troubled. Refuse to be troubled. Mount Guard over your heart; the bible says to do so with all diligence (Proverbs 4:23).

It is in a similar light that Paul writes, "Be anxious for nothing" (Philippians 4:6). Have no anxiety over what is happening, let not your heart be troubled. Only believe in God and in His word. Hold on to the promise that says, "I will not leave you nor forsake you" (Hebrews 13:5). That is a word of assurance that He will see you through and will not disappoint you. Trust in the Lord no matter what comes your way and let not your heart be troubled. He has it figured out. "Be still and know that I am God", says the Lord (Psalm 46:10).

Prayer

> Thank You Lord for your ever-abiding presence. We rejoice in your faithfulness and are confident in your help that is never late. Therefore, our hearts are still as we look to your promises that are sure. In Jesus' name.

Bible in one year // **Isaiah 7-8, Ephesians 2**

SEP 30

> Assuredly, I say to you, unless you are converted and become as little children, you will by no means enter the kingdom of heaven.
> // **Matthew 18:3**

Receive like a child

There is a degree of childlikeness that is commanded if you will experience the Kingdom of God and its blessings. On the other hand, failing in this aspect to have this childlike attitude will be your hindrance to knowing the Lord and experiencing all that He has for you. Matthew records Jesus saying, "Assuredly, I say to you, unless you are converted and become as little children, you will by no means enter the kingdom of heaven" (Matthew 18:3).

That was a statement of fact by Jesus: "Unless you change and become like little children, you will never enter the kingdom of heaven". In this regard, it has to do with being teachable. That's a characteristic of children, particularly toddlers. It is the age where they recognize how naïve they are about their environment, about life, even the basics about how things are called. They are willing and ready to learn from someone who is available to teach them. They are open to knowledge with little resistance. In short, they are gullible. They don't trust themselves to know better, and this is some trait the Lord wants in us, that we be childlike. For the Kingdom of God is for such persons.

> **It is childlike to be gullible and naïve, recognizing you don't know any better than the Lord. Then He will bring you into the full experience of all He has for you. It is for the childlike.**

In Luke 10:21, Jesus prayed a prayer of thanks. Jesus, full of joy through the Holy Spirit, said, "I praise you, Father, Lord of heaven and earth, because you have hidden these things from the wise and learned, and revealed them to little children. Yes, Father, for this is what you were pleased to do". Jesus made it clear that it pleases the Father to conceal things from those who think of themselves to be wise and clever but reveals to the childlike. This is the reason those who think the bible is a lie will remain in their darkness, those who say there is no God might remain in their ignorance, those who think we are stupid for believing in Jesus might not experience him. And even if you have come to know the Lord, there is a degree of Childlikeness you must maintain to experience him more and more. As the writer of proverbs cautions us, "Do not be wise in your own eyes" (Proverbs 3:7).

Prayer

Father, thank you for the illumination in your word that teaches us daily. We receive grace to be humble, ready to learn and conscious of our need for you. Like babies, we are open to explore the vastness of your knowledge and the wonders of your Kingdom as your take us by the hand. In Jesus' name.

Bible in one year // Isaiah 9-10, Ephesians 3

OCTOBER

> Blow the trumpet in Zion and sound an alarm in My holy mountain! Let all the inhabitants of the land tremble; for the day of the Lord is coming, for it is at hand. // **Joel 2:1**

OCT 1

Announcing a dispensation

Joel made a call, "Blow the trumpet in Zion, and sound an alarm in My holy mountain! Let all the inhabitants of the land tremble; for the day of the Lord is coming, for it is at hand: a day of darkness and gloominess, a day of clouds and thick darkness, like the morning clouds spread over the mountains. A people come, great and strong, the like of whom has never been; nor will there ever be any such after them, even for many successive generations" (Joel 2:1-2).

Why blow a trumpet in Zion? To announce a new dispensation. For trumpets are spiritual alarms that sound an alert to a move of God. That is why Joel would cry out, "Blow a trumpet in Zion, sound an alarm in my holy mountain". It was a call to sound an alarm for a new dispensation, a set time under heaven when the Lord is accomplishing a thing, or a measured-out time for a given course of events to take place. That is a dispensation. And spiritually, they are usually announced by the sounding of a trumpet. You see a practical example in Revelation. John recounts his vision, "I saw the seven angels who stand before God, and seven trumpets were given to them. Then the seven angels who had the seven trumpets prepared to sound them" (Revelation 8:2 & 6 NIV). And if you read from there onwards, you see that each angel got to sound their trumpet. And when they did, a set of events took place. They each were sounding an alarm to announce a move of God or a dispensation, the set time for certain events.

> Joel saw our dispensation ahead of his day and announced it. Now we are here and should recognize the prophetic words over us that we might walk in them.

So the prophet Joel was announcing a dispensation, the set time of the Lord to bring forth a new people, such as never existed before and after whom there would not be another, a people great and strong. Joel was announcing us, he was announcing our coming, the arrival of the new creation. And this dispensation was going to begin with the resurrection of Jesus. Joel saw us coming and announced it. And we would be doing ourselves much good to recognize this, see who we are and reflect what a prophetic life was written concerning us.

Prayer

Heavenly Father, Thank you for all my days were written before I came on the scene. And in Christ, all your promises for us are "yes" and "amen". As we meditate in your word and see ourselves in the light of prophecy, let the manifestations be evident in our lives in Jesus name.

Bible in one year // **Isaiah 11-13, Ephesians 4**

OCT 2

> If anyone is in Christ, he is a new creation; old things have passed away; behold, all things have become new. // **2 Corinthians 5:17**

An unprecedented generation

In Joel's prophecies, he talked about "A people come, great and strong, the like of whom has never been; nor will there ever be any such after them, even for many successive generations" (Joel 2:2). Joel talked of an unprecedented generation, a generation that had never existed before, and the like of which was not going to be repeated. What was he really saying, and what was it he saw? And how does this apply to us? In a general context, a generation is defined as "All of the people born and living at about the same time, regarded collectively". This is what is registered in our minds as the meaning of generation.

> **We the new creation in Christ make up the unprecedented generation Joel talked about, a people that did not exist before, and their likes will never be again. We are recreated in Christ.**

However, there is a second usage of the word generation. In this case, it refers to things that were brought forth by the same process, like a batch of a product in a line of production. So even though they might have been brought forth at different times, they make a generation because they all came through the same process. In this regard, as far as man is concerned, there are only two generations. The first generation is the generation after the likeness of Adam, and the second generation is the generation after the likeness of Christ. Paul wrote, "The first man Adam became aliving being. The last Adam became a life-giving spirit... The first man was of the earth, made of dust; the second Man is the Lord from heaven. As was the man of dust, so also are those who are made of dust; and as is the heavenly Man, so also are those who are heavenly" (1 Corinthians 15:45-48).

Paul puts side by side, two classes of people -the adamic generation and the Christ generation. The first generation are a people born of natural decent and by nature inheriting the likeness of Adam. They were all brought forth by the same process, thus making them all a generation. But like Christ, the second generation is from above and are born again, proceeding from the Father, and therefore heavenly. Just as Galatians 4:26 says, "The Jerusalem that is above is free, and she is our mother". Therefore, we who are born again are from above, born of the Spirit, born again by God. Just like Jesus, we were brought forth by the same process, born of the word (James 1:18). We are a new creation (2 Corinthians 5:17).

Prayer

Almighty God, thank you for the privilege to be numbered in the new creation, after the likeness of Christ. We receive grace to comprehend these realities fulfilled in us. In Jesus' name.

Bible in one year // **Isaiah 14-16, Ephesians 5:1-16**

For we are God's masterpiece. He has created us anew in Christ Jesus, so we can do the good things he planned for us long ago.
// **Ephesians 2:10 NLT**

OCT 3

Like a factory recall

You will remember we are talking about two generations, the Adamic generation and the Christ-like generation, the latter being the new creation. The new creation, as mentioned in writing yesterday, is an all-new man that never existed before the resurrection of Jesus. And this new man is not a converted version of the old one, it is an all-new creation. The new creation is more than a converted soul, it is more than a conversion. The new creation is what it is. It is a new creation – something made totally new from scratch.

Think of it like a factory recall. I remember for example, many years ago, when the first Toyota hybrid cars were produced, their first owners reported a malfunction. The manufacturer saw it to be substandard and failing to represent the company's values and quality. So, they made a recall to fix the issue. Now when you think of a company like this, what they would do is to piece-off, if necessary, these cars and remake them, correcting every fault before sending these products back into the market. The customers don't get to keep the old malfunctioning car and the new, the old is taken away and a completely new one is restored to them.

This is the picture of the new creation with regards to the old. God found fault with the old creation. The bible tells us in Genesis, "The Lord saw how great the wickedness of the human race had become on the earth, and that every inclination of the thoughts of the human heart was only evil all the time. The Lord regretted that he had made human beings on the earth, and his heart was deeply troubled. So the Lord said, 'I will wipe from the face of the earth the human race I have created'" (Genesis 6:5-7 NIV). But every effort to fix that condition of wickedness proved futile until Christ. God took away the old you, crucified it to the cross with Christ and brought forth an all-new man that never existed before ((Romans 6:6, Ephesians 2:10).

> **You do not have two natures. The old adamic nature was nailed to the cross and an all-new man in Christ, created to be like God in true holiness and righteousness was made.**

Prayer

Heavenly Father, thank you for recreating me in Christ Jesus that I might do the good works that was planned for me long ago, taking paths that were prearranged and living the good life made ready for us – a life above Satan, above sicknesses, a life of glory and power in the Holy Ghost. In Jesus' name.

Bible in one year // **Isaiah 17-19, Ephesians 5:17-33**

OCT 4

> You are a chosen generation, a royal priesthood, a holy nation, His own special people, that you may proclaim the praises of Him who called you out of darkness into His marvelous light. // **1 Peter 2:9**

A divine breed

A teacher of the law once met Jesus and was baffled with the concept of being born again. This was Nicodemus who came to Jesus by night. He was a teacher of the law, supposedly knowledgeable in the revelations of God until that time. But he grappled with the concept of being born again. It is sadly still the struggle of many believers today; they have a glimpse of understanding of what it means to be born again but are often estranged to the implications thereof. It is my experience too, that as I share with others, I often realize that even those that have been in the faith so long, and sometimes themselves ministers, are yet to get it. Maybe we were just taught wrong.

After informing Nicodemus of the necessity of the new birth, Nicodemus wondered and asked, "How can a man be born when he is old? Can he enter a second time into his mother's womb and be born?"... "How can these things be?" (John 3: 4 & 9). Then Jesus answered saying, "Are you the teacher of Israel, and do not know these things? (John 3:10-12). And this is the burden the Lord has put on my heart, to shine the light of His word for the illumination of the saints that they might know who they are in Christ Jesus, what they have received in Him and the glorious riches of their inheritance (Ephesians 1:8). And through Your Daily Light, we break these great truths into small assimilable bits.

> **The new birth brought forth a new species, a people who together make a divine breed, separate and distinct from the human race.**

Your Christian experience and your walk with God are so dependent on a full understanding of the fundamentals of our faith, it sets the ball rolling and determines the ultimate experience you can have. And one such understanding that is good for today is the knowledge that by the new birth, God brought forth a divine breed that is different from the human race. The new creation in Christ is not another human being. The new creation is a divine being, proceeding from the Father (1 John 4:4), bearing a divine nature (2 Peter 1:4). His genealogy is no longer traced to his natural family but to God. If you are born again, can rightly say like Jesus, "I am from above... I am not of this world" (John 8:23). Together as those born again, and offsprings of God, we make a divine breed – a chosen generation.

Prayer

Heavenly Father, as we grow in the knowledge of you and the knowledge of who we are in Christ, let these truths become evident and clear to all as your word continues to flood our understanding with Light. That we might comprehend the glorious riches of your inheritance for us. In Jesus' name.

Bible in one year // **Isaiah 20-22, Ephesians 6**

I said, "You are gods, and all of you are children of the Most High".
// **Psalms 82:6**

OCT 5

The gods are here

Luke narrates an event that occurred during the missionary journey of Paul and Barnabas as they passed through Lystra. While they were at Lystra, Paul and Barnabas came upon a man with crippled feet. He had been that way from birth, so he had never walked. He was sitting and listening as Paul preached. Looking straight at him, Paul realized he had faith to be healed. So Paul called to him in a loud voice, "Stand up!" And the man jumped to his feet and started walking. When the crowd saw what Paul had done, they shouted in their local dialect, "These men are gods in human form!" (Acts 14:8-11). These men saw the supernatural manifestations of the Kingdom life we are called to live, and shouted, "The gods are here". And this was no lie. The gods are truly here.

> The implications of the new birth are far reaching. It brought forth a divine breed, a generation of gods, people who are a direct offspring of God with supernatural traits.

This was not the last time such a thing happened. On the Island of Malta, Paul was bitten by a venomous viper. But he shook off the creature into the fire and suffered no harm. However, they were expecting that he would swell up or suddenly fall dead. But after they had looked for a long time and saw no harm come to him, they changed their minds and said that he was a god (Acts 28:5-6). Once again at this instance, there was a supernatural manifestation of the divine life in Paul, just as Jesus had declared of us, "They will take up serpents; and if they drink anything deadly, it will by no means hurt them; they will lay hands on the sick, and they will recover" (Mark 16:17-18).

And this is what the scripture says : „You are gods; you are all sons of the Most High'" (Psalm 82:5-6). And Jesus even emphasized that this was written to God's people when He quoted this passage in response to those saying He was blaspheming. Jesus answered saying, "If He called them gods, to whom the word of God came (and the Scripture cannot be nullified), are you saying of Him whom the Father sanctified and sent into the world, 'You are blaspheming,' because I said, 'I am the Son of God'" (John 10:35-36). The principle at work here is simple; it is the law of procreation, that everything gives birth to its kind. Therefore, by the new birth, God brought forth a generation of gods. Indeed, the gods are here.

Prayer

Heavenly Father, thank you for your life at work in me, giving me the ability to live above the limitations and capacity of the natural man as I bring your power to my world. That indeed my light will shine, and men will see my good works and glorify you, my Father. In Jesus' name.

Bible in one year // **Isaiah 23-25, Philippians 1**

OCT 6

> As was the man of dust, so also are those who are made of dust; and as is the heavenly Man, so also are those who are heavenly.
> // 1 Corinthians 15:48

A characteristic people

We have emphasized that we are a divine breed, a generation of gods, a people brought forth by the same process, a people who are direct offsprings of God, distinct from humans – a people with supernatural traits. And when we talk of supernatural traits, it is different from spiritual gifts. We are referring to our characteristics, such things that are true for all because we are of the same breed. Just as in elementary biology, we had lessons on characteristics of different species of animals, so also there are characteristics of the new generation, things that are true for all. Such that any deviation in any member of the species that fails to align with these traits is but abnormal.

There are certain things that are characteristic of the new creation we are in Christ Jesus, things that are true for all and a deviation from it is the abnormal.

Paul wrote, "As is the heavenly man, so also are those who are of heaven". In a breed, there are traits that if true for one, are true for all. We are a characteristic people. Peter declares, "A peculiar people" (1 Peter 2:9). Paul wrote, If the part of the dough offered as firstfruits is holy, then the whole batch is holy; if the root is holy, so are the branches (Romans 11:16 NIV). It highlights same principle above, because it is from the same batch, what is true for one is true for all. In this light, Christ Jesus is the firstfruit of the new generation, the blueprint of what every other member of the breed should be like. He is called the first born from the dead (Colossians 1:18), just as we too were given life from spiritual dead after him (Colossians 2:13). "For God knew his people in advance, and he chose them to become like his Son, so that his Son would be the firstborn among many brothers and sisters" (Romans 8:29 NLT).

Indeed, there are certain traits which if true for one, are true for all because we are of the same breed. Keep this is in mind. Joel talked about a people coming and went forth to detail what they would be like. The prophet Isaiah spoke prophetically of us too, it was a prophecy of Jesus speaking of himself and the new generation. Jesus speaks as the first fruit of this divine breed, "Here am I and the children whom the LORD has given me! We are for signs and wonders in Israel from the LORD of hosts, who dwells in Mount Zion" (Isaiah 8:18). We are for signs are wonders in the world. Hallelujah!

Prayer

Heavenly Father, thank you for the blessing of a new day and the opportunities it brings to glorify you in the earth. Your grace is sufficient for us today to walk in your paths, and to do your will as we serve our world as a unique people of peculiar characteristics. In Jesus' name.

Bible in one year // **Isaiah 26-27, Philippians 2**

> Who being the brightness of His glory and the express image of His person, and upholding all things by the word of His power, when He had by Himself purged our sins, sat down at the right hand of the Majesty on high. // **Hebrews 1:3**

OCT 7

Expressions of the divine

It is written of Jesus, "He is the radiance of God's glory and the exact representation of His nature". A lot can be said from this verse. But I would like to draw your attention to the fact that the Son is the express image of the Father, an exact representation of the Father. In other words, Jesus was a full expression of the divine. No doubt Jesus could say, "You have seen me, you have seen the father" (John 14:9).

It is common to hear people say we are all humans, and they say this often to justify their limits or weaknesses. But the greater truth is that we are not all humans, not in that sense. The divine life we have received in Christ Jesus gives us the nature of God and makes us divine beings, a nature the Father delights to see in full expression. In this new life, the divine nature superimposes itself over the natural human life and its tendences, supplanting that life and making us expressions of the divine. And this is what God has made of us in Christ Jesus, He has made us to be full expressions of the divine. Galatians 3:27 tells us, "For as many of you as were baptized into Christ have put on Christ".

Paul admonished the Romans, "Put on the Lord Jesus Christ, and make no provision for the flesh, to fulfill its lusts" (Romans 13:14). So too we must put on the Lord Jesus, that simply means, give the divine nature expression. In this setting of being clothed with Christ, we are made true expressions of the divine. Our strengths become amplified, and natural weaknesses are swallowed up in His strength. We are turned into another person, fully enabled to live holy lives, willing and equipped to serve God. This reminds me of Gideon. He had such an experience of being clothed with God. We read from Judges 6:34, "The Spirit of the Lord clothed Gideon with Himself and took possession of him" (AMP). Fearful and timid Gideon was turned into a bold and courageous general, he became an expression of the divine with which he was clothed. Gideon lived it for a moment. But this is our everyday reality when we are born again, for we have put on Christ.

> **In Christ, you have been made an expression of the divine. Give that divine nature expression as you live by the word of God and become yielded to the Holy Spirit who manifests through us in all places.**

Prayer

Heavenly Father, thank you for the privilege to represent you and be an expression of your divine person to my world. Thank you for the Holy Spirit who is at work in me, whose power also is available to work wonders as I go about the service to which I am called in your Kingdom. In Jesus' name.

Bible in one year // **Isaiah 28-29, Philippians 3**

OCT 8

> Whereby are given unto us exceeding great and precious promises: that by these we might be partakers of the divine nature, having escaped the corruption that is in the world through lust. // **2 Peter 1:4**

Great and precious promises

Regarding Joel's prophecies, he saw what it looked like ahead and behind this new creation: „A fire devours before them, and behind them a flame burns; the land is like the Garden of Eden before them, and behind them a desolate wilderness" (Joel 2:3). What Joel saw is nicely pictured by Peter in his writing: "Whereby are given unto us exceeding great and precious promises". When Joel had a revelation of the new creation, it was shown to him what their future looked like. They were a people arrayed on a march with a fruitful end ahead of them, like the garden of Eden. By this, he was referring to the great and precious promises given to us in Christ Jesus.

It helps to go back to the beginnings and consider what the garden of Eden was. It was the enabling environment in which God placed man after his creation – a place that was richly furnished with all he needed for life, a refreshing environment in which he could thrive with his descendants. And when Adam and Eve fell for the devil's tricks, they were sent out of this place to toil. But in Christ Jesus, we were once again restored to a life of hope; a people who can always look forward to good things coming. For before us, it is like the garden of Eden. These are indeed the great and precious promises we have in Christ Jesus. Much more, the promises are as good as fulfilled (2 Cor 1:20).

> **Never let anything lure you back into the world: there is nothing there to go for; it is a desolate place with fading glories. Focus on the great and precious promises in Christ and be steadfast in the Lord.**

The second point to note in Joel's prophecy was the desolateness behind these people, like a place scotched down by fire with nothing to return to. Joel talked of a desolate wilderness behind us. This is a picture of the world we leave behind us, like Peter puts it in that verse above, "Having escaped the corruption that is in the world". Corruption, meaning a state of decay that only gets worse – a decay that rubs on anything it comes into contact with and reduces it to rubbish. Like it is commonly said, one bad fruit in a basket will spoil the rest; or bad company corrupts good character (1 Cor 15:33). Never look back at the world and desire it's filth and seeming glories. What is ahead of us in Christ Jesus is far greater and better than anything you could ever gain from the world (Luke 9:62).

Prayer

God almighty, thank you for the great and precious promises in Christ Jesus, the guarantee of salvation, the assurance of provision, the confidence in protection, the hope of success, the joy of the Holy Spirit, strength for every day and the hope of life forevermore with you in eternity. In Jesus' name.

Bible in one year // **Isaiah 30-31, Philippians 4**

He brought them out with silver and with gold and there was no one who was weak among their generations. // **Psalm 105:37**

A strong people

Regarding the new creation, Joel declared, "A people come, great and strong" (Joel 2:2). And that is true about us. We are strong people in Christ Jesus. Not just strong together, but also strong because it is an assembly of strong people with no one weak among us. Now for some people, this will come across as a false teaching because they are so familiar with a mindset of weakness and gladly boast about it. And it is scriptural; however, often applied wrongly. They delight in the verse as Paul recounted, "He said to me, 'My grace is sufficient for you, for my power is made perfect in weakness.' Therefore I will boast all the more gladly about my weaknesses, so that Christ's power may rest on me" (2 Cor 12:9 NKJV). But when you follow the life of Paul, he did not go about proclaiming weaknesses. He spoke always of the strength of God at work in him. And this is what scripture commands: Let the weak say, "I am strong" (Joel 3:10).

> In Christ, you are a strong person. Never see yourself as weak but always profess His strength at work in you to enable you fulfill all He has called you to do and to endure whatever challenges you encounter.

Recounting the journey of the Israelites, the Psalmist wrote, "There was no one who was weak among their generations". If this was true under the Old Testament, how much truer it is in Christ. Take it for a fact: There are no weak persons in Christ, there are only persons who have not known how strong they are by the Spirit of God and are yet to learn to take advantage of His presence as our strengthener. There are also persons who like strong soldiers, are wounded in battle, and need their strength to be renewed or need support. There people going through challenging times with a new demand placed on their strength. As it is written, "If you faint in the day of trouble, your strength is small" (Proverbs 24:10 NET).

Although Paul talked of delighting in weaknesses, he boasted more in strength. He said he delighted in weaknesses so the strength of God might be made manifest. As for Paul, he declared rather "I can do all things through Christ who strengthens me" (Phil 4:19). He wrote, "To this end I strenuously contend with all the energy Christ so powerfully works in me" (Col 1:29). Paul also exhorted the Romans at a time they were fainting under trial, "Take a new grip with your tired hands and strengthen your weak knees" (Romans 12:12). And this is the reality, it doesn't matter what the Lord has called you to do or what you are going through, you have sufficient strength in Christ.

Prayer

> Heavenly Father, thank you for the Holy Spirit at work in us as our source of unlimited strength, empowering us to do the things you have called us to do and fulfill our destinies. In Jesus' name.

Bible in one year // **Isaiah 32-33, Colossians 1**

OCT 10

Let the weak say, "I am strong". // **Joel 3:10**

How to activate divine strength Pt. 1

There is no one in Christ without strength. You have more than all the strength you could ever need because God indwells you by His Spirit. And His strength is in exhaustible. "Have you never heard? Have you never understood? The Lord is the everlasting God, the Creator of all the earth. He never grows weak or weary (Isaiah 40:28). His strength never fails, and same God lives in you. Therefore, you have a reservoir of inexhaustible strength because of His Spirit in you. Now you do not have to pray and ask God to give you strength. A thousand times no! You will be asking for what he already gave you. You can only pray like that when it is for others, like Paul prayed for the Ephesians saying, "I pray that he may grant you, according to the riches of his glory, to be strengthened with power in your inner being through his Spirit" (Ephesians 3:16 HCSB). This is called intercession when you pray for God to strengthen others.

> Even if you feel weak, always declare strength, for in doing so, you activate divine energy resident in you. It is a spiritual switch that works through the law of creation by words.

However, when it comes to you drawing on divine strength, you don't ask God to give you strength because He already gave you all you could ever get. You rather have the responsibility to activate that strength. You might say "That prayer works for me". But it is God responding to the cry of a Child. It is not the way to activate divine strength. Activating divine strength is like the use of a switch. When you have a home that is powered by electricity and everything is fine, you don't call the power company to light the bulbs. You simply turn on the switches. It is a similar thing with divine power resident in us, we have a responsibility in activating divine energy. There are three principles I will share with you.

The first principle is to speak strength. It is a switch that turns on divine energy in you. It is a law of the spirit. That is why the Lord spoke to the Israelites saying, "Let the weak say ,I am strong'" (Joel 3:10). It is a spiritual switch to activate divine energy in you. You do not always say I am strong because you feel strong. You say I am strong because in saying so, you will be strengthened. It is the law of creation through words. The bible speaks of God saying, "He calls those things which do not exist as though they did" (Romans 4:17 NKJV). Why? Because in calling them, he brings them into being. In like manner, you will be strengthened when you speak strength.

Prayer

Heavenly Father, thank you for your strength at work in me, energizing me to run and not grow weary, to walk and not faint. Thank you for the Holy Spirit who renews my strength daily. In Jesus' name.

Bible in one year // **Isaiah 34-36, Colossians 2**

A wise man is strong, yes, a man of knowledge increases strength.
// **Proverbs 24:5**

OCT 11

How to activate divine strength Pt. 2

We saw the first key to activating divine strength yesterday. As we emphasized, if you are in Christ and full of the Holy Spirit, God already gave you all the strength you could ever need. However, like a switch we have the responsibility to activate that strength. And the first principle is by speaking strength, declaring that you have strength. You do not always say I am strong because you feel strong. You say I am strong because in saying so, you will be strengthened. It is the law of creation through words. As scripture enjoins us, "Let the weak say "I am strong" (Joel 3:10).

The second key to activating divine strength resident in you is by increasing in the knowledge of God through meditation in His word. As simple as these principles may sound, they are powerful switches that make manifest divine strength in you. These are like the simple instructions behind the miracles of Moses or Jesus. For example, once Moses was asked to strike a rock in the wilderness to get water. God could have made the water flow without Moses striking the rock. But outof God's sovereignty, at this instance, striking the rock was going to act like the switch to unlock a floodgate in the wilderness and provide water for the Israelites (Exodus 17:1-7). This you must understand in the word of God. It is about principles, doing as you are commanded to see the results promised you.

> **Meditating in the word of God activates in you God's supernatural energy, for it is spiritual food to your spirit just as physical food gives strength to the physical body. Continue therefore in daily meditation.**

In this regard, the author of proverbs wrote, "A wise man is strong, yes, a man of knowledge increases strength" (Proverbs 24:5). Just as we know, man must not live by bread alone but by every word that comes from the Spirit. Just as Physical food gives strength to your physical body, so the word of God energizes your spirit. When you spend quality time meditating in the word of God, you will increase in knowledge and that knowledge increases your strength. And that is one blessing of having Your Daily Light, that it brings to you daily something for meditation, an illumination from the word of God, and with it, supernatural strength for your day.

Prayer

Heavenly Father, thank you for your word that comes to me daily. I am energized and strengthened in my spirit as I meditate in your word. Therefore, I run and do not get weary, I walk and do not faint because my strength is renewed daily. In Jesus' name.

Bible in one year // **Isaiah 37-38, Colossians 3**

OCT 12

He who speaks in a tongue edifies himself, but he who prophesies edifies the church. // 1 Corinthians 14:4

How to activate divine strength Pt. 3

Paul's second letter to Timothy nicely defines the purpose of scriptures. He wrote to the young minister, "All Scripture is given by inspiration of God, and is profitable for doctrine, for reproof, for correction, for instruction in righteousness, that the man of God may be complete, thoroughly equipped for every good work" (2 Timothy 3:16-17). It is God's manual for life to us, it is the manufacturer's manual for human existence; in it you understand life from the point of the creator and find a lot of instructions on "How to...". But unfortunately, sometimes because we are poorly taught or have not yet known, we wait on God for things He has already given us responsibility on how to get them

Although not the last, one more point I will bring to your attention as a switch to activate divine energy is praying in tongues; that is praying with the spirit. Paul wrote, "Anyone who speaks in a tongue edifies themselves" (1 Corinthians 14:4). Another rendition of the same verse says, "A person who speaks in tongues is strengthened personally" (NLT). That is rightly so because the word translated edify, is a word more associated with architecture, as in building, when a structure is built up, fortified to stand strong. Paul lets us know that the person who prays in tongues strengthens himself.

> Spiritual tongues is the language of the recreated human spirit with which we commune with God and in the process, draw on His reservoir of inexhaustible strength. We are edified through speaking in tongues.

Although Paul emphasized the need to focus on the gift that edifies the Church, he did not make light of the tongues that edifies the individual (1 Cor 14:1-2). He said He who speaks in tongues speaks to God and speaks mysteries, he speaks undisclosed spiritual and intelligible things to God. It is the language of the recreated human Spirit, a language for communion with the divine. Now that is important, because communion also means intercourse, a time of exchange between two persons in intimacy. So, in that communion with God when you spend time praying in tongues, you are positioned to draw on God's strength as you exchange his strength for your weakness, His wisdom for your ignorance and His visions for your dreams. Speaking in tongues strengthens the one who does, it edifies them as they spend time communing with God.

Prayer

Father, thank you for the blessing of a spiritual language for communion with you. Today, as we pray in tongues we are invigorated, energized, revived, and strengthened to do your will. In Jesus' name.

Bible in one year // **Isaiah 39-40, Colossians 4**

God has not given us a spirit of fear, but of power and of love and of a sound mind. // **2 Timothy 4:7**

A breed like horses

Taking one step further on our study of Joel's prophecies, we consider this text from his writing, a description of these people he saw coming. Joel wrote, "Their appearance is like the appearance of horses; and like swift steeds, so they run. With a noise like chariots. Over mountaintops they leap, like the noise of a flaming fire that devours the stubble, like a strong people set in battle array (Joel 2:4-5). What was Joel talking about? We do not need to emphasize again the last sentence in this passage, about a strong people arrayed for battle.

We will focus on the breed of people like horses. To understand this, it is good to look at the characteristics of a horse, what God himself thinks of a horse, one of His creatures. God said to Job, "Do you give the horse its strength or clothe its neck with a flowing mane? Do you make it leap like a locust, striking terror with its proud snorting? It paws fiercely, rejoicing in its strength, and charges into the fray. It laughs at fear, afraid of nothing; it does not shy away from the sword. The quiver rattles against its side, along with the flashing spear and lance. In frenzied excitement it eats up the ground; it cannot stand still when the trumpet sounds (Job 39:19-24 NIV).

> **In Christ, we are a breed like horses, fearless and bold, courageous and confident, charging forward into destiny and turning back from nothing.**

From time immemorial, horses were used for battle. And in these battles, the people really had to come close to fight with swords and spears, the weapons of the times. And for this, the horse proved the most valuable creature for war, for it would not turn away from the sound of fighting nor the clanging of swords. It charged forward into the fiercest battles, galloping, and looking unstoppable. God said of this His creature, "It laughs at fear, afraid of nothing; it does not shy away from the sword". That is a nature God has given us in Christ Jesus, a nature that is not fearful. We don't fear the devil, we don't fear men. We don't fear the systems, we don't fear the future. When fear arises on your journey as God leads you in life and destiny, remember to define FEAR as False Evidence Appearing Real. The bible tells us, "God has not given us a spirit of fear, but of power and of love and of a sound mind" (2 Timothy 1:7).

Prayer

Heavenly Father, thank you for not giving me a spirit of fear or timidity, but of power, boldness and courage. Therefore, I dare out in faith on the things you call me to do, knowing always that you have commanded angels concerning me, to bear me up in their hands. In Jesus' name.

Bible in one year // **Isaiah 41-42, 1 Thessalonians 1**

OCT 14

You therefore must endure[a] hardship as a good soldier of Jesus Christ. // **2 Timothy 2:3**

God's great army

In Joel's prophecies, he mentioned of the coming people, "With a noise like chariots over mountaintops they leap, like the noise of a flaming fire that devours the stubble, like a strong people set in battle array... The Lord gives voice before His army, for His camp is very great (Joel 2:5-11). In the light of today, Joel so us, God's great army, set out in battle, with the Lord himself as commander at the head of his army. This is what the Church is in the world, we are God's great army and you as an individual is a soldier in this great army. Have you embraced the thought of being a soldier in God's army, and do you carry yourself about as one?

> **You are one soldier in God's great army with a vital role to play in the overall victory. Therefore, be fully armed and don't get entangled in civilian affairs. Rather commit yourself to please our commander.**

We are a people arrayed in battle against the forces of darkness, against lawlessness, a people set for war to prevail over the devil and free the souls of men in bondage. There is a military call upon us in Christ Jesus, not one that takes away life, but one that brings life and enforces the divine will in the earth. Paul nicely paints this picture of men and women in battle when he admonished us, "Finally, my brethren, be strong in the Lord and in the power of His might. Put on the whole armor of God, that you may be able to stand against the wiles of the devil. For we do not wrestle against flesh and blood, but against principalities, against powers, against the rulers of the darkness of this age, against spiritual hosts of wickedness in the heavenly places. Therefore, take up the whole armor of God, that you may be able to withstand in the evil day, and having done all, to stand (Ephesians 6:10-13).

Not only are you called upon to take up your full armor as a soldier in Christ Jesus and stand your ground, you are also called to live the life fitting of a soldier. Paul wrote to Timothy, "Join with me in suffering, like a good soldier of Christ Jesus. No one serving as a soldier gets entangled in civilian affairs, but rather tries to please his commanding officer" (2 Timothy 2:3-4 NIV). There is a way of life for soldiers, and that includes you. Others may be doing it, indulged in unbridled quest for fleshly pleasures, but there is more at stake for a soldier to join in. Have this mindset and be sold-out as a soldier of Christ.

Prayer

Heavenly Father, thank you for enlisting me as a soldier in your great army and giving me full armory in Christ with which I can face the enemy and quench all his fiery darts. I receive grace to be disciplined. That I might use my time and resources wisely for the Kingdom. In Jesus' name.

Bible in one year // **Isaiah 43-44, 1 Thessalonians 2**

Arise, shine; for your light has come! And the glory of the Lord is risen upon you. // **Isaiah 60:1**

OCT 15

A time of great glory

It is very exciting to get into the word of God and to realize the times we are living in. As much as it announces woe and doom, it also announces glory and victory. You choose which side you want to experience by either choosing to be a part of God's great army or not. When God told Noah there was a flood coming, it was not to scare Noah, but to prepare him for the times, to be fully equipped to weather the season. Eventually the rains came. But while there was a perishing on the outside, there was preservation with abundance on the inside, Noah and his family had a different experience to tell through the stormy weather. They had chosen righteousness, they had chosen the ways of God. It is a similar thing with the times we are living in.

Prophet Isaiah saw these dark days coming and declared, "Arise, shine; for thy light is come, and the glory of the Lord is risen upon thee. For, behold, the darkness shall cover the earth, and gross darkness the people: but the Lord shall arise upon thee, and his glory shall be seen upon thee. And the Gentiles shall come to thy light, and kings to the brightness of thy rising" (Isaiah 60:1-3). He saw a time of gloom, a time of great darkness, but parallel to it, he saw a people outshining with light, radiating the glory of God – such glory that calls the attention of men and draws even kings from the ends of the world.

> We are living in a time of prophecy, a time of greater glory. A time that makes for excitement towards life as we dare out to accomplish all that God has set us here for.

We are in times of great glory, and the glory of today is greater. We are better positioned to experience God than ever before. This is one reason we have been in the book of Joel, making a journey into his prophecies, understanding how that connects to us and how we can live it out. It was proclaimed of Jesus saying, "Look, I have come to do your will, O God –as is written about me in the Scriptures" (Hebrews 10:7). We also have the responsibility to understand the prophecies of our times as written of us in scripture, and to walk in them. One truth to bear in mind is that we are living in a time of great glory, a time of glory greater than what the patriarchs and the apostles ever experienced, we are living at the consummation of the age, a time when everything is being manifested at its peak. As darkness unfolds like never before, even so parallel to it, a glory the world has never known is being revealed.

Prayer

Father, thank you for the times we live in, the unveiling of prophecies long foretold. We align ourselves with these truths and are positioned to shine your glory to the saving of our world. In Jesus' name.

Bible in one year // **Isaiah 45-46, 1 Thessalonians 3**

OCT 16

Every kingdom divided against itself will be ruined, and every city or household divided against itself will not stand. // **Matthew 12:25**

No need for contentions

In Joel's visions, he saw a people coming who had no need for contentions, that is no need for arguments and fights over positions. He wrote about us, "They never jostle each other; each moves in exactly the right position. They break through defenses without missing a step" (Joel 2:8 NLT). Joel said we would not jostle or push each other around as if to fight for positions, we will not have the quarrels of "That is my place, that is not your place". Because everyone will know their place and take their positions. And like a very organized army in a parade, we will match forward without needing to push one another. But sadly, this is the norm among some Christians; they incite misunderstandings and fight over leadership positions. And if someone else is in authority, someone they don't like, they try to work against every agenda of that leader. They set themselves up against the person as if in a political war.

Such contentions are not from God. They are often inspired by pride, envy, or jealousy. Like James wrote, "What is causing the quarrels and fights among you? Don't they come from the evil desires at war within you? You want what you don't have, so you scheme and kill to get it. You are jealous of what others have, but you can't get it, so you fight and wage war to take it away from them" (James 4:1-2).

It is of God to raise and position people. And if he wants you to be in authority, in due season he will make the way and grant you smooth entry. Until then, humble yourself and work for the good of any group in which you find yourself, be part of a divine vision and work constructively towards its fulfillment, regardless of how you feel about the leader. And if you think you indeed have a leading from the Lord, share with the rest. Every true spiritual leader will evaluate and act on divine inspiration. This is what makes God's army complete, that we are united on one common front. Remember, "Every kingdom divided against itself will be ruined, and every city or household divided against itself will not stand" (Matthew 12:25).

> If we will simply find our place in the body of Christ, we will each march in our lane and there will be no need for fighting. We must be united as one solid front to be victorious as the Church.

Prayer

Heavenly Father, thank you for your love and guidance, that leads us into our unique offices and positions in Christ. Inspire those in leadership positions to lead your people right and grant us grace to overcome every form of selfishness that could be the reason for contentions. In Jesus' name.

Bible in one year // **Isaiah 47-49, 1 Thessalonians 4**

Pray without ceasing

As Joel's prophecies unfold, he calls the people to prayer with fasting. Now the will and purpose of God was made plain. "Well, the Lord should just make manifest the word", some people say. Why do we have to pray? And this sometimes is the cause of failed prophecies and divine visions. Sometimes they fail, not because they were false but because we were not rightly positioned through prayer. Prophecy unveils a divine plan and sometimes spells out what the Lord will accomplish, with or without our participation. But other times, the purpose of prophecy is to unveil to us divine plan so we can be rightly positioned and partner with the Lord to make the word manifest.

Joel said to the people, "'Now, therefore,' says the Lord, 'Turn to Me with all your heart, with fasting, with weeping, and with mourning.' So rend your heart, and not your garments; return to the Lord your God, for He is gracious and merciful, slow to anger, and of great kindness; and He relents from doing harm. Who knows if He will turn and relent, and leave a blessing behind Him – a grain offering and a drink offering for the Lord your God? Blow the trumpet in Zion, consecrate a fast, call a sacred assembly" (Joel 2:12-15).

> **Knowing God's purpose is not a call to sleep so he can accomplish it, rather it is a call to prayer as we enforce the divine will in the earth and gain insight on our responsibility to make the word a reality.**

In Christ Jesus, we also, after receiving great and precious promises, are not called to sleep. In fact, we have a greater call to prayer. For through prayer, we enforce the divine will in the earth, giving heaven the legal license to intervene in the affairs of men and establish the purpose of God. It is also a call to prayer because in the process, we receive instructions and inspiration on what we must do to make these things a reality in our lives. Just as Jesus said, "Men ought always to pray and not give up" (Luke 18:1). Even much more is the call to us to pray as the world seems to hang on loose bearings, as the earth seems to spin out of control with wars, diseases, natural disasters, famine, and political instabilities. We have a call to continue in prayer, knowing that our prayers work. Even when change seems slow, stay at it, for the results will soon speak forth. In fact, it just might have been worse without prayers. Therefore, "Pray without ceasing" (1 Thessalonians 5:17).

Prayer

Heavenly Father, thank you for today and the blessings laid therein for us. We receive grace to continue in prayer until we see every manifestation of your promises in our lives and communities. In Jesus' name.

Bible in one year // **Isaiah 50-52, 1 Thessalonians 5**

OCT 18

> It shall come to pass afterward that I will pour out My Spirit on all flesh; your sons and your daughters shall prophesy, your old men shall dream dreams, your young men shall see visions. // **Joel 2:28**

Live with a vision

Life only takes on true meaning when you have a vision for life, when you have found a purpose for living. No life is without purpose. God who made you created you for a purpose. Your parents might not have been expecting you, but God was waiting for you. Even if the circumstances surrounding your birth were not ideal, God chose that moment to let you come into this world, and that for a reason He knows best. And now that you are here on the earth, there is no greater fulfilment than to live for your purpose, to live with God's vision for you.

> **Living with a vision gives life true meaning and brings you fulfillment.**

Joel Prophesied of these days saying, "And it shall come to pass afterward that I will pour out My Spirit on all flesh; your sons and your daughters shall prophesy, your old men shall dream dreams, your young men shall see visions" (Joel 2:28). We are living in days of multiplicity of visions, when God is distributing visions to all His children, a time when God is putting his dreams and plans in our hearts for us to fulfil them in the earth. Have you taken hold of a vision from the Lord, a vision for life? If not, this is the season to ask him such questions. Ask like Paul, "Lord what do you want me to do?" (Acts 9:6). The Lord is willing to make known to you a vision for your life; that one thing He wants you to spend your life doing. And wherever His fingers point, you go and make that your number one business.

Don't just go through life. Live with a vision. Don't just fall into the cycle of going through life with its routines of the natural man. Have a divine vision at heart. Now you must not receive a very independent vision. If you are a member of a local church, then the driving vision of that spiritual family to which the Lord has joined you becomes your vision, you find your place in it and make it your vision. In this regard, Your Daily Light is part of a Lighthouse vision given to me, a vision you can also embrace and run along with us as a partner. And if you were to forget everything, always remember the reason why we are here. God has placed us in the world as beacons of light to reflect his glory to our world (Matt 5:14).

Prayer

Heavenly Father, thank you for the gift of the Holy Spirit by whom we can receive visions and be inspired with your plans and purposes. We receive grace to see what you are calling us to do that we might live purposeful lives, fulfilling your plans for us. In Jesus name.

Bible in one year // Isaiah 53-55, 2 Thessalonians 1

They are like trees planted along the riverbank, bearing fruit each season. Their leaves never wither, and they prosper in all they do.
// **Psalms 1:3 NLT**

Prospering in all things

The blessedness of the Word of God is that it gives us the opportunity to choose our life experiences. Jesus commissioned the disciples to preach saying, "Go ye into all the world, and preach the gospel to every creature. He that believeth and is baptized shall be saved; but he that believeth not shall be damned (Mark 16:15-16). We even choose where we want to spend eternity. Now if God leaves such a big decision in our hands, how much more the lesser things. The earlier we understand that God has put our lives in our own hands as a gift of trust, the easier we will take it on Him when things go differently from expectations. We will learn more to take responsibility over our lives and influence the results and experience in the direction we want it to go.

One such decision that is left in our hands is the decision to prosper in all things. The Psalmist writes, "Blessed is the man who walks not in the counsel of the ungodly, nor stands in the path of sinners, nor sits in the seat of the scornful; but his delight is in the law of the Lord, and in His law, he meditates day and night. He shall be like a tree planted by the rivers of water, that brings forth its fruit in its season, whose leaf also shall not wither; and whatever he does shall prosper (Psalm 1:1-3). He shows us by this text that we can choose to make our way prosperous in all things by making the word of God our daily meditation and walking in its truths. And that is the reason for Your Daily Light, placing at your doorstep every morning a word for the day.

> **We can choose to be prosperous in all things by choosing to delight in the word of the Lord daily, meditating in it and doing according to what is written.**

This was nothing new when David declared that one who lives in the word of God will make his way prosperous. The Lord himself had said so to Joshua many years earlier on. He said to him, This Book of the Law shall not depart from your mouth, but you[a] shall meditate in it day and night, that you may observe to do according to all that is written in it. For then you will make your way prosperous, and then you will have good success (Joshua 1:8). How He declares, "You will make your way prosperous and have good success". This is my prayer for you today, that you will prosper in all things as you meditate daily in the word.

Prayer

Thank you, Father, for your wisdom revealed to us through the word. As we meditate therein day and night, we find the truths that will shape and mold our lives for prosperity in all things. In Jesus' name.

Bible in one year // **Isaiah 56-58, 2 Thessalonians 2**

OCT 20

God is our refuge and strength, always ready to help in times of trouble. // **Psalms 46:1**

Find refuge in God

The Psalmist found refuge in God. He was so confident in His protection that he declared, "In the Lord I take refuge, how can you ask me to flee to another hiding place?" (Psalm 11:1). He declared in Psalm 46:1, "God is our refuge and strength, A very present help in trouble". Not only was he confident in the Lord as his refuge, but he was aware of how present God was. He is very present. Even with all the Chaos in the world, you don't have to ask, "God where are you". His answer will be simple, "Right here with you".

The Psalmist wrote about the secret place of the Most High: "He who dwells in the secret place of the Most High shall abide under the shadow of the Almighty. I will say of the Lord, He is my refuge and my fortress; my God, in Him I will trust" (Psalm 91:1-2). Then he continued to assure us that such a person abiding in the shadow of the almighty would be spared from the arrow by day or the pestilence of the times. When you look carefully, you will discover that the secret place of the most high is not the temple, it is now disclosed to us, it is to be in Christ.

> Find refuge in the Lord and be con-fident in his protection as your shelter. Also act and move with wisdom remembering it is a wild world out there.

Paul wrote to the Colossians, "Your life is hidden with Christ in God" (Colossians 3:3). If you are in Christ, you have found that secret place and should abide therein. Even at a time in the world of political instability, national unrest, terrorist activities and the lawlessness of armed men, you can find refuge in God. Continue in prayers and be sensitive to His leading so you can keep yourself out of harm's way. Like Jesus said, "Behold, I am sending you out as sheep in the midst of wolves, so be wise as serpents and innocent as doves" (Matthew 10:16).

Prayer

Heavenly Father, thank you for preserving our lives in our travels, for delivering us from harm's way, and keeping us safe. We receive grace to be sensitive to your leading for us and our loved ones, that we will not be victims. But we shall live to declare your works in the land of the Living. In Jesus' name.

Bible in one year // **Isaiah 59-61, 2 Thessalonians 3**

For I am sure of this very thing, that the one[b] who began a good work in you will perfect it until the day of Christ Jesus. // **Philippians 1:6 NET**

OCT 21

He will perfect His works

It is not unusual to look at our lives and see areas where we need a completion, places where things are not where we would like them to be, like unfinished projects. That rightfully so, for it is always a work in progress, a journey in prophecy as our lives unfold. On this journey, there could be seasons of despair, times when things seem stagnant or even worse, things are on the decline. It is times like this that you must remind yourself, "The Lord will perfect His work in my life, He will bring it to completion. It is in His nature to do so". For faithful is He that calls, who also will do it (1 Thessalonians 5:24).

> **Be confident in the Lord to bring to completion the good work He has started in your life and remain faithful and true, living according to His will.**

God demonstrated this His character of not leaving unfinished the works He started from the very beginnings. As you read the creation story, you realize He continued his work until everything was not just good, but very good. He only rested after all perfect (Genesis 1:31). The Lord Himself said to Jacob same words He will say to you today. He told Jacob, "I am with you and will watch over you wherever you go... I will not leave you until I have done what I have promised you" (Genesis 28:15). The Psalmist understood this when He wrote, "The LORD will perfect that which concerns me" (Psalm 138:8).

I believe it was looking back at all that God had done in His life and God's records from scriptures that Paul wrote to the Philippians, "I am confident of this very thing, that He who began a good work in you will perfect it until the day of Christ Jesus" (Philippians 1:6). So today, no matter where you are and what is going on in your life, be encouraged and strengthened to know that God who began a good work in you will perfect it to finishing. He does not abandon the works of His hands. As the author of Hebrews writes, "Do not throw away your confidence; it will be richly rewarded. You need to persevere so that when you have done the will of God, you will receive what he has promised" (Hebrews 10:35-36).

Prayer

Heavenly Father, thank you for your Faithfulness towards us that inspires commitment and dedication, knowing that it has a great reward if we do not give up. Today we receive grace to be patient, serving you until we see all your promises made a reality in our lives. In Jesus name.

Bible in one year // **Isaiah 62-64, 1 Timothy 1**

OCT 22

> Now out of His mouth goes a sharp sword, that with it He should strike the nations. // **Revelation 19:15**

The sword of the Spirit

It is not uncommon that a Christian going to bed in fright over demonic activity does so with a bible next to them. Not because they plan to open and read it first thing in the morning, rather as "The sword of the spirit". It is there at the bedside as a warning to the devil to stay off. We are instructed, "Take the sword of the Spirit, which is the word of God" (Ephesians 6:17). And it is this verse that is being wrongly practiced when someone takes the bible in their hand as a weapon. I did that too as a babe in the Lord until I found out it doesn't work. After a demonic encounter, I would get up and reposition the bible only to go back to sleep and have an even stronger oppression. This might have been your experience too. The devil is not afraid of a closed bible lying next to you. To the devil, it is nothing but another pile of papers with print. That is not the sword of the Spirit – a hard copy of the bible.

> *The word of God that is potent is the one spoken from your mouth out of an understanding of what God said, that is the sword of the spirit.*

The Sword of the spirit is the word of God that has been meditated upon, processed in your spirit, digested, and spat out in your on words. The sword of the spirit is the word of God chanted out of a heart that has understood the implications of what was said. The sword of the spirit is the word of God on your tongue, the one proceeding from a heart of understanding that has grasped the revelation of what was said. Talking about Jesus, John made this clear when he wrote, "From his mouth comes a sharp sword with which to strike down the nations" (Revelation 19:15).

The sword proceeding from his mouth was the word. And this is the word with power as we read in Hebrews, "For the word of God is living and powerful, and sharper than any two-edged sword, piercing even to the division of soul and spirit, and of joints and marrow, and is a discerner of the thoughts and intents of the heart" (Hebrews 4:12). The sword of the Spirit is not a closed bible in your hands. The sword of the spirit is the word of God you have received in your spirit, when spoken out to situations as needed. That is the word that is powerful, able to move mountains as Jesus declared (Mark 11:23).

Prayer

Heavenly Father, thank you for your word that is potent on my lips, to create, restore, demolish, and establish your purpose in my life as I speak forth scripturally inspired words. In Jesus name.

Bible in one year // Isaiah 65-66, 1 Timothy 2

> There is salvation in no one else! God has given no other name under heaven by which we must be saved. // **Acts 4:12 NLT**

OCT 23

Only in Jesus

The apostles were talking about Jesus, and this is a statement of fact. It is not the Christian version of the path to salvation. There is only one way to salvation, through Jesus the mediator. Jesus spoke of Himself saying, "I am the way and the truth and the life. No one comes to the Father except through me" (John 14:6). Jesus was the one appointed by God to represent humanity before him and to be a mediator of a reconciliation covenant. Be sure to check that you are holding to the right path. For there are many false religions in the world with nice doctrines. So, it is important to be sure you are on the right path. For "There is a path before each person that seems right, but it ends in death" (Proverbs 14:12).

In a generation that advocates for religious tolerance, we must remain conscious that we owe our neighbor the responsibility to help them escape a fire. What would you do if your neighbor's house was on fire and you could see the fire but they were unaware? Would you say it is not my business? This is how some people see it. It is not their business what another person believes, they say. Well, Jesus made it our business when he commissioned us saying, "Go into all the world and preach the Good News to everyone. Anyone who believes and is baptized will be saved. But anyone who refuses to believe will be condemned" (Mark 16:15-16 NLT).

> There is no other name given under heaven by which we must be saved except the name Jesus. So, find salvation in Jesus and take responsibility to share this truth with those around you.

The way to salvation is simple. As it is written, "If you declare with your mouth, "Jesus is Lord," and believe in your heart that God raised him from the dead, you will be saved. For it is with your heart that you believe and are justified, and it is with your mouth that you profess your faith and are saved" (Romans 10:9-10). Someday the Lord will hold you accountable for the souls that perished, souls he placed around you so you could help them find the truth. Therefore, He has left us in the world, to continue to be witnesses for him until the end.

Prayer

Heavenly Father, thank you for the call to salvation. We believe in our hearts that you raised Jesus from the dead and proclaim His Lordship in our lives and therefore are saved. We receive grace to be effective witnesses for you in our world, bearing your light to the lost for their salvation. In Jesus name.

Bible in one year // **Jeremiah 1-2, 1 Timothy 3**

OCT 24

> Therefore, do not cast away your confidence, which has great reward. // **Hebrews 10:35**

Hold your firm hope

The author of Hebrews admonished us to hold firm our hope. He wrote, "So do not throw away your confidence; it will be richly rewarded. You need to persevere so that when you have done the will of God, you will receive what he has promised. For, 'In just a little while, he who is coming will come and will not delay'. 'But my righteous one will live by faith. And I take no pleasure in the one who shrinks back.' But we do not belong to those who shrink back and are destroyed, but to those who have faith and are saved" (Hebrews 10:35-39). Thank God we are of those who hold firm their hope, have faith, and are saved. You have the capacity to hold firm till the end.

Life situations sometimes can announce hopelessness, giving us reasons to stop thinking the alternative outcome is ever going to be possible. Rather it is in moments like this that we must remember whom we have believed, we must remember the God we serve and His power that is able to do and undo. In fact, the more hopeless a situation seems, the greater and more evident will be the miracle. This is the reason why sometimes things will first deteriorate before they get better. The setup is arranged for a greater miracle. It reminds us of when Jesus heard of Lazarus' illness. He stayed a few days on, not because he cared less. When He finally decided to go, it was to raise him up from the dead. There was a setup for a greater miracle (John 11:1-44).

> **Because things seem to deteriorate does not mean you should lose hope. Rather find excitement in the possibility of a greater miracle and hold firm your confidence in God who is faithful.**

Learn from Abraham. The bible tells us, "Even when there was no reason for hope, Abraham kept hoping–believing that he would become the father of many nations. For God had said to him, "That's how many descendants you will have!" (Romans 4:18 NLT). The more hopeless the situation got, the stronger His faith grew, because He was fully persuaded that God was able to keep His promise. Let this be your confidence now and always. No matter what, hold firm your hope. For it has a rich reward.

Prayer

Almighty God, maker of heaven and earth and possessor of everything there in, thank you for the hope we have in you, a hope that does not disappoint. Today, we are confident in your love, your presence, your provision, your leading, your plan and your power. Thank you for victory is ours over every situation. In Jesus' name.

Bible in one year // Jeremiah 3-5, 1 Timothy 4

Come to Me, all you who labor and are heavy laden, and I will give you rest. // **Matthew 11:28**

OCT 25

Come into His rest

These were the words of Jesus. It was a call with a guaranteed outcome. And that call still stands today. God wants you to live a life of rest, a life in rest. Rest is not the absence of activity, although that is one definition. Rest is a state of tranquility, a state of undisturbedness from where you live. So you are busy about life, actively going about things that should be done but doing so in rest. This is God's desire for you. It is synonymous to an absence of anxiety and panic. It is a rest that comes from the knowledge that everything is checked, and all things are under control.

> The more of God's word you receive and believe in an area of your life, the more rest you experience in that domain. Come into His rest.

The call to come into His rest still stands. Concerning this rest, the writer of Hebrews had a lot to say. He admonished, "Today, if you hear his voice, harden not your heart" (Hebrews 3:7). Then he goes ahead to share the wilderness experience of the Israelites. He explains to us why they could not enter the Lord's rest. They could not enter His rest because of unbelief (Hebrews 3:19). He continues in the next chapter with more elaboration of this rest, letting us know it is for now. He wrote concerning the Israelites emphasizing that the rest was not about entering the promised land. There was more to that rest, the reality of which is in Christ Jesus. Hebrews 4:8 & 9 tell us, "For if Joshua had given them rest, then He would not afterward have spoken of another day. There remains therefore a rest for the people of God".

We get this strong call, "Let us labor therefore to enter into that rest, lest any man fall after the same example of unbelief" (Hebrews 4:11). What a paradox! Let us labor, that is, let us make every effort to enter that rest. For the rest is here, and you are to live in this rest. But how do you enter His rest? By believing God's word for your life and living in the consciousness of that reality. The more of His word you believe concerning an aspect of your life, the more of His rest you will experience in that domain. The more of His word you master concerning your health, the less anxious you will be over your health, the more rest you will experience, irrespective of the doctor's report. As it is written, "For we who have believed do enter that rest" (Hebrews 4:3).

Prayer

> Father, thank you for the rest offered us in Christ. We cast all our cares upon you because you care for us. We receive your word for us in every area of our lives, and with it, the rest it brings. In Jesus' name.

Bible in one year // **Jeremiah 6-8, 1 Timothy 57:20-40**

OCT 26

> How we thank God for you! Because of you we have great joy in God's presence. // **1 Thessalonians 3:9**

The joy of a minister

Paul wrote, "Now Timothy has just returned, bringing us good news about your faith and love. He reports that you always remember our visit with joy and that you want to see us as much as we want to see you. So we have been greatly encouraged in the midst of our troubles and suffering, dear brothers and sisters, because you have remained strong in your faith. It gives us new life to know that you are standing firm in the Lord. How we thank God for you! Because of you we have great joy as we enter God's presence (1 Thessalonians 3:6-9 NLT). Paul expresses His joy and comfort from the testimonies of the saints. That is the true joy of a true minister. Our joy is in seeing the fruits of our labor in the lives of those we minister to.

> **As much as you are impacted by the works of those God sends your way, do well to share your testimony of that impact. For it is to them a cause of great joy and a booster to their faith as they labor for the Lord.**

I can relate with the joy of Paul from the positive feedback, being reminded that his labor and work had not been in vain. As I labor daily with commitment for the spiritual nourishment and strengthening of the saints around the world through Your Daily Light, my joy is always in the impact it is making in the lives of those reading. It is always great joy when someone writes to say, "This word was for me". It inspires joy and serves as affirmation that it is truly someone's light for the day. To be reminded that our labor of love and faith is not in vain is always comforting and encouraging as ministers. Not that we seek human appraisals, for our labor is on assignment to Him that has called us, who also will reward us. However, it is a great booster to the zeal and commitment of a minister, when they are reminded that their labor towards you is yielding fruits.

Make it a habit to share your testimonies with those who minister to you and let them know the impact their work is making in your life. Don't act indifferent when the result is evident. You will be ministering encouragement to them. Even today, you can share with us a testimony of the impact of Your Daily Light in your life. The lack of such encouraging feedbacks is the reason many, who lacked a full understanding of their calling and purpose, have left the work of the Lord to pursue ordinary lives. They became convinced that their work was in vain, and their time could benefit them elsewhere.

Prayer

Heavenly Father, thank you for the ministers you have sent our way, those who inspire us in your paths and build us for greater effectiveness in the Kingdom. Strengthen them today. In Jesus' name.

Bible in one year // **Jeremiah 9-11, 1 Timothy 6**

> Encourage one another every day, as long as it is still called "today," so that none of you will be hardened by the deceitfulness of sin.
> // **Hebrews 3:13 NASB**

OCT 27

Be an encourager

Scripture commands us to encourage each other daily. The writer reiterates this again in the same book of Hebrews. He adds, "Let us not neglect our meeting together, as some people do, but encourage one another, especially now that the day of his return is drawing near" (Hebrews 10:25). We are called to encourage and inspire one another as we journey together in Christ. Be an encourager, that's your true nature in Christ. See the best in others and inspire them to be better.

It is easy to criticize, that is very easy to do. It is easy to see faults and things we would like differently. There is room for that. There is room also for rebukes and corrections. However, don't become a critic. Let it always stand out that the reason for which you point out something negative is for the purpose of building, improving, or making it better. By this, we are particularly considering a church setting, a home setting or work setting, your interaction with those in your world, those you have an opportunity to influence for the better. Sometimes people just don't know better, they just need someone to point them in the better direction. If you must criticize, the best approach is to make it as a rule. Before you criticize anything, find a compliment to start with.

Parents, learn to encourage your kids. Being critical of everything with little encouragement is the reason some kids become recalcitrant. They come to think that nothing they do is ever correct, they come to learn they could never measure up and stop trying. Encouraging one another has its place too among couples. It can bring the best out of a partner. Don't put another down with your words, don't break their spirit or quench the zeal in an individual for the good they are trying to do, just because it needs some improvement. Encourage them, at minimum, for the thought of a good action. The food might not taste good, at least they tried to cook. The voice might have been coarse, at least they put themselves out there to sing. Don't be the reason someone gives up on doing some good. Be an encourager.

> **Let us encourage one another in the way of the Lord and for greater and better results in life.**

Prayer

Heavenly Father, thank you for making me one who encourages and brings out the best in others. By your Spirit, we are helped in our dealings with others, to be a source of inspiration and encouragement for them to continue in good works for your glory. In Jesus' name.

Bible in one year // **Jeremiah 12-14, 2 Timothy 1**

OCT 28 — Let the one who boasts boast in the Lord. // **2 Corinthians 10:17 NIV**

Boast in the Lord

Boasting in the Lord is a Holy thing to do. There is godly boasting that is commended. God Himself recommended that we boast of Him and our knowledge of Him. Jeremiah declared, "This is what the Lord says: "Let not the wise boast of their wisdom or the strong boast of their strength or the rich boast of their riches, but let the one who boasts boast about this: that they have the understanding to know me, that I am the Lord, who exercises kindness, justice and righteousness on earth, for in these I delight" (Jerimiah 9:23-24).

This was the life of David. When you consider most of his Psalms, you will realize they were his boastings in the Lord. He boasted about the Lord being his shepherd, declaring He will not be in want (Psalm 23:1). He boasted in his fearlessness, because the Lord was the strong tower of his life (Psalm 27:1). He boasted of God's works, recognizing he was Himself wonderfully and beautifully made (Psalm 139:14). The truth is, like David, we are braggers in the Lord. Just don't brag wrongly, like those who do not know God but pride themselves in fleeting glories of the earth.

> Boast in the Lord, proclaim your knowledge of Him and do not be hesitant to testify of his wonders in your life. It is all boasting in the Lord.

David so boasted in the Lord that his brothers took offense. When he arrived the battlefield as the Israelites stood off against the Philistines, he boasted in his ability to bring down Goliath. He recounted how he had slain a lion and a bear, he boasted in the Lord's presence with Him, granting Him victory in all things. But when David's oldest brother, Eliab, heard David talking to the men, he was angry. "What about those few sheep you're supposed to be taking care of? I know about your pride and deceit" (1 Samuel 17:28). Worthy of note: You cannot boast in the Lord without seeming prideful in the process and making a show-off of what He has made you. Like Paul would boast in the Lord, "I can do all things through Christ who strengthens me". Second, sometimes it will be other believers who will see your boasting in the Lord for pride just like David's older brother misjudged him.

Prayer

Heavenly Father, thank you for the life I have in Christ Jesus, the excitement of the spirit and hope of the future. Therefore, I speak gladly of who you are to me, what you have made of me, and can do for others. Thank you for a glorious life made ready for all who will come to you. In Jesus' name.

Bible in one year // **Jeremiah 15-17, 2 Timothy 2**

Pray without ceasing, in everything give thanks; for this is the will of God in Christ Jesus for you. // **1 Thessalonians 5:17-18**

OCT 29

Continue in prayer

Jesus said, "Men ought always to pray and not give up" (Luke 18:1). Then He went on to illustrate the power of continuing in prayer particularly when the expected outcome seems not forth coming. You can read the whole story from Luke 18:1-6. An unjust judge grants a widow's request because of her persistence. Then the Lord said, "Shall God not avenge His own elect who cry out day and night to Him, though He bears long with them? I tell you that He will avenge them speedily. Nevertheless, when the Son of Man comes, will He really find faith on the earth?" (Luke 18:7-8).

A good example is seen in the life of the prophet Elijah. After he declared the word of God to the king Ahab concerning a downpour, he went in to enforce the manifestation of the prophecy through prayer. The bible tells us, Elijah said to his servant, "Go and look out toward the sea." The servant went and looked, then returned to Elijah and said, "I didn't see anything." Seven times Elijah told him to go and look. Finally the seventh time, his servant told him, "I saw a little cloud about the size of a man's hand rising from the sea." Then Elijah shouted, "Hurry to Ahab and tell him, 'Climb into your chariot and go back home. If you don't hurry, the rain will stop you!'" And soon the sky was black with clouds. A heavy wind brought a terrific rainstorm... (1 Kings 18:43-45).

> **Though an expected outcome seems to tarry, continue in prayer, and do not quit praying. For your prayer is accomplishing something in you and for you.**

Continue in prayer, even when your expected outcome seems tarrying. Don't give up. Your prayer is prevailing. It is working out something. At minimum, it is working patience in you already. Don't quit now. Jesus guaranteed, everyone who asks, receives, everyone who seeks, finds and to everyone who knocks, the door is opened. Jesus' concern was if your faith will hold out till the end. That is the reason he ended that parable with the question. Will He still find people holding out in faith and praying when He comes? He is trusting you to not quit for He has enabled you by His Spirit. Continue in prayer until you have a note of victory in your spirit or a divine verdict on the situation.

Prayer

Heavenly Father, thank you for the privilege to pray. Thank you for the grace to continue in prayer, knowing that the effectual fervent prayer of the righteous makes available tremendous power, dynamic in its working. Therefore, we rejoice in hope of answered prayers. In Jesus' name..

Bible in one year // **Jeremiah 18-19, 2 Timothy 3**

OCT 30

If you can believe, all things are possible to him who believes.
// Mark 9:23

Anticipate miracles

The life in Christ is a miraculous one. We are not ordinary; we are supernatural people. Therefore, live with the consciousness of the miraculous. Have no limitations in your mind, walk in the consciousness that all things are possible with God. Always anticipate miracles. Jesus said, "These signs shall follow them that believe; In my name shall they cast out devils; they shall speak with new tongues; They shall take up serpents; and if they drink any deadly thing, it shall not hurt them; they shall lay hands on the sick, and they shall recover" (Mark 16:17 - 18).

> As a child of God, miracles are but natural. Live with this consciousness and always anticipate miracles in all situations and at all times.

Never be one such child of God who is critical about miracles. The abnormal thing is when we don't expect them. It does not matter what the situation is and how impossible it seems, there is always a possibility for a change if only you will believe. It is a law. Jesus Himself declared, "All things are possible to him who believes" (Mark 9:23). Don't put limits on God. Don't put limits on what He can do. He is still raising the dead, God is still healing the sick, He is still giving His people information regarding things to come, He is still providing for His Children through supernatural means. There is no miracle recorded in scripture that God cannot do again. And even if a miracle was needed, such as never happened before, you can place the demand on heaven. Jesus even said we will do greater things than He did.

The fact that some people have abused miracles and used gimmicks for selfish ends does not discredit the reality that miracles still happen. God is still in the miracle business and in Christ, He wants to make known His glory through your miraculous life. The woman who suffered from prolonged bleeding shows us how to anticipate miracles. The bible tells us, "She said within herself, If I may touch but his garment, I shall be whole" (Mark 5:28). She believed to see miracles and her expectations did not fail her. This is the mindset you should have in Christ Jesus, a mind that always sees possibilities even in the most hopeless situations, knowing that such situations are occasions for the supernatural. Always anticipate miracles.

Prayer

Almighty God, thank you for your power at work in my life, available to work wonders at all times in all situations. Therefore, I anticipate miracles, knowing that you are able to do exceedingly abundantly above all I can ever ask, think or imagine. Receive all the praise. In Jesus' name.

Bible in one year // **Jeremiah 20-21, 2 Timothy 4**

Don't act thoughtlessly, but understand what the Lord wants you to do.
// **Ephesians 5:17 NLT**

OCT 31

Understand the times

It is very important to understand the times we are living in. And it is in your capacity to discern the times – God has made it so. Without an understanding of the times, we will miss the move of God and divine opportunities prepared for us. It was said of a tribe in Israel, "From Issachar, there were men who understood the times and knew what Israel should do" (1 Chronicles 12:32 NIV). This is what God expects of us, to discern the times and be in step with His move in our individual lives, likewise His move in the earth.

Jesus mourned over Jerusalem saying, "If you had known, even you, especially in this your day, the things that make for your peace! But now they are hidden from your eyes. For days will come upon you when your enemies will build an embankment around you, surround you and close you in on every side, and level you, and your children within you, to the ground; and they will not leave in you one stone upon another, because you did not know the time of your visitation" (Luke 19:41-44). The people in that city did not recognize the time of a divine visitation and so they missed the blessing it was bringing.

> Understand the times and be alert to what the Lord is doing in your world. Join the move and don't miss out on your time of divine visitation.

Ephesians 5:17 tells us, "See then that you walk circumspectly, not as fools but as wise, redeeming the time, because the days are evil. Therefore, do not be unwise, but understand what the will of the Lord is" (Ephesians 5:15-17). Now is the set time for certain things in your life and you must be about them. Now is the time to dare out on some of the visions the Lord has placed on your heart, a more convenient time is not guaranteed. In fact, with delay only comes loss of zeal. If you are going to write a book, start now. If you are going to help an orphan, reach out now. If you will partner with Your Daily Light, join the train today. Understand the times and what the Lord is tugging your heart to do. Get busy on it for the sure reward that awaits you. Do not be like the Israelites who missed the hour of their visitation. Use today's opportunity while it lasts, tomorrow is not guaranteed.

Prayer

Heavenly Father, thank you for the Holy Spirit who leads us into all truths and brings to us the discernment we need. Today we are alert to your move. We receive grace to understand the times and what you are accomplishing so we can be rightly positioned for the blessings. In Jesus' name.

Bible in one year // **Jeremiah 22-23, Titus 1**

NOVEMBER

Patient endurance is what you need now, so that you will continue to do God's will. Then you will receive all that he has promised.
// **Hebrews 10:36 NLT**

NOV 1

He is never late

God is never late. He is always on time. He said to Habakkuk, "Write the vision and make it plain on tablets, that he may run who reads it. For the vision is yet for an appointed time; but at the end it will speak, and it will not lie. Though it tarries, wait for it; because it will surely come, it will not tarry" (Habakkuk 2:2-3). Has the Lord promised you something, do you have a word of prophecy you are holding to, and it seems not forthcoming? It is not time to give up. If you can ascertain it was a word from the Lord, you can confidently wait for its fulfilment. He will honor His word, and that in time. He is never late.

If you look at the word to Habakkuk, you will see what seems a contradiction. The Lord told him the vision was for an appointed time. And though the vision tarries, he should wait for it, for it will not delay. Delay and tarry are synonyms. Seems quite a contradicting statement. But it is not contradicting. The Lord was referring to man's agenda and His agenda. As far as man is concerned, it seems it tarries, for we often have in our own minds a timeline that is not necessary in line with the divine plan. Therefore, it will seem to tarry. However, as far as God is concerned, it is right on schedule.

> **The Lord is never late on the fulfilment of His promises. Exercise patience and get busy with the things He has called you to do. For in just a little while you will obtain what was promised.**

Martha sent words to Jesus saying Lazarus was sick. However, it was not until days later that Jesus responded to the call. When matter saw Jesus, she regrated, "Lord, if You had been here, my brother would not have died". But Jesus had a profound response, "I am the resurrection and the life". Then He went on to demonstrate He wasn't late. Though Lazarus was four days dead, Jesus knew the man was as much alive (John 11). Whenever Jesus arrived was going to be the right time. He is never late. He is the Lord of the time. The clock starts ticking with Him. And if He needs to undo time to work out something, He will. It does not matter what word of promise you are holding to; it will prove true and in time. Don't cast away your confidence. Exercise patience as scripture instructs (Hebrews 10:35-37).

Prayer

Heavenly Father, thank you for all the great and precious promises we have in Jesus. We rejoice because they are as good as done. Therefore, we serve you in confidence and patience, for though any might tarry, they will not delay in the time of manifestation in our lives. In Jesus' name.

Bible in one year // **Jeremiah 24-26, Titus 2**

NOV 2

> I press on toward the goal to win the prize for which God has called me heavenward in Christ Jesus. // **Philippians 4:13**

A heavenly calling

The writer of Hebrews wrote, "Therefore, holy brethren, partakers of the heavenly calling" (Hebrews 3:1). Then He went ahead to show them the faithfulness of Jesus as a son in God's house; and a lot of other things we could be glad to look at. However, I wish to draw your attention on how the author addressed his readers. He called them "Partakers of the heavenly calling". There is a heavenly calling for us all. There is a heavenly calling for you, God calling us heavenwards. And what a blessing that is, to share in a heavenly calling when we say yes to the Lord.

> God's call is to all of humanity, a heavenly calling to be united with Him in Christ Jesus; and to discover and fulfill His plans for our individual lives.

It is first a heavenly calling because God is calling all men to Himself through Christ Jesus, He wants to be united to all men. There is no single person in the world who is not loved and desired by God. It is like God himself dialing your mobile, calling you to Himself. All we have to do is answer the call and say yes to Jesus. It is a call out of the world and its bondage to sin, a call into relationship with God and freedom from sin. He says, "Come out from among them and be separate, says the Lord. Do not touch what is unclean, and I will receive you." "I will be a Father to you, and you shall be My sons and daughters, says the Lord Almighty" (2 Corinthians 6:17-18). It is a call to be part of His family, a heavenly family, Holy and accepted in His presence. Have you accepted that call? Have you received Jesus?

How Paul declared, "We are ambassadors for Christ, as though God were making an appeal through us; we beg you on behalf of Christ, be reconciled to God" (2 Corinthians 5:20). This is the call we extend daily to the world as we invite them to receive Christ. It is a heavenly calling, God Himself is inviting humanity into a fellowship with Him. Then there is a second implication to that call, that is the call to fulfill God's plan for your life. You are not a product of chance. God made you for a purpose He wants you to live for. Have you discovered that purpose? Are you living for it? What are you doing towards its fulfillment? It is a heavenly calling with a glorious reward. Paul wrote of himself in this light, "I press on toward the goal to win the prize for which God has called me heavenward in Christ Jesus" (Philippians 3:14).

Prayer

Heavenly Father, thank you for the call to be your Children and to fulfill the purpose you had for us before the foundations of the earth. As we say yes to the call and yield to your will, the paths are made straight for us, and all our needs richly supplied for the fulfillment of our destinies. In Jesus' name.

Bible in one year // **Jeremiah 27-29, Titus 3**

Let us lay aside every weight, and the sin which so easily ensnares us, and let us run with endurance the race that is set before us.
// **Hebrews 12:1**

NOV 3

Lay aside every weight

If you have been a Christian and exposed to the word of God for a while, then Hebrews 12:1 will not be a strange verse to you for sure. It is a very explicit verse; it loudly speaks for itself. It paints the picture of a runner who will only hinder themselves in winning a race if they drag along with them unnecessary weights. Talking about sins, if there be any that you are consciously meddling with, you sure know. That would not be our emphasis. However, it is good to know that you only harm your spiritual progress and cheat yourself in God's presence. You put yourself in a place where you won't have total freedom in his presence, and your feeling of guilt, if your conscience is not seared, will make your faith ineffective.

The principal class of weights to consider laying aside today is such weights that are not necessarily sins, but things on your agenda, relationships in your life and commitments that do not necessarily add to your progress or make your steps swift in destiny. For example, not every classmate is your friend. Not every school mate must remain a close contact as you age. Sometimes as our persons develop and we find our paths in life, we should be able to recognize those whose paths no longer cross with ours as much. Not that you make them enemies, but because you know that there can no longer be any healthy and meaningful relationship with certain persons, it is ok to lighten some bonds.

> Some weights are pleasurable to carry along, you must recognize such and lay them down alongside any sin that might hamper your walk with God.

You cannot be in Christ and your best friend is an unbeliever, just because you knew each other for so long. If you can win their soul over, that will be great. The friendship can blossom even more. But if they despise your beliefs and make mockery of your new faith, it is time to find a new best friend, one who will help your faith. Destiny is far more important and calls you to choose associations based on where you are going not where you are coming from. That is why the Lord could say to Abraham, "Go from your country, your people and your father's household to the land I will show you" (Genesis 12:1).

Prayer

Heavenly Father thank you for the grace available in Christ Jesus, that enables us to mold our lives by your word. Today we receive grace to lay aside every weight that slows us down that we might gain speed on our journey as you lead us along with the right connections for life and destiny. In Jesus' name.

Bible in one year // **Jeremiah 30-31, Philemon**

NOV 4

> However, when He, the Spirit of truth, has come, He will guide you into all truth; for He will not speak on His own authority, but whatever He hears He will speak; and He will tell you things to come. // **John 16:13**

The agent of revelations

Revelation is the unveiling of things concealed, things we would otherwise have no access to perceive. It comes from the Greek word "Apokalupsis" which means to make naked or lay bare things that were once hidden; it means to unveil. Without revelation, we would be blind to spiritual truths and our best knowledge of spiritual things would be guesses and mere human opinions. For the natural man is spiritually blind and deaf to the spiritual world. He is dead to the spiritual world though they are alive in body. Therefore, "The natural man does not receive the things of the Spirit of God, for they are foolishness to him; nor can he know them, because they are spiritually discerned" (1 Corinthians 2:14).

The natural man was cut off from spiritual truth through separation from God by sin. Sin brought death into the world and all men were cut off from God – the source of all truth. Knowledge about God, the origin of life and life after death, such things beyond the scrutiny of the natural man became out of reach, leaving man oblivious or unconscious to spiritual truths – things beyond the scrutiny of science. But God, through Christ Jesus is bringing men back to life, making us alive spiritually so we can perceive spiritual truth. Paul wrote, "And you [He made alive when you] were [spiritually] dead and separated from Him because of your transgressions and sins" (Ephesians 2:1 Amplified). You pass on from spiritual dead back to life when you become born again. Once again you can perceive spiritual truths.

> **Get to know the Holy Spirit and learn to fellowship with Him. He is the agent of revelation sent to bring you trust-worthy information for your walk in life and destiny.**

This is one reason the Holy Spirit was sent into the world, as the agent of revelations. Jesus spoke of the work of the Holy Spirit saying, "When He, the Spirit of truth, has come, He will guide you into all truth; for He will not speak on His own authority, but whatever He hears He will speak; and He will tell you things to come. He will glorify Me, for He will take of what is Mine and declare it to you" (John 16:13-14). The Holy Spirit came into the world to unveil to you the knowledge of the God and spiritual things, knowledge you would never be able to access by yourself. He is God's agent of revelation.

Prayer

Heavenly Father, thank you for the gift of the Holy Spirit. Thank you for the Spirit of truth who guides us into all truths. We receive grace to know and walk with the Holy Spirit as He teaches us. In Jesus' name.

Bible in one year // **Jeremiah 32-33, Hebrews 1**

> While we do not look at the things which are seen, but at the things which are not seen. For the things which are seen are temporary, but the things which are not seen are eternal. // **2 Corinthians 4:18**

NOV 5

Accept God's Report

Isaiah cried out, "Who has believed our report?" (Isaiah 53:1). The prophet had borne testimony of things he had seen and heard spiritually but not all believed him. He had been proclaiming a divine report about Jesus, "He was wounded for our transgressions, He was bruised for our iniquities; The chastisement for our peace was upon Him, and by His stripes we are healed" (Isaiah 53:5). He gave a detailed report of spiritual realities which were established in the sight of God. The physical manifestation of the report might not have been evident, but the report was valid and binding.

God has a report about every situation that concerns us. He has a report concerning your health. It doesn't matter what the medical report says and what the medical specialists call it. It does not matter the signs and symptoms that are present. All these won't nullify God's report. God's own report is final. And that report says, "By his wounds you were healed" (2 Peter 2:24). Note when Peter wrote of its fulfilment. And this is the greater truth and your present-day reality. If you are in Christ, you are the healed of the Lord, no matter what is going on. This should be your testimony and confidence. Accept God's report and nothing else. Then every condition will align with the word of God. For that word will not prove false. Hebrews 11:2 tells us, "Through faith, the elders obtained a good report".

> God's report concerning anything about your life is final. Accept it and confess it. Refuse to endorse anything contrary until the divine report over-writes everything contrary.

God has a report on your finances, God has a report on your family and everything else that concerns you. Now if circumstances do not look like what God's report suggests, it is not for you to say the word is not accurate. On the contrary, that is the call to exercise your faith, hold fast your confession until you see the full manifestation of God's own report. Continue proclaiming God's word until the divine report overwrites the present situation. Remember the words of Paul, "We do not look at the things which are seen, but at the things which are not seen". Accept God's report and settle for nothing less.

Prayer

Heavenly Father, thank you for your report on my life, my health, my career, family, and all that concerns me is good. As I proclaim your word, I overwrite contrary reports in the name of Jesus.

Bible in one year // **Jeremiah 34-36, Hebrews 2**

NOV 6

Let the word of Christ dwell in you richly in all wisdom, teaching and admonishing one another in psalms and hymns and spiritual songs, singing with grace in your hearts to the Lord. // Colossians 3:16

A rich deposit of God's word

Such a profound word of instruction. "Let the word of Christ dwell in you richly". This is the secret to a victorious life in Christ. You cannot thrive as a Christian without a rich deposit and good understanding of the word of God. The bible is more than a religious document. The bible is more than a moral code of conduct, it is God's manual for life. You can't take the bible and its teachings lightly and experience God fully. You cannot separate a great experience in Christ from a rich deposit of God's word in your Spirit.

> Let the word of Christ dwell in you richly. Like a seed planted, the results will speak for itself in due time.

Jesus declared, "Abide in Me, and I in you. As the branch cannot bear fruit of itself, unless it abides in the vine, neither can you, unless you abide in Me" (John 15:4). He connected your fruitfulness as a believer to how well you can abide in him as a branch must remain on a vine to be fruitful. However, how do you abide in Jesus? You abide in Jesus by having in you a rich deposit of His word and conducting your life by it. And Jesus abides in you through the Holy Spirit and a rich deposit of the word of God in you. Remember, "The word became flesh". So the more of Jesus you want to experience in your life, the more of His word you must imbibe into your spirit. Longing for an experience of Christ without a corresponding desire to grow in the knowledge of His word will only expose you to demons. For you will lack the knowledge and discernment to differentiate spirits.

Let the word of Christ dwell in your richly. Cultivate a personal relationship with the word of God and grow in your knowledge of it. Never become familiar with scriptures that you assume you already know enough. Just like in the natural world, yesterday's spiritual meal does not suffice for today's hunger. Don't live on expired food. Go for the word of God each day like someone reading it for the first time. Be open to learn and receive new truths always like one who newly came to the Lord. Make rich deposit of God's word in you through daily meditation in scriptures and the results will speak for itself. Jesus assured us, "If My words abide in you, you will ask what you desire, and it shall be done for you".

Prayer

Heavenly Father, thank you for the insatiable hunger for your word that keeps us coming for more each day. Thank you for daily inspiration for the day through Your Daily Light. As we receive your word into our spirits and make a rich deposit, it brings forth fruit in due season for your glory. In Jesus' name.

Bible in one year // **Jeremiah 37-39, Hebrews 3**

People ruin their lives by their own foolishness and then are angry at the LORD. // **Proverbs 19:3 NLT**

NOV 7

Take responsibility

When you question some atheists why they believe there is no God, the answer often is the same: if there is a God, why are there such terrible things happening in the world? In their minds, if there was a good God such as is supposed, then everything would be in order. This is because they, like many others, have not understood God's relationship with humanity. God is like a landlord who has leased out the earth to humanity. It is not as much His responsibility what we do with it while it is on lease. The bible tells us, "The heavens belong to the LORD, but he has given the earth to all humanity" (Psalm 115:16 NLT). We can choose to set it on fire or care for it. God is not responsible for what goes on in the world, though He influences things for the better when we give Him the opportunity to do so by invitation through prayer.

The same is true with our lives. God is not responsible for everything that becomes of us. Your life is also a gift of trust to you from God. It is up to you what you make of your life. The author of proverbs understood this as seen in the verse of the day. This is a reality, that people make bad choices and blame God for the consequences. You must take responsibility over your life and over the world. God has called you to partnership with Him on a journey through life. You will have to know your responsibilities in that relationship.

> **Take responsibility in your walk with God and partner with Him to see the full manifestation of His plans. Else you will end up blaming God for your own folly or failure to take responsibility.**

Taking responsibility applies to us in many regards. Even the promises of God to us are as good as done. However, you have responsibilities to make them a reality in your life. My sister, Mbapah Beatrice, nicely covers this aspect of how to appropriate your inheritance in Christ in her book, INHERITANCE. You should get a copy. Even concerning something like healing, God has already healed you in Christ Jesus. God is not going to heal you. He already did, even if your body speaks otherwise. It is now for you to exercise your faith and make that word a living reality in your life. Take responsibility and learn not to wait on God for things He has made you responsible over.

Prayer

> Heavenly Father, thank you for the opportunities to glorify you today. We receive grace to know our responsibilities as you lead us and make manifest your glorious plans for our lives. In Jesus' name.

Bible in one year // **Jeremiah 40-42, Hebrews 4**

NOV 8

> Do you not know that those who run in a race all run, but one receives the prize? Run in such a way that you may obtain it. // **1 Corinthians 9:24**

Run to win

Do you not know that in a race all the runners run, but only one gets the prize? Run in such a way as to get the prize. Everyone who competes in the games goes into strict training. They do it to get a crown that will not last, but we do it to get a crown that will last forever. Therefore, I do not run like someone running aimlessly; I do not fight like a boxer beating the air. No, I strike a blow to my body and make it my slave so that after I have preached to others, I myself will not be disqualified for the prize (1 Corinthians 9:24-27 NIV).

Paul in his writing, used himself as an example to show what He was doing in that regard. He had self-discipline. He recognized he was not His body. He recognized his body was a separate entity from him, the real spiritual being. The bible calls the real you, the hidden man of the heart (1 Peter 3:4). That is your spirit. Your spirit is the one that is born again, your spirit is the one that is going to heaven, your spirit is the one in union with God. Your body is only its shell. Your body is not you, like the shell of a snail is not the snail. Your body is a tent, the habitation of your spirit and the temple of God. However, that body can be unruly, with its own cravings that do not necessarily conform God's purpose.

> **Subject your body to the necessary discipline, deprive it of sensual satisfaction, if need be, and run as to win the prize of the high calling in Christ Jesus.**

If it were up to our bodies, it would have anything, go anywhere, and have sexual intimacy with anyone we got attracted to. It is an unruly entity. It is with such an understanding that the words of Paul make sense. He disciplines his body, he does not let himself be ruled by the body and its tendencies, for that body has no prize to win. From dust it came and to dust it will go. When we fast, it is in part to subdue the flesh and its tendencies and to give our spirits preeminence over the body. It is part of putting the body to subjection. When we live by God's word against the dictates of the flesh, it is all part of striking the body with blows. It is in such a life, reflected in righteousness that winning the prize is guaranteed.

Prayer

Heavenly Father, thank you for the race set before me. Thank you for Jesus the forerunner who has gone before us. We set our gaze on him and run with endurance our race, knowing that there is a crown of righteousness prepared for us. We receive grace to be true to the end. In Jesus' name.

Bible in one year // Jeremiah 43-45, Hebrews 5

Be kind and compassionate to one another, forgiving each other, just as in Christ God forgave you. // **Ephesians 4:32 NIV**

NOV 9

God forgave you

Paul exhorted the Ephesians to forgive each other just as God had forgiven them in Christ Jesus. This is true for you too. God has forgiven you in Christ Jesus. He forgave all your sins and made forgiveness available to you. God is not holding any sin against you. For "God was reconciling the world to himself in Christ, not counting people's sins against them" (2 Corinthians 5:19 NIV). "He has removed our sins as far from us as the east is from the west" (Psalm 103:12, NLT). Just as you cannot look towards the east and see the west, even so in Christ Jesus, God doesn't see your sins when He looks at you. How God declared in another place, "Their sins and lawless acts I will remember no more" (Hebrews 10:17).

> **God forgave you in Christ Jesus. You should forgive others because you have yourself received forgiveness.**

Now there is a wrong teaching that has prevailed in the church for so long. Though it finds its origin from the teachings of Jesus, it is wrongly applied to the Church. This was before the cross. Jesus was talking to a people who were not born again. He was talking to a people under the law of Moses. These people lacked a revelation and understanding of the love of God. As a result, they were called to "Do unto others what they would like done to them" (Matthew 7:12). They had to be constrained in this manner. It was in the same light that Jesus said to them, "If you do not forgive others their sins, your Father will not forgive your sins (Matthew 6:15).

After Jesus' death and resurrection, a new covenant was enacted by His blood. His blood was shed for the remission of our sins. And as many as believe in Jesus are forgiven because of His sacrifice. That is why Paul writes and tells the Christians in Ephesus, "Forgive each other, just as God forgave you in Christ". Under the Old Covenant, they had to forgive so that they could be forgiven. But not so under the New Covenant. We forgive because we have been forgiven. God is not holding your sins over your head and waiting for you to forgive those who wronged you before He forgives you. No! God forgave you already in Christ Jesus. You forgive others because you have yourself experienced mercy.

Prayer

> Gracious Father, thank you for not dealing with us according to our sins, but removing them from us as far as the east is from the west. Thank you for the forgiveness we have in Christ Jesus because of His finished work on the cross. We receive grace to forgive those who wrong us. In Jesus' name.

Bible in one year // **Jeremiah 46-47, Hebrews 6**

NOV 10

> Well done, good and faithful servant; you have been faithful over a few things, I will make you ruler over many things. Enter into the joy of your lord. // **Matthew 25:23**

A gift to trust

It is not unusual to hear someone say, "My life is in God's hands". That is great truth and very scriptural. The Lord said to Jacob the same words which are true for you today. "Now, thus says the Lord, who created you, O Jacob, and He who formed you, O Israel: "Fear not, for I have redeemed you; I have called you by your name; You are Mine. When you pass through the waters, I will be with you; and through the rivers, they shall not overflow you. When you walk through the fire, you shall not be burned, nor shall the flame scorch you. For I am the Lord your God, The Holy One of Israel, your Savior (Isaiah 43:1-4).

Your life is a gift of trust to you from the Lord. It is in your hands what you do with it. Therefore, use it wisely for the fulfillment of God's purpose.

Such an assurance from the Lord that gives us confidence that our lives are in His hands. That confidence is boosted even more when we consider Paul's testimony to the Colossians. He wrote to them, "Your life is hidden with Christ in God" (Colossians 3:3). Yes, your life is in God's hands. However, God placed that life into your own hands as a gift of trust. Your life is in your hands. Your destiny is in your hands. God placed that life into your hands and gave you time in the earth to use it for His Glory. He gave you life and is counting on you to use that life for His purpose and for His glory.

Think of the parable of the talents. Each one received according to their capacity. But it was only for a season and a gift of trust. They were going to be called to accounts on what they had done with that talent. Even so it is with our lives, what we do with it. Jesus made it clear with the illustration of the talents, that the wise thing to do is to use your life for the purpose and service of God. It is investing your life in this way that will guarantee you the words, "Well done, good and faithful servant; you have been faithful over a few things, I will make you ruler over many things. Enter into the joy of your lord" (Matthew 25:23).

Prayer

Heavenly Father, thank you for the gift of trust to be alive for your purpose and your glory. Thank you for your power at work in us to will and to do according to your good. Therefore, we invest our lives for your purpose and glory as faithful servants. In Jesus' name.

Bible in one year // **Jeremiah 48-49, Hebrews 7**

Blessed is she who believed, for there will be a fulfillment of those things which were told her from the Lord. // **Luke 1:45**

NOV 11

The blessedness of believing

Jesus said, "Thomas, because you have seen Me, you have believed. Blessed are those who have not seen and yet have believed" (John 20:29). God wants us to be easily convinced by His word, He wants us to be quick to believe. To believe means to accept something to be so even when you do not have personal evidence for it. You accept it to be so because you trust the informer, not because you have proven it to be so. That is believing. And God wants us to have an open spirit towards His word, quick to accept whatever it says as truth. "Blessed are those who have not seen and yet have believed".

There is a blessedness in believing in God's word, even when you have no personal evidence to accept that to be true. And that blessedness, is that the one who believes gets to experience what was believed. Elizabeth said to Mary, "Blessed is she who believed, for there will be a fulfillment of those things which were told her from the Lord" (Luke 1:45). The actual law in believing is this: "When you believe, you will experience what you believe". This is why many atheists remain in darkness. They have said, "When I see, I will believe". But God's mode of operation is this, "When you believe, you will see". Just as Jesus said to Martha, "Did I not say to you that if you would believe you would see the glory of God?" (John 11:40). We believe to see, we don't see to believe.

> **The blessedness of believing in the word of God to you is that there will be a fulfillment of those things you believe in your life.**

The Thomas way of life is not God's ideal. Do not be the one who only operates like Thomas. Who only waits to be able to ascertain things for themselves before accepting them to be so, particularly things that are clear in the word of God. There are those who still question life after death, they question the existence of hell. You don't want to find out for yourself when you die. It is a risky venture. You will be there when you find out and will have no way to avoid it. Believe the word of God today and accept it to be so, and there will be a fulfilment of the things you have believed in your life.

Prayer

Heavenly Father, thank you for your word that is true and forever settled. Thank you for the Holy Spirit who gives us discernment so we are not swayed away but can prove all things and hold on to that which is true. We receive and accept your word for us today and always. In Jesus' name.

Bible in one year // **Jeremiah 50, Hebrews 8**

NOV 12

Jesus said to His disciples, "If anyone desires to come after Me, let him deny himself, and take up his cross, and follow Me. // **Matthew 16:24**

Your pure devotion

Jesus demands nothing from us less than total and pure devotion to Him. He said to those wanting to follow Him, "If anyone desires to come after Me, let him deny himself, and take up his cross, and follow Me" (Matthew 16:24). He requires nothing less than that. Jesus wasn't soft with words when He talked about following Him. He hardly pampered or coerced anyone. He was blunt on the quality of our following. He required us to pick up our cross, deny ourselves and follow Him. A following that has no alternative agenda outside His plans and purpose, a following at all costs. This is pure devotion, when you are fully given to the Lord, denying yourself and taking up your cross daily no matter the cost in your time, resources, and relationships.

Jesus said, "Whoever desires to save his life will lose it" (Matthew 16:25). This also applies to your job, career, marriage, and everything else that can get in the way between you and your true devotion to the Lord. What you try to preserve at the detriment of your walk with him will end up slipping through your fingers. You will lose. Jesus added on another occasion, "If anyone comes to Me and does not hate his father and mother, wife and children, brothers and sisters, yes, and his own life also, he CANNOT be My disciple" (Luke 14:26). The good news is this: whatever you sacrifice for Him, you will find it. That He guaranteed. "Whoever loses his life for My sake will find it". It applies to everything as well.

Jesus desires nothing less than a pure and total devotion to him, a life where you daily carry your cross, deny yourself and follow Him. That is your pure devotion with guaranteed rewards.

Jesus told the disciples, "Assuredly, I say to you, there is no one who has left house or brothers or sisters or father or mother or wife or children or lands, for My sake and the gospel's, who shall not receive a hundredfold now in this time–houses and brothers and sisters and mothers and children and lands, with persecutions–and in the age to come, eternal life" (Mark 10:29-30). Your devotion and sacrifices have guaranteed rewards. So let your devotion be pure and total. Paul worried for the Corinthians, "I am afraid that just as Eve was deceived by the serpent's cunning, your minds may somehow be led astray from your sincere and pure devotion to Christ" (2 Corinthians 11:3). Don't let that happen in your life.

Prayer

Heavenly Father, thank you for buying us with a price. Our eyes are on Jesus, that in true devotion and following, we will walk in His paths and live the good life pre-arranged for us in Christ. In Jesus' name.

Bible in one year // **Jeremiah 51-52, Hebrews 9**

Fear not, for I am with you; be not dismayed, for I am your God. I will strengthen you. Yes, I will help you, I will uphold you with My righteous right hand. // **Isaiah 41:10**

NOV 13

Fear not

While there might often be cause for fear, we do not have to respond to them in fear. We need not entertain fear. In fact, we have no reason to fear. Time and again, the Lord tells us, "Do not be afraid". And that for good reason. He has assured us of better things even through the worst situations. He has guaranteed our wellbeing, no matter what we face. Just like He said to Jacob, "Fear not, for I am with you; be not dismayed, for I am your God. I will strengthen you; yes, I will help you, I will uphold you with My righteous right hand" (Isaiah 41:10).

If you listen to the news, particularly with the pandemic and recurring new variances of the virus, they only inspire fear. But you don't have to give in to the fear. Not the fear of life or fear for your job. Whatever the case might be, He will bring you through. Just like David declared, let this be your confidence and confession. Just this time, really mean it when you say it. For you have made these declarations in time past, it is probably one of your favorite Psalms too. It is time you made this declaration and meant it. Then act like it and do not be afraid. David declared, "Though I walk through the valley of the shadow of death, I will fear no evil. Lord, for you are with me" (Psalm 23:4).

> Fear not! It is an instruction from the Lord to us this season, an instruction that comes because He has guaranteed our wellbeing through every situation we are facing. And we shall come through victorious.

Don't fear the authorities. Your heavenly Father is the head of all authorities. Don't fear people. Like the Psalmist asked, "What can mere mortals do to me?" (Psalm 118:6). Jesus said do not fear who can destroy the body but cannot destroy the soul" (Matthew 10:28). Don't fear the pandemic. You are above it in Christ Jesus. Like the Psalmist declared, you will not fear the terror of night, nor the arrow that flies by day, nor the pestilence that stalks in the darkness, nor the plague that destroys at midday. A thousand may fall at your side, ten thousand at your right hand, but it will not come near you" (Psalm 91:5-7). Only be cautious and take necessary responsibility. Above all, let your confidence be in God and His word.

Prayer

Heavenly Father, thank you for the confidence we have in you. We are quick in understanding the times and discerning the things we should do. Therefore, we have no fear of the seasons. For in all these things, we are more than conquerors through you who loved us. To you be glory. In Jesus' name.

Bible in one year // **Lamentations 1-2, Hebrews 10:1-18**

NOV 14

Blessed are the peacemakers, for they shall be called sons of God.
// **Matthew 5:9**

Pursue peace with all

"If it is possible, as much as depends on you, live peaceably with all men" (Romans 12:18). This is the word of the Lord to us today. As much as it is in your power, strive to live at peace with all men. Don't be the one that causes disharmony, don't be the one who enflames misunderstandings. Be the peacemaker in every relationship, as much as it depends on you. Maintaining peace with others is very important. It is true some people will not make it easy. However, choose to be the one that seeks to restore peace. Remember the words of Jesus, "Blessed are the peacemakers: for they shall be called the children of God" (Matthew 5:9). If you are not at peace with someone, use today to initiate a reconciliation.

> As much as it depends on you, pursue peace with all men. Be the one who pursues peace and initiates reconciliation. And you will be blessed.

It is part of your identity as a child of God to be a peacemaker. Don't wait on the other party when it is in your power to initiate reconciliation. Even if you were wronged, don't wait until they approach for reconciliation when you can initiate it. They might never do it. This is the gospel and the life we are called to live. That is what it means to pursue peace. As we are commanded in another place, "Pursue peace with all people" (Hebrews 12:14). Don't let your emotions get in the way of God's purpose for you and those around you. We have been given the ministry of reconciliation, a call to reconcile all men unto God (2 Corinthians 5:18). But we can only share the gospel with those with whom we are at peace.

What is at stake is more than your pride. It is a soul for whom Jesus died. Maybe you are just the only one that would ever share the good news with that person. Don't say, "I will never have anything to do with that one again". That will be your flesh talking. Walk by the Spirit and make no room for the flesh. Paul was appalled by the lawsuits among the Corinthian Christians that he asked them, "Why do you not rather be wronged? Why do you not rather let yourselves be cheated?" (1 Corinthians 6:7). Remember, "Vengeance is the Lord's" (Romans 12:19). The compromises and sacrifices you make for the sake of peace with others will not go unrewarded. That is why Jesus declared, "Blessed are the peacemakers".

Prayer
Heavenly Father, thank you for reconciling us to yourself and giving us the ministry of reconciliation to bring all men to you. Thank you for your wisdom at work in us to deal wisely with one another. We receive grace to be quick to apologize and quick to forgive for the sake of peace. In Jesus' name.

Bible in one year // **Lamentations 3-5, Hebrews 10:19-39**

> God is not unjust to forget your work and labor of love which you have shown toward His name, in that you have ministered to the saints, and do minister. // **Hebrews 6:10**

NOV 15

A labor of love

I remember walking home one day and thinking to myself. I had made much sacrifice of my time and stepped out of my comfort zone to run a home fellowship. This day, feeling tired, I pondered to what good it was all these sacrifices, particularly at a time some of my expectations seemed too slow coming. Then I heard a reassuring verse in my spirit, "God is not unjust to forget your work and labor of love which you have shown toward His name, in that you have ministered to the saints, and do minister".

"God is not unjust to forget your labor of love". These words spoke to me greatly and I pray it does to you too. That you will find renewed strength in your service for the Lord and His people. It is a labor of love. It is labor because it is work. It is demanding on your time and energy; it is demanding on your resources. Sometimes and very often, it is sacrificial. For it is service that anyone can hardly reward you for. In fact, your quickest path to frustration is to expect a reward from men for work the Lord has called you to do. There are more people who will not sure gratitude for the work we do in their lives. Jesus healed ten leppers and only one returned to show appreciation (Luke 17:11-19).

> Continue in your labor of love and never be discouraged especially when your labor is not matched by appreciation. God is not unjust to forget your reward.

Do it because you love the Lord and His people. Like Paul puts it, "The love of Christ compels us" (2 Corinthians 5:14). The love of Christ and their love for the saints was the driving force compelling the apostles. I can identify with that when I write daily for your spiritual progress. It is love for the Lord and my love for God's holy people. It is my joy to see you make spiritual progress through the illumination that comes from the word of God. Paul wrote to the Church in Thessalonica, "We remember before our God and Father your work produced by faith, your labor prompted by love, and your endurance inspired by hope in our Lord Jesus Christ" (1 Thessalonians 1:3). Paul saluted their labor prompted by love. And that is the bed rock of true commitment in Kingdom service – Love for God and love for the saints.

Prayer

Almighty God, thank you for your love that is in our hearts, that we have the capacity to love you and to love your people unconditionally. Let this love inspire our commitment in labor in your vineyard as we work, knowing that the reward is sure. Thank you for such assurance. In Jesus' name.

Bible in one year // **Ezekiel 1-2, Hebrews 11:1-19**

NOV 16

[...] whatever things are true, whatever things are noble, whatever things are just, whatever things are pure, whatever things are lovely, whatever things are of good report, if there is any virtue and if there is anything praiseworthy–meditate on these things. // **Philippians 4:8**

Think of these things

Paul defines for us the scope of things we should think about. Such things that are true, noble, just, pure, lovely, things are of good report, things with virtue, and things that are praiseworthy. He said, "Meditate on these things". He spells out what things we should let our minds dwell on. Do these descriptions qualify the kind of thoughts you dwell upon? What thoughts do you entertain?

This is one reason God gave you His word, to give you material for meditation. For what you meditate upon ultimately shapes and defines your life. He said to Joshua, "This Book of the Law shall not depart from your mouth, but you shall meditate in it day and night, that you may observe to do according to all that is written in it. For then you will make your way prosperous, and then you will have good success (Joshua 1:8). Don't spend time pondering on your inadequacies, limitations, and problems. These are not the things the Lord wants you to focus your thoughts on. It only leads to depression. He gives you His word as materialfor meditation. And if you go into the word, you will come out rejoicing. For you will find out that whatever it is that seems to impose itself as an obstacle has been dealt with.

> **The word of God gives you material for meditation, helping you to focus your mind on such things that are praiseworthy and have power to impact your life for the better.**

This is one blessing of Your Daily Light. It provides you with daily spiritual substance on which you can fix your thoughts, pondering on such noble things that will inspire faith, build courage, and propel you in the strength of the Holy Spirit to accomplish more. As you read, don't just look away. Take the word with you along in your day. It is something I started long ago in my life. I had a verse for my day. Sometimes I have my headphones with me, listening to edifying content and keeping my thoughts on the Lord, pondering on all that He has made us in Christ Jesus. How He has made us righteous, given us an inheritance, filled us with the Holy Spirit and commissioned us into the world, such thoughts that put springs in your steps. Think on these things and keep your mind stayed on the Lord.

Prayer

Heavenly Father, thank you for your word that gives me material for meditation and gets my mind on the right things. I denounce unhealthy thoughts and bring to captivity any that exalts itself against your knowledge. I have the mind of Christ. I think divine thoughts and find ease to set my mind on the right things. In Jesus name.

Bible in one year // **Ezekiel 3-4, Hebrews 11:20-40**

God also bound himself with an oath, so that those who received the promise could be perfectly sure that he would never change his mind.
// **Hebrews 6:17 NLT**

NOV 17

Don't doubt his promise

The writer of Hebrews shows us why we should not doubt God's promises to us. Are you holding on to a divine promise, then you can cling to it with all that is in you. don't doubt His promise. It always proves true. We read from the writer of Hebrews, "God also bound himself with an oath, so that those who received the promise could be perfectly sure that he would never change his mind. So, God has given both his promise and his oath. These two things are unchangeable because it is impossible for God to lie. Therefore, we who have fled to him for refuge can have great confidence as we hold to the hope that lies before us" (Hebrews 6: 17 - 18 NLT).

> **Don't doubt the promise of God to you. He has bound Himself by oath to fulfill every promise He makes. You can bank your life on it. It will prove true.**

The writer's logic is simple. It is common that people in an effort to justify their honesty or prove their sincerity, do so by oath. They say, "I swear to God". In fact, this is the reason in some courts of law, the witness is first presented a bible to take an oath. They bind themselves to a higher authority to show the audience or jury that their words can be trusted. So also, God took an oath, it was the oath to Himself since He can't swear by anyone else. He bound Himself by oath to convince us beyond any doubt that His promise is sure.

So now we have two things: First we have His promise which in itself is an infallible word. And we have His oath that binds Him to honor that unfailing promise. And the author shows us why God took an oath on His own promise. He did this so we who have fled to him for refuge might have great consolation and confidence that His promise will not fail. You can plan your life based on His promises and be sure you will not be disappointed in the end. That is why Paul could write, "For no matter how many promises God has made, they are "Yes" in Christ. And so, through him the "Amen" is spoken by us to the glory of God" (Corinthians 1:20 NIV).

Prayer

Heavenly Father, thank you for precious promises given to us and your oath that guarantees the promises. We are confident in you and unshaken in the face of adversity, knowing your word will prove true. Thank you for the manifestation of your promises are guaranteed in our lives. In Jesus' name.

Bible in one year // **Ezekiel 5-7, Hebrews 12**

NOV 18

It is written, "The first man Adam became a living being." The last Adam became a life-giving spirit. // **1 Corinthians 15:45**

A life-giving Spirit

When God formed Adam from the ground, the bible tells us, He "breathed into his nostrils the breath of life; and man became a living soul" (Genesis 2:7). This then became the first man with a human nature. This nature became passed on to every other descendant of the man, forming the humankind. This is the natural human nature, the Adamic nature. More so, this nature became subject to bondage after the sin of Adam. So the bible tells us, "Wherefore, as by one man sin entered into the world, and death by sin; and so death passed upon all men, for that all have sinned" (Romans 5:12).

> You are a life-giving spirit, that is the nature you have. And by that you are a communicator of divine life, virtues, and blessings.

This natural man became subject to bondage, sickness, poverty and all ills of sin in the world. But God in Christ Jesus had a game-changing plan, to raise up a new breed of people with a new nature – a divine nature. "By which have been given to us exceedingly great and precious promises, that through these you may be partakers of the divine nature, having escaped the corruption that is in the world through lust" (2 Peter 1:4). If you are in Christ, you have a new nature, a divine nature, distinct from the Adamic nature inherited at birth. Your new nature is recreated in the likeness of God (Ephesians 4:22-24).

Paul shares striking thoughts about this new nature we have. "The first man Adam became a living being... As was the man of dust, so also are those who are made of dust; and as is the heavenly Man, so also are those who are heavenly". Put together: Just as Christ is a life-giving Spirit, we also who now bear the same nature are life-giving spirits. This is true for you. You are a life-giving spirit. Particularly at this time of a pandemic, it is still God's plan for you to bring healing to those around you. don't be conscious about having a natural human nature that is subject to infection and spreads it to others. You bring life and health, you are a life-giving spirit, bringing divine life to those around you. Let this be your consciousness and your faith will prevail even at a time like this.

Prayer

Heavenly Father, thank you for the life we have in Christ Jesus, one that is not subject to bacteria and viruses. Rather, we will lay hands on the sick and they shall recover. We are not communicators of diseases and sicknesses because of the life-giving spirit in us. Our faith prevails. In Jesus' name.

Bible in one year // **Ezekiel 8-10, Hebrews 13**

For I know the thoughts that I think toward you, says the Lord, thoughts of peace and not of evil, to give you a future and a hope.
// **Jeremiah 29:11**

NOV 19

Your life matters

"I know the plans I have for you, plans of good and not of evil, to give you a hope and a future" (Jeremiah 29:11). This is the word of the Lord to you today. The very fact that you are alive is evidence that He is not done with you yet, He wants you on this side of life, He wants you on the earth. He has a plan for your life. Your life is not just a meaningless existence, your life matters to God. He values you as one of His vessels, prepared and relevant in the earth at a time like this.

Never let anyone convince you that you are useless. They might not see or find a use for you, but God does. You might not be important to them, and your life might not mean much to them, but it means everything to the Lord. He has positioned you as one of the runners in a relay race, He has given you a baton in your hand, a baton you must run along with until you meet the next person ahead of you who will pick it up from where you end. The Lord is counting on you. You are valuable for the success of that team in which He has placed you. Just as in a relay race; another team might not need you, that does not make you useless. It is not your team, that is why. Focus on your team, the environment, and people the Lord has associated with you, those you can impact.

Never give in to the lies of the devil that your life is worthless. Your life was worth the blood of Jesus, and much more, God can give up the whole world for you. Just as scripture assures us, "He who did not spare His own Son, but delivered Him up for us all, how shall He not with Him also freely give us all things? (Romans 8:32). The devil knows your value to God, He understands you being alive is a threat to his wicked schemes in the earth. The devil will prefer you were gone. However, he has no power over your life to take it. That is why he comes with lies of worthlessness to convince one about suicide so they can end their life. Never accept that. God wants you alive for His glory.

> **Your life matters to God and all those He wants you to impact with His word. Never let anyone make you think less of yourself, never let the devil convince you about ending your own life.**

Prayer

Heavenly Father, thank you for the gift of life. Thank you for the value you have given my life and the purpose for living. For through your word, I am made a messenger of goodwill and hope to my world, pointing the way of salvation to my family, friends, colleagues and those I can reach. In Jesus' name.

Bible in one year // **Ezekiel 11-13, James 1**

NOV 20

Do not be deceived: "Evil company corrupts good habits."
// **1 Corinthians 15:33**

Choose your associations wisely

Your associations are those you surround yourself with, those you keep a close walk with. As much as you are to pursue peace with all men and seek every opportunity to reach people with the good news of the gospel, you cannot be friend to everyone. You must choose your close associations wisely. The bible tells us, "He who walks with wise men will be wise, But the companion of fools will be destroyed" (Proverbs 13:20). Paul cautioned the Corinthians, "Do not be deceived: 'Evil company corrupts good habits'" (1 Corinthians 15:33). Your association has an impact on your life, for the better or for the worse. Don't deceive yourself by keeping a wrong association and saying it doesn't affect you. Choose your association wisely.

If an association is not contributing to your progress, and you are neither impacting the other person for the better, then it is time to evaluate its value and purpose. It should be serving one of you in faith, in career, in community life or something. If it is not inspiring your output or giving you an opportunity to be a blessing to others, then it is time to check again. It is ok to outgrow some connections. If after giving your life to Christ and being so long in the faith, your closest friends are still unbelievers, it is time for new close friends. For if you are not helping them find the Lord, they are definitely helping to cripple your faith in the Lord.

> While you pursue peace with all men, recognize you can not have all people in close association. Choose your associations wisely for it will impact your life.

Sometimes, it is a godly thing to end certain connections. Because they can only harm you. That is why Jesus said, "If your right eye causes you to sin, pluck it out and cast it from you; for it is more profitable for you that one of your members perish, than for your whole body to be cast into hell. And if your right hand causes you to sin, cut it off and cast it from you; for it is more profitable for you that one of your members perish, than for your whole body to be cast into hell" (Matthew 5:29-30).

Prayer

Heavenly Father, thank you for discerning hearts to choose our associations wisely. That we might identify and associate with the wise for our safety and wellbeing. That fools we will recognize, and in caution keep ourselves from harm's way. In Jesus name.

Bible in one year // **Ezekiel 14-15, James 2**

Don't do anything from selfish ambition or from a cheap desire to boast, but be humble toward one another, always considering others better than yourselves. // **Philippians 2:3 GNT**

NOV 21

Let this mind be in you

"Let this mind be in you which was also in Christ Jesus, who, being in the form of God, did not consider it robbery to be equal with God, but made Himself of no reputation, taking the form of a bondservant, and coming in the likeness of men. And being found in appearance as a man, He humbled Himself and became obedient to the point of death, even the death of the cross" (Philippians 2:5-8). That is humility, when you forget your high placement, when you forget who you are or what you have and act towards others of supposed lesser placement without exalting yourself above them.

It helps to look at the preceding verses from where this call comes. "Let this mind be in you which was also in Christ Jesus". The author was exhorting the believers, "Don't do anything from selfish ambition or from a cheap desire to boast, but be humble toward one another, always considering others better than yourselves" (Philippians 2:3 GNT). Do not be prideful. Do not use your position or resources against others, in a bid to prove your importance. If you are one in high office serving the community, serve them in humility. Do not act in pride as the one who holds the key to their future. Serve them in humility. Much so even should you act in humility towards those in the faith.

> **Be humble in your dealings towards others and do not let pride rule you. For the Lord resists the proud but gives more grace to the humble.**

Remember, "God resists the proud, but gives grace to the humble" (James 4:6). When the Lord is the one opposing you, no one can help you. And that is what you get when you choose not to be humble. Conversely, when you choose humility, you will find more grace and lifting with God. With Jesus our role model, having humbled Himself, the bible tells us, "Therefore God also has highly exalted Him and given Him the name which is above every name, that at the name of Jesus every knee should bow" (Philippians 2:9-11). This will be your story too as you walk in humility towards others, the Lord will lift you beyond your imagination.

Prayer

Heavenly Father, thank you for we have the mind of Christ. This season we receive the grace to relate with each other in humility, esteeming others better than ourselves. We humble ourselves in your presence, submitting to your will in all things so you will lift us up in due season. In Jesus' name.

Bible in one year // **Ezekiel 16-17, James 3**

NOV 22

> Assuredly, I say to you, whoever says to this mountain, "Be removed and be cast into the sea," and does not doubt in his heart, but believes that those things he says will be done, he will have whatever he says.
> // **Mark 11:23**

Maintain your confessions

Jesus assured us we will have whatever we say. If we speak words of faith, we will change situations and command supernatural results. And this is truly the way miracles are performed. Throughout scriptures, from creation till the end of the apostles' ministries as we have it on record, there was hardly a miracle performed without words spoken. It is the same law at work, the creative power of words.

Do not change your confessions of God's word because of unchanging circumstances. The circumstances will soon align with the divine proclamations if you do not quit confessing God's word.

Now it may happen sometimes that your declarations of faith seem to fail, and circumstances seem hesitant to change according to your proclamations. It is not for you to conclude that it does not work. In fact, if ever you were to change your mind and say this whole thing about words having power is a lie, it would already highlight the lack of faith that was there at the beginning. That might be the reason it proved a lie; because the faith needed for the words to prevail was never there. You should know already from the start there are no alternative outcomes – that is faith; when you know like you know your name, that it must be as it was declared. It is rather such times when you maintain your confessions irrespective of the unchanging circumstance. Something is definitely shifting already in the spirit. As Hebrews 10:23 assures us, "Let us hold fast the confession of our hope without wavering, for He who promised is faithful".

God did not design it for you to admit defeat and failure of His word if the situation seemed stubborn to change. It was never for you to change your confessions and embrace the situation. If you feel sick in your body, you are needing money for a divine vision and confessing healing or supplies, don't change your confession because change seems slow. Maintain your confession. Sometimes that is what it means to resist the devil. As the bible declares, "Resist the devil and he will flee from you" (James 4:7).

Prayer

Heavenly Father, thank you for the words on my lips are potent to cause supernatural changes in my life, my family, my health, my finances, my career and all that concerns me. As we continue to declare the word in faith, we will live to see the manifestation of the things proclaimed in Jesus' name.

Bible in one year // **Ezekiel 18-19, James 4**

Come out from among them and be separate, says the Lord. Do not touch what is unclean, and I will receive you. // **2 Corinthians 6:17**

NOV 23

A vessel unto honor

The young minister Timothy received a letter from His mentor. In it were written these words, "In a great house there are not only vessels of gold and silver, but also of wood and clay, some for honor and some for dishonor. Therefore, if anyone cleanses himself from the latter, he will be a vessel for honor, sanctified and useful for the Master, prepared for every good work. Flee also youthful lusts; but pursue righteousness, faith, love, peace with those who call on the Lord out of a pure heart" (2 Timothy 20-22).

In the words of Paul, he paints a picture of what we all are like in God's big family – we are vessels. As different as we are by our makeup, unique in our own ways, we can be likened to the different vessels you will find in a household – some of gold, some of silver and some of clay. But what is more striking is this: irrespective of the kind of vessel, the vessel that cleanses itself from iniquity will be a vessel for honorable use in the hands of the Master. It is the individual who decides if they will be a vessel unto honor or unto dishonor.

Paul was writing to Timothy regarding the necessity of a sanctified life, a life separated unto God. Yes, He has made us righteous; yes, He has made us Holy; yes, He has sanctified us. However, there is a separation from the world that is needed of us, when we consciously flee iniquity and the lusts of the flesh and conduct ourselves in righteousness. Some people miss the message of grace. They take it to mean we no longer have a moral code or standard for life. God has standards, standards for living. And we can live up to that standard when we learn to conduct and guide our lives by the word of God and be yielded to the Holy Spirit. Like He declared, "Come out from among them and be separate, says the Lord. Do not touch what is unclean, and I will receive you." "I will be a Father to you, and you shall be My sons and daughters, says the Lord Almighty" (2 Corinthians 6:17-18).

> **Irrespective of the individual we are, if we will set ourselves apart for the Lord, we will be vessels of honor, fitted for good works.**

Prayer

Heavenly Father, thank you for the Holy Spirit who works in me to will and do according to your good pleasure. Sin has no dominion over me. I walk in righteousness and flee from all that defiles. Therefore, I am a vessel in your hands, prepared for good works. I receive grace to be true always. In Jesus' name.

Bible in one year // **Ezekiel 20-21, James 5**

NOV 24

Do not remember the former things, nor consider the things of old.
// Isaiah 43:18

Don't hold onto it

For who, having heard, rebelled? Indeed, was it not all who came out of Egypt, led by Moses? Now with whom was He angry forty years? Was it not with those who sinned, whose corpses fell in the wilderness? And to whom did He swear that they would not enter His rest, but to those who did not obey? So we see that they could not enter in because of unbelief (Hebrews 3:16 - 19).

It was their past, the glory of their experience as slaves in Egypt that kept them from seeing what glory was ahead and awaited them in the promised land. They therefore became hesitant about moving and doing the things they ought to do to enter the glory that laid ahead of them. They became rebellious. For they mourned, "Who will give us meat to eat? We remember the fish which we ate freely in Egypt, the cucumbers, the melons, the leeks, the onions, and the garlic; but now our whole being is dried up; there is nothing at all except this manna before our eyes" (Numbers 11:4 -6).

> Do not let a glorious or negative past blind you from the glories of your future in Christ. There is always more in store!

The things they ought to be thankful for had become the very reason for their complains and their grip on the past was blinding them from the glory ahead. It was their past that cheated them out of God's best. And this is something we should watch against. Be it a glorious or a hurtful past, don't hold onto it. It only becomes a stumbling block for the future. God always has something better in store for us, better than the past and good enough to make for every loss. So, He says, "Do not remember the former things, nor consider the things of old. Behold, I will do a new thing, now it shall spring forth; shall you not know it?" (Isaiah 43:18 -19).

Prayer

Thank you, Heavenly Father because of your great love and plans for us. Thank you because the path of the just is like a shining light that gets ever brighter to the perfect day. Thank you for counting me a just one. Therefore, my path shines from glory to glory for the praise of your name. In Jesus name.

Bible in one year // **Ezekiel 22-23, 1 Peter 1**

> These trials will show that your faith is genuine. It is being tested as fire tests and purifies gold–though your faith is far more precious than mere gold. // **1 Peter 1:7 NLT**

NOV 25

Your faith is precious

Peter wrote, "To those who through the righteousness of our God and Savior Jesus Christ have received a faith as precious as ours" (2 Peter 1:1 NIV). He was talking to them about the same precious faith you also received when you heard the Gospel. It is the same faith you have. And that faith is precious. Don't underestimate its value. It is your most-prized possession. Romans 12:3 tells us, "God has dealt to each one a measure of faith" (Romans 12:3). God has given to each one of us a measure of faith.

Peter wrote to his readers at a time of difficulties, "These trials will show that your faith is genuine. It is being tested as fire tests and purifies gold–though your faith is far more precious than mere gold. So when your faith remains strong through many trials, it will bring you much praise and glory and honor on the day when Jesus Christ is revealed to the whole world" (1 Peter 1:7 NLT). He qualified your faith to be far more precious than gold, and that for good reason. Your faith is your most valuable possession as a Christian. For without faith, it is impossible to please God (Hebrews 11:6). And with that faith, nothing shall be impossible for you (Mark 9:23).

> Your faith is precious. It is your direct ticket to God and your shield against the devil. With your faith alive, you are invincible in all circumstances.

Before Jesus would ascend to heaven, one of His greatest concerns was for his disciples to have enduring faith. He said to Peter, "Indeed, Satan has asked for you, that he may sift you as wheat. But I have prayed for you, that your faith should not fail" (Luke 22:31-32). In another place, Jesus pondered, "When the Son of Man comes, will He really find faith on the earth?" (Luke 18:8). This is one reason the devil comes at you so strongly with challenges. He is seeking to bring you to a place where you totally lay down your faith. For your faith is a shield that can quench all his fiery darts. If you have faith, the devil cannot prevail against you. So do all to keep your faith alive. And fan that faith to be stronger. For with your faith, you are invincible.

Prayer

Heavenly Father, thank you for your word that inspires my faith and makes me invincible. With my shield of faith, I stand my ground against all the darts of darkness, prevailing in every battle and bringing glory to you. In Jesus' name.

Bible in one year // **Ezekiel 24-26, 1 Peter 2**

NOV 26

> Now thanks be to God who always leads us in triumph in Christ, and through us diffuses the fragrance of His knowledge in every place. // **2 Corinthians 2:14**

An aroma of God

Paul continues, "For we are to God the fragrance of Christ among those who are being saved and among those who are perishing. To the one we are the aroma of death leading to death, and to the other the aroma of life leading to life" (2 Corinthians 2:15-16). What a blessed assurance, that God always leads us in triumph in Christ. This means winning every battle, winning every course, coming through victorious in all circumstances. Another bible rendition puts it this way, "In the Messiah, in Christ, God leads us from place to place in one perpetual victory parade" (The Message).

> **We are God's aroma to our world as we bring in every place a fragrance of His knowledge. But those to whom our message is delivered will make their choice of what fragrance they receive, of life or death.**

Through us, God diffuses the fragrance of His knowledge in every place. We bring with us an aroma from God to our world. We are an aroma of God in every place we go, wherever we bring His knowledge. We change the atmosphere when we walk in. We bring in a sweet-smelling flavor of God's presence. We do not leave the room the same. We come in with a divine presence and power to cause changes in the lives of men. However, that aroma will be perceived differently by those we encounter.

To one group of people, we are an aroma of life, bringing to them the life of God. These are those who are open for salvation and respond in faith to the message we bring. These ones are saved unto eternal life. To them we are an aroma of life that leads to life. But to a second group of individuals who abhor our message, we are a stench of death. They see our life-saving message as a lie and path to bondage. These are the people who oppose our work and try to silence our voices. To them, they suppose we bring death. This second group of people resent our message and deny the life offered them in the gospel. They deliberately are choosing death. Therefore, to this second class of persons, we are an aroma of death leading to death. As for us, we remain an aroma of God in our world and continue to spread the fragrance of His knowledge to all.

Prayer

Heavenly Father, thank you for the victorious life we have in Christ Jesus. As your aroma to our world, we bring a fragrance into every place. We pray that the hearts of men will be yielded to our message so that we will be to them a fragrance of life leading to life. In Jesus' name.

Bible in one year // **Ezekiel 27-29, 1 Peter 3**

> Let him ask in faith, with no doubting, for he who doubts is like a wave of the sea driven and tossed by the wind. // **James 1:6**

NOV 27

The prayer of faith

My mom was once so sick and needing a life-saving surgery. I was a teenager and unskilled in the word of God. My mom was a teacher with a Christian mission at that time. Her colleagues gathered in our house before she would be brought away for the surgery to pray with us. This was something scriptural. Just as James wrote, "Is anyone among you sick? Let him call for the elders of the Church and let them pray over him, anointing him with oil in the name of the Lord. And the prayer of faith will save the sick and the Lord will raise him up" (James 1:14-15).

It was not long after this occasion of prayer that we received information from the educational board of the mission with which my mom was employed. It was a report from her manager who had received information that my mom would not survive, it was calling for her replacement as a teacher. Someone from the same group of people who prayed had gone away hopeless, that there was ever a possibility to recover. That one prayed, but it was never a prayer of faith. And this is the kind of prayer many people make. To them, prayer is just a form of wishful expressions to a God that is far off. They have no expectations of a result of the requests they make. Such prayers go unanswered. James tells us, "That person should not expect to receive anything from the Lord" (James 1:6-7).

Thank God my mom lived through her surgery. About two decades later, she is alive and strong, living for the glory of God. Others prayed with faith and God proved himself true. He saved her. It is not all praying that is a prayer of faith. Only a prayer of faith gets the job done. But what is a prayer of faith? A prayer of faith is one that is informed about God's will over a situation. As a result, the prayer is made with all confidence and full expectation of a change. Such a prayer expects no alternative answer. If it is a prayer for rain like Elijah did, then rain it must be. The prayer of faith is the prayer that does not take "No" for an answer. The prayer of faith stops at nothing until the desired result is obtained (Mark 7:24-30).

> **A prayer of faith is what gets the job done. It is the kind of prayer made based on knowledge of the will of God, such as inspires unshakable confidence and expectation of the desired outcome.**

Prayer

Heavenly Father. Thank you for the guarantee we have that our prayers are heard and answered. For everyone who asks, receives. In faith, we rejoice in expectation of answered prayers. In Jesus' name.

Bible in one year // **Ezekiel 30-32, 1 Peter 4**

NOV 28

> He who did not spare His own Son, but delivered Him up for us all, how shall He not with Him also freely give us all things?
> // **Romans 8:32**

He is willing

Sometimes it seems God is unwilling to answer our hearts' cries. But it is never true. He is willing. You might be looking at the year coming to an end with goals unrealized, prayer points seemed unanswered and expectations seeming far-fetched. Don't be convinced otherwise that God is unwilling to intervene. There is the account of a leper who was not too sure that the Lord was interested in his situation. He approached Jesus saying, "Lord, if You are willing, you can make me clean." Then Jesus put out His hand and touched him, saying, "I am willing; be cleansed." And his leprosy was cleansed (Matthew 8:2-3).

God is interested in your wellbeing; He is interested in your joy and is willing to bring His plans and purposes for you to full manifestation. Romans 8:32 tells us, "He who did not spare His own Son, but delivered Him up for us all, how shall He not with Him also freely give us all things?". There is nothing any more valuable than what He already gave up for us. He will stop at nothing. Remember this as you look forward to celebrating Christmas soon, it is also a reminder that He is more than willing to give us everything.

> **God is willing to fulfill His plans for you. He is willing to answer your prayers. He proved it all when He gave up Jesus for our sake.**

Maybe you just need to find out what the Lord is saying if a promise seems long coming. Or maybe you just need more patience as the writer of Hebrews tells us, "For you have need of endurance, so that after you have done the will of God, you may receive the promise: 'For yet a little while, and He who is coming will come and will not tarry'" (Hebrews 10:36-37). Don't let passing time kill your expectations in the fulfillment of divine promises or your confidence in the power of prayers. Know that God is willing and can do exceedingly more than all we can ever ask or think (Ephesians 3:20).

Prayer

Heavenly Father, thank you for your love that you so much lavish on us. We rest assured in your faithful promises and rejoice in your willingness and readiness to fulfill in us more than we can ever ask or think. To you be glory. In Jesus' name.

Bible in one year // **Ezekiel 33-34, 1 Peter 5**

Blessed is the man who trusts in the Lord, and whose hope is the Lord.
// **Jeremiah 17:7**

NOV 29

Trust in the Lord

The prophet Jeremiah cried out, "Cursed is the man who trusts in man and makes flesh his strength, whose heart departs from the Lord. For he shall be like a shrub in the desert, and shall not see when good comes, but shall inhabit the parched places in the wilderness, in a salt land which is not inhabited" (Jeremiah 17:5-6). The people were warned to not let their hearts depart from the Lord to trust on flesh. Same is the call for us today. Don't count on people like your God. Don't let anyone compete for placement with God almighty in your life. It is dangerous for you, and it is dangerous for them.

Now there are certain people who are great blessings to us, such people who have come into our lives purposed by God to help us fulfill our callings. Such people are valuable pillars of support and should be appreciated in that regard. However, do not expect from any of them what only God can be or do. Sometimes it is in human nature to prove unreliable. And this is one reason why you need to be cautious not to count on people in such a way that when they act in that nature you will be shaken.

> As much as you recognize and appreciate those people God has blessed you with, let not your heart depart from the Lord in trust. Trust in the Lord and let your hope remain in Him only.

God wants you to trust in Him. And there is where the magic is, trusting in the Lord and not letting your heart depart from him to trust in other things. Then Jerimiah completes his prophetic declarations, "Blessed is the man who trusts in the Lord, and whose hope is the Lord. For he shall be like a tree planted by the waters, which spreads out its roots by the river, and will not fear when heat comes; But its leaf will be green, and will not be anxious in the year of drought, nor will cease from yielding fruit (Jeremiah 17:7-8).

Prayer

Father thank you for the reminder that you are the source of all things. The earth is yours and its fullness altogether. The world and its people all belong to you. Help me to see in my heart any idols I have raised, that I might demolish them and give you the place you alone deserve. In Jesus' name.

Bible in one year // **Ezekiel 35-36, 2 Peter 1**

NOV 30

> We know that all things work together for good to those who love God, to those who are the called according to His purpose.
> // **Romans 8:28**

There is hope

It is never all lost so long as you are alive. Even in death, depending on if you had accepted Jesus, there is gain. Just like Paul said, "For me to live is Christ, but for me to die is gain". However, the focus here today is not on gaining in death. It is on embracing a new beginning particularly after an unpleasant turn of events. The scriptures says, "There is hope for a tree, If it is cut down, that it will sprout again, and that its tender shoots will not cease. Though its root may grow old in the earth, and its stump may die in the ground, Yet at the scent of water it will bud And bring forth branches like a plant" (Job 14:7 - 9).

> **No matter what situation we are in, there is sure hope if we are in Christ. A better future is guaranteed if we stay on course with Him.**

How much more you, a tree of righteousness, the planting of the Lord. There is hope for the righteous in all circumstances. And this is not a hope that disappoints. It is the hope of the realization of the sure word of God. That in the end, we will have more reasons to glorify Him. Just abide in the Lord like the tree planted by the waters, for at the scent of the living water, a regeneration is guaranteed (Psalm 1:1-3).

For indeed, "We know that all things work together for good to those who love God, to those who are the called according to His purpose". (Romans 8:28). We can hope for the better, even after we think we lost the greatest ever knew. There is hope for the one that is in Christ, that it will only get better. As it is written, "The path of the just is like the shining sun, that shines ever brighter unto the perfect day" (Proverbs 4:18). It doesn't matter how good the past might have been and how hopeless things seem now, there is an assurance of hope, a guarantee for better days to come. If only you will stay on the paths of the just.

Prayer

Heavenly Father thank you for the hope and assurance we have in Christ Jesus – a hope that does not disappoint. Thank you for your everlasting arms that bear us up in all things. Visit us at the points of our needs and help us to dream where we don't see a future. In Jesus' name.

Bible in one year // **Ezekiel 37-39, 2 Peter 2**

DEC EM BER

I have other sheep, too, that are not in this sheepfold. I must bring them also. They will listen to my voice, and there will be one flock with one shepherd. // **John 10:16 NLT**

DEC 1

Bring them in

These were the Words of Jesus, He was concerned about the lost. They might not have known him or accepted him yet, but among them, He sees His own. He longs to bring them in that they might be part of the fold where they truly belong. "For God knew his people in advance, and he chose them to become like his Son, so that his Son would be the firstborn among many brothers and sisters. And having chosen them, he called them to come to him. And having called them, he gave them right standing with himself. And having given them right standing, he gave them his glory" (Romans 8:29 - 30 NLT).

That was once your situation until someone through the sharing of the Gospel brought you in. "Once you were dead because of your disobedience and your many sins. You used to live in sin, just like the rest of the world, obeying the devil – the commander of the powers in the unseen world. He is the spirit at work in the hearts of those who refuse to obey God. All of us used to live that way, following the passionate desires and inclinations of our sinful nature. By our very nature we were subject to God's anger, just like everyone else. But God is so rich in mercy, and he loved us so much, that even though we were dead because of our sins, he gave us life when he raised Christ from the dead. It is only by God's grace that you have been saved" (Ephesians 2:1- 5 NLT)

> We are Christ's ambassadors; God is making his appeal through us. We speak for Christ when we plead, "Come back to God!" (2 Corinthians 5:20 NLT)

The testimony is shared of Benny Hinn, how he gave his life to Christ at a school where a few students gathered to worship the Lord. His encounter with the Holy Spirit at a Kathrin Khulmann meeting was also a result of a friend's invitation. Many may never get to know the friends of Benny Hinn by whom these invitations came, but the world impact of his ministry cannot be denied. Someone brought him in. It is time we accepted the responsibility to bring others in. You might never know what a generational impact you might be initiating.

Prayer

Almighty God thank you for making us ambassadors of Christ by whom you reach and bring in the lost sheep. We pray for willing hearts to go and for listening ears and ready hearts that will listen and receive your salvation so we can win and bring in the lost. In Jesus name.

Bible in one year // **Ezekiel 40-41, 2 Peter 3**

DEC 2

For as the Father has life in Himself, so He has granted the Son to have life in Himself. // **John 5:26**

Life as God has it

There is the popular Christmas Carol with lines, "And man will live forevermore because of Christmas day". That is great truth butt it is a partial truth. It echoes the very words of John 3:16. That is a very familiar verse. However, depending on the translation you use, some truth could be missed out like in the song above. John 3:16 says, "For God so loved the world, that he gave his only begotten Son, that whosoever believeth in him should not perish, but have everlasting life". This phrase, "Everlasting life" is the picture that stays with many – a life that lasts forever. And when other translations use the phrase "Eternal life", they are still using a synonym that emphasizes the same thing – living forever.

> **Because Jesus was born, man can have Zoe – the same life as God has it. You can therefore celebrate Christmas with understanding and great joy.**

Eternal life as used in John 3:16 means more than a life that does not end, it means more than everlasting life, although that is an aspect of the life. The word used there is the Greek word, "Zoe". This is the life we get by believing in Jesus. Zoe is the life of God, it is the God-kind of life. It is the life that makes God who He is. Zoe is divine life; it is life as God has it. This is what we get by believing in Jesus.

Just as Jesus said, "For as the Father has life in Himself, so He has granted the Son to have life in Himself" (John 5:26). This is exactly your story in Christ Jesus. As the Father has life in Himself, even so Has he given you to have life in yourself. You have life as God has it, exactly same life. You have Zoe. As Peter wrote, "Whereby are given unto us exceeding great and precious promises: that by these ye might be partakers of the divine nature, having escaped the corruption that is in the world through lust" (2 Peter 1:4). This indeed calls for celebration of Christmas this season with understanding that not only will man live forevermore, but much more, man can have life as God has it, because of Christmas day.

Prayer

Almighty God, thank you for a new day and the blessings with it. Thank you for sharing your life with us, making us partakers of the divine nature. Sickness and diseases have no dominion over me because of your life in me that is superior. I walk in health. I am a distributor of divine virtues. In Jesus' name.

Bible in one year // **Ezekiel 42-44, 1 John 1**

We have seen and testify that the Father has sent his Son to be the Savior of the world. // 1 John 4:14

DEC 3

A call to celebration

It is not new what December signifies to the world and what an event is commemorated in this season. It is the month of Christmas, the season of commemoration of the birth of Jesus, the savior of the world. There is indeed a call to celebration this season to everyone. While people might have different motives for celebration, and even others unmoved by the events, it does not pass anyone unnoticed. Therefore, more than ever before, we have an opportunity to give it its true meaning and redefine its purpose as believers in Christ Jesus.

December still announces a celebration for many including non-Christians. As Christmas is increasingly commercialized, businesses stand to make profit. As families reunite across the globe for the holiday, people will be meeting loved ones after a long time and in the process, enriching travel agencies with all the tickets bought. Yet for others, it is just the joy that a rough or a blessed year is coming to an end, a time to take accounts and be ready for a new page as January announces itself in the horizons.

> There is a call to celebration because the savior of the world was born. And though we have a thousand other reasons, Jesus is indeed the reason for the season.

While there be a million reasons to celebrate, Jesus remains the reason for the season, and on account of His birth we celebrate. Like the angel announced, "I bring you good news that will cause great joy for all the people. Today in the town of David a Savior has been born to you" (Luke 2:10-11). A world that had been subjected to bondage and decay finally had a glimpse of hope in the horizons. Humanity that had been enslaved by the devil was going to have eternal freedom. A new era of relationship with God was going to begin. That is such a call to celebration – the savior of the world was born! After the Samaritan woman had borne witness of Jesus and invited the whole city out to the well, the people after encountering Jesus agreed, "We now believe not only because of your words; we have heard for ourselves, and we know that this man truly is the Savior of the world." (John 4:42).

Prayer

Father, thank you for the grace to be alive this season; for lives preserved, families kept, visions realized, goals achieved, and expectations met. We also thank you for the challenges that made us look up to you. Thank you for a wind of celebration and all the blessings of this season. In Jesus' name.

Bible in one year // **Ezekiel 45-46, 1 John 2**

DEC 4

> You have come to Mount Zion and to the city of the living God, the heavenly Jerusalem, and to myriads of angels [in festive gathering].
> // **Hebrews 12:22**

A festive gathering

This passage describes your current location and state in the spirit – a reality many have not grasped. When you were born again, you were born into Zion, the heavenly Jerusalem. That is your present-day location. Spiritually, that is where you exist and from where you live. Just as at natural birth a child is born into this physical world, so at the point of new birth you were born into this heavenly environment called Zion with angels in festive Gathering. And this is not an occasion, it is the everlasting atmosphere of this new world into which you are brought when you make Jesus Lord of your life.

This Christmas season, while we seem to turn on a festive mood and get set for celebrations in a special way, it is important to know that we are just making special a celebration that is a daily thing, this season. We should celebrate the fact that Christ was born in every day. It is like commemorating your birthday. The fact that loved ones celebrate with you on your special day doesn't mean they value you any less on the other days. In fact, your birthday only provides a special occasion for them to reflect that value in a special way, in gifts, well wishes and declarations of love.

> **This festive season provides us an earthly opportunity to bring others into the experience of a daily heavenly atmosphere of festivity in the presence of God withChrist at the center of all celebrations.**

Even so is Christmas. It is not more valuable than any other day, nor does it make more meaningful the value of Christ's birth to the true believer. No! This is only a season in the earth when we try to bring the world and men to a special notice of the birth of our Lord and savior Jesus Christ. We seek to use it to bring others together into a glimpse of the experience of the festive gathering we should already be experiencing in every passing day – a festive gathering and celebration in Zion, a celebration in the company of myriads of angels, the spirits of righteous men made perfect, God the judge of all men and Christ Himself the mediator of the new covenant, the very center and focus of our celebration (Hebrews 12:22-24).

Prayer

Gracious and everlasting Father, thank you for bringing us into a foretaste of heaven's glory through the new birth in Christ Jesus. Open our eyes by your spirit to see the realities thereof that we might rejoice and sing even through the darkest nights, knowing that we are part of festive gathering. In Jesus' name.

Bible in one year // **Ezekiel 47-48, 1 John 3**

> Therefore let no one pass judgment on you in questions of food and drink, or with regard to a festival or a new moon or a Sabbath.
> // **Colossians 2:16 ESV**

DEC 5

Hijack the feasts

It is not uncommon during this season to come across people calling believers in Christ Jesus to boycott Christmas celebrations. Once I came across an elaborate writing with goal to dissuade Christians from celebrating Christmas. And this is not new. It is a parallel story regarding the 14th of February. Usually, same class of people have the same advocacy: Christians should have nothing to do with these feasts, they say. For both occasions, they have one justification. They argue that Christmas day like the Valentine's Day, have their origins in pagan feasts and celebrations.

However, if you go through scriptures to answer this question, you will only have the resolution to hijack the feasts. To hijack literally means to steal by stopping and interrupting the course of a moving vehicle and taking command to direct it to the destination of your interest. That is what peter did with the feast of Pentecost. It was a Jewish feast that wasn't about Jesus. It had been commanded by God and was an occasion of thanksgiving for the first fruits and more. The disciples of Jesus had joined in as part of a tradition, nonetheless this time they were using the opportunity to commune together as believers in Christ Jesus as they waited for the outpouring of the Holy Spirit.

> **Do not let anyone dissuade you with deluded philosophies about celebrating Christmas this season. Hijack the feast and make Christ the center of it all. Don't shun it but give it the meaning it is due.**

God chose that moment to send the Holy Spirit, baptizing all of them with fire like Jesus had promised. Then the people heard the believers speaking in tongues and were gathered around them in their thousands, claiming they were drunk (Acts 2:1-14). But Peter seized the moment, he hijacked the feast and made it about Jesus. Peter addressed the people, "Therefore let all Israel be assured of this: God has made this Jesus, whom you crucified, both Lord and Messiah... Repent and be baptized, every one of you, in the name of Jesus Christ for the forgiveness of your sins. And you will receive the gift of the Holy Spirit" (Acts 2:36-41 NIV). Like Paul cautioned, let no one pass judgement on you regarding festivals or celebrations, observations based on shallow opinions which lack spirituality (Colossians 2:16-18).

Prayer

Thank you Father for your mercies that are new every morning. We receive the wisdom to hijack moments like peter and make you the center of diverse feasts and gatherings. In Jesus' name.

Bible in one year // **Daniel 1-2, 1 John 4**

DEC 6

> One person esteems one day above another; another esteems every day alike. Let each be fully convinced in his own mind. // **Romans 15:5**

The Lord of the Sabbath

When you read through the bible, you will realize that the laws that were given to Moses were for a purpose. In certain portions of scriptures, we get insight into some of the reasons behind the instructions God gave His people. However, just like many today, the religious teachers in the days of Jesus missed out on God's line of thoughts and were caught up in the instructions of dos and don'ts. And one such example was about the Sabbath. The reason the Lord commanded the Sabbath as a day of rest was emphasized in Exodus 23:12, It was for the people, their servants, and their farm animals to rest and be refreshed. The Sabbath was also a day to worship because everyone could be off the fields for the Lord.

> *If you choose not to commemorate Jesus's birth at Christmas, let it be your decision. But know that it is also a godly thing to do so and don't judge others for celebrating.*

Jesus under attack with His disciples for searching for food on the Sabbath, called the attention of his accusers to realize that on that same day the people were commanded not to work, that was the day priests were called on duty. The priests worked on the Sabbath but did not transgress the law, they were innocent of sin in God's sight. Jesus also goes ahead to refer to David when he violated a heavenly protocol but was in effect blameless in the eyes of the divine. Jesus concludes by saying if they understood the ways of God, they would not condemn the innocent. (Matthew 12:1-8, 1 Samuel 21:1-9)

Today there are those making a religion out of the day of worship. They argue if Saturday or Sunday is the correct day to worship. Totally off course. Even so it is this season with all the religious people making loud calls and calling Christians away from commemorating the birth of Jesus, they are starting a pointless religious battle. But Paul said, „Who are you to judge another's servant? To his own master he stands or falls. Indeed, he will be made to stand, for God is able to make him stand. One person esteems one day above another; another esteems every day alike. Let each be fully convinced in his own mind. He who observes the day, observes it to the Lord; and he who does not observe the day, to the Lord he does not observe it (Roman's 14:5-6).

Prayer

Lord God almighty, thank You for Your grace and love continually lavished upon us. Thank you for the freedom to choose in Christ Jesus. We pray indeed that we may be of one mind as your people, tearing down all walls of division raised by erroneous human understanding of your word. In Jesus' name.

Bible in one year // **Daniel 3-4, 1 John 5**

Stand fast therefore in the liberty by which Christ has made us free, and do not be entangled again with a yoke of bondage. // **Galatians 5:1**

DEC 7

The snare of religiosity

Before Jesus came, God had called and set apart Israel as His chosen people and through Moses as the mediator of the first covenant, handed over to them sets of rules and regulations. These were laws full of dos and don'ts, ceremonial cleansing and sacrifices for different kinds of offenses. And all these were not instituted because God delighted in them. Someone wrote of the Lord, „In burnt offerings and sin offerings You have taken no delight" (Hebrews 10:6).

God was not as interested all the laws and sacrifices He commanded but he instituted them anyway with all the burdensome requirements. Why? For several reasons we can't share on today. One reason was to institute a guardian or tutor, a guide that could serve the people into right-living until Jesus came. That's why Galatians 4:3 says of the Jews and the law, „So we [Jewish Christians] also, when we were minors, were kept like slaves under [the rules of the Hebrew ritual and subject to] the elementary teachings of a system of external observations and regulations". Galatians 4:3 (AMPC).

Jesus came and the laws and its regulations becameobsolete – a lesson we should consider in the future (Hebrews 8:13). However, there were the Jews still trapped in the old covenant and its religious observations which in themselves had no power to save. These Jews were now trying to bring upon the new gentile believers this burden which they nor their fathers had been able to bear. And this is the kind of doctrines some ministers are trying to teach today, subjecting God's people to a life of bondage in religiosity over discussions of Christmas celebrations. So, I also find need just like Paul found to address this in his letter to the gentiles (Read Galatians 4). He was calling them to stand firm in the freedom Christ brought and not to let themselves be burdened with a yoke of slavery from teachers with a skewed understanding of scriptures.

> There is a freedom that was given us in Christ Jesus, a freedom from the law and religious burdens, a freedom you should not let anyone take from you.

Prayer

Heavenly Father thank you for the Illumination by your word that delivers us from the skewed understanding of others that we might walk in your ways and enjoy life while at it. Not being subject to bondage and the snares of religiosity. Thank you for teaching us rightly by your Spirit. In Jesus' name.

Bible in one year // **Daniel 5-7, 2 John**

DEC 8

> God demonstrates His own love toward us, in that while we were still sinners, Christ died for us. // **Romans 5:8**

Just in time

This Christmas season is one of the opportunities to be reminded of God's faithfulness when He said, "I will never leave you nor forsake you" (Hebrews 13:5). For at just the right time, He sent Jesus to die for our sins while we were helpless. We can be confident indeed that He would also show up in time in all things concerning us. He has promised He will not leave nor forsake you. He will not disappoint you. Just as it is written, "For He who spared not His own Son, but gave Him up for us all, how will He not also, with Him, grant us all things?" Romans 8:32.

The Psalmist had this confidence when he wrote Psalm 46. He talked about the security of the city in which God dwells. He declared, "There is a river whose streams shall make glad the city of God, The holy place of the tabernacle of the Most High. God is in the midst of her, she shall not be moved. God shall help her, just at the break of dawn" (Psalm 46:4-5). He was persuaded and knew that the city would not suffers shame, because God would intervene just in time. God was going to help the city at the break of dawn, just before it was bright enough for the world to see her distress and mock at her – at the break of dawn. He had every reason because He had seen God help him in diverse situations. Psalm 34:5 says, "Those who look to him for help will be radiant with joy; no shadow of shame will darken their faces".

> **Let the Christmas season remind you of God's timely interventions in the lives of His people and stir your faith as you hold fast to him for the fulfilment of pending promises, knowing He will intervene in time.**

What are you believing God for this season? What dreams seem unfulfilled even as the year closes out? What situation is it for you that seems to tarry and time passing without divine intervention? Know this day the Lord is with you and is fully involved. And you will see His glory revealed over the situation, and that, just in time. Remember the scripture that says, „You need to persevere so that when you have done the will of God, you will receive what he has promised. For, "In just a little while, he who is coming will come and will not delay." (Hebrews 10:36-37).

Prayer

Most High God, we rejoice in your faithfulness that we can trust you till the end knowing indeed that we will not see shame because we have trusted in your name. For every need and concern, we rest assured in your intervention that is always in time. We give you praise. In Jesus' name.

Bible in one year // **Daniel 8-10, 3 John**

Oh, clap your hands, all you peoples! Shout to God with the voice of triumph! // **Psalm 47:1**

DEC 9

A psalm of celebration

All you nations, clap your hands! Shout out to God in celebration! For the sovereign Lord is awe-inspiring; he is the great king who rules the whole earth! He subdued nations beneath us and countries under our feet. He picked out for us a special land to be a source of pride for Jacob, whom he loves. God has ascended his throne amid loud shouts; the Lord has ascended his throne amid the blaring of ram's horns. Sing to God! Sing! Sing to our king! Sing! For God is king of the whole earth! Sing a well-written song! God reigns over the nations! God sits on his holy throne! The nobles of the nations assemble, along with the people of the God of Abraham, for God has authority over the rulers of the earth. He is highly exalted! (Psalms 47:1)

> Make the season one of praise and thanksgiving as you celebrate the Lord like a Psalmist – with hymns and Psalms.

Paul exhorted the Ephesians, „Do not get drunk with wine, which is debauchery, but be filled by the Spirit, speaking to one another in psalms, hymns, and spiritual songs, singing and making music in your hearts to the Lord, always giving thanks to God the Father for each other in the name of our Lord Jesus Christ (Ephesians 5:18

This is not a call for those who have everything going well for them, it is a call to everyone as the very first line of that Psalm says. Paul was himself a good example in this light while locked up with his companion Silas. Luke wrote in Acts, „About midnight Paul and Silas were praying and singing hymns to God, and the rest of the prisoners were listening to them" (Acts 16:25 NET). And we know how it ended. The power of God was made manifest, and the prison gates were opened. They were set free. This is what you need to do, even when things seem contrary to expectations. Celebrate the season and sing songs of praise to the Lord while at it.

Prayer

Almighty God, Lord over all nations and people, be magnified in our hearts and in our eyes this season. That like the Psalmist, we will well up in praise and celebration, giving glory to your name. All the while knowing that You who has begun a good work in our lives will bring it all to completion. In Jesus' name.

Bible in one year // **Daniel 11-12, Jude**

DEC 10

He who did not spare His own Son, but delivered Him up for us all, how shall He not with Him also freely give us all things? // **Romans 8:32**

All things are yours

This is such a profound thought from the writer, he uses a very simple logic. If God gave up already the most precious thing you could ever imagine, what else would He withhold from you? And this Christmas season calls to remembrance this truth – God is not trying to withhold good from you, there is nothing in this world you desire that is not yours to have in Christ Jesus, so long as it is godly, brings glory to the Father and does not lead you into sin. He already gave you his possession of greatest worth, nothing else would be a difficult thing to give away.

> The Christmas season is a reminder that God who did not spare His son for your salvation will, with Him, make all things abound towards you as required for your life and destiny.

No doubt Paul writing to the Corinthians called their attention to the vast and boundless wealth God has for us in Christ Jesus. He wrote, "So don't boast about following a particular human leader. For everything belongs to you– whether Paul or Apollos or Peter, or the world, or life and death, or the present and the future. Everything belongs to you, and you belong to Christ, and Christ belongs to God (1 Corinthians 3:21-22 NLT). And in another place, it is written, „By his divine power, God has given us everything we need for living a godly life. We have received all of this by coming to know him, the one who called us to himself by means of his marvelous glory and excellence" (1 Peter 1:3 NLT).

This season, despite the challenges that the year might have brought, you have all reasons to hope for a blissful Christmas and a glorious new year, with every need supplied and all things made available for your advancement in destiny. Remember God can do exceedingly, abundantly above all you could ever ask, think, or imagine. Therefore, make room in your life to receive more and raise your expectations higher. Even as this season brings to you the reminder that He who did not spare His son but gave Him up for you will indeed supply all your needs according to His glorious riches in Christ Jesus (Philippians 4:19).

Prayer

Heavenly Father thank you for your daily load of benefits. You have given to us all things that pertain to life. We receive grace to see the opportunities and avenues by which they are delivered to us this season so that we would not miss out on that which you have for us. In Jesus' name.

Bible in one year // **Hosea 1-4, Revelation 1**

> Seek first the kingdom of God and His righteousness, and all these things shall be added to you. // **Matthew 6:33**

DEC 11

One thing is needful

Jesus had paid a visit to the sisters. While one sat at His feet, the other was caught up with all the preparations that had to be done (Luke 10:38-42). It was still about Jesus and for Jesus, however, she was missing out on the most important part of the occasion, she was missing out on the person of Jesus and the attention to His teachings, she was missing out on the central thing of the occasion. Was Jesus saying the other things were not important? Totally not. It was a matter of priority, He wished He first had the full attention of Martha. The preparations and food could come later.

There is such a tendency this season to fall into this trap without realizing. Particularly if you were raised up in a family where Christmas means gifts and new dresses, it is particularly easy to make this season a nightmare for others with wild expectations and demands of gifts and clothing, things that are in themselves not bad. However, remember only one thing is needful, a commemoration of Christ's birth and the salvation it announced.

> This Christmas season, only one thing is needful, a true commemoration and celebration of the birth of Jesus and a proclamation to the world its true meaning and the message of salvation.

Don't let the side things and aspects of the celebration take central stage. There are people who will get too busy cooking that they would not be able to make it for the Christmas Church service. There are people worrying over gifts for loved ones to whom they have never presented the gospel and who themselves might not be saved. And there are many with unbelieving friends who will not use the occasion to share the gospel and meaning of Christmas with them, though they will invite them over for dinner. Do not make these mistakes this season. Let Jesus be central stage, and the salvation He brought for all be our message. Seek first the Kingdom of God and the promotion of God's agenda while you celebrate (Matthew 6:33).

Prayer

God almighty, thank you for the opportunity to make amends and progress in our walk with you. This season as we celebrate and remember Christ's birth that brought us salvation, we receive grace to set our focus and priorities aright. That in it all, we will bring glory to you in our celebrations. In Jesus' name.

Bible in one year // **Hosea 5-8, Revelation 2**

DEC 12

Let us fix our eyes on Jesus, the author and perfecter of our faith.
// **Hebrews 12:2 BSB**

A journey of faith

Matthew recounts of wise men who saw the star announcing to them the birth of Christ. While they are most remembered for the gifts they brought, I want to highlight the very aspect of faith in operation that brought them through this journey. If you read the whole account (Matthew 2:1-12), you will have a clearer picture. Matthew wrote, "After Jesus was born in Bethlehem in Judea, during the time of King Herod, Magi from the east came to Jerusalem and asked, 'Where is the one who has been born king of the Jews? We saw his star when it rose and have come to worship him.'" (Matthew 2:1-2).

These men were discerning enough to recognize the star of the Christ when it appeared. They did not try to justify or explain away the supernatural manifestation. They leaped up in response to go worship Him, bringing with them gifts for the one, born King. However, they lacked full information regarding where the baby would be. Probably as a matter of reasoning, they imagined if a king were born, it would be in the palace. This is a plausible explanation for why they went to inquire from the King's palace. They did not realize the number of lives that would be jeopardized by their visit to Herod. He would later seek to kill every male child under two years of age in that region.

> Do not try to complete by human reasoning, a journey that was born of faith. Rather fix your eyes on Jesus, the author and finisher of your faith, and He will guide you all the way.

I am fully persuaded that the star was their guide all the while, but their minds fixed for the palace would not get them to just follow the star they saw without inquiring from men. After a failed attempt at the palace to get directions, they saw the star again and followed it in faith until their journey's end. The star was with them all the while, just at some point when they looked to men for direction, they evidently missed out on the divine. The journey that had begun by faith could only go smooth when they remained steadfast in faith with their eyes on the star. This too is true for you. If you began a journey of faith with the Lord, don't get caught up in your own understanding and reasoning on the way. You will have to fix your eyes all the way on Jesus, the author and finisher of that faith (Hebrews 12:2).

Prayer

Heavenly Father, thank you for your word of life that comes to us daily as a light for our path on this journey of faith with you. We receive grace to fix our eyes on Jesus, the author and finisher of our faith. We will not lean on our own understanding but follow as you lead us by your Spirit. In Jesus' name.

> Rejoice in the Lord always. Again, I will say, rejoice!
> // **Philippians 4:4**

DEC 13

A reason for joy

Irrespective of what is going on in the world and in your life, there is a cause for great joy. This was the message of the angel to shepherds, "Do not be afraid. I bring you good news that will cause great joy for all the people. Today in the town of David a Savior has been born to you; he is the Messiah, the Lord" (Luke 2:11 NIV). He urged them to cheer up and come out of their fright, for there was a reason for joy – the Christ was born. Even as we celebrate the season and commemorate the birth of Christ, we have a lot more reasons to rejoice and be exceedingly glad. The Christ was not only born, but much so, He died and rose again, bringing to fulfilment the very mission He had come to accomplish – He brought us out of the dominion of darkness into the Kingdom of God, making us children of God and joint-heirs with Himself to the throne of the Father (Colossians 1:13, Galatians 3:19, Romans 8:17).

> **You have more cause to rejoice today over the birth of Jesus than did the shepherds to whom His birth was announced. Rejoice therefore this season and be exceedingly glad.**

We have cause to rejoice more than the shepherds who heard the good news. To them was the announcement of the Christ's arrival, to us is the testimony of the fulfilment of the purpose of His coming. To them was the hope, to us is the reality and experience of the blessings. Even that much we have more cause to rejoice over the birth of Jesus, not as a helpless baby in a manger, but as the Christ and King of Kings, the author and finisher of our faith, the first born from among the death, the redeemer of our souls, the purchaser of our salvation, the hope of our glory, the bishop and watchman over our souls, our High Priest, the soon-coming king and much more.

Even if this season your joy is being choked by the events around your life, it is time to learn a lesson from Jesus. "Because of the joy awaiting Him, He endured the cross" (Hebrews 12:2). He looked pass the cross to the joy ahead. Jesus said of Abraham, "Your father Abraham rejoiced to see My day, and he saw it and was glad" (John 8:56). Now Abraham did not live in the days of Jesus, but through the eyes of faith He saw beyond his present into the promises of God and therefore welled up in joy. Same too can be true for you. You have reasons to rejoice always (Philippians 4:4). Much so, this season.

Prayer

Thank you, Heavenly Father for you have filled us with more joy than when the harvest of grain and wine of others abound. Thank you for the Holy Spirit and His joy as a fruit manifested in us. Therefore, we sing and dance even through the storms, knowing all will play out for good. In Jesus' name.

Bible in one year // **Hosea 12-14, Revelation 4**

DEC 14

> In Christ God was reconciling the world to himself, not counting people's trespasses against them, and he has given us the message of reconciliation. // **2 Corinthians 5:19 NET**

An opportunity for reconciliation

There is a popular song in some communities with the lies: "Christmas is the time for reconciliation, Christmas is the time for forgiveness". And how true that is! It is the commemoration of God's move to forever reconcile humanity to Himself. That is why Jesus came, so we could be reconciled to God and one to another. For when the love of God finds its way into the hearts of men, it inspires love and unity among them. Christmas really symbolizes this opportunity for a reconciliation between God and man that translates into a reconciliation among people, one with another.

> **Christmas indeed presents you an opportunity to be reconciled to others. Seize the opportunity this season and restore broken relationships as well as build new bonds.**

Therefore, use this season to be reconciled to those who in the year or before now had fallen apart with you. There is always an opportunity for a new beginning and that is even possible this season in your relationship with others. A simple text of „Merry Christmas" can set the ball rolling to restore years of separation and misunderstanding. Don't miss this opportunity to revive a relationship and build bonds of unity in your family and with others around you. Don't wait for the other person to initiate things, you are God's ambassador for reconciliation amongst men, reconciling men to God and reconciling people as well, one with another (2 Corinthians 5:19-20).

There is this interesting record in scripture: „When Herod saw Jesus, he was greatly pleased, because for a long time he had been wanting to see him...Then Herod and his soldiers ridiculed and mocked him. Dressing him in an elegant robe, they sent him back to Pilate. That day Herod and Pilate became friends – before this they had been enemies" (Luke 23:8-12). The occasion of Jesus' sentencing provided them with an opportunity for reconciliation. In like manner, seize the opportunity this Christmas season and be an ambassador for reconciliation with those in your world.

Prayer

Thank you, Heavenly Father, for your love that is poured out in our hearts, teaching us to love unconditionally as you do. We receive grace this season to forgive without reservation just as you have forgiven us in Christ Jesus. That we will look pass the excesses of one another. In Jesus' name.

Bible in one year // **Joel, Revelation 5**

I am confident of this very thing, that He who began a good work in you will perfect it until the day of Christ Jesus". // **Philippians 1:6**

DEC 15

A fulfillment of prophecy

As you read the gospels, particularly the accounts of Matthew, innumerable times, he makes mention of events and connects to the fulfilment of prophecy to demonstrate Jesus as the Christ. From conception, through birth and in His days of ministry, Jesus' life demonstrated a fulfilment of many things that were said by the prophets. For example, "All this took place to fulfill what the Lord had said through the prophet: 'The virgin will conceive and give birth to a son, and they will call him Immanuel'" (Matthew 1:22-23 NIV). Even so the commemoration of this season should be a reminder of God's commitment to make good His word to you in the right season.

It was not only of Jesus. Even your life is a prophecy in God. Just like the Psalmist declared, "You saw me before I was born. Every day of my life was recorded in your book. Every moment was laid out before a single day had passed. Psalm 139:16 (NLT). The Lord himself said to Jerimiah, „Before I formed you in the womb I knew you, before you were born, I set you apart; I appointed you as a prophet to the nations." (Jeremiah 1:5). Then He added in Jeremiah 29:11, "I know the plans I have for you, plans to prosper you and not to harm you, plans to give you hope and a future".

This season, ponder on God's faithfulness and His commitment to make manifest His word in your life. He said to Jacob, I am with you and will watch over you wherever you go, and I will bring you back to this land. I will not leave you until I have done what I have promised you." (Genesis 28:15). He says that same word to you today. Paul understood this. That is why He could wrote to the Philippians and declared, "I am confident of this very thing, that He who began a good work in you will perfect it until the day of Christ Jesus.

> **Just as Jesus was born of prophecy and fulfilled prophecy, even so your life in Christ is the unfolding of a divine prophecy – a prophecy that will not fail.**

Prayer

Thank You dear Lord for the blessing of a new day. Thank you for I am the work of your hands, a product of prophecy. Even as you fulfilled your words of promise in the life of Jacob and Joseph, even so you are watching over the words you have spoken concerning me to bring them to fulfilment. In Jesus name.

Bible in one year // **Amos 1-3, Revelation 6**

DEC 16

A prudent person foresees danger and takes precautions. The simpleton goes blindly on and suffers the consequences. // **Proverbs 22:3 NLT**

A call to watchfulness

The Christmas season provides us with opportunity to revisit the accounts around the birth of Jesus, and with that, many lessons to learn from the circumstances and situations that unfolded. One such lesson is the call to watchfulness, looking out to know what the Lord is saying and what we ought to do. It is written of a tribe of Israel, "From the tribe of Issachar, there were 200 leaders of the tribe with their relatives. All these men understood the signs of the times and knew the best course for Israel to take". (1 Chronicles 12:32 NLT). This was the case of the wise men who followed the star to see Jesus.

First, they had discerned the star announcing the birth of Jesus and responded by setting out to look for the one who had been born king. On their return journey, they were led not to go back the way they had come, and this for the safety of the Christ (Matthew 2:1-12). Like the sons of Issachar, they understood the times and knew what they ought to do. They were watchful and attentive to not miss out on divine instructions. "For God speaks again and again, though people do not recognize it. He speaks in dreams, in visions of the night, when deep sleep falls on people as they lie in their beds. He whispers in their ears and terrifies them with warnings... He protects them from the grave, from crossing over the river of death". (Job 33:18 NLT)

> **There is a need to be watchful and alert to what the Lord is saying in season, for He will bring us words of Guidance and lead us out of trouble.**

In like manner, after they left, Joseph received a warning in a dream, an instruction regarding what He ought to do for the safety of the little boy Jesus - to run to Egypt (Matthew 2:13-15). You see, this reminds us of the many natural disasters and sometimes accidents in which Christians lose property or life. Sometimes the intervention of the Lord is with instructions to run to safety elsewhere. But because people don't perceive, they perish or suffer loss and in the end the question becomes, "Why did God let that happen?". No, it wasn't God's orchestration. Like the bible says, "A prudent person foresees danger and takes precautions".

Prayer

Heavenly Father, thank you for Your Spirit who shows us things to come and guides us in the way of safety and profit. Help us to recognize your messages delivered to us that we would not suffer harm and loss like people without knowledge. But with discerning hearts, we will know your will. In Jesus' name.

Bible in one year // **Amos 4-6, Revelation 7**

> Rejoice with those who rejoice, and weep with those who weep.
> // **Romans 12:15**

DEC 17

A parallel miracle

Parallel to the miraculous virgin birth of Jesus, was the miraculous conception of John the Baptist by Elizabeth his mother. Just the one preceded the other by six months (Luke 1:30-37). As the story unfolds, both pregnant women meet and exult in joy and praise for the wondrous works of the Lord. What strikes me is that two miracles of great blessings had been programmed by the Lord for two separate women, however the one preceded the other by six months. And this is how our lives really play out sometimes.

Particularly if you were to look around as the year draws to a close, as many unfulfilled expectations you might still have, you might look around to realize a friend or a neighbor in celebration over the same things you are still trusting God for. Maybe some finance, maybe a job, a partner or a promotion. Don't get envious and downcast as you look at them, asking the Lord, "Why me?". No! Their blessing is a testimonial that God is working other miracles in parallel, and you are next in line. Join them in celebration for the goodness of God in their lives. And if you are that one who already got the expectation others are still praying, be an encouragement to them and inspire their faith that they might look to the Lord who was gracious to you.

> As you look around this end of year and see others in celebration or mourning, have no complex: envy or pride over them. For God is working other miracles in parallel and will not leave anyone out.

As we wrap of the year there are many whose lives were impacted negatively by the loss of a loved one, a property or a job. As much as there are of those who had a multiplication of blessings, received new babies, some celebrating weddings, promotions, and job bonuses. Let us not in our feasting, ignore the pain of the mourning and hurting. On the other hand, let us not let our grieve becloud everything that we fail to join those in celebration with thanksgiving for what the Lord has done for them. You are in competition with no one and should recognize that. Remember what scripture says, "They, measuring themselves by themselves, and comparing themselves among themselves, are not wise". (2 Corinthians 10:12).

Prayer

Heavenly Father, thank you for bringing us through different paths with different experiences. Be they good or unpleasant. We will rejoice with them that rejoice or comfort those who mourn. Let no root of envy or jealousy spring forth in our hearts, rather in unity and love that wells up in praise. In Jesus' name.

Bible in one year // **Amos 7-9, Revelation 8**

DEC 18

> Though I bestow all my goods to feed the poor, and though I give my body to be burned, but have not love, it profits me nothing.
> // **1 Corinthians 13:3**

Let love lead

Paul was writing to the Corinthian Christians, Urging them to emulate the example of the Macedonian Church in giving (2 Corinthians 8:1-5). To sum it up, he spelled out the driving force behind their ability to give so generously: a giving springing from a place of lack and abounding beyond expectations. They gave themselves first, love was the compelling force – love for God and love for the saints. This was the same example of the Father revealed in John 3:16. God's great love for the world compelled Him to give up Jesus as the sacrifice for our sins.

> **As you overflow in giving this season towards others, let love be the driving force for only then will your giving profit you in heavenly reward.**

When Jesus came on the scene, He didn't fall short in this example. He declared to his disciples, "Greater love has no one than this, than to lay down one's life for his friends". (John 15:13). He first gave Himself. And Paul uses this argument to let us know why we can expect to receive all things freely from God. "He who did not spare His own Son, but delivered Him up for us all, how shall He not with Him also freely give us all things?" (Romans 8:32).

The secret behind the generosity of the Macedonian Church was the love that led them to giving, an emulation of both the Character of the Father and of Christ. This Christmas season is not about gifts but it will not go without them. You sure have a list of persons at heart already. Whatever the gift might be, let love lead. Don't do it as a lobbyist for the benefit it will bring to you in return. Do it with the God-kind of love, the love that gave its best even when it had "nothing" to gain. He gave it all for our sake. Check your heart this season as you distribute gifts and let love lead. Remember, "Though I bestow all my goods to feed the poor, and though I give my body to be burned, but have not love, it profits me nothing".

Prayer

Heavenly Father thank you for such great love that compelled you to give Jesus for our sins. We receive grace this season to emulate that example in our lives as we share in love with one another, putting love first. Let our giving reflect Christ and showcase your selfless love in Jesus name.

Bible in one year // **Obadiah, Revelation 9**

> The Berean Jews were of more noble character than those in Thessalonica, for they received the message with great eagerness and examined the Scriptures every day to see if what Paul said was true. // **Acts 17:11**

DEC 19

New age pharisees

In our walk with God and ministry to the saints, it is easy to not realize how quick we could conceive false doctrines from a twisted understanding of the Scriptures. Without realizing, we easily become the very teachers of the Law in the days of Jesus, the Pharisees and the Sadducees. These were people who had taken upon themselves the responsibility to teach and guide others. They were zealous and committed, but often walking in capital error regarding scriptures. They had many misleading doctrines that did not have their foundation in sound knowledge of the word. Even so today we have new age Pharisees -teachers of the word with erroneous doctrines

In the process, they became blind guides leading people away from the truth of God's word. Here was Jesus, the long-awaited Christ with them, but they could not recognize him (Matthew 23:16-18). In fact, they made themselves an opposition to whatever He taught, finding fault in His teachings, and discrediting Him among the people. Jesus called them blind guides. What was the reason for their blindness and heresies? Jesus once gave them their diagnosis. He said to them, "You are mistaken, not knowing the Scriptures nor the power of God. (Matthew 22:29).

> There are teachers of the word who teach error because of their limited understanding of certain aspects of the Bible. Be yourself one who searches the scriptures to validate the things you learn.

Even so we have teachers of the word who in this season lack a full knowledge of God's word and in their zeal, are misguiding the saints about Christmas. They leave the central theme of the Gospel and are focused on erroneous doctrines about Christmas celebrations, Christmas trees and forbidden foods and drinks. Don't let anyone deceive you. Like the Berean Christians, you have the responsibility to deliver yourself from false teachings and doctrines. It is written of them, "They received the word with all readiness, and searched the Scriptures daily to find out whether these things were so".

Prayer

Thank You Heavenly Father for your unfailing love. Thank you for teachers and ministers in your word. We pray you inspire them aright and guide them in truth that they might not mislead your flock. We receive grace to search the scriptures and the wisdom to discern truth from heresy. In Jesus' name.

Bible in one year // **Jonah, Revelation 10**

DEC 20

*Train up a child in the way he should go, and when he is old he will not depart from it. // **Proverbs 22:6***

Educate the kids

Jesus gave Peter charge to feed His lambs and His sheep (John 21:15-16). It is important to note that it was with a similar emphasis that he gave both instructions. I can even imagine it was with the same tone. This is very important to bear at heart particularly as a parent or one positioned in the life of a kid with an opportunity to influence or educate them. Realize that as much an emphasis as the Lord places on teaching the adult, that same he does on teaching the babes. In fact, if you fail to teach the babes in season, you will have a much harder time training them as adults.

Some parents don't take the opportunity at Christmas to teach their kids foundational truths in Christianity, not even about Jesus' birth and the purpose of His coming. They are focused on all the gifts they can get for them and the feasts around it, but the central theme is ignored. Sometimes, it is even common that when some parents bring their kids with them to church, they drag them along to the adult section and not let them go to the kids' department where they have lessons tailored for their age and level of comprehension. My own father did this. I sat with him many Sundays in adult services as a kid. We would not miss church, but I often attended the adults service, sitting next to my dad through the sermon when I was age 3 until about 6.

> **Even this Christmas season, seize the opportunity to teach the kids within your reach the true meaning of Christmas and build a foundation for life.**

The reality is that many parents and sadly, some pastors along with them, see the kids' department as the place where we should keep the kids busy in play while the adults have their lessons. They have a picture of a nursery, where the babysitters keep the children far from the place where the serious things are happening. If you ever were in this group, God is calling for a change. He places even much more emphasis on the spiritual education of the child. Instruct them in the way of the Lord while they are tender, and you won't need handcuffs on them when they are older (Proverbs 22:6). If Jesus said feed my lambs, it means there is food they can chew, a syllabus for their age and spiritual content for their level. Educate the kid in the Lord!

Prayer

Heavenly Father, thank you for the privilege to be an educator and enlightener of many as the light in my world. I receive grace to help the children you send my way to find Christ and His word. We are enabled to raise a godly generation that will bear the torch of the Gospel in this dark world. In Jesus' name.

Bible in one year // **Micah 1-3, Revelation 11**

Behold, I stand at the door and knock. If anyone hears My voice and opens the door, I will come in to him and dine with him, and he with Me. // **Revelation 3:20**

DEC 21

Make room for Him

There is a classic Christmas carol with these amazing lines: "Joy to the world! The Lord is come. Let earth receive her King! Let every heart prepare Him room!" This song echoes the call from David. He wrote, "Lift up your heads, O you gates! And be lifted up, you everlasting doors! And the King of glory shall come in" (Psalms 24:7). This passage is a call to open the gates for the king. It was prophetic of the ascension. However, it is a parallel truth to the fact that there are doors to open for the unhindered entry of the King.

John wrote in Revelation, speaking of Jesus, "Behold, I stand at the door and knock. If anyone hears My voice and opens the door, I will come in to him and dine with him, and he with Me" (Revelation 3:20). It is the call this season, to evaluate our lives and check our hearts to see if the gates are wide open for the King. He wants to come in and fellowship with us. While we might even have Him already in our lives, there is yet a greater call, to make Him Lord over every aspect of our lives and families.

> While we celebrate the season as if to receive Christ into the world, there is a call to make room for Him as Lord in your heart and in every aspect of your life.

Without realizing, there are times we close other areas of our lives to the Lord. For example, we can give him everything so long as it doesn't touch on our finances. We call him Lord but we have not given him the authority to define the kind of people we should relate with. Some are knowingly going to marry a nonbeliever. It is not acceptable in His sight, and He wants you to do it right. He has to have a say in every area of your life, defining the way you go about everything. Only then is He truly Lord of your life. Make room therefore this season, for the King in all things by opening up all doors for him.

Prayer

Lord God almighty, be magnified above all things this day. We open up our hearts and our lives and give you right of way. We surrender to the Holy Spirit, that like a driver, He will take the wheel in every area of our lives and lead us in the paths of righteousness for His name's sake. In Jesus name.

Bible in one year // **Micah 4-5, Revelation 12**

DEC 22

For with God nothing will be impossible. // Luke 1:37

A miracle

The birth of Jesus was a miracle, one that remains a subject of controversy until today. How could a baby be born of a virgin? It was a miracle. From time immemorial, scholars have contested not only the virgin birth, but even the reality of Jesus ever existing. We might have gone pass the debate of whether Jesus ever lived, but the truth of the virgin birth is thought a myth and yet to be grasped by even some who believe in Jesus. But it happened just as it was prophesied, "The virgin will conceive a child! She will give birth to a son and will call him Immanuel" (Isaiah 7:14).

> God is still presently working miracles, and He will perfect that which concerns you.

It was a miracle. That's why it will forever remain controversial. For miracles are phenomenal happenings that defy logic or normal trends. It beats reasoning and does not fit into the norm. If it can be explained logically as fitting to a known trend, then it is not a miracle. If every logic adds up, it is short of being classified a miracle. But when all facts suggest impossibility, then a miracle is defined. Remember, „With God nothing will be impossible" (Luke 1:37). This is not to make light the little things we gladly call miracles.

During this season, it's a call to remembrance that miracles do happen. It might never have taken place before, but God is still in the miracle business, making the impossible possible, initiating new beginnings and fulfilling His purposes. And He is doing that in your life this season, operating His miracles for your good. Believe in miracles and live in the expectation of miracles. It is God's desire to keep us amazed with the unfolding of His wonders.

Prayer

Thank you, Heavenly Father, for your love and commitment towards us. Thank you for the miracle birth of Jesus for the salvation of our souls. We remain confident that you will perfect that which concerns us through your miracle-working power. In Jesus' name.

Bible in one year // Micah 6-7, Revelation 13

> Honor those who are your leaders in the Lord's work. They work hard among you and give you spiritual guidance. Show them great respect and wholehearted love because of their work.
> // 1 Thessalonians 5:12 - 13 NLT

DEC 23

Honour your ministers

We live in a time and generation when ministers of the gospel and servants of God are treated with such disregard and disrespect more than ever before. And sometimes for good reason. For many who are driven by their own selfish ambitions, preying upon the ignorance of gullible individuals, have misrepresented who a minister is.

Do not let the falsehood in the world by false ministers blind you from all the blessedness of having those sent to minister to you. Recognize them and give them all the respect and honor due them. The scripture declares, "No one can become a high priest simply because he wants such an honor. He must be called by God for this work, just as Aaron was" (Hebrews 5:4 NLT). It is indeed a high calling and an honor to be a minister, one that only comes from the Lord. And God calls you to respect and honor them in that regard, for in it is a blessing for you. Remember the words of Jesus to those He sent, "Anyone who receives you receives me, and anyone who receives me receives the Father who sent me". (Matthew 10:40 NLT)

Ministers, are God's gift to you for your edification and spiritual progress, shepherding and guiding you to the pastures and fountains of life in Christ. Ministers were given to you to prepare you for works of service as we together fulfill God's purpose in the earth. Paul wrote, "Now these are the gifts Christ gave to the church: the apostles, the prophets, the evangelists, and the pastors and teachers. Their responsibility is to equip God's people to do his work and build up the church, the body of Christ. This will continue until we all come to such unity in our faith and knowledge of God's Son that we will be mature in the Lord, measuring up to the full and complete standard of Christ (Ephesians 4:11-13 NLT).

> **Honor those who labor for your spiritual well-being in the Lord and be a blessing to them, particularly this season. Think of ways to be a blessing this season to those who sacrifice for your spiritual wellbeing.**

Prayer

Heavenly Father, thank you for the gifts of ministers and shepherds after your own heart who labor tirelessly for the spread of your word, the expansion of your kingdom and the growth of your saints. This season we receive grace to respect, honor and bless them materially in a worthy manner. In Jesus' name.

Bible in one year // **Nahum, Revelation 14**

DEC 24

> Whoever gives one of these little ones only a cup of cold water in the name of a disciple, assuredly, I say to you, he shall by no means lose his reward. // **Matthew 10:42**

A reward for you

Scriptural principles are simple and time-tested. Irrespective of how you feel about a spiritual truth, your opinion doesn't change its reality. And one such truth that is under attack and misconception today is giving to ministers of the Gospel or for the work they are doing, they that labor in and out of season for your spiritual well-being. They are a blessing to you. Be it the pastor of your local Church or a spiritual instructor from afar, much like we are reaching you with Your Daily Light wherever you are.

Never be mistaken, there is a reward for you, a heavenly blessing that the Father sends your way when you give to His servants or for the work they are doing. What you might never know is the financial challenges and need of resources many ministers have. Sometimes you never realize what other avenues of income they have sacrificed to make themselves available for your edification and spiritual growth. While they might not come to you with an open request, make it your responsibility to check and see how you can be a blessing to them. Like Jesus guaranteed, "You shall by no means lose your reward"

Recognize the opportunity for your blessing in giving to they that minister to you and for the work of the ministry God has entrusted in their charge and use it, even this season.

Recognize the opportunity for your blessing in giving, and learn a lesson from the widow of Zarephath (1 Kings 17:11-16). Even in her lack, she gave in faith to one sent by God. And what was supposed to be her last meal was blessed for her sustenance through a season of famine. The Bible records, "The bin of flour was not used up, nor did the jar of oil run dry, according to the word of the LORD which He spoke by Elijah. (1 Kings 17:16). In same manner, after Paul Received the supplies of the Philippians to Him, he proclaimed the blessings, "My God shall supply all your need according to His riches in glory by Christ Jesus. (Philippians 4:19). In your giving this season, remember those ministers who have been a blessing to you. You can also Contact us for details on how to give to Your Daily Light as we continue to sponsor the distribution of free copies of this devotional and the spread of the Word.

Prayer

Heavenly Father, thank you for blessing us with all things that pertain to life and godliness. As we seek first your kingdom, all other things are added unto us. As we share through giving with them that minister to us this season, our bands will overflow in a rich harvest of blessings. In Jesus' name.

Bible in one year // **Habakkuk, Revelation 15**

The Lord is my strength and my defense; he has become my salvation.
Shouts of joy and victory resound in the tents of the righteous:
"The Lord's right hand has done mighty things! // **Psalm 118:14-15 NIV**

DEC 25

Shout for joy

In certain portions of scripture, we are called to exult for Joy, to burst out in celebration. And that for good reasons. The Psalmist had many reasons to call us to shout for joy. He wrote, "Come, everyone! Clap your hands! Shout to God with joyful praise! For the Lord Most High is awesome. He is the great King of all the earth. He subdues the nations before us, putting our enemies beneath our feet. He chose the Promised Land as our inheritance, the proud possession of Jacob's descendants, whom he loves" (Psalm 47:1 - 47:4 NLT)

Today also provides us who commemorate the birth of Jesus one such reason to shout for joy. Let the sound of joy be heard in your home as you celebrate the birth of Jesus Christ. For it is a testimony to others outside of what the Lord is doing in your home. And even if you be one of those who believe Christmas should not be celebrated, you still have a cause to burst out in shouts of joy if you are in Christ Jesus. For His birth brought you salvation, your freedom from the dominion of darkness.

> Let sounds of joy be heard from your homes as you celebrate the birth of Jesus that brought salvation to us.

It might even be such a season seeming to end on a bad note for you because of the loss of a loved one, a job, or just physical discomfort resulting from a health situation. It is important to remember that "All things work together for good to those who love God, to those who are the called according to His purpose (Romans 8:28). Then you will rejoice even as Paul admonished, "Rejoice in the Lord always. Again, I will say, rejoice! (Philippians 4:4)

Prayer

Glorious God, we rejoice today in the birth of Jesus and the salvation it brought to us. We thank you for the opportunity to bear witness of your love and mercies made available for all men. Even this season as we celebrate, we thank you for new testimonies and fulfilled expectations. In Jesus' name.

Bible in one year // **Zephaniah, Revelation 16**

DEC 26

> If anyone loves Me, he will keep My word; and My Father will love him, and We will come to him and make Our home with him.
> // John 14:23

After the feast

For many, the 24th and 25th of December are the chosen dates to celebrate Christ's birth. In Russia, it actually happens to be celebrated on the 7th of January when compared with the rest of the world. Whichever the date, Christmas is certainly a yearly feast for many. The Israelites had such an annual celebration, it was the feast of the Passover. Now Jesus on the scene, joined in along with His parents to the feast at the age of twelve. But unfortunately, His parents assumed He was with them after the feast and went a day's journey without Him. They left Jesus behind. It was only three days later that the found the child in the temple, sitting and listening to the teachers and asking them questions (Luke 2:41 - 45).

> **Beyond the celebrations, check to be sure you are on course with Jesus. Make no assumptions. It might be very costly!**

It is sad to see the way some people go about Christmas celebration; they have no understanding of the event being commemorated and the sanctity of the occasion. These people make it an opportunity for every sensual indulgence, an opportunity for what the Bible refers to as wild parties, orgies or lasciviousness, all lusts of the flesh (Galatians 5:19). They leave Jesus out. While others truly celebrate Jesus, it is nothing beyond this feast, they leave him behind and lead lives with Him out of the picture.

The call today is for you to consider your ways and examine your life. Be sure that beyond the feast, you are on course with Jesus. Make no assumptions like His parents. Jesus Himself declared what that will be like: "Many will say to Me in that day, "Lord, Lord, have we not prophesied in Your name, cast out demons in Your name, and done many wonders in Your name?" "And then I will declare to them, "I never knew you; depart from Me, you who practice lawlessness!" (Matthew 7:22 -23). Beyond Christmas, continue your walk with the Lord by continuing in the word (John 14:23).

Prayer

Heavenly Father thank you for the gift of a new day. We receive grace to walk with you in the light, even as you are in the light. Beyond the feasts and activities, we receive you into our hearts, our lives, and our families. We receive grace to stay on course with you as you lead us from glory to glory. In Jesus' name.

Bible in one year // **Haggai, Revelation 17**

Teach us to number our days, that we may gain a heart of wisdom.
// **Psalms 90:12**

DEC 27

Take stock

As the year draws to a close, it is a wise thing to take off a moment and take stock of your life. Evaluate what the year meant for you and the resources that were at your disposal. Make a balance sheet of your time, your resources, your relationships and your harvest in all things. Then you will have a better appreciation of how well you managed the blessings of this year, and what you might have to do better in the new year. The Psalmist wrote, "The days of our lives are seventy years; And if by reason of strength they are eighty years, yet their boast is only labor and sorrow; for it is soon cut off, and we fly away... So teach us to number our days, that we may gain a heart of wisdom" (Psalm 90:10-12)

He said this because he understood time was limited and with it also, the things we can accomplish. He was desiring that by learning to number our days, we would become wiser in the management of our time and resources. Nonetheless, this begins with us learning to take stock of our use of time and the resources with it. Jesus gave the illustration of the good Shepherd who will leave the 99 to go look for "the one". How would he have noticed one was missing if he didn't stop a moment to take stock, to count the sheep and be sure they were still all part of the flock?

Jacob was one such accountable shepherd. He said to Laban, "You know how I have served you and how your livestock has been with me. For what you had before I came was little, and it has increased to a great amount; the LORD has blessed you since my coming... These twenty years I have been with you; your ewes and your female goats have not miscarried their young, and I have not eaten the rams of your flock." (Genesis 30:29 - 30 & 31:38 - 40). Jacob kept stock of his life – the resources he had and his use of time. God calls us to do same this season.

> **Evaluate your life and your use of resources this year so you can be better positioned to make necessary adjustments for a better new year.**

Prayer

Thank You Heavenly Father. We can testify that indeed as the mountains surround Jerusalem, so the Lord surrounds and protects His people. We thank you for all that was made available to us for the year and receive grace this season to take stock of all things. In Jesus' name.

Bible in one year // **Zechariah 1-4, Revelation 18**

DEC 28

Trust in the LORD with all your heart, and lean not on your own understanding; in all your ways acknowledge Him, and He shall direct your paths. // **Proverbs 3:5-6**

Face it with the Lord

It is easy to proclaim trust in the Lord, but not to lean on your own understanding, is the difficult part and where real faith begins. This is understandable and easy to see why unbelief takes root. When you start examining the facts and circumstances surrounding an issue and wondering how practically possible an expected outcome will be, you are leaning on your understanding – you are trying to evaluate and make judgment and decisions based on your own comprehension of the situation.

Lean not on your own understanding! That is the word of instruction. To put it plain, "Forget what you know and seek the Lord". Then the scripture guarantees, "He shall direct your path". Joshua being a prophet served a good example for us (Joshua 9). This is the account of the Gibeonites after they heard of the victories of Israel and resorted to deception. They were among the neighboring nations God had commanded the Israelites to destroy. However, they disguised as people who had come from afar and convince Israel into a peace treaty that would exclude them from that destruction.

> Particularly as you look forward to the new year, face it with God. Do not lean on your own understanding which is limited.

The Bible records, "So the Israelites examined their food, but they did not consult the Lord. Then Joshua made a peace treaty with them and guaranteed their safety, and the leaders of the community ratified their agreement with a binding oath. Three days after making the treaty, they learned that these people actually lived nearby" (Joshua 9:14 - 16 NLT). The Israelites depended on what they knew and did not seek the Lord. In the end, they got into a snare and were entangled with an unbelieving nation that led them into idolatry. Don't repeat their mistake as you face the new year. Trust in the Lord and lean not on your own understanding. Face the new year with God, acknowledging Him in all your ways.

Prayer

Heavenly Father thank you for you have not dealt with us according to our sins. Even today we repent from leaning on our own understanding and excluding you in the decisions we make. Thank you for imparting us with grace for this. In Jesus' name.

Bible in one year // **Zechariah 5-8, Revelation 19**

If God is for us, who can be against us? He who did not spare His own Son, but delivered Him up for us all, how shall He not with Him also freely give us all things? // **Romans 8:31-32**

DEC 29

God is for you

Oh what joy to know that God is for you! He is with you, working and operating all things in your favor. He is not in opposition of you. Nonetheless, you could position yourself against Him or be in opposition of what He is doing. But as for God, He is for you! Even if you have not yet made room and place for him in your life, it doesn't make him your opponent. You are the one wrongly positioned, walking in opposition to God's plan for you. Even as scriptures say: "God demonstrates His own love toward us, in that while we were still sinners, Christ died for us" (Romans 5:8). That verse is true even for an atheist or a satanist.

> God is for you, causing all things to work together for your good, so long you are rightly positioned, walking in His plans and purposes for you and His people.

We can easily see what we mean by considering a few examples from scripture. When Israel left Egypt for the Promised Land, Balak the King of Moab hired Balaam to curse the Israelites so He could prevail over them in battle. For before now, the Israelites had proven to be unstoppable; defeating every army on their course that set themselves up against Israel. But God said to Balaam, "You shall not go with them; you shall not curse the people, for they are blessed" (Numbers 22:12)

Balaam however, drawn away by the Kings offer, followed the nobles that had come for him. And on the way, the donkey would not move. As Balaam tried pushing forward, the donkey spoke up. The LORD opened the mouth of the donkey, and she said to Balaam, "What have I done to you, that you have struck me these three times" (Numbers 22:28). Now everything was working against Balaam including his donkey because he was positioned against the Lord and His people. The donkey had seen an Angel with his sword drawn standing in the way, ready to strike. For when God is for you or a people, he causes all things to work for them (Romans 8:28). Even so God is for you now and forever, just check your positioning and align yourself with His plans for you.

Prayer

Thank you, Lord for you cause all things to work together for our good who love you and are called according to your purpose. We receive grace this season to see your plans and purposes for our lives that we might always be rightly positioned for prosperity and progress. In Jesus' name

Bible in one year // **Zechariah 9-12, Revelation 20**

DEC 30

> Be careful how you live. Don't live like fools, but like those who are wise. Make the most of every opportunity in these evil days.
> // **Ephesians 5:15-16 NLT**

It is a continuum

"All the generations from Abraham to David are fourteen generations, from David until the captivity in Babylon are fourteen generations, and from the captivity in Babylon until the Christ are fourteen generations" (Matthew 1:17). This account really depicts the heavenly calendar in writing, time measured in reference to God's purpose and agenda in the earth. We might count the years and mark their beginnings and ends, but the heavenly calendar truly is centered on God's purpose and what He is accomplishing. In two days, though the first day of a new year, will truly be just another day. Calendars marking beginnings and ends of years are intended to help man keep tract of passing time and scale it as a measurable quantity.

Time is a continuum. Whether facing a new year or a new day, have the same commitment and attitude to making the most of the time God has entrusted to you.

As far as heaven is concerned, time is a continuum, a piece of eternity measured out to humanity until we are called to account at the end. Yes, time is a continuum, a continuous sequence in which adjacent elements are not perceptibly different from each other, but the extremes are quite distinct. In that light of a definition, we have eternity past, time, and eternity future. Between these extremes, is the continuous segment we call time.

What is the point? What makes a year different from another is not the number, but the events in it. While a new year might mark a new count and bring so much excitement and anticipation, our attitude towards it should not be any different to the attitude we have towards every new day. Just like every new year, we ought to face every new day with resolutions, visions, expectations, commitments, and thanksgiving. For just like every other day, tomorrow just offers us another blank check from God to write a good story for eternity. Even as scripture enjoins us, "Don't live like fools, but like those who are wise. Make the most of every opportunity in these evil days".

Prayer

Eternal Father, thank you for bringing us this far. We receive grace to be discerning of your will and to do your biddings. We will not just count years but count divinely inspired accomplishments that echo into eternity for our good. Help us to make the most of everyday, starting today. In Jesus' name.

Bible in one year // **Zechariah 13-14, Revelation 21**

The path of the just is like the shining sun, that shines ever brighter unto the perfect day. // **Proverbs 4:18**

DEC 31

It only gets better

This was a declaration of fact, a truth that still stands. For the word of God is forever settled and not a dot of it shall prove false (Psalm 119:89, Matthew 24:35). It helps to understand who this is talking about by defining who a just or righteous one is. A righteous one is the person in Christ Jesus. For apart from Christ, none is righteous. For when Adam sinned, sin entered the world and by that, sin spread to all men (Romans 5:12). But when one believes in Jesus, they are made righteous. Romans 3:22 tells us, "This righteousness is given through faith in Jesus Christ to all who believe" (NIV).

You are that righteous one if you are in Christ. As it is written, "God made him who had no sin to be sin for us, so that in him we might become the righteousness of God" (2 Corinthians 5:21 NIV). You were made righteous by God. You are righteous. Many people only know Romans 3:23 that says, "All have sinned and fall short of the glory of God". They have hardly understood the scriptures in context. The whole context of that passage argues to say that even though man sinned, God now offers the opportunity for man to be made righteous through faith in Christ Jesus. And if therefore, anyone is in Christ, that person is righteous. God declares them righteous (Romans 4:22-24).

You are that just one, that righteous one in Christ Jesus. For the righteousness in Christ Jesus is not one that is earned by keeping the law. It is a gift we receive because of our faith (Romans 5:17). And this does not give us a license to sin, rather it produces in us works of righteousness. What is more, as was our focus for today, is that God has placed us on a path of life that only gets better by the day. It says, the path of the just is like a shining light that gets brighter unto a perfect day. Our lives in Christ are programmed to only go from glory to glory, no matter the challenges we face (2 Corinthians 3:18). All you need to do is to abide in the word of God and be led by the Holy Spirit. And you will see this to be your reality even in the new year. You will look back and testify that your life indeed only got better.

> **If you are in Christ Jesus, you are just and righteous. Moreover, God has programmed your life to only get better by the years from glory to glory.**

Prayer

Heavenly Father, thank you for your preservation. That we have been kept by your power through the year. We glory in your love for us that continues to sustain and uphold us among the living. Even as we continue to make progress in ever-increasing levels of glory as we fulfill our destinies. In Jesus' name.

Bible in one year // **Malachi, Revelation 22**

Join the vision

For the earth will be filled with the knowledge of the glory of the LORD, As the waters cover the sea.
// Habakkuk 2:14

The vision of Your Daily Light is to shine the Light of God's word daily to God's chosen people around the world for a victorious and a fulfilling life in Christ. Together with the Lord, we are providing a daily dose of His word and fulfilling this prophecy that was given through Habakkuk – flooding the earth with the knowledge of God. The Lord has given us a mission to bring this word to millions around the world through distribution of free copies – a mission you can join today. And you have one of many avenues.

Be an ambassador of Your Daily Light: Spread the word, let others know of this new devotional with the potential to impact their walk with God and their work for Him. Be it by word of mouth or social media, help bring this devotional to others within your reach and community. This is God's vision, and together we will be fulfilling it for His glory.

Join the outreach: Reach out to an individual or many others and give them copies of Your Daily Light. We are also happy to share such pictures from you on our social media platforms and ministry webpage as a testimony of what God is doing to bring His word to others.

Sponsor free copies: As a ministry, we will be organizing outreaches with free distribution of the devotional on campuses and institutions, bringing the word to those who are positioned to influence the younger generation and those who are positioned already to shape our communities. Through your giving to Lighthouse Global Missions for the free distribution of copies of Your Daily Light, you will be helping us achieve this goal. For this first year of publication, we have a goal to distribute 10.000 copies, a number we plan to increase exponentially in the years ahead.

Sponsor a translation: Partner with us to sponsor the translation of Your Daily Light into a new language. You will be helping us to reach a new group of people that will otherwise be impossible because of the language barrier. German and French versions are already on the way.

> Contact us using the information on the contact page and be part of this move of God in our generation through your financial partnership.

Radio and television: Radio and television remain traditional avenues for the dissemination of knowledge. And it is part of our vision to secure airtime on Radia and TV in different communities for the daily broadcast of the day's message. Your sponsorship and partnership can make this a reality.

Printed in Poland
by Amazon Fulfillment
Poland Sp. z o.o., Wrocław